EDUCATING for LIBERTY

The First Half-Century of the
Intercollegiate Studies Institute

Lee Edwards

Regnery Publishing, Inc.
Washington, D.C.
2003

Library of Congress Cataloging-in-Publication Data

Edwards, Lee.

    Educating for liberty : the first half-century of the Intercollegiate Studies Institute / Lee Edwards. — 1st ed. — Washington, D.C. Regnery Publishing, 2003.

       p. ; cm.
       ISBN: 089526093X

      1. Intercollegiate Studies Institute. 2. Liberty. 3. Social sciences—United States. 4. Political science—United States.
    I. Title.

JA84.U6 E39 2003   2003113003
320/.01/1—dc22   0310

Published in the United States by:

      Regnery Publishing, Inc.
      An Eagle Publishing Company
      One Massachusetts Avenue, NW
      Washington, DC 20001

Distributed to the trade by:

      National Book Network
      4720-A Boston Way
      Lanham, MD 20706

Book interior design by:

      John M. Vella

Manufactured in the United States of America.

Table of Contents

Acknowledgements

I BEGIN WITH LOUISE OLIVER, surely one of the most persuasive conservatives in America, who approached me two-and-a-half years ago about writing the history of ISI—of which she was then chairman—on the occasion of its fiftieth anniversary. She brushed aside all my objections: I had written three books in three years and wanted a break, I had been talking seriously to Annette Kirk about undertaking a life-and-times biography of Russell Kirk, I wasn't sure I was ready for another institutional history. Within a month, I had begun researching the story of an "indispensable" institution of the American conservative movement.

Next, I thank my lucky stars for one of the best editors I have ever had—Jeffrey Nelson, ISI's vice president for publications, whose many suggestions have produced a far better book. Jeff and Mark Henrie were particularly helpful with their intimate knowledge of all the players, past and present. I am indebted to everyone—especially Brig Krauss—at the ISI headquarters in Wilmington who answered all of my questions and helped me and my wife Anne—my essential amanuensis—to plumb the voluminous files and records of the Institute.

And then there are the remarkable officers and trustees—particularly Vic Milione, Kenneth Cribb, Charles Hoeflich, Edwin Feulner, and Richard Ware—who shared their memories of ISI with me. Nor could I have written the history without the help of staffers, such as John Lulves, Spencer Masloff, Robert Ritchie, Peter DeLuca, Robert Reilly, Robert Schadler, Wayne Valis, Gregory Wolfe, John Vella, and Christopher Long. I wish to acknowledge particularly the hospitality of Mike and Gracia Ratliff who put me up and put up with me on my trips to Wilmington.

I asked several hundred professors and students whether ISI had been a "life-altering" experience for them, and they provided the thoughtful replies and lively anecdotes you will find in the pages of this book. Among those who responded, especially among the Weaver Fellows, I am most obliged to Larry Arnn, Peter Schramm, Claes Ryn, John Lehman, Jeffrey Wallin, and Brad Wilson. Several professors have spent a lifetime working with ISI and their recollections have been most useful, among them those of George Carey and George Panichas.

I have been fortunate to have had several outstanding research assistants, but I want to acknowledge the special assistance of Bracy Bersnak of the Catholic University of America—a former ISI Weaver Fellow—and his seemingly limitless knowledge of American conservatism, American politics, and the permanent things.

With this history, as with almost all of the books I have written in the last seven years, I want to acknowledge my special debt to Ed Feulner and the Heritage Foundation. As a Senior Fellow and now Distinguished Fellow in Conservative Thought for the Foundation, I have been provided the necessary resources that have enabled me to write the histories of several of the most important institutions and individuals of the conservative movement.

Here, then, is the "official" history of the Intercollegiate Studies Institute, an organization which through its unwavering dedication to its mission—to educate for liberty—has become the educational pillar of American conservatism.

CHAPTER I

For Our Children's Children

The particular business and objects of [the Intercollegiate Society of Individualists] shall be to promote among college students and the public generally, an understanding and appreciation for the Constitution of the United States of America, the Bill of Rights, the limitations of the power of Government, the voluntary society, the free-market economy and the liberty of the individual.

Articles of Incorporation[1]

FRANK CHODOROV HAD BEEN tilting against windmills all his life. As a student at Columbia University in the early 1900s, he had fought it out with the socialists, arguing that "man's management of man is presumptuous and fraught with danger."[2] He had voted in 1912 for independent Theodore Roosevelt rather than Democrat Woodrow Wilson or Republican William Howard Taft; he never voted again in a presidential election, arguing that politics was not the solution, but the problem. Born in New York City of immigrant Jewish parents, Chodorov turned to atheism as a young man, stung by antisemitic remarks at Columbia, and asserted that religion was "at the bottom of social discords."[3] But in his later years he came to believe in what he called "transcendence," even writing

1. Meeting of the Boards of Trustees and Advisors, Intercollegiate Society of Individualists, April 21, 1956, ISI Archives.
2. Frank Chodorov, *One Is a Crowd: Reflections of an Individualist*, New York: 1952, 28.
3. Ibid., 20-21.

an essay titled, "How a Jew Came to God."[4]

Chodorov insisted that the income tax was the root of all evil and took up the philosophy of the nineteenth century reformer Henry George, the apostle of the single tax. As editor of *The Freeman* in the 1930s, Chodorov delighted in attacking the economic prescriptions of the New Deal and President Franklin D. Roosevelt—and opposed U.S. involvement in the Second World War right up to Pearl Harbor. Like his near anarchist friend and mentor Albert Jay Nock, Chodorov condemned the state as the enemy. Though uncompromising in his beliefs, he was no ideologue. He was a devotee of Adam Smith, not John Stuart Mill, with a respect for "the integrity of personality and a mistrust of aggregated power."[5] His books and his journalism in the first decade after World War II, wrote the historian George H. Nash, "influenced many younger conservatives, including William F. Buckley Jr."[6]

The socialism that Chodorov saw almost everywhere in postwar America had been inspired by the Bolshevik Revolution. It was presented in the United States under the indigenous banners of Progressivism and secularism and was adopted by the architects of the New Deal in the 1930s. Socialism in America had expanded due to the requirements of World War II. Now, with the war won, wrote the historian Mortimer Smith, postwar planners were insisting that "the individual must surrender more and more of his rights to the state" in exchange for what was "euphemistically called security."[7] To those who believed in the heritage of Western civilization and the principles of the American republic, there could be only one possible answer to such a perfidious proposal.

In 1950, therefore, sixty-three-year-old Frank Chodorov determined to challenge one of the most powerful institutions in the country—the American academy—which he believed was largely responsible for the

4. See "Death of a Teacher," a euology delivered by William F. Buckley Jr. at Frank Chodorov's funeral, December 31, 1966. ISI Archives.
5. M. Stanton Evans, *Revolt on the Campus,* Chicago, 1961: 72.
6. George H. Nash, "Forgotten Godfathers: Premature Jewish Conservatives and the Rise of *National Review," American Jewish History* June 1999 and September 1999: 133.
7. Ibid: 4.

shift from "individualism" to socialism in America. By individualism, Chodorov did not mean a radical laissez-faireism but an "historic liberalism" that accepted the doctrine of natural rights, proclaimed "the dignity of the individual," and denounced "all forms of statism as human slavery."[8] His modest proposal (published in 1950 in his newsletter *analysis*)—to create a network of campus clubs for individualists, to launch a lecture bureau, and to start a publication "directed at the student mind"—would become the Intercollegiate Society of Individualists (ISI). ISI was thus born at the dawn of the Cold War when totalitarian states and command economies threatened the existence of liberal democracy and the free society. And it was born battling John Dewey and the other educrats who viewed schools as the "levers" of social progress.

The collectivization of America, Chodorov wrote, had begun when college students of the early 1900s adopted the slogans of the socialists, impressed by their pretensions to "scientific exactitude."[9] Campus socialists were soon organized into the Intercollegiate Socialist Society (which changed its name to the League for Industrial Democracy in 1921). ISS's members included Clarence Darrow, John Reed, Walter Lippmann, Walter Reuther, Frances Perkins, Norman Thomas, and Stuart Chase. Around the country, speeches were made, pamphlets were distributed, and conventions were held. The "success" of the 1917 Bolshevik Revolution added impetus to the socialist crusade in America. Long before the coming of

8. Frank Chodorov, promotional letter to readers of his newsletter, *analysis,* circa April 1945.

9. Chodorov's article was a variation of a pamphlet he had written, entitled, "A Fifty-Year Project to Combat Socialism on the Campus," later distributed by ISI. The tactics to teach individualism, Chodorov said, readily suggested themselves, beginning with literature and lectures. It would be "superfluous," he said, to lay out the specifics of a long-term agenda. The "new converts," he was confident, would give the campaign momentum and direction as they should. Omitted was any effort to convert the current faculty who had been subjected to "socialist indoctrination" for the past thirty years. They would have to be written off until they were replaced by the "new faculty now sitting in the lecture rooms." Chodorov emphasized the long-term challenge of his proposal—the "redirection of a trend of thought is no quick job." What was needed was the same devotion and patience as those of the socialist pioneers. Frank Chodorov, "A Fifty-Year Project to Combat Socialism on the Campus," Intercollegiate Society of Individualists, 1952.

the New Deal, thousands of college-bred socialists had become labor leaders, ministers, teachers, lawyers, and writers. As heads of college departments, Chodorov wrote, the socialists practiced their peculiar kind of "academic freedom," scrupulously hiring their own kind.[10]

When Franklin D. Roosevelt looked for advice on how to deal with the Great Depression, he chose champions of the Left who had established themselves by their academic books and articles. Businessmen were ignored because they were "bewildered" by the economic collapse and, more importantly, because the socialists had already convinced the public that businessmen "were at the bottom of all the trouble."[11]

Chodorov argued that the only way to stop the descent into ever more statism was not by changing socialist laws through the political process but by inculcating the values which "make such laws impossible." Such a "chore," he conceded, was difficult and lengthy—lasting perhaps as long as fifty years—and called for a "sincerity of purpose amounting to religious fervor." It required the kind of zeal that had first brought socialism to America, and it ought to start where the socialists had begun—on the college campus.[12]

"First-class Radicalism"

Socialism's triumph offered opportunity, Chodorov said. The time was ripe for "something new and different," like the ideas of the free market and individual freedom that socialistic propaganda had "so effectively submerged." To shift the mind of the coming generation in the direction of freedom, argued Chodorov, it was necessary to dig up the old values "out of the ash heap of the current culture" and present them in brand-new garb. "Individualism," he wrote, "must be offered as first-class radicalism—which it is, these days."[13]

Chodorov knew that at least some college students would respond

10. Ibid.
11. Ibid.
12. Frank Chodorov, "For Our Children's Children," reprinted from *Human Events,* September 6, 1950.
13. Ibid.

favorably to a "radical" idea like individualism—he had given well-received talks at schools in New York City and as far away as New Haven, Connecticut. The size of the audience did not matter to him—he considered a crowd of only thirty or forty people "almost massive."[14] What mattered was the students' willingness to listen and to reflect on what he said. As a Yale undergraduate, Bill Buckley remembered Chodorov's manner of speaking as quiet, firm, "resolutely undemogogic." The purpose of teaching individualism, Chodorov emphasized, was not "to *make* individualists but to ... help them find *themselves*."[15] And even if those who discovered they were individualists constituted only "a Remnant" (in Nock's famous phrase), they were worth the effort. Chodorov was a loyal disciple of Nock, who had titled his autobiography *Memoirs of a Superfluous Man* and had become increasingly pessimistic in his later years, concluding that the masses could not be saved. Rather, Nock stated, it was the task of any and every Isaiah (like himself) to preach about the decay and impending doom and to hope that "the members of the Remnant would eventually find" each other.[16]

In 1950, a remnant of those who held to the old values was all there seemed to be. The liberal critic Lionel Trilling confidently wrote that "liberalism is not only the dominant but even the sole intellectual tradition" in America. Conceding that a conservative or reactionary "impulse" did exist here and there, Trilling said dismissively that conservatism usually expressed itself in "irritable mental gestures which seem to resemble ideas."[17]

And yet far more than mental gestures were being expressed by classical liberals like F.A. Hayek and Ludwig von Mises, the philosopher Eliseo Vivas, and the traditionalist Richard Weaver in his seminal work, *Ideas Have Consequences* published in 1948. For many on the Right, *Ideas Have*

14. Nash, *The Conservative Intellectual Movement in America Since 1945*, Wilmington, Delaware, 1996: 356 (footnote 148).
15. As quoted by William F. Buckley Jr., in "Death of a Teacher," a eulogy delivered at Frank Chodorov's funeral, December 31, 1966.
16. George Nash, *The Conservative Intellectual Movement in America*: 14-15.
17. Lionel Trilling, *The Liberal Imagination*, New York: 1950, ix.

Consequences was "the *fons et origo* [source and origin] of the contemporary American conservative movement."[18]

In his seminal book, Weaver argued that ideas like nominalism, rationalism, and materialism had led inexorably to what he saw as the moral dissolution of the West. Man had turned away from first principles and true knowledge and in their stead had eagerly embraced rampant egalitarianism and the cult of the masses. Weaver was scathing in his denunciation of man's intellectual sins, but he was not content merely to write a jeremiad. He suggested three reforms—"old" ideas—to help mankind recover from modernism: the defense of private property, a purification of and respect for language, and an attitude of piety toward nature, each other, and the past.[19] Individualist Frank Chodorov could give two wholehearted cheers for traditionalist Weaver's platform, pausing only over the emphasis on piety.

A Nation in Transition

As for the American campus—Chodorov's chosen field of intellectual battle—it was in a state of flux, like much of America. World War II had ended in unconditional victory for the United States and the Allies, but had soon been followed by another global conflict—the Cold War. Aging New Dealers wanted to keep expanding the federal government, and they partially succeeded. Federal spending in 1950 just prior to the start of the Korean War was quadruple what it had been in 1939, while state and local spending more than doubled between 1945 and 1948. Socialists had to be patient because most Americans, wrote the historian James T. Patterson, did not think that government "could—or should—intervene very far in economic matters."[20] But Americans did not seem to be overly worried about government intervention. What they wanted was to enjoy the nation's astounding economic growth that began in the late 1940s

18. Frank S. Meyer, "Richard M. Weaver: An Appreciation," *Modern Age* 14 (Summer-Fall 1970): 243.

19. George H. Nash, *The Conservative Intellectual Movement in America*: 34-35.

20. James T. Patterson, *Grand Expectations: The United States, 1945-1974*, New York: 1996: 59.

and continued for nearly twenty years, constituting what a British observer called "the greatest prosperity the world has ever known."[21]

With 7 percent of the world's population, America had 42 percent of the world's income and produced half of the world's manufacturing output. Per capita income in the United States in mid-1949 was $1,450, almost double that of the next wealthiest nations—Canada, Great Britain, Switzerland, and Sweden. Unemployment was under 4 percent. William J. Levitt was building homes in peacetime as quickly as Henry J. Kaiser had built ships during the late war. Veterans and their wives wanted everything at once—a house, a car, a washing machine, and children, especially children. By the mid-1960s, the historian William Manchester wrote, there would be between 20 and 30 million more Americans than long-range planners had estimated, with the greatest expansion in the teenage population, "the student generation which was destined to make so much news."[22]

The drastic population shift from the farms to the suburbs, the rapid advances in technology and communication, the breakdown of regional traditions, the tension between a cautious older generation that remembered the Great Depression and an ebullient younger generation that thought the boom would last forever—all created an uneasiness about the direction of the country. As they had throughout their history, Americans looked to their schools and colleges, the historian Diane Ravitch wrote, "to protect the heritage of the past and instill traditional values in the rising generation."[23]

But colleges had their own problems, trying to cope with post-war America on top of a unique experiment in mass higher education known as the G.I. Bill (G.I. for "Government Issue," stamped on the uniform of every serviceman). Campus life had been much simpler before the war. Then, only one-third of the 74.8 million Americans who were twenty-

21. Ibid., 61.
22. William Manchester, *The Glory and the Dream: A Narrative History of America 1932-1972*, volume one, Boston, 1973: 525.
23. Diane Ravitch, *The Troubled Decade: American Education 1945-1980*, New York, 1983: 9.

five years of age or older had gone beyond the eighth grade. Just one-fourth of the population was high school graduates while only one-twen-tieth—just 5 percent—had graduated from four-year colleges or universities. The college population in 1940 was a modest 1.5 million. And then came the Servicemen's Readjustment Act of 1944 (commonly known as the G.I. Bill of Rights), which offered the 16 million men and women who had served in the armed forces during World War II a federal subsidy to continue their schooling or training.

Millions jumped at the opportunity, and by 1956, when the program ended, 7.8 million veterans (about half of those who had served in the Second World War and the Korean War) had participated. A total of 2.2 million went to college, 3.5 million attended technical schools below the college level, and 700,000 took agricultural instruction. The program did at least honor two conservative principles: servicemen were free to select their schools, and schools could control their admission policies and curricula without federal intervention.

Behemoth University

One historian called the G.I. Bill "the most important educational and social transformation in American history."[24] Among its legacies was the acceptance by students, faculty, and administrators of ever larger classes and ever larger colleges—schools with more than 20,000 students became commonplace. As the conservative historian Russell Kirk later put it, "Behemoth University" had arrived.[25] The massive infusions of veterans accelerated the conversion of the American university from a center of classical liberal arts education into an all-purpose "multi-versity."

The change was also assisted by the decades-long missionary work of John Dewey, the most influential educational philosopher in America. Born in Vermont in 1859, the young Dewey subscribed to New England Puritan values and Protestant Christianity. But as a graduate student at Johns Hopkins University and later a teacher at universities in Michigan

24. Ibid: 15.
25. Ibid: 17.

and Minnesota, he became disenchanted with a world shaped by God and His moral will and converted to Pragmatism. He became a founder of Progressivism (which produced political leaders Woodrow Wilson and Franklin D. Roosevelt) and an unrelenting critic of individualism and free enterprise.

Moving to Columbia University in 1904, Dewey and his disciples in the following decades taught thousands of teachers who went on to head schools of education all over America. In Dewey's philosophy of education, the school should assume many of the socializing functions once performed by the family, the workplace, and the community. He believed that the school could become "a fundamental lever of social progress."[26] And he had little time for the old-fashioned fundamentals of education like reading, writing, and arithmetic. Since Dewey believed there was no absolute truth, Frank Chodorov pointed out, standards were meaningless—"education should concentrate on the instrumental facts of life, on the functional disciplines."[27] Dewey was in reality a social engineer while Chodorov was the true educator.

By 1950, most of the "levers" of American higher education were in the hands of an informal but self-cognizant coalition of progressives, pragmatists, and socialists. Challenging them were the administrators of a few private colleges, a scattered handful of classical liberal professors, and a fair number of parents shocked by what their children were learning, and not learning, at their alma mater.

A Will for Freedom?

Frank Chodorov knew, from long experience, how difficult it was to challenge a prevailing consensus. He wondered whether there was in America "a will for freedom of sufficient vigor to initiate the suggested campaign." He published his manifesto, "For Our Children's Children," in *analysis* in mid-1950, but more importantly, the essay was revised and reprinted in *Human Events*, the leading conservative newsletter of the time, on Sep-

26. Ibid: 47.
27. Frank Chodorov, *Out of Step*: 33.

tember 6, 1950. Thus, from the very beginning, ISI was connected to the conservative movement.

The reaction to Chodorov's proposal was immediate and encouraging. Letters poured in, praising the program, although some anxious parents argued that the educating should begin in kindergarten, not in college. Thousands of copies of the *Human Events* reprint were bought and distributed. The names of about one hundred individualistic students, suggested by parents and friends, were collected. However, no organizational steps were taken because there was no seed money and no one to run the proposed program. Chodorov was a writer, not an organizer; he also believed that someone young ought to head the effort.

And so the idea was allowed "to simmer" for more than a year until March 1952 when Chodorov revisited the subject in *Human Events*, of which he had become associate editor. In an essay titled, "The Adam Smith Clubs," Chodorov argued that such clubs were needed "to find and help the submerged individualism" on campus and to provide an opposition "to the collectivism being ladled out by the professors." The reaction was not as dramatic as the one to "Our Children's Children," with one important difference. This time the mail contained a $1,000 check from one of the most generous benefactors of the American conservative movement—Sun Oil Company founder J. Howard Pew.

Defense of the "American system of enterprise" was central to Pew's personal and corporate philosophy. He was an unyielding foe of the "collectivists," saying that "no economic planning authority could ever have foreseen, planned, plotted and organized the amazing spectacle of human progress that the world has witnessed in this country during the last 100 years."[28] Pew was also a fervent believer in the power of higher education and gave generously to a number of colleges and universities. Chodorov's proposal to start an organization of pro-freedom, anti-collectivist college students was good news indeed to the Philadelphia business leader and philanthropist. The Pew family would become one of ISI's

28. J. Howard Pew, remarks at Grove City College Alumni luncheon, June 15, 1946.

most important donors for decades to come.

But Chodorov was uncertain how to respond to Pew's largess: talking about the need for an intercollegiate society was one thing, organizing it was quite another. "To me," he once commented, "the most efficient file is a waste basket, and the best procedure is to do what the other fellow wants you to do, providing it promises to be interesting."[29] Chodorov kept the Pew check in his desk for several days and even considered returning it with his thanks. At last, he showed the $1,000 donation to his boss, Frank Hanighen, a veteran journalist who had built *Human Events* into an influential publication read widely on Capitol Hill. "I have one rule," said Frank to Frank, "never send money back."[30] With Hanighen's encouragement, and after visiting Pew in his Philadelphia office, Chodorov formalized his idea.

And so on April 3, 1952, the Intercollegiate Society of Individualists (ISI) was incorporated in the District of Columbia, with Frank Hanighen, Frank Chodorov, and Patricia Lutz (Hanighen's secretary) as the three incorporators. William F. Buckley Jr. was listed as president, Frank Chodorov as vice president, and Aris Donohoe as secretary-treasurer. Buckley was a logical choice because of his close friendship with Chodorov and because Buckley (at age twenty-six and two years out of Yale) had become a national celebrity with a searing critique of his alma mater.

God and Man at Yale (Buckley's first published work) was one of the most discussed books of 1951—it made number sixteen on the *New York Times* best-seller list one month after publication in October. Dedicating the book to God, country, and Yale, "in that order," Buckley charged that Yale had abandoned both Christianity and free enterprise, or what he called individualism. He said that the faculty members—and he named names—who fostered atheism and socialism ought to be fired. He coupled Darwinism, Fabian Socialism, and Pragmatism with Marxism and Nazism. He recommended instead the ideas of John Locke, Adam Smith,

29. Frank Chodorov to Ivan Bierly, January 16, 1953, ISI Archives.
30. Frank Chodorov, remarks at ISI special meeting, November 19, 1960, Indianapolis, ISI Archives.

Thomas Jefferson, and Jesus. He said, as biographer John Judis points out, that the primary goal of education was to familiarize students with an existing body of truth, of which Christianity and free enterprise or individualism were the foundation. But, Buckley reported, "individualism is dying at Yale, and without a fight."[31]

Ancient Truths

Busy promoting his book, Buckley accepted Chodorov's invitation to head ISI only after being assured that the title was pro forma and his responsibilities would be nil. It would have been difficult for the young author to say no—it was Chodorov, after all, who helped edit *God and Man at Yale* and who recommended it to Chicago publisher Henry Regnery. And it was Chodorov who had published Bill Buckley's first professional article (paying him $25) in the spring of 1951 in *Human Events*. Buckley later wrote of Frank Chodorov's tutelage, "It is quite unlikely that I should have pursued a career as a writer but for the encouragement he gave me just after I graduated from Yale."[32] Neither Buckley nor Chodorov was bothered by the irony of launching an organization of individuals presumably indifferent if not hostile to organization.

The articles of incorporation stated that the organization's objective was "to promote among college students, specifically, and the public, generally, an understanding of and appreciation for the Constitution of the United States of America, laissez-faire (free market) economics and the doctrine of individualism."[33]

In late April 1952, a questionnaire was sent to the original list of one hundred college students. Just under forty responded, stating they were either in "complete agreement" with ISI's objectives or would like to receive ISI materials. They also provided the names of several hundred other

31. John B. Judis, *William F. Buckley Jr.: Patron Saint of the Conservatives*, New York: 1988: 83-85; William F. Buckley Jr., *God and Man at Yale*, Chicago: 1951: 113.

32. William F. Buckley Jr. to E. Victor Milione, June 6, 1960, Buckley Papers, Sterling Library, Yale University, New Haven, Connecticut.

33. "Résumé of Activities of Intercollegiate Society of Individualists, 1952-1953; 1953-1954," ISI Archives.

students who they thought might be interested in ISI. After the 1952 graduates were dropped and the new names obtained from students, parents, and friends were added, ISI had a mailing list of about six hundred undergraduates—out of a total college population of approximately 2.5 million.

The question of what should be mailed to them was resolved when there came calling on Frank Chodorov in the late summer of 1952 an energetic, enterprising undergraduate at Georgetown University. Leonard Liggio was a Catholic libertarian from the Bronx, who had already, at age nineteen, helped form Students for America to carry on "the spirit of Robert A. Taft and Douglas MacArthur." He invited a number of speakers, including Frank Chodorov, to Georgetown, and met with Leonard Read, who headed the Foundation for Economic Freedom (FEE), in Irvington-on-Hudson, New York.

Read, who never hesitated to spread the gospel of free enterprise, agreed to send FEE literature each month to several hundred members of Students for America. "I explained to Frank," recalls Liggio, "what FEE was doing for us and that it would do the same for ISI."[34] For Chodorov, this was manna—from an individualist heaven. He talked with FEE secretary Ivan Bierly, and in the fall of the 1952-1953 academic year, FEE began mailing its literature without charge to ISI members.[35]

What these young individualists received twice a month reflected FEE's interests and concerns—articles titled "The Price of Price Controls" and "The Right to Own Property." Missing from the list, however, were works by traditional conservative authors like Richard Weaver and Peter Viereck, which is not surprising, given FEE's strict focus on the free

34. Author's interviews with Leonard Liggio, August 8, 2001, and April 12, 2002.
35. Eight years later, while reminiscing at a 1960 ISI board of trustees meeting, Frank Chodorov stated that Bierly, not Liggio, had first suggested the distribution of FEE "pamphlets" to students interested in "libertarian literature." Chodorov's confusion of the roles of Bierly and Liggio was understandable in a seventy-three-year-old man who had had one stroke and would soon suffer another. In contrast, Liggio's recollection about the sequence of events as recounted in two separate interviews is quite explicit and more reliable, in the author's opinion, than Chodorov's reminiscenses. See "Excerpts from Remarks by Frank Chodorov," ISI Board of Trustees Meeting, November 19, 1960, ISI Archives. Also interviews of Leonard Liggio by the author, April 13, 2002, and August 8, 2001.

market. ISI membership was (and remains) scrupulously self-selective: every mailing contained a card reminding the student that all he had to do to stop receiving the literature was to sign and return the card. A second card was included which the student was invited to give to a friend who might be interested in ISI materials. Some of the more independent students did drop out, surmising correctly that their names had been submitted by father, mother, or maiden aunt, and expressing resentment at "this intrusion into their lives."[36] But far more students, hungry for an alternative view, asked ISI to keep the literature coming. In that first academic year, FEE mailed 7,500 pieces of literature to ISI members at a cost of $2,000.

From its earliest days, those associated with ISI learned to be flexible. In early 1953, Frank Chodorov informed Bill Buckley in a note, "Am removing you as president. Making myself pres. Easier to raise money if a Jew is president. You can be V-P. Love. Frank."[37] Buckley, who had been a figurehead president and was trying to start up a new magazine, was relieved to be relieved. In later years, he would quote the note—after raising yet another half a million dollars for the perennially financially strapped *National Review.*

On June 22, 1953, Frank Chodorov filed a federal income tax exemption application "for use of religious, charitable, scientific, literary or educational organizations" with the Internal Revenue Service. The form showed that the Intercollegiate Society of Individualists was then located at 1835 K Street, NW, in the District of Columbia. Its briefly stated purpose was "to disseminate among students the doctrines of Individualism." The Society's activities were simply put as well: "publishing and distributing pamphlets, lecturing, etc." Attached to the application was a copy of the Society's first Form 990 tax return for the fiscal year beginning April 1, 1952 and ending March 31, 1953—net worth, $1,233.40.

---

36. Frank Chodorov, "Lest It Be Forgotten: The Intercollegiate Society of Individualists Is Growing—Despite Heavy Odds Against It," *Human Events*, August 20, 1955.

37. "Death of a Teacher: Frank Chodorov, RIP 1887-1966," a eulogy by William F. Buckley Jr., ISI Archives.

(It is this slightly odd fiscal year schedule, determined by the happenstance of a founding, on which the ISI still operates fifty years later.) While the organization was incorporated a year earlier, that was only half of the work. The filing of a tax-exempt application meant that the Society was now, though provisionally for another year, able to execute its business fully as a non-profit corporation and to offer prospective donors federal tax exemptions for charitable gifts. As such, it is this date that the Society took to be its formal "founding"—from thence forward charting its educational course "Since 1953."

Teaching Individualism

Eager to expand the mailing list and trusting that FEE would continue to underwrite the mailings, Chodorov drafted a letter that was sent to some five thousand *Human Events* readers, asking them for the names of college students "who might be interested in reading libertarian literature." The intent of the Intercollegiate Society of Individualists, explained Chodorov, "is to teach individualism—economic, philosophical and spiritual—as a counter-agent to the collectivism to which the students are exposed. The presumption is that ideas have consequences; right action can only come from right ideas."[38]

For parents anxious about the wrong ideas their children were being taught at college, here was an organization whose time had come. Hundreds of letters containing two, three, and more names of students arrived at 1835 K St., N.W., Washington, D.C., the offices of *Human Events* and, for the time being, of ISI. (Actually, the ISI "office" consisted of a desk and a chair on loan from the obliging newsletter.) The unvarying plea of the correspondents was: "save my son from socialism." Several letters included a modest check of $5 or $10, a few considerably more. ISI received a major publicity assist from John T. Flynn, the vehemently anti-New Deal writer and radio commentator, who invited his listeners,

---

38. Frank Chodorov, "The Intercollegiate Society of Individuals," article distributed by the Committee for Constitutional Government, New York, Spring 1953.

if they had a son or daughter "whose mind you would like to see guarded from those evil revolutionary, collectivist influences in the colleges," to send his or her name to the ISI address in Washington.[39]

Among the *Human Events* readers inspired by Frank Chodorov's idea was Donald J. Cowling of Minneapolis, who had been president of Carleton College for twenty-seven years. A businessman as well as an educator, Cowling contributed almost $2,000 to ISI in the first year and had several conversations with Chodorov about practical matters like a budget. In late August 1953, Cowling wrote J. Howard Pew, whom he knew had already given $1,000 to the Society. He explained that ISI needed $10,000 to distribute literature and conduct other business in the academic year 1953-1954. "I agreed to be responsible," Cowling wrote, "for $2,500 of this amount." Could Pew see his way clear to making a gift of $5,000 to help get ISI started? "When I remember," said Cowling, "the leadership (including Felix Frankfurter) which developed from the Socialist Clubs established by Jack London fifty years ago, the present proposal seems to me to have real possibilities."[40]

Pew must have been amused by Cowling's proposal because it was usually he who said he would match someone else's donation. The novelty of being on the receiving end of a challenge grant added to ISI's potential to make a difference in American higher education and led Pew to act. Two months later, Frank Chodorov received five checks for $1,000 each from five different members of the Pew family, including J. Howard and John G. Pew, Jr., who would later become vice chairman and then chairman of the ISI board of trustees. ISI was now truly in business: it purchased its own desk, organized its first campus lectures, and began laying plans for a newsletter. Friends donated copies of books like John T. Flynn's *The Road Ahead*, Henry Hazlitt's *Economics in One Lesson*, and Frank Chodorov's *One Is a Crowd* for distribution to ISI members. Other benefactors made it possible to send *Human Events* to the students every

39. Excerpt from a broadcast by John T. Flynn, September 21, 1953, Henry Regnery Papers, ISI Archives.
40. Donald J. Cowling to J. Howard Pew, August 27, 1953, ISI Archives.

week of the college year.

Meanwhile, during 1953-1954, the Foundation for Economic Education mailed 24,000 pieces of literature (including such essays as "Why Is Social Security a Fraud?") to ISI members at a cost of $9,500. Thanks to the return cards, the ISI list grew quickly until, by the end of the second year of operation, it had a membership of 2,500, representing 210 colleges and universities. ISI clubs, usually with only a handful of members, began to appear on campuses; the tireless Leonard Liggio organized one of the very first at Georgetown University.

A tiny group of ISI lecturers began appearing on campus—asking only for their travel expenses—led by Chodorov, who traveled to the University of Illinois and Kent College, and William F. Buckley Jr., who visited Northwestern University and Union Theological Seminary. From the beginning of the ISI lecture program, the emphasis was on imparting ideas, not on entertaining the audience. It was not the "principal role of the ISI," Buckley wrote Chodorov, to provide "a good scrap" but "a thoughtful examination of the individualist alternative."

Nor did the size of the audience matter. If only people would get it into their heads, Buckley lamented, that "we don't care about crowds of 1,000; a crowd of 30 (provided the 30 are intelligent and conscientious) would serve our purposes better. We don't need the frumperies of a revival meeting."[41] A third ISI speaker was twenty-nine-year-old E. Victor Milione, who was hired by the Society in the fall of 1953, and would remain its chief executive officer and intellectual conscience for the next thirty-five years.

Born in May 1924 in the Philadelphia suburb of Penfield of devout Roman Catholic parents (his father was a sculptor who loved to read, especially the classics), Vic Milione went to public schools as a boy and then to West Catholic High School in Philadelphia. Following Pearl Harbor, he enlisted in the U.S. army air corps and wound up in Colorado. At the war's end, he took advantage of the G.I. Bill and enrolled at St. Joseph's

41. E. Victor Milione, "Ideas in Action: Forty Years of 'Educating for Liberty,'" *The Intercollegiate Review*, Fall 1993: 54.

College, Philadelphia, graduating in 1950 with a BS in political science. He encountered his first Keynesian professor at St. Joseph's, who argued that while government could be small in the "pastoral" world of the eighteenth century when the United States was founded, a large government was now needed "to accommodate the changes" wrought by the Industrial Revolution. Whereupon Milione sought, but failed, to find material to "refute the ideas of centralized government."[42]

For a year and a half following graduation, he was a salesman for a fire equipment distributor. He considered studying law, but then, eager to preach the advantages of the free market, especially to young people, Milione went to work for Americans for the Competitive Enterprise System (ACES), an educational organization supported by Philadelphia businessmen, including the ever-generous J. Howard Pew. He traveled throughout the greater Philadelphia area, visiting mostly high schools but also Rotary, Kiwanis, and other service clubs and even farmers' groups. He also initiated an economic education program for plant employees in Pennsylvania to whom he explained the economic fundamentals of a free Society, stressing that profits were not evil but good—they led to jobs and prosperity.

The Noble Life

At the ACES board meetings, Milione met Charles H. Hoeflich, a successful Philadelphia banker who would become a life-long friend and almost permanent secretary-treasurer of ISI. "It was always his brain," says Hoeflich of Milione, "that fascinated me."[43] That brain was filled to the brim with the ideas of the greatest thinkers and writers of Western civilization. In a single conversation, recalls Hoeflich, Milione would quote *in extensio* John Henry Newman, Alexis de Tocqueville, Seneca, Jacob Burckhardt, Ortega y Gasset, James Bryce, and Richard Weaver, his favorite modern conservative writer. (An ISI staffer once quipped, "Vic

---

42. E. Victor Milione, "Where Would You Go?" Newsletter of the Minute Women of the U.S.A., March 1957: 3.
43. Author's interview with Charles H. Hoeflich, May 16, 2001.

may not have been the most quoted conservative, but he was certainly the most quoting.")[44]

Charles Hoeflich was a prime example of the humane, liberally educated businessman so often drawn to ISI. A graduate of the University of Pennsylvania, he built the Union National Bank (founded in 1876) from a small enterprise with $14 million in commercial loans and a $2.2 million trust into a complete financial holding company with $1.2 billion in commercial paper and a $800 million trust fund. Committed to giving back much of what he had received, Hoeflich founded several non-profit organizations, including the Pennsylvania Foundation for Mental Health, one of the ten outstanding community psychiatric institutions in the country; the Adult Community for Total Health Care, "conservative in its administration and Christian in its attitude"; and Fatima House, a Catholic retreat center. But his overriding commitment—almost a calling—was to ISI and its furtherance of Western civilization among the young.[45]

When talking with Hoeflich, Milione often quoted Ortega's definition of the "noble" life—"Know what's required of you and do it voluntarily."[46] After more than two years with ACES, Milione decided that more was required of him than explaining the basics of capitalism to high school students, and he contemplated enrolling at Temple University's law school in the evenings. But in early 1953, he and Frank Chodorov—whom he had first met as a junior at St. Joseph's College—began discussing ISI and its fifty-year plan to change the intellectual climate on the campus and in America. Here was a worthy challenge for a young Catholic intellectual who believed deeply that ideas were the wellspring of civilization.[47]

Undeterred by the fact, readily admitted by Chodorov, that ISI had some $2,300 in its bank account, Milione signed on as the Society's first and only campus organizer. "Vic," said Chodorov, "I have this money and as long as it lasts, you will get $75 a week and expenses. You'll have to

44. Author's interview with Robert Ritchie, April 30, 2003.
45. Author's interview with Charles Hoeflich, May 16, 2001.
46. Author's interview with E. Victor Milione, July 29, 2000.
47. E. Victor Milione to Clyde H. Slease, June 15, 1955, ISI Archives.

take your chances on the future"[48] (Milione's total wages the following year were $4,325.00). Limiting himself to visiting schools in the East in order to save traveling expenses, the Society's intrepid representative provided college students with "the arguments that support free-market economics, a respect for private property, and self-determination of the individual." It was these ideas that had motivated the Founding Fathers of the Republic, he noted, and they "must be a part of the education of our young people."[49]

Incredibly, at a time when America was the most prosperous country in the world, because it was capitalist, such ideas were not a part of many economics textbooks at leading universities. Based on a careful review of university textbooks, a distinguished professor—and ISI friend—concluded that every single text subscribed "to Keynesian doctrine"; presented a list of indictments of the American economic system without any "counter-balancing list of achievements"; and revealed an "almost blind faith ... in the efficacy of government to solve economic problems."[50] Here was corroboration of a central argument of *God and Man at Yale*—and an indication of the enormous educational task facing ISI and its new employee.

Typically, Milione would spend several days each week, going from college to college, meeting with ISI members, passing out literature, and enlisting recruits by a somewhat unorthodox method. Milione would walk down a campus sidewalk with a large "Taft for President" button prominently displayed on his lapel and wait for someone to strike up a conversation. If the student was friendly and smiling, he was a potential ISI member. If the student was combative and frowning, he gave Milione an opportunity to do what he loved to do—teach. As he explained why he preferred Senator Robert A. Taft of Ohio—who had said in 1951 that the choice for the nation was liberty or socialism—Milione would discuss not only current politics but American history, the founding of the Republic, the glories of Western civilization, and as much else of the history

48. Excerpts from remarks by Frank Chodorov, ISI Board of Trustees Meeting, November 19, 1960, ISI Archives.
49. "Prospectus of the Intercollegiate Society of Individualists," prepared by E. Victor Milione, 1955, ISI Archives.
50. Ibid.

of mankind as the student was willing to take in. Even if they did not agree with him, young people invariably listened to Vic Milione because he took time to talk and listen to them.

The young ISI organizer was constantly on the go, driving from campus to campus in a car filled with pamphlets and books, trying to cover as much territory as possible as quickly as possible, and always conscious of the Society's scant funds. For example, Milione's total expenses for two nights and three days in one week of November 1953 were $54.97. Breakfast was 75 cents, lunch 90 cents, dinner $2.10; the motel room cost $5.05. On that one trip, he drove 395 miles at an estimated gasoline cost of $31.60, the single largest item on his expense account.[51]

The following year brought more change to ISI. Frank Chodorov left *Human Events* in the summer of 1954 to become editor of *The Freeman*, recently purchased by the Foundation for Economic Education and converted into a monthly magazine. Chodorov moved from Washington, D.C., into the FEE offices in Irvington-on-Hudson, New York, taking ISI (and Vic Milione) with him. The Society had a new venue, but it stuck to its policy of free literature, self-selected members, and as little organization as possible.

The First Advisory Board

When Milione proposed the creation of an ISI advisory board, Chodorov responded, "Aristotle and Spinoza are our board." But, consistent with his individualism, Chodorov did not try to prohibit his younger colleague from forming a board whose first members were William F. Buckley Jr.; Brig. General Bonner Fellers (USA-ret.), a former aide to General Douglas MacArthur; Ivan R. Bierly, FEE executive secretary; *Human Events* editor Frank Hanighen; Utah Governor J. Bracken Lee; Adolph Menjou, the veteran Hollywood actor and outspoken anti-Communist; retired Admiral Ben Moreell, chairman of the board of Jones & Laughlin Steel Corporation; economics Professor William H. Peterson of New York

51. "Expenses for the Week Ending Nov. 13th [1953]," submitted by E. Victor Milione, ISI Archives.

University; John G. Pew, Jr., vice president of Sun Shipbuilding & Drydock Company; Professor E. Merrill Root of Earlham College (who would publish in a few years the controversial *Collectivism on the Campus*); and investment counselor Edwin S. Webster, Jr., of Kidder Peabody & Co.

It was an impressive lineup for an organization barely two years old, including as it did the *enfant terrible* of the Right—Bill Buckley, not yet thirty; the editor of *Human Events*, the most widely read conservative publication in the country; two prominent captains of industry (Moreell and Pew); two widely published professors (Peterson and Root); a governor; a well-known film star; a former aide to the redoubtable Douglas MacArthur; and a wealthy Wall Streeter. Their presence testified to ISI's steadily growing impact under Vic Milione, who was named the Society's executive vice president in the fall of 1954.

Between 1953 and 1956, ISI annual contributions went from $2,055 to $36,934.81 while membership increased from 600 to 4,200 students attending over four hundred colleges. About ten thousand students had participated in various ISI activities since its founding. Fund-raising was helped when ISI, with the help of Republican Congressman Ralph Gwynn of New York, received tax-exempt status from the Internal Revenue Service on May 6, 1954. Milione instituted an annual audit by an independent CPA (the national accounting firm of Lybrand, Ross Bros. and Montgomery) as a check on ISI receipts and expenditures. Such accounting diligence was not the accepted practice of many tax-exempt organizations in the 1950s.

Dissatisfied with mailing other organizations' literature, ISI launched its own newsletter, *The Individualist*, in May 1954. The leading article described the founding of "The Independent Library" at Yale, intended to be, explained undergraduate Gridley L. Wright, a "Conservative, Individualistic organ" that "would counterbalance the preponderant atmosphere ... of neoliberalism" on campus.[52] Within two weeks, the Yale radio station WYBC attacked members of the Independent Library as "intellectual isolationists, bigots and idolators" and of attempting "to secede from the normal inter-

52. "The Independent Library," Gridley L. Wright, *The Individualist*, May 1954, ISI, Washington, D.C.

change of ideas." Demanding and receiving e

reported that the majority of visitors to the

including members of the John Dewey Society

the young individualist explained, the library w

tion neglected books, so that they can be consid

The books in the Independent Library, Wrigh

themselves but, rather, presented "the best insig

Reaction to *The Individualist* was generally favorable except for a sting-ing letter from traditionalist Russell Kirk, who had been asked by Vic Milione to join ISI's advisory board. Kirk formally declined on the grounds that he was too busy and then revealed his real reason: He did not like, indeed, he abhorred the word "individualist." Politically, he wrote, individualism "ends in anarchy; spiritually, it is a hideous solitude." He continued, "I do not even call myself an 'individual'; I hope I am a *person*." Kirk went on to say that the first issue of *The Individualist* "shocked" him.[54]

The author of *The Conservative Mind* took special note of ISI's con-sistently agnostic and libertarian advisers, ranging from the Chinese phi-losopher Lao-tse to Albert Jay Nock. He suggested that if ISI had chosen for its pantheon:

> Moses in place of Lao-tse, Aristotle in place of Zeno, Pascal in place of Spinoza, Falkland in place of Locke, Dante in place of Milton, [Samuel] Johnson in place of [Adam] Smith, Ruskin in place of Mill, Burke in place of Paine, Adams in place of Jefferson, [James Fitzjames] Stephen in place of Spencer, Hawthorne in place of Thoreau, Brownson in place of Emerson, you might succeed in capturing the imagination of the rising generation.[55]

"I think," Kirk concluded, "you people really are conservatives in your prejudices, not 'individualists'; and you might as well confess it, and get the credit for it."[56]

53. Ibid.
54. Russell Kirk to E. Victor Milione, May 24, 1954, Regnery Papers, Hoover Institution Archives, Stanford University, Stanford, California.
55. Ibid.
56. Ibid.

he agreed with Kirk that the West faced a crisis *in toto* and that
ght to be concerned with all sides of man, not merely the economic
s reading of Burckhardt and others had already convinced him of this).
But he was barely one year on the job and could not yet take the necessary
steps to expand ISI's stated mission of promoting among college students
an appreciation of the Constitution, the free market, and "the doctrine of
individualism."

Among other things, Milione was occupied with speaking at colleges, managing mailings, raising funds, and getting to know two young
men—M. Stanton Evans of Yale and Donald Lipsett of Indiana University—who had been hired by Chodorov to help him at *The Freeman*.
Evans was assistant editor—at $320 a month—while Lipsett was assis-
tant business manager. To save money, Milione, Evans (who would become a major intellectual figure in the American conservative movement),
and Lipsett (who later served as ISI's Midwest director and was chiefly
responsible for the creation of the Philadelphia Society) briefly shared an
apartment in Tarrytown, New York. Milione enjoyed the long philosophical conversations with his young roommates but did not share their enthusiasm for rock and roll music and Indiana University football (Mozart
and Bach were his composers of choice).

Still under the influence of his prolix Yale professors, Evans was at
first shocked by Chodorov's heavy penciling of his work, but he grew to
appreciate "the wisdom of his editing" and his personal kindness to young
writers like himself.[57] Arriving at FEE in July 1955, Evans enrolled at
New York University in September to begin work on his Ph.D. in economics (one of his NYU professors was Ludwig von Mises). But in November,
Bill Buckley started *National Review* and offered Evans a position, editing a
local edition of the magazine in Louisville, Kentucky. When the Louisville
edition folded the following June due to a paucity of subscribers, Evans
accepted a standing offer from publisher James L. Wick of *Human Events*
and moved to Washington. He reestablished contact with Vic Milione and

57. Author's interview with M. Stanton Evans, October 31, 2001.

became editor of *The Individualist,* eager to document "the liberal bias" on the campus.[58] Evans would become one of ISI's most loyal alumni, ever ready to lecture at a campus or emcee a conservative event.

Meanwhile, the ISI-FEE relationship became increasingly problematic. ISI membership grew so rapidly that FEE informed Chodorov and Milione it could no longer assume all of the Society's clerical and mailing costs. To keep the literature flowing and assuage FEE, ISI agreed to pay the costs of college subscriptions of *The Freeman* for its members. Next FEE began reviewing ISI literature; it questioned and then vetoed the reprint of "Campus Rebels," written by journalist-historian William Henry Chamberlin for the *Wall Street Journal.* Chamberlin, a former leftist sympathizer, reported that today's college rebels were "conservatives fed up with the prevalent collectivist viewpoint." He also noted a tendency to "search for underlying spiritual values and to question the infallibility of agnosticism." Chamberlin singled out ISI as "a sign of changing times."[59] FEE argued, unconvincingly, that the Chamberlin article left the impression that ISI was engaged in political action.

At the same time, there were disagreements over things large and small between the strong-willed Leonard Read, "who liked to have things revolve around him," and the always independent but never ideological Chodorov. They even disputed the topic to be discussed at the foundation's daily luncheon, prepared and served by the staff.[60] Read objected to ISI's plans for a lecture bureau, according to Chodorov, because "the lecturers could not be controlled."[61] ISI's future was effectively decided in December 1955, when FEE decided to stop publishing *The Freeman* as a general audience magazine, although Chodorov had built up its circulation to an impressive 24,000. But the foundation had nevertheless lost $90,000 in the eighteen-month-long venture. After almost selling *The Freeman* to

58. Ibid.

59. William Henry Chamberlin, "Campus Rebels," *Wall Street Journal,* December 19, 1955.

60. Author's interview with E. Victor Milione, April 20, 2001. Leonard Liggio described the relationship between the Midwesterner Read and the New York City-bred Chodorov as "a kind of culture clash." Author's interview, August 8, 2001.

61. Frank Chodorov to Ben Moreell, March 25, 1956, ISI Archives.

Bill Buckley, who was seeking subscribers for his just-launched *National Review*, Read reconstituted *The Freeman* as a monthly journal of libertarian ideas.[62] In the end, Read and Chodorov parted amicably, with the veteran editor suggesting that he would be happy to write for *The Freeman* "part time."[63]

Vic Milione, however, was informed that he was now a full-time FEE staff member. Henceforth, only FEE-approved materials would be sent to college students and in FEE envelopes. Furthermore, all future funds raised would be "under the auspices of FEE rather than ISI." The relationship between FEE and ISI would be "formally terminated" as of June 30, 1956— when ISI would "need another address from which to operate."[64] "I wasn't interested," recalls Milione, "in working for FEE under those circumstances," adding succinctly, "I didn't forgo law school to work for Leonard Read."[65]

Milione consulted members of the ISI board of trustees—Frank Chodorov, Frank Hanighen, and Edwin S. Webster—who agreed that FEE's proposal would mean "the demise of ISI" and instructed Milione to move the organization. "I have secured office space in the Lafayette Building near Independence Square in Philadelphia," Milione informed Leonard Read, and would move in the week of February 12.[66] Chodorov retained the title of president, but the thirty-two-year-old Milione became president in all but name. And he faced the usual problems, starting with an almost empty till. Scrambling for donations, Milione appealed to trustee Edwin S. Webster, Jr., who immediately responded with a check for $10,000. Webster's grand generosity, at this critical juncture in the Society's history, enabled Milione to make the move to Philadelphia. By the annual board of trustees meeting in April 1956, ISI had, for the first time in its history, its own address, 407 Lafayette Building, Fifth and Chestnut Streets, across the square from Independence Hall. Two small

62. See Nash, *The Conservative Intellectual Movement in America*: 28; also "Notes from FEE," March 2, 1956: 1.
63. Daily Journal of Leonard E. Read, November 1, 1955, FEE Archives.
64. Ivan R. Bierly memorandum to Vic Milione, December 30, 1955, ISI Archives.
65. Author's interview with E. Victor Milione, April 20, 2001.
66. Memo from Vic Milione to Leonard Read, February 8, 1956, ISI Archives.

rooms housed the Society's two employees, Vic Milione and his secretary Mary Toelk, but the space was not shared with *Human Events*, FEE, or anyone else. ISI had declared its independence.

At the April trustees meeting, new by-laws were adopted and the "purposes" clause of the old Articles of Incorporation was amended to read:

> The particular business and objects of [the Intercollegiate Society of Individualists] shall be to promote among college students and the public generally, an understanding of and appreciation for the Constitution of the United States of America, the Bill of Rights, the limitations of the power of Government, the voluntary society, the free-market economy and the liberty of the individual.[67]

The changes were subtle but significant. Gone was any mention of "individualism;" added were references to "the voluntary society" and "the limitations of the power of Government." With the new purposes clause, ISI ended its short-lived commitment to an individualism narrowly conceived and committed itself to a more humane all-encompassing understanding of man and society. No longer would there be a singular concern with *homo economicus* but a broad examination of what constitutes the whole man.

The following were elected "Founder Members" of the board: Frank Chodorov, Frank C. Hanighen, John G. Pew, Jr., Charles H. Hoeflich, Edwin S. Webster, Jr., and William F. Buckley Jr. Chodorov, Hanighen, Pew, Hoeflich, Webster, and Buckley were then elected members of the new board of trustees for the ensuing year or until others were chosen in their stead. Unanimously chosen as officers were Frank Chodorov, president; William F. Buckley Jr., vice president; and Charles Hoeflich, secretary-treasurer. Chodorov then announced the appointment of E. Victor Milione as executive vice president.

Getting down to business, Milione proposed a June 1956-June 1957 budget of just over $65,000, covering salaries and office expenses, publica-

---

67. Meeting of the Boards of Trustees and Advisors, Intercollegiate Society of Individualists, April 21, 1956, ISI Archives.

tions, distribution of literature, lectures, and travel. He urged the resumption of *The Individualist* and its expansion to eight pages to include in the first section, news about ISI chapters, student essays, and reviews of college textbooks, and in the second section, essays by college professors and a column by Frank Chodorov. The expanded *Individualist*, Milione explained, would serve to "make the students feel they were more a part of ISI" and afford "conservative professors" a "medium for their academic arguments."[68]

Stating that publication of *The Individualist* would demonstrate that ISI had its "own" literature. Milione also went along, for the time being, with sending *Human Events*, *The Freeman*, and *National Review* to ISI members during the school year. Indeed, the total cost of the subscriptions (*Human Events*, 4,000; *The Freeman*, 2,000; *National Review*, 1,000) was $35,000—more than half of ISI's total budget. Never one to say no to a friend, Chodorov had allowed donors to use ISI's tax exempt status to make contributions earmarked for distribution of *Human Events* and the other magazines. It was technically legal, but Milione resolved to stop the practice, which undermined ISI's independence and adversely affected its fund-raising, as soon as he could. As he wrote to a friend, "Most people fail to realize we have a program of our own, other than providing students with gift subscriptions."[69]

The trustees meeting ended on a strong sense of satisfaction—about the thousands of students who were being exposed to the ideas of liberty; the ambitious program of literature, lectures, and campus clubs for the coming school year; the quiet determination and deep intelligence of the executive vice president; and ISI's location in Philadelphia, the cradle of liberty and a place of political miracles as far back as the Declaration of Independence in 1776. Casting about for a fitting end to the meeting, a trustee quoted from the 1950 Chodorov essay that had started the chain of events culminating in ISI: "What the socialists have done can be undone, *if there is a will for it.*"[70]

68. Ibid.
69. E. Victor Milione to James W. Crockett, November 21, 1956, ISI Archives.
70. Minutes of ISI Board of Trustees Meeting, April 21, 1956, ISI Archives.

CHAPTER II

Educating for Liberty

The man who is grounded in history knows something of the ever-present tension between the ideal and the prudential, so that his judgments should reflect wisdom rather than cleverness or phantasy.

Richard Weaver[1]

IN THE TURBULENT YEARS between 1929 and 1945, America was stunned by the free fall of the stock market, suffered through a Great Depression that initially left 25 percent of the labor force jobless, debated fiercely whether the nation should follow an isolationst or an interventionist foreign policy, recovered rapidly from the infamy of Pearl Harbor, and led the Allies to a decisive victory over the Axis in a great world war. Americans, exhausted, yearned for a return to normalcy, but instead, the "greatest generation" was called upon once more to deal with the multiple challenges of the Cold War and to determine the proper role of their government in an age seduced by collectivism. In this protracted conflict, the conservative movement produced its own great generation—a group of

1. Richard M. Weaver, "The Role of Education in Shaping Our Society," address delivered at the Metropolitan Area Industrial Conference, Chicago, October 25, 1962, published by ISI in 1966.

philosophers, popularizers, politicians, and philanthropists who stubbornly and courageously challenged the prevailing liberal orthodoxy.

Conservatives of high resolve and reputation were in place in key sectors of American society—including the academy—but they were usually isolated. They awaited organization—and organizations like ISI. ISI was the first institution (in 1953) to organize students and professors interested in promoting the ideas of liberty. *National Review* was the first weekly journal of opinion (in 1955) to expound systematically the philosophy of freedom in the universities and the media. Unsurprisingly, from the beginning, ISI and *National Review* were closely joined, with the magazine hiring ISI staffers like Stan Evans and sending student subscriptions to ISI members, and the Society sponsoring appearances by the magazine's editors and contributors (such as Frank Meyer and Russell Kirk) on the campuses. And there was the obvious connection: William F. Buckley Jr., ISI's first president, if only for about six months, was the founding editor-in-chief of *National Review.*

At the same time, "conservative thought became self-conscious and overt" with the publication of Russell Kirk's *The Conservative Mind.*[2] Indeed, books poured forth from right-thinking men and women—many of them ISI lecturers and advisers—like a mighty river: F. A. Hayek's *Capitalism and the Historians*, James Burnham's *Containment or Liberation?*, Merrill Root's *Collectivism on the Campus*, Richard Weaver's *The Ethics of Rhetoric*, Leo Strauss's *What Is Political Philosophy?*, and Eric Voegelin's *New Science of Politics*. Russell Kirk, it seemed, couldn't stop writing, producing six books in five years—*The Conservative Mind* (1953), *A Program for Conservatives* (1954), *Academic Freedom* (1955), *Beyond the Dreams of Avarice* (1956), and *The Intelligent Woman's Guide to Conservatism* (1957) and *The American Cause* (1957). Articulate, self-confident conservatives began fanning out across the country, taking on one and all in freewheeling debates about the state of the union and the world.

Puzzled by the persistent presence of something their usually percep-

---

2. Remarks by T. Kenneth Cribb, Jr., at Collegiate Network conference, November 10, 1995, Arlington, Virginia, ISI Archives.

tive colleague Lionel Trilling had said did not exist, liberals began examining the pesky conservative movement and coming to the most peculiar conclusions. According to Arthur M. Schlesinger, Jr., the "leading conservatives" included McGeorge Bundy, Wayne Morse, and Jacob Javits, all quite contented liberals.[3] Daniel Bell, David Riesman, Richard Hofstadter, and others in *The New American Right* went farther off course, linking Senator Joseph McCarthy and *The Freeman*, a politician and a publication as far removed in philosophy and rhetoric as Democratic presidential candidate Adlai Stevenson and *Human Events*. For such observers, George Nash wrote, conservatism and its proponents were not a serious intellectual challenge but rather "an aberration."[4]

But by the end of the decade, liberals were not so cavalierly dismissing a movement capable of producing serious journals like *Modern Age* (launched in 1957 by Russell Kirk and publisher Henry Regnery), popular politicians like Senator Barry Goldwater of Arizona, influential economists like the University of Chicago's Milton Friedman (a future Nobel laureate), and perceptive intellectuals like M. Stanton Evans, at twenty-six the youngest editor of a daily metropolitan newspaper—the *Indianapolis News*—in America.

As for Vic Milione, while appreciative of all that Buckley, Goldwater, and Kirk were doing to build the conservative movement, he was careful to place some distance between ISI and the movement, in order, he said, to protect the Society's educational tax exempt status. But there was a deeper reason for the separation: Milione preferred to think of himself as "a man of the West" (like Whittaker Chambers) rather than a conservative. "Conservative" seemed to Milione to be more a political than a philosophical term. Western civilization, he remarked, "did not begin with Edmund Burke."[5] Furthermore, the emphasis on politics, especially by well-heeled conservatives, frustrated Milione when he was seeking funds for ISI. "Too many people in the conservative movement," he said, "didn't

3. George Nash, *The Conservative Intellectual Movement in America:*135.
4. Ibid: 138.
5. Author's interview with E. Victor Milione, April 20, 2001.

give a damn about the universities."[6] Milione's policy of keeping ISI at a certain remove—even to locating in Philadelphia rather than in a more political city like Washington, D.C., or New York—served the Society well in the 1950s and early 1960s, when conservatism was often swirling in controversy. The *New York Times*, whenever it could, linked any rising star of the Right with the paranoid writings of Robert Welch, founder of the John Birch Society.

A Utilitarian Citadel

In the 1950s, there was no greater challenge for the gradually coalescing group of conservative thinkers, communicators, and policymakers than the academy, increasingly characterized by what Russell Kirk called a "vulgar utilitarianism" and an early but as ugly version of what came to be known as political correctness. When it was suggested at a faculty meeting at a well-known Midwest university that Professor Sidney Hook of New York University should be invited to speak, a dean cried, "What! That fascist reactionary?"[7] Hook was banned. And what great crime did this outspoken democratic socialist and widely admired scholar commit? He was an anti-Communist who insisted that Joseph Stalin was one of the giant villains and mass murderers of the twentieth century.

The single event that had the greatest impact on American higher education in the 1950s was the launching into near space in early October 1957 of a small aluminum alloy sphere that weighed 184 pounds and was less than two feet in diameter. It had two radio transmitters and was called *Sputnik*, Russian for "fellow traveler." One scientist called the Soviets' launching of *Sputnik* a technological Pearl Harbor. A phalanx of partisan Democrats, anxious Republicans, eager scientists, and tuition-poor educators formed and demanded an immediate response to the national emergency, with emphasis on the needs of higher education. In response, the Republican administration and the Democratic Congress co-produced

---

6. Author's interview with E. Victor Milione, May 16, 2001.
7. Russell Kirk, *Decadence and Renewal in the Higher Learning: An Episodic History of the American University and College Since 1953*, South Bend, Indiana, 1978: 38.

the National Defense Education Act, which declared that "the security of the nation requires the fullest development of the mental resources and technical skills of its young men and women. The national interest requires ... that the Federal Government give assistance to education for programs which are important to national defense."[8]

Unlike the G. I. Bill, which limited its aid to veterans, the NDEA offered federal money to everyone—$295 million in loans to students in higher education and $36.5 million in National Defense Fellowships. At the same time, government research grants and contracts to individuals as well as institutions increased substantially. By 1960, the federal government was spending several billion dollars annually on university "defense" research. At some schools, according to the American Council on Education, federal research yielded three times as much income from student fees and endowment earnings combined.

In the face of these liberal trends—a significantly larger federal presence on campus, an emphasis on utilitarian rather than classical education, 1950s-style political correctness, the private college versus Behemoth University, all of which strengthened the already heavy hand of the collectivists and the secularists in the academy—what could a tiny organization like ISI, with an annual budget of less than $50,000, realistically do? "We are little more than a gnat on the backside of a horse," Milione conceded.[9] The odds against having any measurable impact seemed impossibly long.

And yet, quietly and methodically, Vic Milione began building a national student organization dedicated to liberty, keeping the mailings moving and gradually broadening its intellectual reach. In the 1956-57 academic year, for example, ISI published "Religion and the Social Problem" by Edmund A. Opitz of FEE and "The Sociological Perspective" by Albert A. Hobbs of the University of Pennsylvania. It also offered copies of books—if a student requested them by letter—such as *Economics in*

8. George Roche, *The Fall of the Ivory Tower: Government Funding, Corruption, and the Bankrupting of American Higher Education*, Washington, D.C., 1994: 33.
9. E. Victor Milione to Thomas Molnar, March 8, 1963, ISI Archives.

One Lesson by Henry Hazlitt, *The Road to Serfdom* by F. A. Hayek, *The Mainspring of Human Progress* by H. G. Weaver, *One Is a Crowd* by Frank Chodorov, and *Human Action* by Ludwig von Mises. Students were expected to pay half the cost of the book. *The Individualist* elicited thanks and praise from students who found the newsletter "inspiring and eye opening"—one remarked that "young conservatives and libertarians need an outlet to voice their opinions."[10]

Clearly, the word was getting around. Members reported they were using ISI literature in the classroom, in intercollegiate debates and informal discussion, in forensic and other clubs. ISI material, wrote a New York University student, broadened "my base for give and take discussion with fellow students and friends and in challenging the accuracy, logic, etc., of professorial opinions." Even high school students signed up; one enthusiast was David Franke of Corpus Christi, Texas, who wrote to the editor of the local newspaper inviting students interested in "Judeo-Christian morals" and "the supremacy of the individual" over "the current wave of collectivist doctrines" to join ISI. (Four years later, Franke would be one of the prime movers in the founding of the conservative youth group, Young Americans for Freedom.)[11]

The ISI speakers bureau, composed of educators, businessman, and lawyers of the individualist philosophy, scheduled campus appearances in their immediate area. Among those who agreed to donate their services were John Frenning of the Penn Mutual Life Insurance Company, Boston; Hugh Forster, assistant to the president of Armstrong Cork Company, Lancaster, Pennsylvania; Peter Steele, director of education of the Associated Industries of Missouri; Associate Professor William H. Peterson of New York University; Professor U.S. Dubach of Lewis & Clark College, Portland, Oregon—and Dr. F. A. Hayek of the University of Chicago. The schools visited were equally diverse: the University of Minnesota, the University of Wisconsin, Cornell University, the University of

10. "A Report of the Intercollegiate Society of Individualists," August 1957, ISI Archives.
11. David Franke to ISI, April 26, 1956, ISI Archives.

Omaha, and St. John's University. About 3,500 ISI members in 1956-57 requested and received school year subscriptions to *Human Events* or *National Review* (*The Freeman* was dropped from the list). Students were asked to contribute $1 toward a subscription to *National Review.*

Budding Journalists

In the summer of 1957 and in cooperation with *Human Events*, ISI offered internships to aspiring young journalists, planting yet another mustard seed. The first three interns selected were David Franke, who would become an editorial assistant to Bill Buckley at *National Review*; Douglas Caddy of Georgetown University, a future founder of Young Americans for Freedom and its first executive director; and William Schulz of Antioch College, who would later work for the nationwide radio commentator Fulton Lewis Jr.—the Rush Limbaugh of his day—before joining *Reader's Digest* and eventually becoming its executive editor. Because of ISI, Schulz said, "I first read Hayek, heard Von Mises, worked with Stan Evans."[12] Evans has described ISI's internship program for young journalists as "an embryonic National Journalism Center"—an organization he founded in 1981 and which, by the year 2002, had graduated some one thousand young men and women into the ranks of American journalism—print, broadcast, and cable.[13]

ISI also encouraged the creation of independent student journals of high quality and plain appearance—publications like the *New Individualist Review* (University of Chicago), *Insight and Outlook* (University of Wisconsin), the *Alternative* (Yale), and the *Harvard Conservative.* These campus journals tackled both national and campus issues, offering the opinions of established writers like Russell Kirk and Milton Friedman as well as those of their own student editors. The first issue of the *New Individualist Review* featured a Friedman essay on "Capitalism and Free-

---

12. William Schulz, as quoted in "I Am Proud To Be an ISI Alumnus," published by ISI, circa 1981: 17.

13. Author's interview with M. Stanton Evans, October 31, 2001. Also see "Alumni Update" of the National Journalism Center, January 2002, published by NJC.

dom," and a profile of the eighteenth-century German classical liberal Wilhelm von Humboldt by graduate student and editor-in-chief Ralph Raico. In an editorial, Raico stated that "the party of liberty is steadily gaining adherents among students."[14]

The first issue of *The Conservative Digest* (at the University of Missouri) explored the conservative resurgence on campus as evidenced by the student support of the film *Operation Abolition* about the House Committee on Un-American Activities and the formation of the Missouri Society of Young Conservatives. Some of these student publications—like *Insight and Outlook*—lasted for years, while others disappeared with the graduation of their editors, a casualty of the four-year collegiate cycle. But these early journals were the forebears of the Collegiate Network of newspapers that emerged in the 1980s and achieved national prominence in the 1990s under ISI management.

ISI held its first regional meeting in November 1956 in New York City with members from New York, New Jersey, Pennsylvania, and New England attending. Students were encouraged to form informal discussion groups; some formalized themselves into campus clubs. At Queens College in New York City, Richard Whalen, who would later write the best-selling *The Founding Father* about the Kennedy family, organized the Robert A. Taft Club. Long a liberal stronghold, Queens College tried to ignore the new conservative group, but was forced—due to the persistence of Whalen and other students—to recognize its newsletter *Portfolio* and to allow conservative speakers like author Felix Wittmer to debate "a muddle-minded chap from the American Civil Liberties Union" during the college's Academic Freedom Week. Reflecting the exuberant spirit of a rising generation, Whalen urged young conservatives to reject "self-defeating pessimism" and "approach the task of building a stronger America confidently."[15]

The central role of New York City—the editorial home of *National Review*—in these early days of the conservative movement was reflected

14. "An Editorial," *New Individualist Review,* April 1961: 2.
15. "On Campus," Richard Whalen, *The Individualist*, December 1956: 3.

yet again in the debut in April 1956 of the Collegiate Libertarian Union at Columbia University. What is striking about the Union's founding document is not its staunch endorsement of "a free economy," a constitutional government protective "of even the smallest minority," and opposition to "anti-freedom forces in all their manifestations," but its reference in the first paragraph to "the benevolence of Divine Providence" and the wording of the final paragraph: "We pray that God will aid us and give us success in our efforts."[16] Such transcendent references served to strengthen Vic Milione's determination to include the spiritual as well as the economic dimension in ISI programs.

In that same year of 1956, ISI received a modest but important grant of $1,600 from the Relm Foundation (succeeded by the Earhart Foundation) of Ann Arbor, Michigan. This led to a close relationship between two individuals—Vic Milione and Richard A. Ware, Relm's secretary and later president—which would yield the single most influential ISI program in its fifty-year history: the Richard M. Weaver Fellowship Program.

Milione had written to Relm President James A. Kennedy in 1955 and the following year asking support for a series of pamphlets on a wide range of subjects, to be written by such scholars as Albert Hobbs, Edmund Opitz, and Richard Weaver. "We feel," explained Milione in June 1956, "that we should design our program so it will aid [students] in understanding the philosophy of freedom and its bearing upon economics, sociology, philosophy and education." Hobbs, a sociologist, had agreed to write a condensation of his well received book, *Social Problems and Scientism*. Opitz, a libertarian and ordained minister, would demonstrate that individualism "is a philosophy of responsibility and morality in all human endeavor and that collectivism is a philosophy of irresponsibility and immorality." The rhetorician Weaver would discuss "the philosophical approach of liberty; its roots in natural law, the parallel of which should be human law."[17]

16. "Declaration of the Faith and Purposes of the Collegiate Libertarian Union," April 13, 1956, Columbia University, ISI Archives.
17. E. Victor Milione to James A. Kennedy, May 24, 1956, Earhart Foundation Archives.

In its meticulous way, the Relm Foundation asked for and received a certified audit, an annual budget and report, a copy of ISI's tax exemption, and background on ISI's chief operating officer. Along the way, Milione explained to Ware that ISI believed it should promote "the libertarian view" in every academic discipline, not just economics. "One can never tell," he wrote, "what might interest a student." Although a political science major in college, he recalled, the one book that "gave the most impetus to my interests in freedom" was James M. Beck's *Our Wonderland of Bureaucracy*, published in 1932. Beck, a former U.S. solicitor general, wrote bluntly:

> The constantly growing strength of bureaucracy, the demands of groups for legislation and large appropriations, and the impotence of Congress to maintain its power are leading this American Government toward an absolutism, worthy of Moscow but unworthy of Philadelphia, where the Constitution was framed.[18]

Within the week, Relm approved a $1,600 grant, and in October, Dick Ware visited ISI's office in Philadelphia to "get acquainted." His memo on the meeting stated that ISI had "a simple office," a two-person staff of Milione and a stenographer-clerk, and an annual operating budget—excluding gift magazine subscriptions—of about $32,000. "Ideally," wrote Ware, "there should be a field representative (just out of college) to visit campus groups." Currently, about 4,700 members in some 400 colleges made 700 to 800 requests each school year for books and pamphlets. Milione impressed Ware as "a well-educated and quiet, but effective individual who thoroughly believes in his work." There have been longer and more eloquent descriptions of the man who led ISI for more than three decades, but none more accurate. As proof of Milione's commitment, Ware noted that he remained at ISI at an annual salary of $7,500 although "he has been offered almost twice as much from industry."[19]

Over the next two years, ISI's total annual income jumped to

18. E. Victor Milione to Richard A. Ware, June 15, 1956, Earhart Archives.
19. Memorandum entitled, "Intercollegiate Society of Individualists, Victor Milione, Exec. Vice-President, October 18, 1956," R. A. Ware, October 29, 1956, Earhart Archives.

$80,810.27 in 1957-58, and then to $95,187.75 in 1958-59. But almost all of the increase was for gift subscriptions to *Human Events* or *National Review*, both of which used ISI's tax-exempt status to raise funds for that purpose. Buckley informed the ISI board at the June 1958 trustees meeting that he hoped to bring in as much as $40,000 through ISI for his cash-strapped magazine. Frank Chodorov responded by raising "the possibility of the two publications contributing [to ISI] a percentage of the funds raised through the Society's name."

Human Events agreed that 7 ½ percent of all funds raised through ISI would be retained by the Society. *National Review* offered ISI a full page of advertising in the magazine once a month (actually thirteen times a year).[20] The board of trustees unanimously approved the arrangement, while passing a protective resolution that "all funds" raised for ISI gift subscriptions must be accounted for "by periodic invoices from the publisher(s) providing the subscriptions."[21] Vic Milione welcomed the safeguard but retained his reservations: too many organizations, no matter how worthy their objectives, were borrowing ISI's name. "How do you raise money," Milione recalls asking himself at the time, "when other people are using your tax exemption?"[22] And no one could say exactly how the IRS might react to the arrangement.

Inside the Enemy Camp

Meanwhile, ISI members were going where young conservatives had never gone before. At the University of Wisconsin, then as now one of the most liberal schools in America, Alan McCone, Jr., and his student colleagues started *Insight and Outlook*, which declared boldly in its first issue that the editors "agree with Orwell that the welfare state to which America seems to be heading leads to totalitarian despair."[23] The magazine included advertisements for ISI and FEE, a notice that the Wisconsin Con-

20. Meeting of Trustees and Advisors, ISI, June 9, 1958, ISI Archives.
21. Ibid.
22. Author's interview of E. Victor Milione, May 16, 2001.
23. "A Greeting to Our Readers," *Insight and Outlook*, Volume 1 Number 1, February 17, 1959: 3.

servative Club would debate the Socialist Club on the topic: "Resolved: Socialism would lead to a better world," a review of Russell Kirk's *The American Cause*, and an essay by Richard S. Wheeler (a future *National Review* editor) attacking Southerners for imposing "a totalitarianism upon the Negro" and the federal government for imposing "a dictatorial ultimatum upon the southerners."[24]

At Sweetbriar College in Virginia, the entire student body publicly recited the Pledge of Allegiance, apparently "for the first time in the history of the college," following a year of lobbying by ISI member Mary-Lou Burelle. At Oklahoma A. & M., John D. Farr reported "the growing participation of women in politics and campus leadership" because they realized "the importance and gravity of the Socialist threat even more than men. Women worry about their families." At St. John's University in Brooklyn, Antoinette Campanella said that copies of *National Review* in the student lounge were "sold out in a day" and that the Political Discussion Seminar had announced its topic for the term—"Conservatism."[25]

ISI, for its part, contacted members in 1957 seeking to discover what kind of textbooks and other materials were being used in their classrooms. "What have your professors been pushing at you?" a letter asked. "Have any of them notably associated themselves with collectivist thinking? (The incidents are important, not the names.)" ISI emphasized it was interested in good news as well as bad: "If the situation at your school is encouraging, we want to hear about that too." At a press conference, Arthur M. Schlesinger, Jr., and three other Harvard professors denounced the ISI inquiry in a press conference as "ridiculous," "silly," "trivial," "snooping," "tattling," and "spying" (omitting only the charge of "McCarthyism"). *The Individualist* calmly responded that "the Harvard professors obviously did not cotton to the idea of ISI trying to find out whether or not Cantabridgians were being subjected to collectivist-slanted instruction."[26]

In response to a letter from a Cornell student, *The Individualist* of-

24. Ibid: 12.
25. "On Campus," *The Individualist*, May 1957: 1, 3,4.
26. "Cool Reception," *The Individualist*, February 1957: 2.

fered pointers on how to form an ISI chapter, underlining that the "ideas here set forward should not be considered mandatory." ISI, the newsletter said, stressed "the need for *individual* votaries of freedom, rather than regimented cadres." The prospective organizer might begin by contacting ISI for the names of conservatives at his campus. He could study the school newspaper for letters expressing a conservative point of view. And he should probably attend the political forum at his school and take note of those "arguing the conservative cause." Once a group of conservatives had come together—as few as two, as many as twenty—they could write to ISI expressing their wish to call themselves an "ISI Chapter."

And that was it: ISI issued no charter and made no attempt to control the activities of the chapters. "The programs undertaken to forward conservatism at the various schools," said *The Individualist*, "are left to the initiative and discretion of the students at the scene." (It was early days in the conservative movement, and the level of mutual trust and respect was high.) At the same time, and notwithstanding the laissez-faire philosophy of founder Frank Chodorov, ISI was practical: the Society declared that it was not responsible for the opinions or activities of its "completely autonomous affiliates" and reserved the right "to withdraw the use of its name."[27]

The suggested activities were classic ISI—public meetings featuring conservative "notables," letters to the editor of the campus paper, a chapter newsletter, debates with liberal groups, and a library of conservative books for "the convenience" of interested undergraduates. Perhaps most important was "conservative advocacy" on questions before the campus community.[28]

The consistent use of the word "conservative" rather than "individualist" in ISI's newsletter reflected a new reality of the late fifties—an American conservative movement had gradually come into being. The movement took its name from Russell Kirk's definitive work, *The Conservative Mind*. It received its weekly allotment of shrewd analysis and often outrageous commentary from Bill Buckley's *National Review*—and *Hu-*

27. "How to Start an ISI Chapter," *The Individualist*, March 1957: 3. The author found no evidence of any such withdrawal in his extensive research of the voluminous ISI files.
28. Ibid.

man Events. And it was given political substance by those elected officials who now openly described themselves as conservatives—led by Senator Barry Goldwater, who would title his manifesto, published in the spring of 1960, *The Conscience of a Conservative.* In this new intellectual and political climate, some mused, it might be time for the Intercollegiate Society of Individualists to consider changing its name.

Chapters and Verses

Meanwhile, aggressive ISI members stepped up their organizational activity until by 1960, there were ISI chapters or conservative clubs at more than fifty major colleges and universities, including the University of Pennsylvania, the University of Chicago, the University of Southern California, Ohio State University, Cornell University, Antioch College, Carleton College, Williams College, and Grove City College. In addition, ISI had a working relationship with Princeton's Clio Society, the nation's oldest student conservative group, and Marquette University's Franklin Forum, that school's oldest society. Several clubs published their own journals with finanicial support from ISI. In addition to *Insight and Outlook*, published by the Conservative Club of Wisconsin, there were *Analysis*, published by the Eleutherian Society of the University of Pennsylvania; and *The Entrepreneur*, published by the Conservative Club of Grove City College.

With characteristic chutzpah, ISI began questioning the actions of the National Student Association (NSA), a confederation of student governments on some four hundred campuses comprising about one million students. Founded in 1946, NSA initially concerned itself with the internal problems of the academic community—such as tuition and student participation in school governance—but gradually added the problems of the world at large. "Students should be directed to a greater social awareness," an NSA president proclaimed in Dewey-speak.[29] NSA's policy pronouncements lurched ever leftward, including a fervent plea for more

29. "NSA: Where is it leading American students?" M. Stanton Evans, *The Individualist*, November 1958: 1.

federal aid to education and opposition to the discharge of communist teachers and loyalty oaths for ROTC students.

The organization, wrote M. Stanton Evans in *The Individualist*, seemed to look upon a college education "as a sort of sociological laboratory in which one masters the arts of committeeship, manipulation of groups, and general politicking." Anticipating arguments that would be made by conservative critics Allan Bloom and Dinesh D'Souza decades later, Evans suggested that if NSA's student politicians "spent more time studying, and less bigwigging, they might make a far more valuable contribution to the cause of American education."[30] In the 1960s, Young Americans for Freedom, not bound as ISI was by tax-exemption, directly challenged NSA's political monopoly on dozens of campuses.

In the late 1950s, with the Cold War an increasingly grim reality following the brutal Soviet suppression of the 1956 Hungarian Revolution and the launching of Sputnik the following year, loyalty in America was a consequential issue. The 1958 National Defense Education Act required students receiving government aid to file a loyalty oath and an anti-Communist affidavit. But opponents complained that freedom of belief and conscience were violated by such requirements. Harvard University withdrew from the program because the loyalty clause "singles out students alone in our population"—a position also taken by the NSA which called the oath-affidavit "discriminatory." But David Franke, who along with Douglas Caddy organized the Student Committee for the Loyalty Oath, pointed out in the pages of *The Individualist* that the pledge of loyalty was required only of those who sought financial assistance from the government and in the name of national defense. Franke asked:

> By what conceivable twist of logic can it be held that citizens who are loyal should be taxed to help an unloyal student through college as a defense measure? Nor does the student who is loyal, but ashamed to declare his allegiance, have a claim to the taxpayer's assistance. It is only the student who is proud to declare his loyalty who will readily fight for his country when the cold war turns hot—and this is the only

30. Ibid: 4.

student who has any conceivable claim to assistance from his government.[31]

Describing himself as a "true" individualist (someone concerned with community as well as self), Franke endorsed the principle of a limited government that takes necessary action to protect the citizenry "against subversion and aggression." He quoted Richard Weaver as observing that "for four centuries every man has been ... his own professor of ethics, and the consequence is an anarchy which threatens even that minimum consensus of value necessary to the political state."[32] Franke reflected, in microcosm, the ongoing philosophical development of ISI from a strictly individualist institution as defined by the anti-statist Nock to a broadly conservative organization open to the ideas of traditionalists like Kirk and Weaver as well as classical liberals like Hayek.

ISI members began to make their presence felt far beyond the campus. In September 1960, under the supervision of Bill Buckley and master organizer Marvin Liebman, Dave Franke and Doug Caddy convened— at Buckley's parents' spacious home in Sharon, Connecticut—the founding meeting of Young Americans for Freedom, which would provide a large share of the ground troops of the conservative movement in the 1960s. The principal author of YAF's declaration of purpose, the Sharon Statement, was Stan Evans; an editor of the statement was Carol Dawson, an ISI member at Dunbarton College in Washington, D.C. (Dawson later served as an aide in the Nixon White House and then in the Reagan administration as a member of the Consumer Products Safety Commission.)

In the fall of 1959, as part of its mission to advance "conservative thought on the campus," ISI distributed two telling documents—Bill Buckley's scathing remarks at the Khrushchev Protest Rally at New York City's Carnegie Hall and Richard Weaver's reflective paper, "The Purpose of Education," excerpted in the *Wall Street Journal*. The reprints repre-

31. "The Student Loyalty Oath," David Franke, *The Individualist*, December 1959: 4.
32. Ibid: 4.

sented two major concerns of ISI—the present danger of communism and the muddled state of American higher education.

Addressing an emotional audience wearing black armbands and waving black flags, symbolizing their grief for the millions of victims of communism, Buckley declared that Soviet Premier Nikita Khrushchev's visit to the United States "profaned" the nation. The "national acquiescence" to President Eisenhower's invitation had required, he said, "the lapse of our critical and moral faculties." As long as they were in suspension, Buckley warned, national "regeneration is not possible."[33]

Buckley's cold fury revealed the conservative movement's anti-communist fervor and its sense of betrayal by Eisenhower as well as his vice president Richard Nixon, the man who had put one-time Soviet spy Alger Hiss behind bars. "The President will meet with Khrushchev," *National Review* editorialized scornfully, "as Chamberlain and Daladier met with Hitler at Munich, as Roosevelt and Churchill met with Stalin at Yalta."[34] Many conservatives, and not just members of the ultra-right John Birch Society, applauded the call of *National Review* senior editor L. Brent Bozell for "victory" in the Cold War—a policy that would be articulated by Barry Goldwater in his 1964 presidential campaign and finally implemented successfully by President Ronald Reagan in the 1980s.[35]

The Aim of Higher Education

Expecting perhaps a critique of the Khrushchev visit or an analysis of the sluggish U.S. economy, the readers of the *Wall Street Journal* were given one early October morning a closely reasoned 2,500-word essay about the purpose of higher education. The author was Richard M. Weaver, who wrote the essay at the invitation of ISI, which then offered it to the *Journal*. Author, organization, and newspaper were all agreed as to the profound importance of education to the person, the society, and the nation.

33. "'The Damage We Have Done to Ourselves,'" remarks by William F. Buckley Jr., Carnegie Hall, September 17, 1959, ISI Archives.
34. John Judis, *William F. Buckley Jr.: Patron Saint of the Conservatives*, New York, 1988: 175.
35. Ibid: 176.

Richard Weaver's article proceeded logically from the problem (education suffered from "an unprecedented amount of aimlessness and confusion") to the cause (a failure "to think hard about the real province of education") to the solution (a turning away from "life adjustment" theory to the disciplines that life requires). At the heart of those disciplines, argued Weaver, was language, "the supreme organon of the mind's self-ordering growth." (Neither Weaver nor the editors offered a definition of *organon*— "a set of methods or principles used in scientific or philosophical investigation"—Webster's.)[36] Those who attacked the discipline of language, the author insisted, were attacking "the basic instrumentality of the mind."[37]

Something called "social science" or "social studies" was being substituted for history, and the student was being encouraged to give thought to the "dating patterns" of teenagers instead of the wisdom that explained the rise and fall of nations. With "amazing audacity," Weaver said, so-called progressive educators have turned their backs on the subjects that have provided "the foundations of culture and of intellectual distinction." In their place, they have offered only propaganda.[38]

One of the more pernicious claims made by the progressives, concluded Weaver, was that their kind of education fostered individualism. But true individualism, stressed the author, was "a matter of the mind and the spirit"—it meant "the development of the person, not the well-adjusted automaton." What the progressivists really desired, Weaver insisted, was to produce the "smooth" individual adapted to "some favorite scheme of collectivized living," not the person of "strong convictions, of refined sensibility, and of deep personal feeling of direction in life."[39]

In one of the nation's leading newspapers, then, and with full credit to ISI—"This article is excerpted from a paper prepared for the Intercollegiate Society of Individualists"—Richard Weaver, a respected member

36. *Webster's II New College Dictionary*, Boston, 1995: 772.

37. "The Purpose of Education," Richard M. Weaver, *Wall Street Journal*, October 9, 1959, excerpted from a paper prepared for the Intercollegiate Society of Individualists, ISI Archives.

38. Ibid.

39. Ibid.

of the academy, decried the "educational breakdown" brought about by the "collectivist political notions" of the progressives and offered an alternative—what we now call conservatism, although Weaver did not use the term—a discipline of the mind and the spirit that leads to true freedom. It was just such paradigmatic analysis that caused Vic Milione to say of Weaver that he went "deeper and more thoroughly" into a subject than any other academic he knew.[40]

In May 1960, in the middle of a presidential election year, Weaver was pleased to participate in a remarkable ISI conference held in Chicago and organized by Notre Dame political scientists Gerhart Niemeyer and Rev. Stanley Parry, C.S.C. The organizers explained that the meeting would be "devoted to a hard-driving attempt to formulate a conservative position on the level of general theory" and not "to a political manifesto ordered to the coming elections."[41] In addition to Niemeyer, Parry, and Weaver, the other attendees—all leading conservative intellectuals—were L. Brent Bozell, David S. Collier, F. A. Hayek, Frank S. Meyer, Donald Lipsett, Revilo Oliver, Henry Regnery, E. Victor Milione, and M. Stanton Evans.

At the initial Friday evening session, according to a summary written by Niemeyer, the conferees agreed that laissez-faire economic views were no longer in conflict with a positive view of political authority "in conservative circles" and that any lingering division lay "in underlying philosophical views of man and society." The Saturday sessions revolved around the concepts of man, society, and transcendence and their relations to each other. Niemeyer reported a "surprising amount of agreement," with virtually no one expressing a positivistic view against the relevance of spiritual things. Every conferee "acknowledged that virtue presupposes freedom, and all accepted, in some form or other, the concept of natural law." Everyone, said Niemeyer, "showed concern for an uncoerced individualism."[42]

40. Author's interview with E. Victor Milione, May 16, 2001.
41. Gerhart Niemeyer and Stanley Parry to David Collier, February 19, 1960, ISI Archives.
42. Gerhart Niemeyer summary of the Chicago ISI Conservatism Conference, May 6-8, 1960, ISI Archives.

Disagreements arose, however, over the nature and cause of "our present crisis" and the kind of social order that might bring about uncoerced individualism. Three different views were expressed: the central problem was man's attitude toward the Creation; the difficulty stemmed from a failure to hold in balance the values of virtue and freedom; and civilization provided only a precarious foothold on order and had to be continuously defended against the forces of barbarism. No one, according to Niemeyer, denied the essentially Christian character of "our society" or suggested that anything other than Christianity was "the basis for our individualism." Nevertheless, it was agreed, non-Christians and agnostics had to be accommodated in public life.[43]

Niemeyer's positive assessment of the ISI conference was confirmed by, among others, Weaver, who conveyed to the Notre Dame professor "the great pleasure and profit" he gained from the weekend. Having attended many conferences with equally lofty goals, Weaver admitted that he could not "remember one from which I felt I was taking away more solid instruction and clarification." He praised the organizational skill and intellectual integrity of the two organizers. "I have never been so satisfied," he said, "that conservative leadership is in the right hands."[44]

Weaver was especially pleased at the high degree of agreement. He believed it was primarily due to the focus on "profound principle" rather than practical politics. For the good of the cause, he said, conservatives "have got to avoid making 'last stands' on minor issues." He counseled conservatives to be "flexible" which was something "entirely different" from compromising. He highlighted the need for conservatives to develop a sense of timing and a sense of rhetorical sophistication. "The conservatives," he wrote Niemeyer, "have got to give the impression that they are talking about the real world and about values that are desirable. This is the only way to start cracks in the Liberal dogma."[45]

Frank Meyer also wrote to Niemeyer expressing his pleasure with the

43. Ibid.
44. Richard Weaver to Gerhart Niemeyer, May 18, 1960, ISI Archives.
45. Ibid.

outcome of the conference and singling out three key results: establishing agreement on key issues; clarifying conflicting views that make debate "less irritating and much more fruitful"; and stimulating thought and writing by "all the participants with whom I have spoken."[46]

The Chicago conference did indeed stimulate thought and writing, including the publication in 1964 of *What Is Conservatism?* a collection of probing essays commissioned by ISI and edited by Frank Meyer. Several of the contributors such as Hayek, Bozell, Parry, and Evans participated in the Chicago meeting, and the book was dedicated to the memory of Richard M. Weaver, "pioneer and protagonist of the American conservative consensus."[47] Once again, ISI had helped to shape the conservative arguments of the day.

Invading the Heartland

Wanting to tap into the educational and financial roots of the American heartland, ISI opened a Midwest office in Indianapolis, Indiana, and named the vigorous Donald Lipsett as director. Lipsett had B.S. and M.B.A. degrees from Indiana University and extensive work experience with FEE, *National Review*, the Ingersoll Milling Machine Company, and the Indiana Manufacturers Association—although he was barely 30 years old. In the years to come, Lipsett raised the money for his salary and the expenses of the office, traveled all over the Midwest visiting campuses and setting up ISI chapters (mostly in Illinois, Indiana, and Wisconsin), organized seminars and conferences featuring conservatism's brightest intellectual stars, and bombarded Milione with memoranda about everything from fund-raising leads to a newspaper article that had to be answered *now*. Lipsett liked to quote Gordon Fox—that the attributes of individualism are "the primacy of the individual, the concept of God-given rights, and the concept of limited, delegated governmental powers and dispersed dominion."[48]

46. Frank Meyer to Gerhart Niemeyer, May 20, 1960, ISI Archives.
47. Frank S. Meyer, ed., *What Is Conservatism?*, New York, 1964.
48. Flyer of the Midwest Office of the Intercollegiate Society of Individualists, Don Lipsett, Director, c 1960.

Plans were also laid for ISI's first summer school—four weeks in duration—to be held in July 1960 at Grove City College, under the direction of economist Hans Sennholz and through the generosity of J. Howard Pew, who had graduated from the college in 1900. But first Vic Milione decided that the time had come to cut the deceptively golden cord between ISI and the two magazines, *Human Events* and *National Review*, with which it had long been so closely associated.

The arrangement had undoubtedly boosted the circulation of the two magazines and provided ISI members with some of the best conservative writing—and thinking—of the day, especially on current issues. But it also hampered ISI's efforts to raise money for its own projects, and it clouded the Society's image in the minds of many—was ISI an independent institution dedicated to advancing liberty on the campus or a student adjunct of some other organization? At Milione's insistence, the board of trustees agreed to stop accepting "contributions designated specifically for subscriptions" to outside periodicals. ISI was now obliged to produce its own materials, Charles Hoeflich explained, "geared to helping students get an education despite what they were receiving on the campus."[49]

Warnings by some trustees of a sharp decline in ISI income were justified: ISI contributions plummeted more than 50 percent between 1959 and 1960, from $95,187.75 to $45,195.73. A lesser leader might have panicked and reinstituted the old arrangement, but Milione stood firm—as he would on other occasions when funds were low and someone came calling with an offer that was tempting but inconsistent with ISI's mission. As Milione would say to staff members during lean times when bills went unpaid and salaries were delayed, sometimes for weeks, "Live

49. Author's interview with Charles H. Hoeflich, May 16, 2001. The board of directors was also influenced in its decision by Vic Milione's two weeks in a hospital following what was thought at first to be a heart attack. The diagnosis was "severe stress." Milione informed the board that his stress would be significantly alleviated if ISI would stop "lending" its tax exemption—and mailing list—to other organizations. Shortly after the board's action, both publisher James Wick of *Human Events* and editor William F. Buckley Jr. of *National Review* resigned as trustees. Author's interview with E. Victor Milione, April 12, 2002.

on your acorns."[50] Milione himself once went on half-pay for several months.[51]

But the decision to go it alone (what could have been more individualist?) was proven correct when ISI contributions soared in 1961 to $100,955.27, more than double the previous year, and set a new income high. Contributions doubled again in two years to $206,902.97. The impressive growth was due to the efforts of an expanded and more business-oriented board of trustees, Milione's determination to broaden the donor base, ISI's measurable impact on and off campus, and the challenge of coping with America's ever expanding student population which in 1961 topped 3.5 million—more than double what it had been in 1940.

Organizationally, John G. Pew, Jr., vice president of the Sun Shipbuilding and Drydock Corporation (and brother of J. Howard), replaced Bill Buckley as vice president. Buckley had resigned from the board of trustees in December 1958, pleading the press of *National Review* business and not wishing to "give grounds to any suspicion that there is a conflict of interests" between the magazine and ISI.[52] The new trustees included Indianapolis attorney Albert M. Campbell, who would write many letters and make many telephone calls in the ensuing years on behalf of ISI, and business leaders such as Louis H. T. Dehmlow, president of the Great Lakes Terminal and Transport Corporation, Chicago; James A. McConnell, director of the Corn Products Refining Corporation; and Peter O'Donnell, Jr., a Dallas millionaire and Texas Republican leader, who would later serve as chairman of the Draft Goldwater for President Committee.

Believing that ideas needed organization in order to have consequences, O'Donnell proposed that ISI divide the nation into ten regions and assign an organizer to each region. "Some may feel that we are over-organizing an individualist movement," wrote O'Donnell, but one or two people, "however dedicated and hard-working they may be," could

50. Author's interview with Wayne Valis, October 20, 2001.
51. Author's interview with Robert Ritchie, April 30, 2003.
52. William F. Buckley Jr. to Frank Chodorov, December 4, 1958, ISI Archives.

not carry the ISI message to "the leaders of tomorrow." The price tag for the ten regional "salesmen" and their offices was $120,000, over half of the annual budget.[53] While ambitious and imaginative, O'Donnell's plan was never adopted—other needs always came first.

The ISI Alternative

Over the phone—his favorite means of communication because "you could find out quickly what you wanted to know"—Milione set about persuading wealthy conservatives to support ISI.[54] He usually began by stating what was obvious to any conservative—"the past and present course of America has been that of increasing the sphere of government and decreasing that of individual liberty." A decade earlier, it had seemed as though "America was of one mind in this choice, particularly on the college campuses." Some people even suggested that "it was natural to be socialistic in youth," but Frank Chodorov and the other ISI founders strongly disagreed, arguing that "if young people were socialistic, it was simply a reflection of what they were taught."[55]

What was needed, Milione would explain, was an organization that offered students "convincing literature on the alternative to socialism." And that was what ISI provided year after year on campus after campus. In just eight years, it had distributed books, pamphlets, and reprints to over 40,000 students and professors—about ten thousand members of the academic community were currently on the Society's mailing list. More than one million pieces of literature had been mailed. Newspapers and magazines in the late 1950s often highlighted the high jinks of Jack Kerouac and other spaced-out beatniks, but more perceptive members of the press noted the existence of a less colorful but more substantive group—"the un-beat generation." The *Richmond News-Leader* editorially lauded the young men and women of ISI for their "intellectual independence" and directed students "who like to think for themselves" to the Intercollegiate

53. Peter O'Donnell to Lemuel R. Boulware, March 2, 1962, ISI Archives.
54. Author's interview with E. Victor Milione, May 17, 2001.
55. Message of E. Victor Milione in "The ISI Story as of 1961," published by ISI, circa 1962: 2-3, ISI Archives.

Society of Individualists in Philadelphia.[56]

Among the ISI graduates already making a difference in the public square were M. Stanton Evans, editor of the *Indianapolis News* ("It was only when I enrolled in ISI, I think, that my education really began"); Richard Whalen, editorial writer for the *Wall Street Journal*, Edwin McDowell, editorial writer for the *Arizona Republic* and later book reviewer for the *New York Times* ("ISI was probably the best thing that happened to me during my college career"); Allan Ryskind, assistant editor of *Human Events* ("Just after the professors had shampooed your brain in class, it was thoroughly unshampooed again by the pamphlets put out by ISI [and] read after class"); and William Schulz, reporter for commentator-columnist Fulton Lewis, Jr. ("The Intercollegiate Society of Individualists has contributed more to my intellectual development, to my evolution into a knowledgeable young conservative, than any other single group or organization"). Typical of the student comments received was that of Joseph M. McNally at Seton Hall in New Jersey: "Professors Hobbs' and Weaver's works are powerful, deep and enlightening. Chodorov the same. Please MORE and MORE. Thank you."[57]

Never an advocate of the hard sell, Milione normally ended his telephone conversation with a potential donor by saying that ISI was not trying to "preempt" the credit for such accomplishments. ISI had principally been "a catalyst, a source of encouragement and advice when asked"—it did not force its literature and its views on anyone. At the same time, the Society was pleased with the results of the last eight years, while aware "there is much more to be done" to advance individual freedom in America.[58] If the so-and-so company or foundation or individual wanted to help by sending a contribution or approving a grant, ISI would be grateful, and so, implied its executive vice president, would be the nation.

Even to a bottom-line businessman accustomed to immediate re-

56. "The Unbeat Generation," *Richmond News-Leader*, June 4, 1959.
57. "The ISI Story as of 1961: For the Advancement of Conservative Thought on American College Campuses," c. 1962: M. Stanton Evans quote, 19, Edwin McDowell quote, 20, Allan Ryskind quote, 22, Joseph McNally quote, 7.
58. Ibid.

sults, ISI's mission to educate for liberty and free enterprise, its solid record of accomplishments among students, and the absolute conviction of the messenger ("When Vic has an idea," says Charles Hoeflich, "he *believes* in it") had a powerful attraction.[59] Among the first to respond with a donation and to encourage their friends and associates to give were Southern industrialist Roger Milliken, who underwrote the distribution of John T. Flynn's *Decline and Fall of the American Republic*; Lemuel R. Boulware, retired vice president of General Electric, who opened many doors for ISI in New York City and in wealthy southern Florida where he lived; Milwaukee business leader William H. Brady, Jr., who supported the Midwest office for years; California industrialist Henry Salvatori, Jr., who would give ISI its largest individual contribution in its first thirty years; New Jersey philanthropist Fred Kirby, who would see Milione when he would not see other people, and who in the mid-1990s gave $1.5 million for ISI's new headquarters in Wilmington, Delaware; Californian Kersey Kinsey, whose support enabled ISI to open up a Western office in the 1960s; and Mellon heir Richard Scaife and his Allegheny Foundation.

All these successful conservatives—mostly entrepreneurs rather than corporate managers—agreed with ISI that the rising generation was redeemable. They endorsed the assertion of Arnold Toynbee that "a small group with a clear idea of what it wants to do can have a greater impact than thousands who don't know where they are going."[60] ISI would need every possible ounce of clarity and steadfastness in the decade ahead when it often seemed that young Americans had lost their senses.

59. Author's interview with Charles Hoeflich, May 16, 2001.
60. Author's interview with E. Victor Milione, May 16, 2001.

CHAPTER III

The Other Sixties

The academy is no longer a comfortable fiefdom of the Left; it has
become instead what it ought to be, a battleground of ideas.

M. Stanton Evans[1]

"T̶HE CENTER THAT HAD more or less held in the late 1950s," wrote
the historian James T. Patterson, "cracked in the 1960s, exposing
a glaring, often unapologetic polarization" between generations, races,
genders, and social classes.[2] It split apart because of a seemingly unending
succession of cruel and mocking events. One president was assassinated,
and another decided he did not dare run for reelection. The civil rights
movement transformed the way America looked at its black citizens, but
the leader of the movement was foully murdered in a Memphis motel.
The most powerful nation in the world committed half a million men
and $150 billion to defeating communism in Vietnam and was fought to
a standstill by a tiny Third World nation. Millions cheered John F. Kennedy

1. M. Stanton Evans, *Revolt on the Campus,* Chicago, 1961: 190.
2. James T. Patterson, *Grand Expectations: The United States, 1945-1974,* New York,
1996: 457.

when he declared that "we shall pay any price, bear any burden, meet any hardship, support any friend, oppose any foe to assure the survival and success of liberty," but eight years later, more than 600,000 people were participating in antiwar "moratorium" demonstrations in Washington, D.C. Eight million young people happily enrolled in the nation's colleges and universities which by the end of the decade were riven by anger, fear, violence, and death.

Other historians have taken a less apocalyptic view of the era. For instance, one wrote that the 1960s were "the longest period of uninterrupted growth in United States history." Untouched by either the Great Depression or World War II, the young men and women of the 1960s were more self-confident and self-centered than their parents or grandparents. Many came to believe they had "the knowledge and the resources to create a progressive, advanced society like none before," not only in American but in human history.[3]

The academy shared in the hubris. College and university officials, according to Diane Ravitch, foresaw "no dark clouds on the horizon, not even the problem of financing, which seemed manageable in a thriving economy."[4] No one anticipated that the openness of America's campuses would make them staging grounds for youthful revolutionaries who "tried to destroy the one institution in American society that provided a sanctuary for their views." How ironic, Ravitch pointed out, that the freedom to teach and learn was attacked not from the Right but by "student ideologues" of the Left and "their campus sympathizers."[5]

What many accounts of the 1960s leave out is the remarkable rise of the Right that successfully challenged the liberal political establishment throughout the decade. Conservatives nominated an uncompromising conservative—Barry Goldwater—as the presidential candidate of a major political party (a feat not accomplished since Calvin Coolidge headed

3. Ibid: 451-452.
4. Diane Ravitch, *The Troubled Crusade: American Education 1945-1980,* New York, 1983: 182.
5. Ibid: 183.

the Republican ticket forty years before); elected an enormously attractive if inexperienced candidate—Ronald Reagan—to the governorship of the second most populous state in the union; and helped accelerate the forces which led to the decline and eventual fall of liberalism as the reigning philosophy of American politics.

The 1960s were a heady time for conservatives who came to believe, swept up in the revolutionary spirit of the age, that they too could accomplish almost anything through political action. But there were those who took the longer view that man does not live by politics alone. Writing to the Notre Dame political scientist Gerhart Niemeyer, ISI's Vic Milione argued that the election of a conservative as president would mean little "without an increase in the effort to restore the root values of our civilization in the intellectual center of American life." Milione conceded that such a restoration was "a tremendous task" but not an impossible one, because, he said, quoting Tocqueville, "every fresh generation is a new people."[6] Despite mounting pressure from members and donors, ISI stuck to its mission to educate for liberty and declined to join the political parade.

From its beginnings, ISI had been conceived as an educational institution, not a vehicle for political activism. This fundamental imperative was given concrete form by Milione's educational philosophy, shaped by his reading of such thinkers as John Henry Newman, Ortega y Gasset, and Richard Weaver. From Newman, Milione learned that fragments of the truth are found in many disciplines, so that an approach to the whole truth about man requires the student to confront a variety of perspectives. ISI therefore eschewed a narrow approach in its educational efforts and instead exposed students to the whole of the liberal arts. In an era of increasing specialization and professionalism, ISI insisted on the importance of traditional broad learning.

From Ortega, Milione learned that true education involves the cultivation of cultural norms which are the preconditions of sound judgment. These norms represent the best insights of the past, and Milione believed

6. E. Victor Milione to Gerhart Niemeyer, November 6, 1964, ISI Archives.

that in the twentieth century, it was particularly important to remind the rising generation—hubristic in every age, but especially so in an age of scientific and technical progress—about the great achievements of the Western tradition. ISI necessarily endeavored to distinguish the truly profound truths from passing fads. In so acting, it sought nothing less than to conserve Western civilization itself.

From Weaver, Milione learned a lesson which would distinguish ISI from almost every other educational organization—students are not "objects" but individuals. They should not be used to achieve any political end but should be allowed to develop their own intellectual abilities and cultural interests. Students themselves are the end, and ISI existed for their sake. When students encountered ISI for the first time, they were often baffled by an organization which seemed to have no ulterior motive in dispensing its largesse. But when they discovered that what seemed to be true of ISI was indeed true, they were captivated by the idea of education *qua* education—a reflection of what university learning ought to be but so often was not.[7]

In mid-1961, Frank Meyer drafted and Gerhart Niemeyer revised a statement of principles for ISI which, while never formally adopted, reflected and still does reflect more than forty years later ISI's basic philosophy:

- Man's activities are guided by moral law, founded in the nature of things.

- Political power is legitimate only as it defers to this moral law.

- Government's functions are the preservation of public peace, the maintenance of justice, and the defense of the Republic.

- Free government presupposes the rule of law; personal separation of political and economic power.

- The right of private property is an essential condition of independence.[8]

7. Based on a telephone interview of E. Victor Milione by Mark Henrie, July 15, 2003.
8. Working Draft written by Frank Meyer and revised by Gerhart Niemeyer, March 13, 1961, ISI Archives.

Liberal Harvard

The urgent need to provide an alternative view to the prevailing ethos of the academy was confirmed in a 1960 poll of Harvard undergraduates conducted by the editors of the student-run *Harvard Crimson*, under the guidance of sociologist David Riesman. The paper headlined its report, "'Moderate Liberals' Predominate Politically: Lectures, Course Reading Influence Shift to Left." The *Crimson* pointed out that while a large number of students identified themselves as "liberal," their political views were "decidedly radical"—one-seventh supported "full socialization of all industries," more than a fifth favored socialization of the medical profession, nearly a third believed that the federal government should "own and operate all basic industries," two-thirds supported wage and price controls to check inflation.

Indeed, wrote the *Crimson*: "Federal aid is rapidly gaining the status of a magic word. Surrounded by a climate of liberalism, most Harvard undergraduates seem ready to accept increased Federal activity in almost any area of national life."[9] For the most part, the *Crimson* stated, students did not arrive at Harvard with these beliefs but picked them up from class lectures and assigned textbooks that consistently leaned to the Left. The result was that 70 percent had changed since their freshman year either "from conservative to more liberal" or "from liberal to more liberal."[10]

Although Vic Milione conceded (in a letter to a potential supporter) that what happened at Harvard did not necessarily "happen in equal measure elsewhere," it was safe to assume that *all* students were influenced by their teachers and acquired thereby "beliefs which they will retain, most likely, for life."[11] The Harvard undergraduate poll demonstrated that no school, not even the most tradition-bound, was immune to the virus of collectivism.

ISI stepped up its distribution of pamphlets and books and its spon-

---

9. William F. Buckley Jr., "Harvard Says It Loud and Clear," *National Review*, January 16, 1960: 44.
10. Ibid.
11. E. Victor Milione to Robert Fotte, Jr., January 17, 1964, ISI Archives.

sorship of speakers and seminars and held its first summer school in 1960 at Grove City College in Western Pennsylvania. With total expenses of about $10,000, the school represented a major commitment by ISI. In addition to four-week courses in economics and persuasive speaking by Grove City faculty Hans Sennholz and William Teufel, a veritable Who's Who of American conservatism addressed the thirty-five students (six of them female) who immersed themselves in conservative ideas for a full month. One of the young ladies was Annette Courtemanche of New York's Molloy College, whose very Catholic mother contacted ISI to inquire about the nature of the accommodations. Milione assured Mrs. Courtemanche that her beautiful twenty-year-old daughter would be perfectly "safe"—as indeed she was, except from the subtle blandishments of faculty member Russell Kirk, whom she married four years later.[12]

One-week courses at the Grove City summer school were conducted by political scientist Karl Cerny of Georgetown University, economist David McCord Wright of McGill University, and international relations professor Stefan Possony of Georgtown. Lecturers who spent one or two days were political scientist Anthony T. Bouscaren of LeMoyne College, law professor Sylvester Petro of New York University, the ubiquitous William F. Buckley Jr., FEE president Leonard Read, and ISI trustee Lemuel R. Boulware. As important as the lectures themselves were the frequent opportunities for the students to talk informally with Kirk, Buckley, Sennholz, et al, at breakfast, lunch, dinner, and late into the evening. (Russell Kirk enlivened the nights with his ghost stories.) At this and ensuing summer schools, more than one student summed up his experience by saying simply: "It changed my life."

Out in America's heartland, Don Lipsett was a whirlwind of activity, setting up ISI chapters, arranging for outside speakers, encouraging campus publications, and finding time to establish the Indiana Conservative Club, whose intellectual standards were impressively high. The club's

---

12. Remarks by E. Victor Milione and Annette Kirk at testimonial dinner for Milione at the annual meeting of the Philadelphia Society, April 13, 2002, in Philadelphia.

weekend seminar in early November 1960, for example, featured Milton Friedman, Frank Meyer, and Richard Weaver—all for a seminar registration fee of $20 plus $8.50 a day for room and board. The willingness of the prominent conservatives to accept far less than their normal fee was due to Lipsett's persuasive argument that they would be addressing a group of future conservative leaders.

At the seminar—and a subsequent ISI meeting—Friedman offered the encouraging news that there had been "a drastic change over the last ten or twenty years in the teaching of economics in American universities and colleges." In the late 1930s, he said, the University of Chicago was almost the only U.S. institution "at which there was a substantial group of believers in a free enterprise system." Today, said Friedman, there were "young, able, vigorous teachers of a free market persuasion" widely spread over the country. The reasons for the change, Friedman argued, were the failure of centralized control in Britain and other countries and the widespread "disenchantment with the Soviet Union."[13]

ISI activities in Lipsett's first full year as Midwest director reflected the traditionalist/libertarian/anti-Communist character of the conservative movement. There was a seminar entitled "The Moral and Economic Case for the Free Society," featuring FEE's Edmund Opitz and Dean Ben A. Rogge of Wabash College, and held in Indianapolis. And there were speakers like Representative Donald Jackson of California, a member of the House Committee on Un-American Activities, who showed the riveting documentary film *Operation Abolition* before a capacity audience at Indiana University, and discussed the Left's concerted efforts to abolish the Committee.

Lipsett's $6,000 annual salary and most of the expenses of the Midwest office were paid by Milwaukee businessman William H. Brady, who was impressed by the young Hoosier's unflagging energy and appreciated his quirky humor, seen in the "super-secret" Stephen Decatur Society, which Lipsett founded in 1961. The Society's red, white, and blue letter-

13. Milton Friedman, remarks at a special ISI meeting, November 19, 1960, ISI Archives.

head provided no address, telephone number, or names of officers. An unsigned two-page document explained that the Stephen Decatur Society stood firm for America First and against "Socialism, Liberalism, Atheistic Communism, Foreign Aid Giveaways, The Godless U.N., Egghead Conspiracy, Planned Parenthood, The Urban Renewal Hoax, Fluoridation ... Gnosticism and Entangling Alliances (partial list)." The Society collected no dues or fees, it was explained, because it was comfortably financed by an "extensive holding of Imperial Habsburg Gold Bonds, Imperial Russian Bonds, Chinese Imperial Railway Bonds ... gold bullion, enriched Uranium (for maximum fallout), numbered deposits in the Liechtensteiner Staatsbank and several leading Geneva houses (partial list)."[14] Conservatives vied to become "members" of the nonexistent society and relished letters from "Commodore" Lipsett (the Society's very unofficial secretary) through the years.

Lipsett's industry caught the attention of *National Review* publisher William A. Rusher, an influential mentor to many young conservatives. "Ordinarily I am skeptical about 'field men' as a genre," Rusher wrote Milione, but Lipsett "does a fine, solid job for you, and is worth every cent. I am sure you must be proud of him."[15]

A Special Meeting

Lipsett helped to organize in November 1960 a special Indianapolis meeting of ISI's trustees and advisers at which students from Northwestern University, DePauw University, the University of Wisconsin, and Earlham College reported on the state of conservatism at their schools. Thomas C. Huston was the founder and first president of the Indiana University Conservative League and later chairman of Young Americans for Freedom and a White House aide to President Richard Nixon. He said that while Indiana was considered "basically a conservative school," left-liberal faculty "dominate intellectual discussion on the campus." As a result,

14. Letterhead of and memorandum about the Stephen Decatur Society, Donald Lipsett Personal Archives.
15. William A. Rusher to E. Victor Milione, October 17, 1961, ISI Archives.

students moved to the left during college because "the average student, particularly at the freshman and sophomore level, is much more affected by the teaching of his faculty instructors than he is by his family background." ISI, Huston said, "performs a tremendously important task in getting out the intellectual material." Anne Husted, secretary of the DePauw Conservative Club and future contributor to leading conservative magazines, suggested that the main problem at DePauw was that students knew very little about conservatism. "ISI," she said, "is the only channel through which we are able to obtain ... conservative literature."[16]

Robert Croll of Northwestern University, the organizer of Youth for Goldwater for Vice President at the 1960 Republican National Convention and a future professor of political science, praised ISI for the Chicago seminars and their "noted conservative speakers" and for publishing *The Individualist*, which provided "a vehicle for student writers" like himself. Roger Claus, who helped found the student magazine *Insight and Outlook* at the University of Wisconsin, talked about the difficulties of campus publishing and revealed that financial support was easier to obtain "through advertisers than contributors." When asked for suggestions about possible improvements in *The Individualist* and other ISI publications, the students said they would like "more introductory material" about conservatism, more humor, "ammunition" on academic freedom—a favorite faculty topic—reduced subscription rates for *National Review* and *Modern Age*, and "case studies" on the most current campus issues, like the National Student Association and the United Nations.[17]

A visibly moved Frank Chodorov, now in his seventy-third year and in poor health—he would suffer a debilitating stroke the following year—responded, "This meeting has been like a birthday present to me." Like all old men, he said, "I dote on my grandchildren. But, I get the same pleasure out of hearing you young folks tell me how you are carrying the ball for conservatism. God bless you."[18]

16. Thomas C. Huston and Anne Husted, remarks at ISI luncheon meeting, June 15, 1961, ISI Archives.

17. Minutes of ISI Special Meeting, November 19, 1960, ISI Archives.

18. Frank Chodorov: Ibid.

At the same meeting, Richard Weaver was asked to say a few words about "what students are thinking today." In the main, the University of Chicago professor replied, student thinking reflected the thinking of the faculty because "undergraduate students tend to live in the shadow of their professors." And in general, the undergraduate faculty was thinking "as it has been ... since the 30s, 40s, and 50s," with an occasional "break in the line." More faculty "breaks" would occur, Weaver believed, if books were written that "can not be shaken ... books such as Eric Voegelin's great series on order and history; Professor Friedman's books on economics; Leo Strauss's books on political science; and books like James Burnham's *Congress and the American Tradition.*"[19]

As for students, Weaver concluded, it would not suffice to "invite them to fold their hands and say, 'I'm a conservative, look at me.'" That was, he insisted, too static a role for young people "full of energy and enthusiasm and ideals." ISI, Weaver said, had "to give them some image to fight for, some objective to contend for, some picture of the society we would like to live by, which will require a lot of effort to create, or perhaps recover."[20]

Weaver was reiterating a central argument of ISI founder Chodorov— true individualism had to be presented to restless inquisitive students as "something new and different."[21]

M. Stanton Evans, who would publish *Revolt on the Campus* (describing the conservative renaissance at a growing number of schools) the following year, informed the trustees at the November meeting that conservatism had become a significant presence on many campuses, including his alma mater Yale. He had visited Yale earlier in the year and had been "amazed" to discover conservatives everywhere—writing for the newspaper, running the Political Union, keeping the Calliopean Society going, bringing in speakers nearly every week, and establishing a Young

19. Richard Weaver, remarks at ISI special meeting, November 19, 1960, Indianapolis, ISI Archives.
20. Ibid.
21. Frank Chodorov, "For Our Children's Children," *Human Events*, September 6, 1950.

Republican Club. While admitting that the majority of students were "what we might call liberals," Evans said that 5 percent were "articulate, forceful and resourceful" conservatives. In twenty years, he predicted, they would be "the nation's journalists, teachers, clergy, and leading businessmen." In fact, he said, the conservative movement in fifteen or twenty-five years "is going to be taking possession of the seats of power in the United States." ISI, Evans declared in a final flourish, "has generated this [movement] and made it possible."[22]

Evans was warmly applauded, more for the sentiment expressed than from any conviction that his prediction would come to pass. After all, John F. Kennedy had just been elected president, Fidel Castro ruled Cuba, the captive nations of Eastern and Central Europe, after the brutal suppression of the Hungarian uprising by the Soviets, seemed more captive than ever, Bob Taft and Joe McCarthy were dead, and only Barry Goldwater was consciously articulating the conservative position in the Senate and across the country.

And yet, twenty years later almost to the day, Ronald Reagan, a self-described and proud conservative, would be elected the fortieth president of the United States of America along with a Republican Senate.

A Political Force

By mid-1961, evidence of conservatism's accumulating political power had become abundant. Goldwater's political manifesto, *The Conscience of a Conservative*, made the *New York Times's* best-seller list, and the senator's national approval rating rose sharply in the Gallup Poll. The circulations of *National Review* and *Human Events* steadily increased until both topped 100,000, due largely to the Goldwater phenomenon. Young Americans for Freedom held a rally for Goldwater and other conservative celebrities in New York City's Manhattan Center and turned away thousands, inspiring YAF to lay plans for a rally the following year in historic Madison Square Garden. There was also the far-right John Birch Society, which

22. M. Stanton Evans, remarks at a special ISI meeting, November 19, 1960, Indianapolis, ISI Archives.

distributed so many incendiary books, pamphlets, and bumper stickers (a favorite: "Get the U.S. Out of the UN and the UN Out of the U.S.") that liberals decided to try to bury it.

President Kennedy delivered a major speech in the fall of 1961 in which he urged Americans to reject "fanatics" who found "treason" everywhere and did not trust the people. Although Kennedy did not name the "fanatics," the *New York Times* did so in its front-page story about his speech, mentioning the John Birch Society and the paramilitary Minutemen.[23] Over the objections of William Rusher, Frank Meyer, and new *NR* senior editor William Rickenbacker, editor in chief William F. Buckley Jr., supported by James Burnham, wrote a *National Review* editorial reading Birch Society founder Robert Welch out of the conservative movement.

Noting the criticism of Welch by such respected anti-Communists as Barry Goldwater, Walter Judd, Fulton Lewis, Jr., and Russell Kirk, the *National Review* editorial concluded that a love of truth and country called for the firm rejection of Welch's "false counsels"—the JBS magazine *American Opinion* described America as "50-70 percent Communist-controlled." Anticipating a sharp reaction, Buckley wrote, "There are bounds to the dictum: Anyone on my right is my ally."[24]

But the conservative movement had to accomplish another task before it could operate effectively in the political realm—it had to be philosophically united. Traditionalists and libertarians had been snapping at each other in the pages of *The Freeman* and *National Review* for years. Frank Meyer, the former Communist organizer turned conservative strategist, decided the time had come to seek a consensus of principle. Through articles, books, and long late-evening telephone calls, Meyer communicated his synthesis of the disparate elements of conservatism which came to be called fusionism.

The fundamental idea of fusionism, the historian George H. Nash has written, was that "the freedom of the person [is] the central and primary end of political society." The state had only three limited functions:

23. William A. Rusher, *The Rise of the Right*, New York, 1984: 121-123.
24. "The Question of Robert Welch," *National Review*, February 13, 1962: 83-88.

national defense, the preservation of domestic order, and the administration of justice between citizens. The "achievement of virtue" was not a political question—indeed it was not even the state's business. Freedom, Meyer argued, was the indispensable condition for the pursuit of virtue. Freedom was the ultimate *political* end; virtue was the ultimate end of man as man.

And yet Meyer insisted that modern American conservatism was not classical liberalism, which had been significantly weakened by utilitarianism and secularism. Most classical liberals, he charged, were seemingly unable to distinguish between "the *authoritarianism*" of the state and "the *authority* of God and truth." Although not then a Christian, Meyer declared that conservatives were trying to save the Christian understanding of "the nature and destiny of man." To do that, they had to absorb the best of both branches of the divided conservative mainstream. Moreover, Meyer insisted that he was not creating something new but simply articulating an already existing conservative consensus forged by the Founding Fathers in 1787 with the writing of the Constitution.[25] Regardless of their philosophical orientation, Nash observed, all conservatives—from Hayek to Weaver—thought that the state should be circumscribed and were deeply suspicious of governmental planning and attempts to centralize power. They defended the Constitution "as originally conceived" and opposed the "messianic" Communist threat to "Western civilization."[26]

ISI was the main institution through which this debate took place, sponsoring, for example, a Chicago seminar at which libertarian Ralph Raico of the University of Chicago and conservative Robert Croll of Northwestern debated the question, "Individualist, Libertarian or Conservative—Which Are We?" After quoting Hayek that any connection of individualism with conservatism was always "more or less accidental," Raico declared that the purpose of individualists and libertarians as opposed to the "medieval impulses" of conservatives was "to *transform* existing society into a new order, based—absolutely—on private property and its cor-

25. George H. Nash, *The Conservative Intellectual Movement in America:* 172-175.
26. Ibid: 161.

ollary, individual freedom." Drawing upon Russell Kirk, Croll responded that reason alone, even freedom alone, was not enough. "Conservatism," said the future professor, was founded on concepts about "the nature of man and of society" which did not share "the secular rootlessness and shifting philosophical foundations that are so characteristic of the 'liberal' mind in both its classical and collectivist forms."[27]

In an influencial paper prepared for an ISI seminar, Richard Weaver discussed the "common ground" of conservatives and libertarians—constitutional government with its list of "thou shalt nots" to the governors. Both want, said Weaver, "a settled code of freedom for the individual." In addition to this shared *political* position, conservatives and libertarians agreed philosophically that "there are operating laws in nature and in human nature which are best not interfered with or not interfered with very much." If you tried to change or suspend them by government fiat, Weaver said, "the cost is greater than the return, the disorganization is expensive, the ensuing frustration painful."[28]

Russell Kirk made much the same point about the centrality of the Constitution to conservatism in the closing pages of *The Conservative Mind*, arguing that the principal interests of true conservatism and old-style libertarian democracy were converging. Confronted by collectivists and the architects of the New Society, Kirk said, conservatives must "defend constitutional democracy as a repository of tradition and order" while classical liberals (whom he called "intelligent democrats") must "espouse conservative philosophy as the only secure system of ideas with which to confront the planners of the new order."[29]

Although both traditional conservatives and libertarians chafed at and often challenged fusionism in the years to come (young libertarians attempted a takeover of YAF but were decisively defeated at the 1969

27. Ralph Raico and Robert Croll, "Individualist, Libertarian or Conservative—Which Are We?" *The Individualist*, May 1960: 1-2, 4.

28. Richard M. Weaver, "Conservatism and Libertarianism: The Common Ground," *The Individualist*, May 1960: 1-4.

29. Russell Kirk, *The Conservative Mind from Burke to Santayana*, rev. ed. Chicago, 1953: 413,424.

national convention in St. Louis), it prevailed as an effective synthesis for more than a quarter of a century, until the collapse of communism in Eastern and Central Europe in 1989 and the disintegration of the Soviet Union in 1991.

A New President

In November 1962, slowed by a stroke and other health problems, Frank Chodorov stepped down as ISI president. It had been twelve years since he had written "For Our Children's Children" outlining a fifty-year plan to challenge the collectivist zeigiest on the American campus and a decade since J. Howard Pew's $1,000 check had led to the incorporation of the Intercollegiate Society of Individualists. Chodorov had watched ISI grow from a borrowed desk, a mailing list of six hundred, and barely $2,000 in the bank into a thriving organization with a national headquarters in Philadelphia, regional offices in Indianapolis, Indiana, and Menlo Park, California, a mailing list of some 18,000 (the great majority of them students), and an annual budget of $200,000. He had watched, with no little pride, as his modest proposal blossomed into a comprehensive program of books, pamphlets, publications (*The Individualist*, *ISI Campus Report*, and *Under 30*), campus clubs, speakers (including, in 1962-1963 alone, respected scholars such as Milton Friedman, Russell Kirk, Martin Diamond, Thomas Molnar, Benjamin A. Rogge, and Francis G. Wilson), one-day seminars, and "life-changing" summer schools.

As Chodorov had hoped, ISI was challenging and transforming the minds of young men and women who would assume positions of leadership across the country, especially in the academy. A 1963 brochure included encomiums from several dozen students and professors. "ISI has become a nearly indispensable stimulant in American college life of informed political debate," commented Garry Wills, assistant professor of classics at Johns Hopkins University and future best-selling author and critic. "I can think of no organization," said Philip M. Crane, assistant professor of history at Bradley University, and later member of Congress from Illinois, "quite so effective and urgently necessary in precipitating a renaissance of belief in the worth of the free society at the present time than ISI." "For the creation of today's solid movement of student conservatism—not yet triumphant, but surely militant," remarked J. D. Futch, assistant professor of history at Washington and Lee University, "we have, I believe, to thank ISI above all others."[30]

Satisfied that his children's children would find a spirit of true individualism almost regardless of where they went to college, the seventy-five-year-old Chodorov gratefully relinquished the ISI presidency to the man responsible for most of the organization's success—E. Victor Milione. Always more interested in furthering the cause than himself, Milione cut short the trustees' congratulations, obtained their approval of the next year's program—and budget—and set to work implementing it. "Liberty," he stated in an ISI brochure, "requires good character, integrity, responsibility, self-discipline, initiative and perseverance." He might have been describing himself.

Milione also came up with a new—and enduring—motto for the Society: "To Educate for Liberty." ISI had employed several different mottos in the late 1950s and early 1960s, including "Every Fresh Generation Is a New People" (from Tocqueville) and "For the Advancement of Conservative Thought on American College Campuses." While satisfactory, none of them evoked a cry of "eureka!" And then one day, while sitting in his small cluttered office across the mall from Independence Hall, Milione recalled the exhortation etched at the base of the Liberty Bell—"Proclaim Liberty throughout all the Land unto all the Inhabitants thereof" (Leviticus 25:10).[31] Wasn't that, he thought, what ISI did—proclaim the blessings and the duties of liberty through literature, speakers, clubs, conferences, all the means of education? And while ISI did not try to reach every inhabitant of the land, it did focus on one of its most important constituencies—the student. The more he reflected the more Milione decided that "To Educate for Liberty" was a motto consonant

30. Comments by Garry Wills, Philip M. Crane, J.D. Futch, "The ISI Story—1963," published by ISI, circa 1964, ISI Archives.

31. The following is based on the author's interviews with E. Victor Milione, May 16, 2001, and February 29, 2003.

with the ideas of the founders of the Society and the founders of the Republic.

John Adams, for example, believed that the American "spirit of liberty" required certain "*sensations* of freedom" and certain "*ideas* of right." Liberty for Adams, contends historian C. Bradley Thompson, meant freedom from foreign domination, unjust government coercion, other individuals, and "freedom from the tyranny of one's own passions."[32] For James Madison, writes political scientist Colleen Sheehan, dedication to the principle of liberty meant "a common commitment to the idea of responsibility and the practice of self-government."[33] For Vic Milione, liberty could not be obtained nor maintained "except by those who are willing to accept individually the responsibilities which it imposes." To emphasize the critical importance of education in distinguishing between "sound and unsound economic measures" and which form of government is most "conducive to a preservation of individual liberty," Milione superimposed the motto, "To Educate for Liberty" on the open pages of a book.[34]

Moving ISI into a small suite on the first floor of the Public Ledger Building (a few blocks from Independence Hall) in the spring of 1962, Milione assembled a team of committed young men and women. Robert Ritchie, an erudite graduate of George Washington University, filled the crucial post of director of publications; the indefatigable Don Lipsett became national field director; Robert S. Luckock was named Eastern director; Frederic N. Andre (who would later serve in the Reagan administration as vice chairman of the Interstate Commerce Commission) filled the post of Midwestern director; and Peter L. DeLuca III (who would help found Thomas Aquinas College in California) became Western director. Milione hired a very young Brigitte Vogel in August 1964 as his secretary and office manager; almost four decades later, the unflappable and indispensable Brig Krauss was still with ISI as assistant to the president, T. Kenneth Cribb, Jr.

32. "Atlas of American Independence," C. Bradley Thompson, *The Founders' Almanac,* edited by Matthew Spalding, Washington, D.C., 2002: 70.
33. "Father of the Constitution," Colleen Sheehan, *The Founders Almanac:* 116.
34. Preface, E. Victor Milione, "The ISI Story 1963": 3, ISI Archives.

"Vic was an early starter," recalls Krauss, "who often had lunch at his desk. He used the telephone a lot and made many of his calls himself." Milione was a mentor as much as a boss; almost every morning he would step out of his office to begin a conversation with someone about a book or article he had read, and soon everyone would be standing in a doorway or leaning against a wall, listening to him. "It was like a little seminar," Krauss says.[35] There was very little ceremony—everyone answered the phone, did correspondence, opened the mail, made bank deposits.

"It was like a family," says bookkeeper and later chief receptionist Patricia Mangano, who arrived in 1968 and stayed into the early 2000s. In these early years, "we did a lot of socializing together," she says, going to concerts, the ballet, opera. "I had parties at my house and nearly everyone would come." While "Vic didn't take himself too seriously," says Mangano, he took the work and mission of ISI very seriously, including the question of funding. "Vic was always adamant about keeping away from government," she recalls. "He always said we could have gotten more money that way, but there were those strings."[36]

Another early enlistee was John F. Lulves, Jr., who went to ISI lectures and summer schools in the early 1960s as an accounting major at Quincy College in Illinois and while earning a master's in accounting at Southern Illinois University. Lulves first encountered conservatism as a teenager when he read *The Conscience of a Conservative* by Barry Goldwater and joined the activist group, Young Americans for Freedom. He discovered a deeper conservatism when he bought a paperback edition of Russell Kirk's *The Conservative Mind* and began attending ISI events. Hired in the spring of 1965 as Midwestern director, Lulves immediately impressed Milione with his administrative talents and "voracious" reading.[37] The following year, at age twenty-five, John Lulves became ISI's national director. Over the next two decades, Milione and Lulves forged a close working relationship that allowed Milione to serve as ISI's chief executive

35. Author's interview with Brigitte Krauss, July 9, 2001.
36. Author's interview with Patricia Mangano, May 10, 2001.
37. Author's interview with E. Victor Milione, May 16, 2001.

officer and the primary contact with major donors while Lulves functioned as chief operating officer, managing the organization's day-to-day affairs, especially the finances. In 1970, in recognition of his many contributions, John Lulves was named ISI's executive vice president.

But Lulves was always more than a numbers cruncher. James B. Taylor, who served as Eastern director in the mid-1970s, remembers that "John was a very good writer and was always available to critique an essay you had written." More personally, "if you had a problem, any problem, you went to John."[38] ISI staffers quickly discovered that Lulves was a man of broad interests—a member of the Philadelphia Society and the Society for American Baseball Research, and an avid user of the Oxford English Dictionary and his personal computer. Among his avocations, besides books and baseball, were vegetable gardening, philately, and short-wave radio. He required little encouragement to talk about the transforming power of the written word—"the jolting insights of Burke's *Reflections,* the awesome realization that Chesterton could unlock Thomism, the plain truth that Richard M. Weaver's 'Education and the Individual' was superior to most courses in education."[39]

Christopher Long, ISI vice president for programs in the first half of the 1990s, credits Lulves and national director James Gaston, now a professor of humanities at Franciscan University of Steubenville in Ohio, with personally maintaining "life support lines to faculty representatives" on dozens of campuses when there was "little money" for lectures and "sporadic publishing" of journals. In his seven years at ISI, says Long, who today manages a major investment company, "I learned to be a salesman, to write, to edit, to speak, to think, and to manage people. I learned an enormous amount from ... Vic and especially John Lulves."[40]

Reflecting ISI's close-knit culture, Lulves says the same thing about the man who hired him. "I was tremendously impressed by Vic," says Lulves, by "his integrity, his interest in ideas, his ability to integrate knowl-

38. Author's interview with James B. Taylor, May 15, 2002.
39. "Spotlight On ISI," *Eastern Region Newsletter,* Vol. 1, No. 2, January 1984: 1.
40. Author's interview with Christopher Long, September 17, 2002.

edge" into the everyday work of the organization. Lulves says that Milione was often ahead of his time, as when in the mid-1960s he foresaw the demise of the core curriculum, then still in place. In response to the coming crisis, Lulves says, Milione emphasized two things: the "idea of quality"—ISI would go to a campus with the best possible speakers and scholars; and the "idea of self-selection"—students were allowed to pick what they wanted and needed on their campus in the way of books, pamphlets and publications. "He believed in and allowed the marketplace of ideas to operate."[41]

Acknowledging that ISI "didn't pay very much," Lulves says that "working with Vic was psychic income." And ISI's president kept his head, even amid the spreading political excitement surrounding Barry Goldwater and his quest of the presidency. ISI, Milione reiterated, was in the business of education, not electoral politics. When others might have been tempted, Lulves recalls, "Vic turned down a donor when his proposed project was off mission."[42]

New Trustees—and a New Name

To help stay on track intellectually, ISI in 1963 added three trustees with strong academic credentials—James W. Wiggins, professor of sociology at Emory University and an expert on the aging; William S. Stokes, senior professor of comparative political institutions at Claremont Men's College and an authority on Latin America; and Thomas Molnar, professor of French and world literature at Brooklyn College and one of ISI's most popular campus lecturers. (In 1962, Chodorov had been named honorary chairman and John G. Pew chairman of the board of trustees.) And, propelled by his own convictions and a slighting reference by *Wall Street Journal* editor Vermont Royster to ISI's "long-winded title," Milione initiated a lengthy debate which eventually produced a new name but retained the same initials for the organization.[43] Milione was propelled by

41. Author's interview with John F. Lulves, Jr., February 26, 2001.
42. Ibid.
43. Vermont Royster, "The Taft Spirit: Conservatism Is Still a Force at the G.O.P. Convention," *Wall Street Journal*, July 27, 1960.

philosophical as well as pragmatic reasons. Philosophically, the word "individualist" did not accurately represent the broad spiritual, political, and economic view of man and society that animated ISI's mission and publications. Pragmatically, hardly anyone on the Right used the word "individualist" any more—"conservative" had become the term of choice by philosopher, popularizer, politician, philanthropist, and student.

Many in and out of the Society chimed in with an opinion about the matter. Trustee and major donor William H. Brady wrote in 1960 that if it were his choice alone, "I would leave ISI's name exactly as it is, because I am first and foremost an individualist." But the Milwaukee industrialist admitted that "individualists and individualism just don't seem to have any frame of reference for most people." On the other hand, Brady said, "conservative and conservatism are words that carry some meaning ... [and] are gaining in popular acceptance." He found that among businessmen, in particular, "the word conservative is respected," even among the more liberal.[44]

Frank Chodorov, still president in name but deferential to Vic Milione in operational matters, wrote in 1961 that if a majority of the board voted to change the name of ISI, "I shall go along. I don't place weight on a name; it's the substance that counts." But since he gave the Society its name, he wanted to explain why he had used the word "individualist." Individualism, he said, "describes a philosophy" while conservatism "is essentially a political creed." The basic tenet of individualism "is that in the scheme of things man is endowed by his God with free will, and as a consequence, is a responsible being—responsible to himself, to society and to his God." It therefore followed, Chodorov said, that man "is self-reliant and is capable of enterprise and initiative. He is not a product of his environment but rather makes his own environment."[45]

Although no longer a trustee, Bill Buckley wrote a long letter explaining why he believed the Society should drop the word "individualist" in favor of "conservative." Based on his experience as a lecturer—

44. William H. Brady, Jr., to E. Victor Milione, August 29, 1960, ISI Archives.
45. Frank Chodorov to William H. Brady, Jr., January 14, 1961, ISI Archives.

"twenty to thirty campuses a year"—he could report that "'individualist' ... is simply not used." On several occasions, in fact, mention of the "Intercollegiate Society of Individualists" brought "a spontaneous outburst of laughter, as though one had referred to a society of Rosicrucians or phrenologists." Buckley was also convinced that "the term 'individualist' scares people who might otherwise contribute money." He recounted how a wealthy friend had begun a presentation to a foundation board on behalf of ISI with "a lengthy apologia for the title of the organization." "I do not feel," wrote Buckley, "he would have [done so] had he, say, solicited funds in behalf of the College Society of Conservatives."[46]

Asked for counsel, *NR's* Frank Meyer wrote that philosophically speaking, he knew no better word than "individualist" to express "the emphasis on freedom and the person" which he viewed as vitally necessary to contemporary conservatism. "Liberal" had been "stolen" and "libertarian," he said, was "awkward and smelling of sectarianism." But with regard to the name of an organization like ISI, "individualist" emphasized only "one side" while "conservative" was becoming the word to describe both sides—"the authority of the tradition of Western civilization and the freedom of the person." As fierce a defender of the individual as anyone in the movement, Meyer "reluctantly" agreed that conservative should replace individualist in the title of ISI.[47]

Publisher Henry Regnery, who would later serve as chairman of the board of trustees and who often dispatched an emergency check to ISI headquarters when receipts were down and salaries were due, said bluntly that he had never liked the term "individualist." For him, the word had "overtones of crackpotism"—"it reminds people, somehow or other, of nudists, etc." He thought that ISI should drop "individualist" and use "conservative"—which had become accepted, mainly through the efforts of "our friend Russell Kirk."[48] Although not the last word, donor W. Russell Fawcett of Rancho Mirage, California, summed up the view of

46. William F. Buckley Jr. to E. Victor Milione, September 1, 1960, ISI Archives.
47. Frank S. Meyer to E. Victor Milione, October 22, 1960, ISI Archives.
48. Henry Regnery to E. Victor Milione, October 6, 1960, ISI Archives.

many when he wrote that the need for ISI was "more than imperative" and it would continue to receive his support despite its "almost impossible name."[49]

And there the matter rested for nearly six years while Vic Milione dealt with more pressing problems, such as dissuading pro-Goldwater donors who wanted ISI to become more political, adding campus programs and an ambitious new publication, *The Intercollegiate Review*, raising money (always a challenge), and dealing with the unexpected death of a longtime trustee and valued mentor.[50]

Death of a Scholar

A native of North Carolina and an admirer of the Southern Agrarians, fifty-three-year-old Richard M. Weaver died of a heart attack in early April 1963, on the south side of Chicago, where he was a professor of English at the University of Chicago. Weaver published just two books during his lifetime, noted his longtime friend Russell Kirk, but they "made their mark in this land." The first, published in 1948, was *Ideas Have Consequences*, a devastating dissection of modern nominalism and one of the first and most enduring works in modern American conservatism. *The Ethics of Rhetoric*, which appeared in 1953, demonstrated, in Kirk's words, how "men's words both reflect and form their actions," reminding us all that "the Word may still be either holy or diabolic." According to Kirk, Plato was Weaver's mentor among philosophers, Lincoln among American statesmen.[51]

Normally reclusive, Weaver formed a special attachment for ISI,

49. W. R. Fawcett to E. Victor Milione, September 23, 1960, ISI Archives.

50. Vic Milione would complain to visitors at considerable length about the failure of the American businessman to appreciate the importance of education and the need to be patient about results. After a visit to ISI's offices in August 1963, Richard Ware wrote, in a private memorandum for the Relm Foundation files, that Milione had discussed "the difficulty of raising money from business because of name and the tendency of businessmen to become more cautious at the same time that 'old standby' supporters want a more militant approach and less concern with scholarship." R. A. Ware, September 19, 1963, Private Relm Foundation Archives.

51. Russell Kirk, "Richard M. Weaver, RIP," *The Individualist*, September 1963: 2 (reprinted from *National Review*).

writing original essays for the Society (including one on academic free-dom), speaking at its seminars and summer schools for expenses and a tiny honorarium, and faithfully attending trustee meetings where fellow trustees often strained to hear his soft-spoken comments. He suggested book reviewers to the editor of *The Individualist* and, despite his heavy teaching schedule, found time to undertake writing assignments for the Society. One week before his death, he wrote Robert Ritchie, ISI director of publications, whom he had met recently, "I hope that the wonderful work the ISI is doing will bring us together again in the future."[52]

Weaver's most enduring contribution to ISI, perhaps, was an ad-dress, "The Role of Education in Shaping Our Society," which he deliv-ered in the fall of 1962 and which became a guiding document of the Society. Weaver argued against the modern tendency to make all educa-tion "an exercise in immediate relevancies or numerous courses in con-temporary journalism." Weaver's emphasis, as usual, was on history. "The Man who is grounded in history," Weaver wrote, "knows something of the ever-present tension between the ideal and the prudential, so that his judgments should reflect wisdom rather than cleverness or phantasy."[53]

"This is not only a great personal loss," wrote Henry Regnery, Rich-ard Weaver's publisher, to Vic Milione, "but also a great loss to the Con-servative movement. He was a dedicated man and a profound thinker, and I think we should all feel privileged to have known him."[54]

Mourning the death of his friend and mentor and worn out by the daily demands of administration, programming, and fund-raising, Vic Milione reluctantly informed the board in the spring of 1963 that he intended to resign as president of ISI. For almost a decade, he had done it all, and with little or no help, and he was no longer able to do so. A sympathetic Henry Regnery asked Milione to reconsider his decision— "you have made ISI one of the more effective, if not the most effective,

52. Richard M. Weaver to Robert Ritchie, March 30, 1963, ISI Archives.

53. Richard M. Weaver, "The Role of Education in Shaping Our Society," an address delivered at the Metropolitan Area Industrial Conference, Chicago, October 25, 1962, and first published by ISI in 1966.

54. Henry Regnery to E. Victor Milione, April 5, 1963, ISI Archives.

organizations on the right." And he suggested that "some reorganization should be considered so that you won't have to be responsible for administration." Regnery revealed that he had already written to the chairman John G. Pew and that he himself would attend the upcoming trustees meeting. "I hope very much," he wrote to Milione, "that things can be reorganized so that you won't feel it necessary to go through with your decision to resign."[55] And in fact help would arrive before long in the person of John Lulves and other administrative staff, enabling Milione to remain with his beloved ISI and concentrate on what he did best—educating for liberty.

Genesis of the Weavers

In a follow-up essay to his original 1950 article proposing an individualist response to the collectivist climate on the campus, Frank Chodorov had written that "it would be a waste of time to try to re-educate" the professors who had been subjected to socialist indoctrination for thirty years. The faculty, Chodorov said, would "have to be written off" until it was replaced by the "new faculty now sitting in the lecture rooms."[56] But Vic Milione did not want to wait twenty or thirty years; he wanted to begin *now* to produce young liberty-minded teachers who would challenge and ultimately replace "the socialist pioneers"—Chodorov's phrase—in the classroom. This was Milione's dream, but without the necessary money, a dream it remained.

And then in the fall of 1963, Relm Foundation executive Richard Ware asked Milione if ISI might be interested in managing a graduate fellowship program for "college seniors who hold promise of becoming outstanding scholars or teachers in the related fields of economics, history and political science."[57] Milione enthusiastically responded with a proposal, explaining that he had had "a great interest" in such a project

55. Henry Regnery to E. Victor Milione, April 25, 1963, ISI Archives.
56. Frank Chodorov,"A Fifty-Year Project: To Combat Socialism on the Campus," distributed by the Intercollegiate Society of Individualists, c 1952, ISI Archives.
57. Internal memorandum of Richard Ware to Relm Foundation staff, November 1963, Private Archives of Relm Foundation.

for a number of years. But when he had asked businessmen for support, they had typically responded, "The hell with education; when they get out into the business world they will learn better." Such "thinking" reminded Milione of Tocqueville's admonition: "Nations [which] can only obtain truth as the result of experience may forfeit their existence whilst they are awaiting the consequences of their errors."[58]

Milione proposed an annual program of between five and ten fellowships, each worth $1,500 plus tuition, covering a year of graduate work in economics and related disciplines. He suggested a Fellowship Awards Committee composed of William H. Peterson, New York University; Yale Brozen, University of Chicago; and Louis Spadaro, Fordham University, all economists. A week later, he wrote that he had contacted Peterson, Brozen, and Spadaro as well as Father Stanley Parry at Notre Dame University, and all had agreed to serve on a fellowship awards committee.[59]

Accustomed to moving quickly when their minds were made up, the Relm trustees approved the program, and Richard Ware informed Vic Milione in late January 1964 that the foundation was giving ISI "up to Fifteen Thousand Dollars ($15,000) plus up to ten tuitions" for a maximum of ten fellowships in graduate study in economics and related disciplines.[60] Relm laid down the following conditions. Each fellowship would offer $1,500 plus tuition for an academic year. ISI would accept and screen student applications that would be presented to a fellowship awards committee which would select the fellows. Fellowships would be granted "only to fully qualified candidates." If the candidates that year were not qualified, Ware stipulated, "awards will not be made." There was a final request—that the fellowships not be designated "Relm Foundation Fellowships" or "H. B. Earhart Fellowships" to avoid confusion with the

58. E. Victor Milione to Richard Ware, December 23, 1963, Private Archives of Relm Foundation.

59. E. Victor Milione to Richard Ware, December 23, 1963, and January 7, 1964, Private Archives of Relm Foundation.

60. Richard A. Ware to E. Victor Milione, January 29, 1964, Private Archives of Relm Foundation.

programs already being operated by Relm.[61]

A delighted Milione gratefully accepted the Relm Foundation grant and its conditions and set in motion the process which in August 1964 produced the first ten fellows of the Richard M. Weaver Fellowship Awards Program. There had been nearly unanimous agreement within ISI that the program should be named in memory of the educator, author, and trustee who had contributed so generously to the Society and for whom Milione had almost unbounded admiration. Seeking to describe Weaver, Milione quoted his favorite historian, Jacob Burckhardt: "The only unique and irreplacable human being ... is the man of exceptional intellectual or moral power whose activity is directed to a general aim, i.e., a whole nation, a whole civilization, humanity itself."[62]

Over the years, Weaver Fellows would head departments at influential schools, write widely praised books, direct powerful research organizations, and serve in high governmental positions, but the first Weavers were a truly exceptional group, setting a high standard for those who followed. They included Edwin J. Feulner, Jr., the future head of The Heritage Foundation, arguably the most infuential think tank in Washington, D.C.; James D. Gwartney, co-author of the textbook *Economics: Private and Public Choice*—which has been used by more than one million students in the last two decades—and professor of economics at Florida State University; and John F. Lehman, Jr., secretary of the navy in the Reagan administration and later head of his own New York investment firm. "The Weaver fellowship," says Feulner, "was seminal for me. It enabled me to attend the London School of Economics and sit at the feet of men like Peter Bauer, F. A. Hayek, who was an occasional lecturer, and Kenneth Minogue, who is acknowledged as the successor to Michael Oakeshott in political philosophy. None of that would have been possible without the Weaver."[63] "Without the [Weaver] Fellowship," admits Gwartney, who took a leave of absence from Florida State University from

61. Ibid.
62. E. Victor Milione, "The Uniqueness of Richard M. Weaver," *The Intercollegiate Review*, Vol. 2, No. 1, September 1965: 67.
63. Author's interview with Edwin J. Feulner, August 22, 2001.

1998-2000 to serve as chief economist for the Joint Economic Committee of the U.S. Congress, "I would not have continued on to complete a doctoral program."[64]

"It was Vic Milione and ISI," Lehman says, "that persuaded me to pursue a Ph.D. at the University of Pennsylvania and saved me from a dull career as a Philadelphia lawyer." Lehman remembers how Milone would take the time—sometimes for hours—to talk and debate with him and other young conservatives who visited the Society's cluttered offices in the Public Ledger Building, drawn by the "intellectual ferment" that flowed from ISI. Today, says Lehman, who serves on the University of Pennsylvania's board of visitors, "there is more intellectual diversity and representation of the views that ISI stands for than in my day.... ISI gets a lot of credit for that."[65]

During the next four decades, ISI selected nearly five hundred Weaver Fellows, including Larry Arnn, president of Hillsdale College ("While I had the Weaver Fellowship, I was taking classes at [Claremont Graduate School that] remain the dominant fact in my understanding");[66] Claes Ryn, professor of politics at the Catholic University of America and one-time president of the Philadelphia Society; William Allen, professor of political science, Michigan State University ("My Weaver Fellowship made it possible for me to ... study with H. V. Jaffa, Martin Diamond, and Leo Strauss");[67] Peter W. Schramm, director of the John M. Ashbrook Center at Ashland University ("ISI had a profound impact on me—I became a political animal in the best sense. I began a life of the mind");[68] John C. Goodman, president and CEO of the National Center for Public Analysis ("I was in the Columbia University graduate program in economics, and the Weaver Fellowship was very important in [its] financial support");[69] Larry W. Reed, president of the Mackinac Center for Public Policy; Paul

64. James D. Gwartney in his response to the author's ISI questionnaire, July 1, 2001.

65. Author's interview (via telephone) with John F. Lehman, Jr., May 7, 2002.

66. Larry P. Arnn to Lee Edwards, August 24, 2001.

67. William B. Allen's response to the author's ISI questionnaire, July 2001.

68. Author's telephone interview with Peter W. Schramm, December 7, 2001.

69. John C. Goodman's response to the author's ISI questionnaire, July 2001.

A. Rahe, J. P. Walker professor of American history at the University of Tulsa ("The Fellowship helped me get through my first year in graduate school at Yale without getting into debt");[70] Bruce Fingerhut, founder of the St. Augustine Press; and Gerald P. Dwyer, Jr., vice president, Federal Reserve Bank of Atlanta ("I could not have attended the University of Chicago without the additional money from ISI.... It was a dream come true").[71]

"The success of the Weaver Fellowships," says President David Kennedy of the Earhart Foundation, the primary sponsor of the Weaver Fellowship program since its beginning, "is just amazing. About 90 percent of the Fellows go on to teach or write and otherwise participate in the marketplace of ideas—that's a much greater success rate than our own Earhart Fellows."[72]

Integral to the continuing success of the Weavers were the members of the awards committee who took their responsibilities seriously, reviewing dozens of applications each year. A typical member was Peter Stanlis, professor of English at the University of Detroit and then distinguished professor of humanities at Rockford College. A widely-recognized authority on Edmund Burke and editor of *The Burke Newsletter,* Stanlis was a frequent contributor to *The Intercollegiate Review* and *Modern Age* and a popular lecturer at several of ISI's earliest summer schools. "Ken Cribb was a student at two of my ISI programs," he recalls—at Rockford and Hartford University. The Hartford program was divided between Will Herberg and Stanlis, and "we heard from students on what we said for weeks afterwards."[73]

Defeat But Not Defeatism

While many of the mass media recorded in admiring detail the student Left's permissiveness in ethics and its enthusiasm for statist politics during the sixties, a few detected what *Time* called "a sharp turn to the political right" on campus. The student editor of the *Michigan Daily* explained

70. Paul A. Rahe's response to the author's ISI questionnaire, July 2001.
71. Gerald P. Dwyer Jr.'s response to the author's ISI questionnaire, July 2001.
72. Author's interview with David Kennedy, November 5, 2001.
73. Peter J. Stanlis to Jeffrey Nelson, August 6, 2003, ISI Archives.

there was "a revival of interest in individualism and decentralization of power—principles espoused by John Locke and Thomas Jefferson and rekindled by Senator Barry Goldwater."[74] *Newsweek* reported that Milton Friedman was lecturing from Northwestern to the University of California under the auspices of the "paradoxically" named Intercollegiate Society of Individualists and "is to campus conservatives what Harvard's John Kenneth Galbraith is to campus liberals."[75] Stan Evans, in his book-length survey of the American campus, concluded that "the academy is no longer a comfortable fiefdom of the left; it has become instead what it ought to be, a battleground of ideas."[76] The rejection of collectivist nostrums that Frank Chodorov had seen as possible if students were given the right alternative seemed to be occurring. "My parents thought Franklin D. Roosevelt was one of the greatest heroes who ever lived," remarked Robert M. Schuchman, chairman of Young Americans for Freedom and a Yale law student. "I'm rebelling from that concept." Roger Claus, the president of Wisconsin's Conservative Club, admitted, "You walk around with your Goldwater button, and you feel the thrill of treason."[77]

But what do you do when your political champion is trounced in the 1964 presidential election—winning only 38.5 percent of the popular presidential vote and just six states—and the media proclaim your principles to be irrelevant in a modern society (columnist Walter Lippmann opining that "the Johnson majority is indisputable proof that the voters are in the center"), and your hero's slogan "In your heart, you know he's right" is mockingly converted into "In your guts, you know he's nuts"? Do you take early retirement from the political wars, or do you take heart from the reassuring words of a new leader rising in the West? Writing in *National Review*, Ronald Reagan said that "the landslide majority did not vote against the conservative philosophy, they voted against a false image our liberal opponents successfully mounted." The ever-resilient Frank

---

74. "Campus Conservatives," *Time*, February 10, 1961.
75. *Newsweek*, January 13, 1964.
76. M. Stanton Evans, *Revolt on the Campus*, Chicago, 1961: 190.
77. "Campus Conservatives," *Time*, February 10, 1961, reprinted and distributed by ISI.

Meyer pointed out that despite the campaign to make conservatism seem "extremist, radical, nihilist, anarchic," two-fifths of the voters still voted for the conservative alternative. "In fact," Meyer insisted, "conservatives stand today nearer to victory than they ever have since Franklin Roosevelt."[78] Conservatives publicly welcomed Meyer's defiant rhetoric while wondering privately if victory anytime soon was possible.

Meanwhile, midway between the political enclaves of New York and Washington, Vic Milione kept a steady hand on the ISI tiller. Immediately after the Goldwater rout, he wrote Gerhart Niemeyer he was heartened that so many outstanding scholars had agreed to serve on the editorial board of a new ISI journal *The Intercollegiate Review* (the name suggested by editor-to-be Robert Ritchie), that would be launched in January 1965. His spirits were not dampened by the electoral results because "what occurred was what I expected." The critical thing, he said, was to continue to assert the importance of education, not politics, "in shaping the course of future events."[79]

Ever-increasing numbers of students agreed that a college education was critical in shaping their future. At the time of Pearl Harbor, only 15 percent of Americans of college age were attending a college or university. By the fall of 1965, 40 percent—over five million youths—were enrolled. Within four years, the figure would rise to 6.7 million, aided by the Higher Education Act of 1965, which created a $1 billion Guaranteed Student Loan program. For the first time, federal aid for higher education was approved on its own merit and not as a response to a crisis, like the launching of Sputnik. Nearly half-a-million bachelor degrees were now awarded every year. More than $30 billion was spent annually on education—making going to class "the largest industry in the United States" and students "the country's biggest single interest group."[80]

78. Walter Lippmann column, *Washington Post*, November 5, 1964; Ronald Reagan, *National Review*, November 17, 1964; Frank Meyer, *National Review*, December 1, 1964: 1057.

79. E. Victor Milione to Gerhart Niemeyer, November 30, 1964, ISI Archives.

80. William Manchester, *The Glory and the Dream: A Narrative History of America 1931-1972*, Vol. Two, Boston, 1974: 1342.

Even the far-sighted Milione did not anticipate how severely ISI and the other advocates of a classical liberal arts education would be tested in the sixties. The testing, in fact, had already begun at what was then the most radical school in America—the University of California at Berkeley.

CHAPTER IV

A New Radicalism

ISI is the only national organization working exclusively with students on the campus to bring to them scholarly and educational material designed to retain all that is good in our Western heritage, all that makes up a free society—at a time when the assault from the unprincipled forces of the Left is stronger than ever.

Richard A. Ware[1]

MODERN LIBERALISM, RUSSELL KIRK POINTED OUT, meant different things to different people. To some, it meant antireligious opinions; to others, socialism or a managed economy; to still others, "absolute liberty of private conduct, untrammeled by law or tradition." To yet another group, liberalism meant perpetual doubt for the sake of doubting; for advanced liberals, it meant "humane" Marxism.[2]

Modern American conservatism proceeded from a sharply different set of beliefs as set forth by ISI and other institutions: Free will and moral authority come from God. Political and economic liberty are essential for the preservation of free people and free institutions. Government must be strictly and constitutionally limited. The market economy is the system

1. Richard A. Ware to Harold W. Luhnow, October 25, 1966, Earhart Foundation Archives.
2. Russell Kirk, *Decadence and Renewal in the Higher Learning*, South Bend, Indiana, 1978: 42-43.

most compatible with freedom. Communism must be defeated, not simply contained.

Liberalism's lack of a philosophical core prepared the way for radicals like C. Wright Mills and Paul Goodman. Mills was an avowed Marxist who argued that decision-making in America rested with powerful elites in government, business, and the military. His conspiratorial thesis appealed strongly to the Left because, wrote one historian, it suggested "that they might in fact be part of the great mass of hoodwinked citizenry rather than a lonely minority."[3] Responding to Mills' idea that students might become the "radical agency of change," Students for a Democratic Society (the successor organization to the League for Industrial Democracy and the Intercollegiate Socialist Society) wrote the Port Huron Statement. The statement was a far-ranging denunciation of American society which SDS said was characterized by racial injustice, reflexive anticommunism, an ever-present fear of nuclear war, the maldistribution of wealth, and the exhaustion of liberal "centrist" thinking. The universities were identified as the "potential base and agency in a movement of social change"—i.e., radical change.[4]

Paul Goodman was a professed anarchist and radical populist who charged that "semi-monopolies" in business, unions, and government were more concerned with profits and jobs than personal freedom and "genuine" culture. Goodman argued that "if ten thousand people in all walks of life will stand up on their own two feet and insist, we shall get back our country."[5] His words inspired radical students, who, for their first major battleground, chose the University of California at Berkeley.

Only five hundred of the university's 27,000 students were political activists, but this small minority—led by a twenty-one-year-old junior in philosophy named Mario Savio—was committed to the fundamental change of American society. Beginning in September 1964, according to Diane Ravitch, a series of events "plunged the Berkeley campus into a

---

3. Diane Ravitch, *The Troubled Crusade*, New York, 1983: 186-187.
4. Ibid: 188.
5. Paul Goodman, *Growing Up Absurd: Problems of Youth in the Organized Society*, New York, 1962: 14-15.

crisis unprecedented in American higher education."[6] Returning students encountered an impassioned "Letter to Undergraduates" that urged them to "organize and split this campus wide open!" Demands included the immediate abolition of undergraduate grades and a permanent student role in the running of the university.[7]

The conflict climaxed in early December in a giant night-time rally and sit-in at Sproul Hall, the administration building. An alarmed Chancellor Edward Strong called in police to clear the hall, and 773 people were arrested. Much of the campus was instantly radicalized. Over 800 professors protested, calling for the dismissal of all charges against the demonstrators. Students carried picket signs reading, "I am a student. Do not fold, spindle, or mutilate." University President Clark Kerr attempted to negotiate a ceasefire between all parties, but the radicals were interested in conflict, not its resolution. The Free Speech Movement morphed into the Filthy Speech Movement, "a loose alliance of radical students, hippies, and street people" who kept alive the spirit of protest at UC-Berkeley for the rest of the decade.[8]

The radical rhetoric and militant tactics of the Free Speech Movement—idealistic slogans, deliberate confrontation, catering to a sympathetic news media—became a model for SDS and other leftist groups. After Berkeley, one thing seemed sure: "America had a new radicalism, a new left spawned on the campuses among middle-class youths."[9] Student activism was reinforced in the spring of 1965 when President Johnson sent the first large contingent of American ground troops to Vietnam, and his administration began using the draft for manpower. Campus demonstrations against the Vietnam War spread—in April, SDS led some 25,000 antiwar demonstrators in Washington, D.C.—although a majority of students supported the war, as did the mass media and other main-

6. Diane Ravitch, *The Troubled Crusade*: 191.

7. Bradford Cleaveland, "A Letter to Undergraduates," in *The Berkeley Student Revolt: Facts and Interpretations,* eds. Seymour Martin Lipset and Sheldon S. Wolin. New York, 1963: 72, 80.

8. Ravitch: 203.

9. Ibid: 197.

stream institutions, until the unexpected Tet offensive in January 1968. "The fear of being labeled radical, leftist, or subversive," the author Harvey Swados observed of the academy in the early 1960s, "seems to have all but disappeared."[10]

The mid-1960s also marked the birth of the "counterculture," which rejected traditional American values such as faith, family, work, and community. The counterculture championed sexual experimentation and instant gratification, enabled by the Pill and guided by *Playboy* (which by the early seventies was reaching an estimated 20 percent of adult American men). Young people dropped out and turned on; many openly smoked marijuana, some graduated to harder drugs. Two Harvard psychologists, Timothy Leary and Richard Alpert, began experimenting with LSD, a new "psychedelic" drug alleged to expand the mind. Leary and Alpert were dismissed from Harvard, but "taking a trip" became the cool thing to do on many an American campus. A rock concert in 1969 at an upstate New York farm attracted some 400,000 mostly young people who, in pursuit of nirvana, gorged themselves for three days on hard rock, soft drugs, and casual sex. "Woodstock," wrote the historian James T. Patterson, "was the culminating event of 'countercultural' celebration in the 1960s."[11]

It was also a time of political trauma, induced by the assassinations of John F. Kennedy, Martin Luther King, Jr., and Robert F. Kennedy, and sustained by the escalating Vietnam War and the continuing civil rights revolution. The political historian Michael Barone wrote that Americans who had taken justifiable pride in "rebounding from the depression and winning the war" were now finding rot in the foundation of their basic institutions. Confidence in government, business, labor unions, the press, and almost every institution declined sharply and did not recover until 1980 and the election of a conservative president.[12]

---

10. William Manchester, *The Glory and the Dream*, Vol. 2: 1345.

11. Robert T. Patterson, *Grand Expectations*: 447; Marty Jezer, *The Dark Ages: Life in the United States, 1945-1960*, Boston, 1982: 3; George Will, cited in Arlene Skolnick, *Embattled Paradise: The American Family in an Age of Uncertainty*, New York, 1991: 78.

12. Michael Barone, *Our Country: The Shaping of America from Roosevelt to Reagan*, New York, 1990: 386.

Revolution or Reason?

As the virus of radicalism spread from campus to campus, ISI offered students the antidote of reason. Rejecting the anarchic notions of Mills, Goodman, and Herbert Marcuse, ISI literature insisted that freedom in any society "was diminished or extended" according to the quality of the education of the individual, an education that ought to be firmly grounded in Western thought and experience. That the modern university was failing to provide such learning was obvious, ISI said, especially to students "who have experienced its crucial shortcomings first hand." At least some of the shortcomings could be overcome through ISI's programs which were based on "the principles and values essential to good citizenship, the preservation of liberty, and the humane life." The absence of these values, stated a Society brochure, "leaves men prey to panaceas which offer utopia but inevitably lead to despotism." ISI rejected utopian remedies and offered instead sound scholarship in philosophy, political theory, economics, history, and related disciplines. ISI was throwing down its gauntlet before the American academy and offering an educational alternative to the dissatisfied American student. Indeed, a 1966 brochure said that ISI had sought from its inception to be "the first 'alternative university.'"[13]

An alternative university. Here indeed was a grand vision, far advanced from Frank Chodorov's modest suggestion to plant the seeds of individualism in the minds of a few receptive undergraduates. It was the first time, as far as the author can determine, that the phrase "alternative university" appeared in Society literature. The idea of ISI as a conservative alternative to the modern university—replete with deconstructionism, postmodernism, and political correctness—undergirded much of ISI's thinking in the following years, and would be taken up seriously by its officers and trustees in the mid-1990s and early 2000s as the practice of long-distance learning through the Internet and other means of modern communication spread through the academy.

13. "Reason or Revolution?" ISI promotional pamphlet, c 1966, ISI Archives.

Most educational organizations in America have publications of varying size and frequency, but the truly influential publish a serious journal for their members and supporters. After experimenting with a newsletter, *The Individualist*, and then briefly with a magazine, *Under 30*, which reprinted the best writing of young conservatives on and off campus, ISI committed itself to *The Intercollegiate Review*. Launched in January 1965—two months after Barry Goldwater's resounding defeat and the alleged "end" of conservatism—the *IR* was offering insightful analysis and commentary on the past, present, and future of conservatism nearly forty years later, making it one of the oldest intellectual journals on the Right.

In the first issue, an editorial explained that *The Intercollegiate Review* was dedicated to "the pursuit of academic truth" and, to that end, would be revolutionary and conservative. It would be revolutionary in that it would "challenge ideas which have been unquestioned by the prevailing academic orthodoxy" and conservative in that it would promote an appreciation of those things in Western civilization which are "consonant with the moral underpinnings of the free society." The *IR* held high the importance of individual freedom and agreed with Irving Babbitt that Americans "should in the interests of democracy itself seek to substitute the doctrine of the right man for the doctrine of the rights of man."[14]

The mature, self-confident language was that of the founding editor, Robert Ritchie, who learned about ISI by reading *Human Events* as a student at George Washington University in the late fifties. Born in Dallas and growing up in Houston, Ritchie's natural conservatism was strengthened intellectually by his friendships with M. Stanton Evans and other young conservatives in Washington, D.C. Upon graduating from George Washington, Ritchie entered military service and was stationed at nearby Fort Belvoir, where he edited the base newspaper and moonlighted as book editor of *The New Guard*, the monthly magazine of Young Americans for Freedom. When he told Stan Evans in 1962 he would be getting out of the army "soon," Evans suggested that the twenty-six-year-old

14. "By Way of Introduction," *The Intercollegiate Review*, January 1965, Vol. 1, No. 1:4.

Ritchie call Vic Milione, who was "looking for a director of publications." Milione had tried earlier to hire Ritchie and now told the young editor (who read books as some people eat potato chips) to "come on up" to Philadelphia. "I wasn't sure," recalls Ritchie, "whether I had the job or not, but I showed up at the Public Ledger Building" in April 1962. And there he would remain for six years, fashioning an impressive publications program in the face of "an overwhelmingly hostile intellectual environment in the academic community," and with inadequate and sometimes nonexistent funding. "It's a wonder we survived," Ritchie remarks, "and were able to bequeath a legacy of some intellectual substance for others to copy, criticize, build upon, and profit from."[15]

Ritchie considers his founding editorship of *The Intercollegiate Review* (a name he proposed) to be his most significant ISI accomplishment. He set a very high standard for the editors who followed. He began by assembling a twenty-six-member editorial advisory board that included such diverse conservative academics as Yale Brozen of the University of Chicago, Colin Clark of Oxford University, Donald Davidson of Vanderbilt University, Gottfried Haberler of Harvard, Will Herberg of Drew University, Gerhart Niemeyer of Notre Dame, and Leo Strauss of the University of Chicago. Among the young conservatives who assisted Ritchie editorially were Edwin J. Feulner, Jr., John Lehman, Jr., Angelo Codevilla, who persuaded Raymond Aron to write for the *Review*, and Richard V. Allen, responsible for an article by Eric Voegelin.

The debut issue in January 1965 was comprised of a lead article by economist Colin Clark on the facts and fallacies of "growthmanship," a book review of Hannah Arendt's *On Revolution* by Oxford graduate student Robert Schuettinger, an analysis of Rolf Hochhuth's anti-Pius XII play, *The Deputy*, by cultural critic Kenneth Paul Shorey, and a discussion of American conservatism's "schizophrenia," as evidenced in the continuing split between traditionalists and libertarians, by George Washington University senior Paul Cole Beach, Jr.

15. Author's interview with Robert Ritchie, April 30, 2003; Robert Ritchie to Lee Edwards, April 26, 2003.

Quoting Frank Meyer, Alexis de Tocqueville, and Lord Acton, Beach suggested that a unifying vision for conservatives and libertarians could be found in the coupling of the "human person as the necessary center of political and social thought" and "the historical essence of American conservatism"—constitutionalism and federalism. Beach's proposed "fusionism"—although he did not use the word—acknowledged the importance of individualism, or libertarianism, but stated that, by itself, it failed "to cope adequately" with "the existing spiritual crisis." That crisis required a more comprehensive philosophical answer, Beach argued, which could be found in the religious insights of such conservatives as Tocqueville and Acton, proponents of what Russell Kirk called "ordered liberty."[16]

The Beach article reflected Vic Milione's core belief that "Western civilization and thought [were] being undermined in more than the economics classroom." The articles in *The Intercollegiate Review* were written to explicate "first principles" to a younger generation often encountering them for the first time. The articles were interdisciplinary so as to counteract the liberal orthodoxy and intellectual "fragmentation" on campus. As Milione would later remark, "some of the most important essays in the [modern] intellectual conservative movement" were published in *The Intercollegiate Review.*[17]

From the beginning, the *IR* was edited with "an eye to an undergraduate audience, albeit a highly intellectual one." One way of ensuring that the articles were intelligible was to publish the best lectures by ISI faculty, thus avoiding excessively technical language. Aware that an undergraduate generation spans only four years, the *IR* undertook to reintroduce the major themes and figures of the conservative intellectual movement to succeeding generations of conservatives. The "art" of editing the *IR* involved doing so "while also providing intellectual nourishment" for the "thousands of ISI faculty who also read the journal."[18]

16. Paul Cole Beach, Jr., "Renascent American Conservatism," *The Intercollegiate Review*, January 1965: 27-29.

17. E. Victor Milione, "Ideas in Action: Forty Years of 'Educating for Liberty,'" *The Intercollegiate Review*, Vol. 29, Vol. 1, Fall 1993: 53.

18. Mark Henrie to Lee Edwards, March 19, 2003.

Action Intellectuals

Knowing that ideas do not have consequences all by themselves, ISI encouraged its members to get out of the armchair. By mid-1965, there were almost eighty associated ISI campus clubs with membership ranging from a dozen to over one hundred students. There was one mandatory requirement—that the club function "*solely* ...[as] an educational group" and "*refrain from political activism*" (emphasis in the original). The reasons were both practical and philosophical. Political activity would endanger ISI's tax-exempt status. Excessive activism would embroil its members in the transitory issues of the day rather than the enduring ideas of Western civilization. ISI was content to let members of the rambunctious Young Americans for Freedom (YAF) take the lead in organizing student activities from debates about academic freedom to blood drives in support of the Vietnam War.

The rapid growth of ISI clubs was attributable in large part to the skills and energy of regional directors like Peter L. DeLuca III, based in San Francisco. DeLuca (and his successors) arranged for visiting—and local—lecturers, distributed ISI publications and tape recordings of ISI lectures, and provided a "bookshelf" of basic books on conservative thought. Sometimes a local student, like Eric Brodin at UC-Berkeley, would respond to the ISI program in an extraordinary way.

Born in Sweden, Brodin had come to America as a teenager and was doing graduate work in English literature at the California university. He was a founding member of the University Society of Individualists at Berkeley, helped to start the club journal, *Man and State*, and was a weekly columnist for the liberal student newspaper, the *Daily Californian*. His most impressive achievement, perhaps, was the USI library, known as the Center for Conservative Studies. In two years, Brodin built the library "from nothing" to a collection of over 800 books, cross-indexed and catalogued, plus 1,500 pamphlets and 100 periodicals, filed by subject. It was the largest collection of conservative literature "attached to any conservative college club in the United States," and provided a rational alternative to the revolutionary impulses of the Berkeley radicals.[19]

Not long after the Free Speech Movement shut down the University, Brodin extended an invitation to the thinking student in his *Daily Californian* column: "Should you be tired of the conformity of the left, with its ranting and emotional obfuscation of issues, perhaps your place is in one of the conservative organizations on campus," like the University Society of Individualists.[20] In short order, USI's membership increased dramatically, and Brodin became ISI's Western director, succeeding Peter DeLuca, who moved to Philadelphia to become, at age twenty-five, the Society's national field director and Vic Milione's right-hand man. "All I owned," DeLuca remembers, "were a couple of rumpled summer suits. The first thing Vic did was to take me to his haberdasher to get a new suit."[21]

DeLuca did everything—organized programs, oversaw publications, talked to creditors (who rarely got paid on time), and raised money, including through a relatively new method for nonprofit organizations, direct mail. Conservatives discovered the tremendous potential of direct mail fund-raising in 1964 when presidential candidate Barry Goldwater attracted more than 650,000 individual contributors. (By contrast, Richard Nixon had received fewer than 50,000 individual contributions in his 1960 presidential campaign.) Stan Evans signed an ISI fund-raising letter which elicited a $1,000 contribution from Henry Salvatori. "I flew out to California," recalls DeLuca, "and visited [Salvatori] personally." It was the beginning of a close relationship between the wealthy industrialist and conservative Republican (one of a small group of Californians who persuaded Ronald Reagan to run for governor of California in 1966) and ISI, which lasted more than thirty years until Salvatori's death in 1997 at the age of ninety-six.

DeLuca stayed in Philadelphia less than two years ("it was frustrating because we never had the money to do all we wanted"), moving back

19. Peter L. DeLuca to E. Victor Milione, October 28, 1964, ISI Archives. "Conservative's Directory," Eric Brodin, February 10, 1965, *The Daily Californian*.
20. Ibid: Brodin, "Conservative's Directory," February 10, 1965.
21. Author's telephone interview with Peter DeLuca, October 5, 2001.

to California where he went to work for Salvatori and served again as ISI's Western director.[22] In December 1967, DeLuca was running a meeting of the Philadelphia Society at a Los Angeles airport hotel when he heard a talk on higher education by Doyle Swain, a fund-raiser at Pepperdine College. He approached Swain afterwards and was joined in the discussion by Ronald McArthur of St. Mary's College, a frequent ISI lecturer. The two young men asked so many pointed questions that Swain finally said to them, "Why not start your own college?" "You're crazy!" was the quick response. But this exchange, says DeLuca, was "the genesis of St. Thomas Aquinas College"—now nationally respected for its intellectual rigor and unswerving commitment to the basics of Western civilization.[23] It was a sign of ISI's growth and maturation that other organizations, such as the Philadelphia Society, Thomas Aquinas College, and, later, the formidable Claremont Institute, developed as offshoots from its institutional trunk.

From 1967 to 1969, Vic Milione allowed DeLuca to devote part of his time and some ISI resources to the challenge of launching a new college, and in June 1969 (with a donation of $10,000 from Henry Salvatori) Pete DeLuca became the one and only employee of the as-yet unnamed school. "I have been here ever since," DeLuca says, who serves as vice president for finance and administration and is a faculty member at Aquinas College. DeLuca reveals that it was the experience of running the ISI summer schools in California that "convinced me to start a college." He observed that for students like Mike Antonovich, later speaker of the California State Assembly, and Michael M. Uhlmann, who served in the Reagan White House, the ISI summer school was "a life-changing experience." "What could you do in four years," DeLuca asked himself, "if you could accomplish that much in a summer school?"[24]

Because of the spirited efforts of DeLuca and other regional directors in the field and the steady flow of publications out of Philadelphia, ISI

22. Ibid.
23. Ibid.
24. Ibid.

steadily grew. In the 1965-1966 academic year, the national ISI mailing list totalled more than 20,000, including three thousand faculty members. Two-thirds of the students were located in the Midwest and the Northeast, with one-fifth in the West, and only 15 percent in the South. Since ISI's founding in 1953, it was estimated, some 83,000 people had received literature free of charge and benefitted from the Society's programs—and on an annual budget that only approached $200,000 in the mid-1960s.

Ever in pursuit of income, ISI came to an agreement with the Acme News Company of New York to test newsstand and book store sales of *The Intercollegiate Review* in selected cities across the country. The organization also sought *Review* advertising, especially from book publishers, "guaranteeing" a circulation of 22,000 and charging a modest $150 for a full page. ISI also took a small step into the information age by converting its membership list from addressograph plates to Automatic Data Processing (ADP). An Alumni Committee was established with M. Stanton Evans as chairman. A questionnaire sent to ISI graduates revealed that at least fifty were already teaching economics, physics, and other subjects at institutions ranging from Barnard College to the University of Santa Clara.

A Life-Altering Experience

Continuing a program begun in 1960, one-week summer schools were held in the early and late summer of 1965 at the University of Pennsylvania, Rockford College in Illinois, and Claremont Men's College in California. The schools, Vic Milione stressed, were not meant to provide attendees "with all there is to know about freedom or the free society." Rather, they were intended to embark the student on an "intellectual voyage ... that should absorb a major portion of [his] lifetime."[25] One hundred and five students, representing eighty-five colleges and universities, attended the schools, paying only their own transportation. The total cost of the three sessions (described as life-altering by more than one participant) was

---

25. E. Victor Milione, "A Word from Our President," excerpted from the brochure of the fourth annual Western ISI Summer School, Claremont Men's College, August 29-September 4, 1965, ISI Archives.

$11,000, about $100 per student. Albert H. Hobbs, a University of Pennsylvania sociologist, wrote Milione that "in more than twenty years of university teaching I have never met with a more capable group of students." "I believe," said the University of Michigan's Stephen J. Tonsor of the program, "that when the fads, the political follies, the movements have broken down and disappeared, a program which is intended, not for tomorrow only but for a generation, will have demonstrated its validity." Student Bruce Weinrod, who would later serve as a deputy assistant secretary of defense in the George H.W. Bush administration, emphatically agreed: "It has been the most intellectually stimulating week in my life."[26]

Among those who did the stimulating were Russell Kirk, then a professor of political science at C. W. Post College in New York; Robert Strausz-Hupe of the University of Pennsylvania, the founding director of the Foreign Policy Research Institute and later ambassador to Turkey; political scientist Harry V. Jaffa of Claremont Men's College, who wrote Barry Goldwater's memorable acceptance speech at the 1964 Republican national convention; and Martin Diamond, another Claremont political scientist and a national authority on the American Founding.

Ten graduate students were named Weaver Fellows for the 1965-1966 academic year, including Robert A. Hessen, who, after receiving his Ph.D. from Columbia University and teaching at Columbia's graduate school of business, joined the Hoover Institution at Stanford University and is today a senior research fellow at Hoover; Tom Pauken, who would serve as director of the federal agency ACTION under President Reagan and is today a member of ISI's board of trustees; and James T. Kolbe, elected in 1984 to the U.S. House of Representatives from Arizona's 5th Congressional District and today is a ranking member of the House Appropriations Committee. "My ISI experience," says Pauken, who also served as chairman of the Texas Republican Party, "gave me the philosophical grounding with which to make decisions in public policy."[27]

26. Albert H. Hobbs to E. Victor Milione, October 8, 1965; Stephen J. Tonsor to Peter DeLuca, as quoted in a "Contributors' Report," October 29, 1965, Bruce Weinrod, as quoted in the same contributors' report, ISI Archives.

27. Author's interview with Thomas Pauken, April 12, 2001.

Weaver Fellow Carl Grafton went on to earn a Ph.D. from Purdue University and is distinguished research professor of political science and public administration at Auburn University. Thomas Jefferson Meeks, after receiving a Ph.D. from Duke University, taught economics at Virginia State University for over thirty years. William C. Wooldridge, after studying history at the University of St. Andrews in Scotland, joined the Norfolk Southern Railroad, becoming its vice president for law. And Michael J. Tonsing received an M.A. in political philosophy and government from Claremont Graduate School and a J.D. from the University of San Francisco Law School before founding his own law firm and then his own company.

On the administrative side, ISI chairman Charles H. Hoeflich announced the election of three prominent businessmen and a noted educator to the board of trustees: R. H. Borchers of Armour and Company, Chicago; J. Jerome Thompson of Charles Pfizer and Company; Harold L. Severance of Standard Oil Company of California (a major financial supporter of the Western office); and John H. Davis, vice chairman of the board of trustees of the American University in Beirut.

To learn why people gave to ISI, the Society surveyed its major foundation and corporate donors, finding a common characteristic—"they were family-owned companies and foundations that were still controlled by the donor or a first- or second-generation family member."[28] They included well-known entrepreneurs and philanthropists such as the Pews of Sun Oil and the Glenmede Trust (Philadelphia), the Donners of the Donner Foundation (Philadelphia), Phillip McKenna of Kennametal (Pennsylvania), Milwaukee businessman William H. Brady, Roger Milliken of the Deering Milliken Foundation (South Carolina), J. K. Lilly of the Lilly Endowment (Indianapolis), Jaspar Crane of the Curran Foundation, Harry Bradley of Allen-Bradley (Milwaukee), James Kennedy of the Relm/Earhart Foundation (Ann Arbor, Michigan), Harold Luhnow of the William Volker Fund, Pierre Goodrich (Indianapolis), and the Scaifes of Pittsburgh.

By the mid-60s, nearly every major conservative foundation was sup-

28. E. Victor Milione, "Ideas in Action: Forty Years of 'Educating for Liberty,'" *The Intercollegiate Review*, Fall 1993: 55.

porting ISI. "Through the years," remarked veteran fund-raising consultant Robert Russell, "ISI donors have represented the 'first families' of the conservative movement."[29] The constant challenge was to persuade them to increase the amount of their contribution.

Moving On Up

On an average day, with telephones ringing, electric typewriters clicking, and an old mimeograph clanking, with letters being opened, publications being edited, contributions being counted, and lunches being eaten at the desk, the cramped ISI offices in the Public Ledger Building in downtown Philadelphia resembled the filled-to-overflowing hotel room in the Marx Brothers' classic film *Room Service,* where Groucho keeps welcoming every additional repairman, waiter, visitor, and friend. ISI headquarters had clearly exceeded maximum capacity (and perhaps warranted a citation from the fire marshal because of the ever-increasing piles of pamphlets and publications). The former conference room was now Peter DeLuca's office; two people shared space in another medium-sized office. There was serious discussion about moving out of rented offices in the city into a house, perhaps on Philadelphia's Main Line. In addition to the need for more space for the expanding staff and their expanding work, a house would provide "tangible evidence" of ISI as "a permanent element of the academic scene."[30]

Although a property was not purchased (the asking price for one possibility was $100,000, a sum equal to half the Society's annual budget), ISI did move to a modest suite of six small offices in a squat red-brick building surrounded by blacktop and located at 14 S. Bryn Mawr Avenue, in Bryn Mawr, thirty minutes from downtown Philadelphia. "We would tell first-time visitors," remembers former national director Christopher Long, that the ISI suite "looks like a dentist's office."[31] (In fact,

29. From the Executive Brief of the Final Report of "A Fund Raising Situation Analysis and Feasibility Study" by Robert Russell & Associates and the Geneva Group, December 11, 1992: 3, Personal Papers of Robert Russell.
30. "Contributors' Report," October 29, 1965, ISI Archives.
31. Christopher Long to Lee Edwards, September 5, 2002.

there was a dentist next door.) ISI would remain in Bryn Mawr for nearly thirty years until the generosity of New Jersey philanthropist Fred M. Kirby and others enabled the Society in 1996 to open a true national headquarters just outside Wilmington, Delaware.

In April 1966, at a trustees meeting in Chicago, ISI took care of some long deferred business (first broached in 1960) when it changed its name but not its initials from the Intercollegiate Society of Individualists to the Intercollegiate Studies Institute. Director of Publications Robert Ritchie recalls that before the meeting, Milione asked him to come up with "a list of possible names." One of Ritchie's suggestions was the Intercollegiate Studies Institute.[32] The final impetus for change came when Mario Savio and other radicals at Berkeley began calling themselves "individualists." Potential donors now associated ISI with the leftist unrest on campus, and fund-raising, never easy, became even more difficult. The name change, Milione said, enabled ISI to present its case simply on the merits of its mission, vision, and programs. Ritchie says that the new name "made a difference" also with academics uncomfortable with the "individualist" label.[33] A few supporters questioned whether the change indicated "a weakening commitment" to individual freedom and a free market economy, but the majority echoed the opinion of the Relm Foundation's Richard Ware, who wrote Milione that the Intercollegiate Studies Institute "connotes exactly the right idea."[34]

At the same trustees meeting, publisher Henry Regnery and Richmond industrialist Richard C. Holmquist joined the board. Regnery had been a faithful and bountiful supporter of ISI from its birth—"I called Henry more than once," recalls Vic Milione, "to help us meet the payroll or pay an overdue bill."[35] In 1971, Regnery became chairman of the board of trustees, replacing a grateful Charles Hoeflich (who had been

32. Author's interview with Robert Ritchie, April 30, 2003.
33. Ibid.
34. E. Victor Milione, "Ideas in Action: Forty Years of 'Educating for Liberty,'" *IR,* Fall 1993: 55-56. Richard A. Ware to E. Victor Milione, April 29, 1966, Earhart Archives.
35. Author's interview with E. Victor Milione, May 16, 2001.

doing double duty as chairman and secretary-treasurer) and served in that position for almost twenty years. Annual ISI income slowly rose, topping $270,000 in the fiscal year 1966-1967, due to new donations from corporations such as Koppers Company, Caterpillar Company, General Electric, and Motorola and from wealthy individuals such as DeWitt Wallace of *Reader's Digest*, George Champion of Chase Manhattan, Clifford Backstrand, and Dudley Swim of National Airlines. That same year, ISI's mailing list reached 33,000, an increase of five thousand over the previous year. Of the total, 23,000 were undergraduates, 3,500 graduate students, and 4,400 were faculty.

Amid the increasing cacophony on the campus, these students and professors were attracted to an organization committed to a free society and the proposition that individual freedom requires "not only an understanding of man but also of the universe and its Creator."[36] It was the commitment to the founding principles of Western civilization that persuaded at least some businessmen, normally concerned only with quarterly statements, to take a longer view and support ISI. This understanding of what was truly at stake in the campus rebellion inspired Richard Ware to write:

> ISI is the only national organization working exclusively with students on the campus to bring to them scholarly and educational material designed to retain all that is good in our Western heritage, all that makes up a free society—at a time when the assault from the unprincipled forces of the left is stronger than ever.[37]

Midwestern director John F. Lulves Jr. went so far as to claim that "'New Left' hoopla to the contrary ... student conservatism is experiencing boom conditions." He pointed to the large turnouts for conservative speakers at the University of Texas and Southern Illinois University and the strong response at the University of Wisconsin to a semester-long weekly seminar on liberty, intended to "fill the intellectual gap created by the picketers."[38]

36. E. Victor Milione, introduction to brochure for 1967 Midwestern Summer School, Rockford College, August 20-26, 1967: 3. ISI Archives.
37. Richard A. Ware to Harold W. Luhnow, October 25, 1966, Earhart Archives.
38. "The Return of the Campus Conservative," John F. Lulves Jr., *Indianapolis News*, February 24, 1966.

But the Institute did not limit itself to examination of first principles. As the size of the American military presence in South Vietnam steadily grew, Georgetown University Professor James D. Atkinson and David Martin, legislative assistant to Senator Thomas J. Dodd (D-CT), appraised U.S.-Vietnam policy in 1966 at a George Washington University ISI seminar. Martin stated that withdrawing from South Vietnam would mean "the improvisation of another line of defense" in an adjacent country and expenditures of money and men "infinitely greater than are presently required." Answering those who warned that Communist China might enter the Vietnam conflict, Atkinson described the Chinese military as weak and lacking in strategic supplies.[39] Speaking before 1,200 students at Vanderbilt University, newspaper editor Stan Evans described "peaceful co-existence" as a "Communist formula for formal conquest" and said that "Vietnam cannot be understood outside the context of the Communist cold war which has been going on the past 20 years." Evans expressed guarded optimism that U.S. commitment in Vietnam might lead to "a policy of strength and resolution" against communism.[40]

Death of a Teacher

On December 28, 1966, Frank Chodorov, author and lecturer, salesman and teacher, varsity football player at Columbia and lover of cowboy movies ("because the good guys always win"), radical libertarian and atheist Jew who came to God in his last years, editor and founder of the Intercollegiate Society of Individualists, died in New York City at the age of seventy-nine.

He always spoke, said William F. Buckley Jr. at Chodorov's funeral, "from a heart full of belief, enlightened by a mind keen and observant and understanding." There was praise aplenty about someone who had touched the hearts and minds of many in his several careers. He was "a man who breathed controversy," said his publisher Devin A. Garrity, "who

39. "U.S. Vietnam Policy Praised, Appraised at GWU Seminar," Frank Forlini, Jr., *ISI Campus Report*, Vol. 4, No. 1, Winter 1966: 7.
    40. Ibid: 8.

was obviously fearless at a time when fear was commonplace."

"How fiery, how dynamic, your classes were," recalled a former student, Jack Schwartzman, who quoted a favorite Chodorovism: "A teacher is a conductor of electricity." "He offered," said Robert LeFevre, head of Rampart College at which Chodorov frequently lectured, "an unforgettable picture of kindness and intellect working together as a team." "He wrote and spoke without rancor," reflected Admiral Ben Moreell, "but with the courage of a lion. He was constantly and relentlessly on the prowl in search of truth." But truth, Chodorov had cautioned fellow teacher Sydney A. Mayers, "is like mumps or measles. A lot of people are immune. All you can do is expose them to it. If they 'catch' it, that's fine; but if they don't, it isn't your fault."[41]

Chodorov had sounded a more optimistic note about the receptivity of young people to truth in his autobiography, *Out of Step*. Looking at history, he ventured that it was possible to anticipate "a renaissance of individualism" after fifty years of modern collectivism. But the renaissance wouldn't just happen—"we must do a selling job," he insisted, especially among the younger generation. "Youth will not buy us out lock, stock and barrel," he wrote, "but will be rather selective about it." They will take "what seems good to them, modernize it, build it into a panacea and start a revolution. God bless them."[42]

Vic Milione summed up the life of his mentor and friend, with whom he had seen many a Tom Mix cowboy movie, in this way: "His primary interests in life were individual freedom and the assurance that younger generations would have some exposure to the values which comprise the free society, in the hope that it would secure their support and they its blessings."[43]

41. William F. Buckley Jr., "Frank Chodorov, RIP," eulogy delivered at Frank Chodorov's funeral, December 31, 1966; Devin A. Garrity, "Frank Chodorov: Prophet"; Jack Schwartzman, "A Letter to Frank"; Robert LeFevre, "Frank Chodorov: Teacher"; Ben Moreell, "Frank Chodorov: Man of Honor"; and Sydney A. Mayers, "F.C.—A Recollection;" all published in *Fragments*, October-December 1966.
42. Frank Chodorov, *Out of Step*: 260-261.
43. E. Victor Milione, "Frank Chodorov: Questing Spirit," *The Intercollegiate Review*, Vol. 3, No.3.

Fanning the Flames of Liberty

Despite the critical distance that Vic Milione strove to place between ISI and the conservative movement, the Institute continued to influence the movement meaningfully. The primary creator of the Philadelphia Society, American conservatism's premier organization of intellectuals, was ISI's Don Lipsett. Initially, the idea was to have an organization that would keep ISI "graduates" involved in the battle of ideas. And so in the spring of 1964, with Milione's approval, Lipsett organized regional meetings of the Philadelphia Society in Indianapolis, Philadelphia, and San Francisco, featuring such ISI stalwarts as Russell Kirk, Thomas Molnar, and Stefan Possony. The need to keep conservative ideas alive took on added urgency that fall following Barry Goldwater's horrific presidential defeat.

To strengthen the Philadelphia Society, Lipsett proposed a New York City meeting in December 1964 of editor-author William F. Buckley Jr., representing the traditionalist wing of the conservative movement, and economist Milton Friedman, representing the libertarians. Also present were Frank Meyer of *National Review*, Edwin J. Feulner, then a graduate student at the University of Pennsylvania's Wharton School, and Lipsett himself. Remarkably, recalls Feulner, "This was the first time that Buckley and Friedman [had] ever met each other."[44] Buckley and Friedman agreed to lend their names to "an American multi-discipline organization patterned after the Mont Pélerin Society," started in 1947 by F. A. Hayek, Friedman, and other free-market advocates when socialism seemed to be sweeping across Western Europe and much of the free world. Buckley also put up $100, Feulner recalls, so "we could open a bank account."[45]

Lipsett served as secretary of the Philadelphia Society from the beginning and organized its first national meeting in February 1965 in Chicago. Speakers Milton Friedman, Father Stanley Parry of Notre Dame, and Frank Meyer—all frequent ISI lecturers—explored "The Future of

44. Ed Feulner to Heritage Foundation staff, October 30, 1995.
45. Lee Edwards, *The Power of Ideas: The Heritag Foundation at 25 Years*, Ottawa, Illinois, 1997: 187.

Freedom," reflecting in their remarks the diverse strains of American conservatism. Friedman, calling himself a classical liberal, discussed freedom in terms of the free market economy based on "cooperation." He said that classical liberalism represented a "healthy" breaking away from the authoritarianism and traditionalism of the past. Father Parry disagreed, stating that man must perceive the metaphysical rather than the economic basis for freedom. This being so, he said, conservatives "are the heirs of Western civilization." Fusionist Meyer suggested that American conservatism was a "blending" of traditional values and individual freedom. The *raison d'etre* of the Philadelphia Society, he emphasized, should be to abandon "partisan concepts of truth" and exchange ideas "frankly."[46] In succeeding meetings, Philadelphia Society members enthusiastically followed Meyer's advice, often exchanging ideas so frankly as to alarm first-time participants.

For three decades, Lipsett and his devoted wife Norma kept the books, looked after the membership, developed the programs, and found the young people (most of them ISI members) who attended the national and regional meetings. Those who were privileged to drink "from the refreshing waters" of the Philadelphia Society's meetings, wrote the *Detroit News*, knew how fortunate they were.[47] The leading role of Don Lipsett, Ed Feulner, Leonard Liggio, M. E. Bradford, William Campbell, and many others in the Philadelphia Society provides further proof of the saliance of ISI's intellectual contributions to the conservative movement.

Translating Ideas into Action

Meanwhile, conservative ideas inspired two quite different men to become political candidates, strengthening conservatism on opposite coasts of the country. In February 1965, a group of influential California Republicans (including ISI guardian angel Henry Salvatori) called on Ronald Reagan. They told him that he was the only person around whom Re-

46. Don Lipsett, notes on the first national meeting of the Philadelphia Society, February 26-27, 1965, Chicago, Private Lipsett Papers.
47. Ibid.

publicans could rally in the 1966 gubernatorial race, and that they were convinced he could defeat the incumbent governor, Edmund (Pat) Brown. Reagan had always preferred to campaign for someone else, but now people whom he respected were insisting that it was his turn. He agreed to travel throughout California for the next six months to discover if the people— not just the Republicans—really wanted him as their governor.[48] They did, and by the time Reagan finished campaigning eighteen months after he had first been approached, he had stunned the politicians, but not the people, by being elected governor of the second most populous state in the nation.

Three thousands miles away, William F. Buckley Jr. was mulling over whether to run for mayor of the largest and most liberal city in America— New York City. Certainly, the conservative movement could use a political boost after the Goldwater defeat—a strong showing by a conservative candidate in the citadel of liberalism would do that. And Buckley had some provocative ideas about how the affairs of a large city would be conducted from the Right. Where better to debate the proper role of government and the inherent responsibility of the individual citizen than in New York City, home of the liberal establishment and headquarters of the nation's media?

In early June 1965, although not yet a candidate, Buckley suggested a ten-point platform on which a mayoral candidate might run, revealing the lasting impression that Albert Jay Nock and Frank Chodorov had made on him. He recommended that "anti-narcotic laws for adults" be repealed, gambling be legalized, anyone without a police record be allowed to operate a car as a taxi, and that communities be encouraged to finance their own "watchmen," relieving the municipal police force of what he called "an almost impossible job."[49]

On election day that fall, an impressive 13.4 percent of the New York City electorate (341,226 voters) voted for conservative Bill Buckley

48. Lee Edwards, *The Conservative Revolution: The Movement That Remade America*, New York, 1999: 144.

49. William F. Buckley Jr., *The Unmaking of a Mayor*, New York, 1966: 91-93.

while Republican John Lindsay eked out a narrow win, receiving 45.3 percent to Democrat Abe Beame's 41.3 percent. Buckley's mayoral effort sketched the outlines of a winning political coalition of ethnic Catholic Democrats and middle-class Republicans. In his landmark 1969 study *The Emerging Republican Majority*, Kevin Phillips cited Buckley's vote in New York's Catholic assembly districts as a "harbinger" of Richard Nixon's new majority in 1968.[50]

While Ronald Reagan and Bill Buckley were engaged on the field of politics, ISI had plenty to do on the campus. Generously funded by the federal government, American higher education swelled in the next decade. The number of colleges and universities soared by 50 percent, from 2,040 to 3,055. The number of students tripled from 3.6 million in 1960 to 9.4 million in 1975, the majority of them in public schools. Few predicted that educational performance would fall as sharply as it did. The College Board reported in 1975 that scores on the Scholastic Aptitude Test (SAT), taken each year by more than one million high school students, "had declined steadily since 1964."[51]

The life of the university was fundamentally transformed. According to John Henry Newman, the university was intended to develop a philosophical habit of mind "of which the attributes are freedom, equitableness, calmness, moderation, and wisdom." But instead, as President Gordon Chalmers of Kenyon College foresaw, American higher education slid "into technological hustling for some" and "a lazy egalitarianism for others."[52] The university's sense of purpose became more diffuse, and the sense of community was diminished. Even Clark Kerr, who hailed the coming of the "multiversity," agreed that undergraduates had been neglected and "recent changes ... have done them little good."[53]

As it had been from its founding, ISI's response was philosophical, not political. "The crisis of our age," said Eastern director Wayne Valis,

50. Kevin Phillips, *The Emerging Republican Majority*, New Rochelle, N.Y., 1969: 168. John B. Judis, *William F. Buckley*: 256.

51. Ravitch, *The Troubled Crusade*: 311.

52. Russell Kirk, *Decadence and Renewal in the Higher Education:* x-xi.

53. Clark Kerr, *The Uses of the University*, New York, 1977: 103-104.

"is a crisis in human values." It was therefore incumbent on the individual student "to seek the truth" and attempt to determine "the nature of man."[54] To help students find the truth at its 1966 Eastern summer school, ISI offered lectures by political science professor David Nelson Rowe of Yale, economics professor Paul Craig Roberts of Virginia Polytechnic Institute, neo-Thomist philosophy professor Frederick D. Wilhelmsen of the University of Dallas, and the grand old man of the Austrian school of economics, eighty-five-year-old Ludwig von Mises of New York University, who stated that the prospect of a "world market"—today's global economy—was one of "the greatest ideas of Western man."[55]

At ISI's 1967 Midwestern summer school, students explored "Man, the State, and Freedom," applying Christopher Dawson's principle that liberty flows from civilization and "enculturation"—"the process by which culture is handed on by the society and acquired by the individual." The faculty included economist Yale Brozen of the University of Chicago, historian Thomas Molnar of Long Island University, Gerhart Niemeyer of Notre Dame, political scientist Jerzy Hauptmann of Park College, and M. Stanton Evans, who asked those assembled, "Can laissez-faire economics be reconciled with the religious and ethical precepts of Western religious teaching?" Ever the fusionist, he proceeded to demonstrate that they could.

In his seven lectures on philosophy and literature, the European-educated Molnar dealt, among others, with Bergson, Heidegger, Kafka, Camus, Sartre, Malraux, Orwell, Huxley, Homer, Dante, Balzac, Beckett, and Genet, intellectually exhilarating and exhausting his audience at the same time.[56] Molnar said that literature through the centuries had reflected "a solid belief in universals," as in Homer, Dante, and Racine. But modernity brought an end to realism in literature as the Romantic "turned from the world toward himself," as in the writing of the existentialist

54. "Reflections of Modernity," Wayne H. Valis, brochure of 1966 Eastern Summer School, ISI Archives.
55. "Summer School Lectures Tied to 'Modernity' Theme," John A. Faylor, *ISI Campus Report,* Vol. 5, No. 1, Fall 1966: 6.
56. Brochure of 1967 Midwestern Summer School, Rockford College, Rockford, Illinois, August 20-26, 1967, ISI Archives: 17, 14-15.

Jean-Paul Sartre. But Molnar saw a tendency back to a belief in reality in "the new novel," as reflected in the works of Ernest Hemingway, John Dos Passos, and their successors.[57]

Under new editor Wayne Valis, *The Intercollegiate Review* published in the summer of 1968 one of its most important and oft-quoted articles—"What Is the Moral Crisis of Our Time?" by Will Herberg of Drew University. Often described as America's most distinguished Jewish philosopher, Herberg wrote that the crisis was not "the widespread violation of accepted moral standards"—which everyone conceded—but "the repudiation" of the standards themselves. "The very notion of morality or a moral code," he said, "seems to be losing its meaning for increasing numbers of men and women in our society." Herberg traced the beginning of the long slide into moral anarchy to the midnineteenth century when intellectuals turned away from the ancient Hebrew and Greek concept of truth—"grounded in a higher law and a higher reality"—and substituted a relative, conditional truth. The end result was the creation of a pseudo-ethic predicated on an "urge for pleasure or power." And that in turn placed "the humanity of man" in jeopardy. "We are losing," Herberg concluded on a somber note, "the tradition of the higher law and the higher reality—and are therefore also losing our standards."[58]

Running Wild

It also seemed that many students were losing their minds. Between January 1 and June 15 of 1968, 221 major demonstrations flared up, involving nearly 39,000 students, on 101 American campuses. Buildings were dynamited, administrative offices were invaded, professors were intimidated, classes were suspended. Historian William O'Neill observed that prior to the student protests of 1968, many universities, for all their flaws, had at least required hard work and discipline—helping to train students for life in the real world. By contrast, in some post-protest universities, O'Neill

57. "Students, Lecturers Explore Theme, 'Man, State, Freedom' at ISI Midwestern Session," John R. Hicks, *ISI Campus Report,* Vol. 5, No. 2, Spring 1968: 10.

58. Will Herberg, "What Is the Moral Crisis of Our Time?" *The Intercollegiate Review,* January-March 1968: 63-69. Herberg would develop this theme in future issues.

lamented, echoing Will Herberg, "The Protestant Ethic gave way to the pleasure principle."[59] The aphorism, however, placed too much of the blame on the student rather than on those who ran the university—the teachers and the administrators.

It was "the free floating journalist," stated Herberg, "the *litterateur,* or the junior academician" who was attempting to subvert and destroy "the existing social order." Gerhart Niemeyer agreed, arguing that it was not "youth" that was causing the upheaval but a "radical ideology." English professor Jeffrey Hart of Dartmouth College referred to "the habitually antagonistic, and sometimes even treasonous, relationship" of intellectuals "to their surrounding society."[60] Stan Evans hammered away at the theme that the root premises of the New Left—collectivism, moral permissiveness, militant egalitarianism, antipatriotism—were the ideas of "American liberalism writ large." Whittaker Chambers had earlier made the same point, writing, "Every move against the Communists was felt by the liberals as a move against themselves."[61]

Evans, Hart, Niemeyer, and similar critics were all building on the wisdom of Richard Weaver (ISI's primary intellectual influence in its first decade), who had written in the early sixties that America was the victim of a "systematic attempt to undermine a society's traditions and beliefs through the educational establishment." Weaver went on: "Gnostics of education" were determined to perfect the evil world around them, and in so acting, they would produce a "secular communist state." Needing recruits, he said, the modern gnostics found them in students who would be carefully conditioned "for political purposes."[62] The result, according to conservative sociologist Robert Nisbet, was the sixties—"the single most critical, crisis-ridden decade in the history of American higher education."[63]

59. William O'Neill, *Coming Apart: An Informal History of America in the 1960s,* Chicago, 1971: 302.

60. Will Herberg, Gerhart Niemeyer, and Jeffrey quotations from George H. Nash, *The Conservative Intellectual Movement in American Since 1945:* 299-300.

61. Ibid: 301; Whittaker Chambers, *Witness,* New York, 1952:741-742.

62. Richard M. Weaver, *Visions of Order: The Cultural Crisis of Our Time,* Baton Rouge, La., 1964: 114.

63. Robert Nisbet, "Dismal Decade for the Academy," *National Review,* December

The ISI Response

Vic Milione had anticipated Barry Goldwater's defeat in the 1964 presidential campaign because of the overwhelming political forces arrayed against the conservative senator. So, too, Milione was prepared for the campus chaos of 1968 because through his deep reading of historians like Hermann Rauschning and Jacob Burckhardt, he perceived the signs of "a great crisis." As Rauschning wrote in *Time of Delirium* such a crisis is marked by "the breakdown of the intellectual and ethical norms, of the ideas and principles, of the creeds and ideals which comprise the content of a civilization."[64]

As disquieting as the breakdown was, the proper response, Milione believed, was to concentrate on the root causes and offer root solutions. "If you want to win in the current conflict in regard to freedom and civilization," he wrote trustee Albert M. Campbell, "then you get the best minds possible" and bring them into contact with the best students possible. That was what ISI had been doing for fifteen years, Milione said, and what it would continue to do, even if such a long-range intellectual approach lacked sufficient "sex appeal" for some businessmen. "Considering the stakes," he wrote, "it would be disastrous to sacrifice substance for sex appeal."[65]

And so, ISI lecturers calmly challenged the destructive trend. Professor Lewis Feuer, who had taught at the University of California-Berkeley and once publicly debated Mario Savio, said the New Leftists "were possessed by a terrible, compulsive irrationality which corrupted their idealism." He suggested that the modern intellectual should turn to men like Thomas Jefferson and Benjamin Franklin, who tested their ideas by action, and were prepared to answer for their actions. "This," he said, "is the tradition we must try to recapture by working through American democratic institutions."[66]

29, 1970: 1409.
  64. E. Victor Milione to Albert M. Campbell, November 27, 1968, ISI Archives.
  65. Ibid.
  66. Tim Nagler, "Feuer Hits 'Apprenticed Intellectuals,' Cites 'Irrationality' of New Leftists," *ISI Campus Report,* Spring 1968: 9.

The most serious obstacle to promoting liberty on many campuses, reported ISI's field representatives, was not the political agenda of the radicals, whose numbers were comparatively few, but the general attitude of students who were expressing an increasing hostility to Western values and free enterprise—the very system which enabled them to go to college. Midwestern director Lawrence Pratt (who would later serve as executive director of the American Conservative Union and then director of Gun Owners of America) said the reason for the anti-Americanism was philosophical. The students' "'education' too often informed them that government has been too limited" and individuals "have been too free," thereby producing "unprecedented grave problems." As a result, Pratt said, "the free enterprise system is not only not understood but it is very often the object of intense hatred."[67]

An urgent note was struck by Western director Charles Heatherly (who would later fill top posts at the Heritage Foundation and in the Reagan administration in the 1980s). "Each day," he wrote to ISI headquarters, "sees an acceleration in the rate of politicization and radicalization on the campuses and each day sees the task of *education* rendered more difficult." Heatherly saw the academic year 1970-71 as a "turning point"— either ISI would significantly increase its impact on the campuses "or the situation will be beyond repair." Students and teachers alike, he said, looked to ISI "for leadership."[68]

Aware of its responsibilities, ISI extended its reach on the campus and beyond. In 1968, the Institute distributed, upon students' requests, more than 300,000 pieces of literature, assisted campus representatives at 190 schools, published three issues of *The Intercollegiate Review,* and maintained a list of over 30,000 members. ISI was especially proud of what the Weaver Fellowship program had accomplished after only three years. Of the thirty Fellows, 24 percent were already teaching full-time; and 88 percent were studying for an advanced degree, with many of them

67. Lawrence Pratt, as quoted in "Report on the Programs of the Intercollegiate Studies Institute During the 1969-70 Academic Year," prepared for R. Daniel McMichael and the Scaife Family, ISI Archives.
68. Ibid.

in the final stages of a Ph.D. candidacy. Assistant professor Douglas K. Adie at Ohio University said that the Weaver Fellowship was "particularly valuable because it provided support ... *before* I [had] 'proved' myself." "Many graduates ... would turn their backs on graduate education," said John F. Lehman Jr., then at the Foreign Policy Research Institute, and "would be lost to the professions of teaching and research, were it not for the Weaver program." "It is certainly true," added Lehman, "to paraphrase Voltaire, that if ISI did not exist we would have to invent it." Paul Cole Beach, teaching at Johns Hopkins University, said that because the Weaver program "aimed at promoting genuine scholarship," it "strikes me as more important in the long run than mere political action in arriving at solutions to current problems, political and otherwise." William C. Dennis II, a teaching assistant at Yale, who would later become a program officer at Liberty Fund, wrote that he could "think of no better program to encourage conservative youth to become teachers in the nation's colleges where their effect may be felt for generations."[69]

A continuing strength of ISI was its board of trustees, judiciously balanced between men and women of the academy, business, and politics. "The trustees reminded me of the Founding Fathers of the American Republic," says Wayne Valis, who spent six years with ISI as Eastern director and publications director in the late 1960s and early 1970s before moving to Washington, D.C., and serving in both the Nixon and Reagan administrations. Valis now heads his own lobbying firm. "Those initial ISI trustees," he says, "were amazingly unselfish and indifferent to public recognition—they did what they did to help bring about a humane society. They set a high standard for those who followed."[70] Valis was inspired by their example: he has been an ISI trustee and major donor since 1984.

The Institute enlarged the board in 1968 to include California industrialist Henry Salvatori, U.S. Senator George Murphy of California, and William Bogie, editor and publisher of *Banking,* the journal of the

69. "The First Three Years: A Report," Richard M. Weaver Fellowship Awards Program, May 1968, ISI Archives.
70. Author's interview with Wayne Valis, November 20, 2001.

American Banking Association. Also added were educator Philip M. Crane (who would be elected to the U.S. Congress from Illinois within a year and is still serving in 2003); best-selling author Richard Whalen; economics professor H. E. Michl of the University of Delaware; and Richard V. Allen, a senior staff member of the Hoover Institution at Stanford (who would become President Reagan's first national security adviser). Rejoining the board were economist William H. Peterson of U.S. Steel and sociology professor Albert H. Hobbs of the University of Pennsylvania, both of whom had worked with ISI in its earliest days. Dick Allen did double duty for the Institute by agreeing to serve, along with M. Stanton Evans, as co-chairman of the newly formed ISI Alumni Committee. Their mission was to maintain a continuing relationship with "the over 100,000 individuals who have participated in the ISI program as students."[71]

The burgeoning activities—the Weaver Fellowships, the lectures and summer schools, *The Intercollegiate Review* and other publications, the clubs and books—elicited yet more student requests, producing a painful paradox. ISI's success, reported national director John Lulves at a board of trustees meeting, had "financially weakened it." The Institute, he said candidly, was not "able to service properly the minimum requests of students who come to ISI—to say nothing of the untold thousands yet to be approached."[72] The Institute's chief financial officer estimated that expenditures for 1968-1969 would probably be around $350,000. That was, he pointed out, double the ISI budget six years earlier but still far less than what was needed to service adequately the thousands of young conservatives who believed, with Plato, that the purpose of education was to assist the student to gain wisdom and virtue.

As he had generally done since he joined ISI in 1953—when it had all of $2,000 in the bank—Vic Milione responded calmly to the latest financial challenge (he declined to characterize the situation as a "crisis").

71. "M. Stanton Evans, Richard V. Allen Head Newly-Formed ISI Alumni Committee, *ISI Campus Report*, Spring 1968: 1.

72. Remarks of John F. Lulves Jr., at a meeting of the ISI Board of Trustees, February 3, 1968, ISI Archives.

He told trustees that several of the major foundations that supported the Institute were receptive to a "one-time grant of additional funds for the purpose of building an ISI Reserve Fund." He reported that Neil McCaffrey, president of the Conservative Book Club and "very experienced in successful fund-raising," was helping them with a test mailing for a national direct-mail campaign.[73] Through trustee Henry Salvatori, he hoped to meet Patrick Frawley, Blanche Seaver, and other potential major donors on an up-coming California trip. He also intended to submit new proposals to foundations that had not yet supported ISI. A series of "corporate support luncheons" would be held in Pittsburgh, Indianapolis, Washington, D.C., and Chicago. As a result, ISI entered the 1970s "in a much more healthy financial condition than it has enjoyed during the recent years."[74] But as Milione wrote Henry Salvatori after giving him the good news, "we do not intend to sit on our duffs during the present year or the rest of the seventies."[75]

73. E. Victor Milione to Charles Dana Bennett, January 12, 1968, ISI Archives.
74. E. Victor Milione to Richard A. Ware, March 14, 1972, ISI Archives.
75. E. Victor Milione to Henry Salvatori, September 15, 1972, ISI Archives.

CHAPTER V

Staying the Course

[ISI] has been more effective than all the radical student organizations put together.

Russell Kirk[1]

"WHY CAN'T SCHOOL BE LIKE THIS all the time?" the student cried out at two in the morning. The young man was coming off a full week of interacting personally and at length with teachers like Russell Kirk, Gerhart Niemeyer, Thomas Molnar, Mel Bradford, Arthur Shenfield, and Frederick Wilhelmsen at an ISI summer school that Robert Reilly, then ISI's Western director, had organized at Pepperdine University in Southern California.[2] Wherever it was held, East, West, North, or South, an ISI summer conference was one of the most intellectually exhilarating and exhausting experiences in the lives of the fifty or so young conservatives in attendance.

The first "class" was at 9 A.M.—an early hour for college undergradu-

1. As quoted in M. Stanton Evans, "The ISI Story: Ideas Have Consequences," *ISI Campus Report,* Vol. 7, No. 1, Fall 1978: 5.
2. Author's interview with Robert Reilly, August 30, 2001.

ates—affording them just enough time to shower, dress, and grab a do-
nut before the opening lecture by, perhaps, Gerhart Niemeyer. The two
morning sessions, divided by short breaks and coffee, would be followed
by a speaker-less lunch during which the students would begin debating
the morning topics ("Of course the Declaration of Independence is the
most important of the Founding documents;" "No, I don't agree that
Lincoln was the greatest president, starting with his suspension of habeas
corpus"). During the two afternoon sessions—often featuring Russell Kirk,
whose day began and ended late—students who had stayed up most of
the previous night began to sag and yearn not for a coffee break but for a
nap. But by the time dinner was over, the young conservatives had recu-
perated and were ready for the best "class" of the day—an informal, intense, and extended debate with the faculty and other students on the
current crises of the West.

The rigor of the schedule led one conferee to complain, "It's a conservative bootcamp." But the great majority of the students reveled in the
total intellectual immersion, saying that "by staying up until the wee hours
of the morning discussing eternal verities, ISI students and faculty participated in a Socratic dialogue reminiscent of Plato's *Symposium*."[3] There
were debates between traditionalists and neoconservatives, conservatives
and libertarians, Catholics and Protestants. "The intellectual battles of
the past," recalls one participant, "were very much present to us." Holding on to T. S. Eliot's dictum that "there are no lost causes because there
are no gained causes," the summer school graduates sallied forth—even
as Frank Chodorov had decades before—to contend with their most formidable adversary, modernity. "Perhaps the single greatest feeling that I
took away" from an ISI conference, says Bracy Bernsnak, who attended
as a Miami University student, "was the realization that I was not alone.
There were other students my age who believed the same things I did and
were as determined to fight to preserve them."[4]

From its first days, ISI was blessed with dedicated regional directors

3. Memorandum of Bracy Bersnak to Lee Edwards, April 1, 2003.
4. Ibid.

who, like modern circuit riders, carried the good news of conservatism from campus to campus. The men and women who composed the national headquarters staff were equally committed to implementing the Institute's manifold informational programs. The causes of their dedication were several: they were, first of all, believers in a conservatism broad enough in its humanism to include Frank Chodorov and Richard Weaver. They were adamantly opposed to the dead hand of collectivism and determined to preserve the living ideas of Western civilization. They were inspired by the example of their boss, E. Victor Milione, who "never lost sight of ISI's mission to educate for liberty, even in the hardest of times."[5] Not that working for ISI required formal vows—except perhaps that of poverty. The ISI offices in Bryn Mawr, Indianapolis, and Claremont often echoed with laughter. A sense of equanimity also helped, particularly on campus where the carefully laid plans of ISI members sometimes went agley.

In the 1960s, for example, when much of Rutgers University in New Jersey was in turmoil, undergraduate Wayne Valis brought the courtly Gerhart Niemeyer to his campus for a lecture. Valis and another undergraduate met the impeccably dressed Niemeyer at the New Jersey airport in a huge 1940 Packard sedan with a faded but still elegant velvet interior. With his appreciation for *les choses anciennes*, Professor Niemeyer was visibly impressed with the means of transportation—until the nervous young driver went the wrong way on the New Jersey Turnpike and wound up in New York City.

Turning around, amid profuse apologies by Valis, the small party made for New Brunswick until the venerable Packard suddenly developed a flat tire. Repairs were hastily made. Resuming their journey, the professor and his two young escorts had no sooner begun discussing the future of Western civilization than the Packard slowed and came to a dead stop. The young conservatives had neglected to check the fuel tank, and the car had run out of gas. In desperation, Valis and his embarrassed

5. Author's interview with Wayne Valis, November 20, 2001.

ISI trustee Albert M. Campbell (r) thanks Rev. Edmund Opitz for his December 1961 Indianapolis lecture. Below: Richard M. Weaver talks to Campbell and Thomas F. Huston, president of the Indianapolis University Conservative League, at the 1960 ISI board meeting. Previous page, l to r: Leonard Read, Foundation for Economic Education president, with Russell Kirk, and ISI trustee Prof. Hans F. Sennholz.

Roy Gilbert, president of the Michigan State University Conservative Club (l) with U.S. Senator Barry Goldwater and club advisor Prof. Daniel K. Stewart (r). Below: A Goldwater syndicated column devoted to ISI reprinted from the March 31, 1961 Indianapolis News. Right: A March 28 letter to Don Lipsett from ISI alumnus and Arizona Republic editorial writer Edwin McDowell reporting his meeting with Goldwater staffer Steve Shadegg.

THE ARIZONA REPUBLIC

120 EAST VAN BUREN STREET
PHOENIX, ARIZONA

March 28, 1961

Dear Don:

About 10 days ago I spent a few hours with Steve Shadegg advising him of the activities of the I.S.I. The meeting was for the purpose of giving I.S.I. a plug in Barry's column. So, if it hasn't appeared already, don't dispair, for it surely will appear sometime in the future.

Best regards.

Sincerely,

Ed McDowell

Vic — Ed takes good care of us.
Don't bother to return.

HOW DO YOU STAND, SIR?

Freedom Movement Led by Young Conservatives

By Barry Goldwater
United States Senator

I AM CONSTANTLY amazed by Republicans who tell me the presidential election of 1960 indicates we will never re-establish conservative constitutional government in the United States.

My political enemies like to pretend there is something outrageously old-fashioned about conservative beliefs and I understand they even put out a bumper sticker which said "Goldwater for President—1864."

Conservative political ph...

Goldwater

The League for Industrial Democracy, which began as the Intercollegiate Socialist Society, is a notable example of the kind of left-wing liberal organization which has contributed so much toward the establishment of the welfare state in this republic.

The picture has changed radically. The revolutionaries on American campuses today are conservative. The Intercollegiate Society of Individualists, born in 1953 with an initial mailing list of over 400 students, now has some 12,000 active members with chapters on most American campuses. Victor Milione, one of the founders of this movement, says; "Individual men should be their own agents in all things respect-

The Wall Street Journal, Time Magazine and columnist John Ackelmire of The Indianapolis News among other reporters of the American political scene have taken notice of the rapid spread of conservatism among college students.

The Young Americans for Freedom, which might be regarded as a political-action group parallel to the Intercollegiate Society of Individualists, publishes a directory listing activities on 95 college campuses as of the spring of 1961. In addition to their publications these two organizations sponsor seminars, debates and speeches by the leading conservative thinkers.

The home office of ISI is located at ... te Building, Philadelphia,

New York University economist Israel Kirzner lectures at an ISI Eastern summer school at LaSalle College in 1967. Middle: All eyes are on Ludwig von Mises at the 1966 Eastern summer school at Bard College. Below: Paul Craig Roberts joins von Mises at the same summer school.

Milton Friedman with ISI students. Below: Frank Meyer (l) with Northwestern University philosopher Eliseo Vivas joke with Minor Meyers, Jr. (l) of Carleton College and John Ferguson (r) of Abilene Christian College at the 1961 Lake Forest College ISI summer school.

National Review *columnist and author Erik von Kuehnelt-Leddihn of Austria holds court following an ISI-sponsored lecture in the early 1960s. Below, l to r: Businessman James Evans and ISI trustee Louis H.T. Dehmlow with William F. Buckley Jr. and ISI midwest director Don Lipsett in 1960.*

William F. Buckley Jr. signs copies of Up From Liberalism *for (l to r) Nellie Hill, Phyllis Painter, and Susan Regnery who attended the first ISI summer school at Grove City College in 1960. Below, l to r: M. Stanton Evans, ISI trustee and former G.E. vice president Lemuel Boulware, and ISI founder Frank Chodorov at the 1960 board meeting in Indianapolis.*

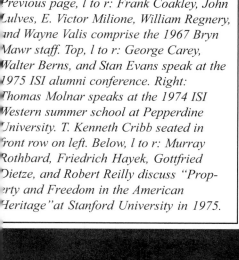

Previous page, l to r: Frank Coakley, John Lulves, E. Victor Milione, William Regnery, and Wayne Valis comprise the 1967 Bryn Mawr staff. Top, l to r: George Carey, Walter Berns, and Stan Evans speak at the 1975 ISI alumni conference. Right: Thomas Molnar speaks at the 1974 ISI Western summer school at Pepperdine University. T. Kenneth Cribb seated in front row on left. Below, l to r: Murray Rothbard, Friedrich Hayek, Gottfried Dietze, and Robert Reilly discuss "Property and Freedom in the American Heritage" at Stanford University in 1975.

Top, l to r: David Schaefer,
William Dennis, John Alvis,
Hadley Arkes, Harry Jaffa, and
Russell Kirk discuss "The
Future of American Conserva-
tism" at ISI's 1980 Western
summer school at Claremont
Men's College. Left, l to r:
Harry Jaffa talks to Ernest
Fortin, Richard Kennington,
and Harvey Mansfield following
a 1980 ISI lecture at Harvard.
Bottom left, William Kristol
lectures at the 1988 ISI Eastern
summer school at Catholic
University of America. Bottom
right: Ken Cribb (r) with
Russell and Annette Kirk at
Durie House, Scotland, 1973.

The Bryn Mawr office, circa 1967. Notable ISI staff at work, counter-clockwise: E. Victor Milione, 1978; Ken Cribb along with Robert Schadler & John Lulves, 1973.

Top, l to r: E. Victor Milione joins Stan Evans and former staff members Charles Heatherly, Robert Reilly, and Robert Schadler at a 1982 ISI alumni meeting. Below, l to r: Former ISI staff members Peter DeLuca, Charles Heatherly, Peter Schramm, Robert Reilly, and Eric Brodin attend the 1980 national Philadelphia Society meeting.

Top, l to r: Malcolm Muggeridge and Russell Kirk participate in a symposium at Dartmouth College in 1977 entitled "The True Crisis of our Time." Allan Bloom gives a lecture on Richard II at the "Poetry and Politics in Shakespeare" conference in 1978 at the University of Dallas.

Top, l to r: Robert Reilly with "Role of Business in Society" (ROBIS) conference faculty Walter Williams and William Peterson in North Carolina, 1978. Bottom left: Frequent ISI lecturer and future U.S. senator Phil Gramm at a 1975 ROBIS summer school. Bottom right: Irving Kristol addresses the question "Capitalism vs. the Economists?" at a Stanford University ROBIS banquet in August, 1977.

colleague began pushing the ancient machine toward a garage only one block away. Professor Niemeyer, a practical man as well as a political theorist, got out and helped them push. "I knew," remembers Valis, "that my career in the conservative movement was over."[6]

Finally arriving on campus, the imperturbable Niemeyer took a few minutes to "compose" himself before delivering a brilliant lecture on "The Communist Mind" to about thirty students, never mentioning any of the misadventures. He came to Valis's small student apartment afterwards where he talked for hours about the need to marry moral ideas with economic interests if you wanted to change the world. Remember, Niemeyer said, "the imperfectability of man" and that every "solution carried with it the next problem." "The words and the ideas," Valis remembers, "seemed to explode out of him." "That evening," says Valis, "changed my life."[7]

Upon graduation in 1966 from Rutgers, Valis was approached by ISI's Charles Heatherly, who asked him about his future plans. In short order, he met with Vic Milione "and the ISI crew," and was offered and accepted the position of Eastern director. "I had just gotten married," recalls Valis, "and was flat broke. I had to borrow the train fare to get to Philadelphia."[8] His first major responsibility was to plan a summer school featuring the legendary economist Ludwig von Mises.

Although von Mises spoke in a high voice with a thick Austrian accent, he was a "riveting" lecturer with sparkling eyes, recalls Valis. His topic at the ISI school, held at Bard College in New York, was "Man and Property." His lecture notes, Valis noted with awe, consisted of just three words—"Capitalism," "England," and "Industrial Revolution." Von Mises talked without interruption for more than an hour. "It was as though," said one audience member to Valis afterwards, "he were speaking to each and every person in the room individually."[9]

Valis spent six years with ISI, from 1966 through 1972, as Eastern director and then publications director and editor of *The Intercollegiate*

6. Ibid.
7. Ibid.
8. Ibid.
9. Ibid.

Review, after Robert Ritchie left to join Van Nostrand publishing as an editor. While bombs burst on campus and ISI countered with books, and funds for the Institute ebbed and flowed ("we ate a lot of jello and white bread"), Valis formed enduring friendships with Charles Heatherly, Kenneth Cribb, James Taylor, Robert Reilly, and Robert Schadler—a "band of brothers," like those who fought so bravely for young King Henry on Saint Crispin's Day. But the young warriors of ISI were concerned not just about the fate of a nation, but of a civilization.

Robert A. Schadler was a conservative in 1964 when he entered Georgetown University. His father and mother, who had immigrated to America from Austria after World War II, were strong anti-Communists who imparted their traditional Christian values to their son. As a teenager, Schadler read *Masters of Deceit* by J. Edgar Hoover and *The Conscience of a Conservative* by Barry Goldwater, and invariably took the conservative side in high school debates. He remembers listening to Fred Schwarz's anti-Communist broadcasts on a local radio station in Columbus, Ohio, where his father was teaching at Ohio State.[10]

Marginally involved in the Goldwater presidential campaign, Schadler moved off-campus in his sophomore year at Georgetown University to a house on Q Street that became "a hub" for young conservatives, particularly of an intellectual bent. Georgetown professor Joseph Schiebel had had some contact with ISI as had James Riley, one of Schadler's housemates, and before long Wayne Valis and Charles Heatherly came calling. In 1967, Schadler coordinated an ISI summer school at Georgetown featuring such ISI regulars as Gerhart Niemeyer, Will Herberg, Stanley Parry, Francis Graham Wilson, and George W. Carey. Carey liked one of Schadler's research papers so much that he encouraged him to attend graduate school (Schadler picked the University of Pennsylvania) and arranged for him to receive an Earhart Fellowship.

Schadler started at Penn in the fall of 1968, but the Vietnam war was changing the lives of many young Americans—"I was drafted almost im-

10. Author's interview with Robert Schadler, April 7, 2003.

mediately." Out of the army the following year, the young conservative learned that ISI was looking for an Eastern director. "I was interviewed by Vic and John Lulves," recalls Schadler, "and offered a very nominal salary of $500 a month."[11] But he was content: the ISI job got him back to Philadelphia, his Earhart Fellowship was restored, and he recommended his studies at the University of Pennsylvania from which he received a master's degree in international relations.

For the next ten years, Bob Schadler was one of ISI's most effective people at national headquarters, serving as Eastern director, national director, and from 1972, director of publications. In his spare time, Schadler edited *The Intercollegiate Review,* administered the Weaver Fellowships, and, when necessary, went calling on Richard Larry of the Scaife Foundation and other officials of grant-giving foundations. "Earhart, Scaife, Salvatori, and Pew," he says, "were the Big Four of ISI fund raising." In all that he did, Bob Schadler tried to "give bright undergraduates intellectual nourishment and to keep in contact with them," knowing how lonely it could be for a conservative on campus.[12] He also served as a recruiter for ISI, one of his most auspicious "finds" being a young South Carolinian—T. Kenneth Cribb, Jr.

The Making of a Conservative

When the eighteen-year-old Kenneth Cribb arrived at Washington and Lee University in 1966, he was already a complete conservative by reason of his intellectual and cultural upbringing in Spartanburg, South Carolina. His father, Troy Kenneth Cribb, was the president of a successful produce distribution company and was well-known as a civic leader. But the elder Cribb was far more than a leading businessman. Taking great interest in higher education, he had been elected to numerous terms as a trustee of Clemson University by the South Carolina legislature. He was well read, with a particular fondness for C. S. Lewis, and had become through intense personal study and research an expert on the Dead Sea

11. Author's interview with Robert Schadler, September 6, 2001.
12. Ibid.

Scrolls. "He was," recalls his son, "a kind and gentle man" who inculcated a love for language in his namesake. Ken's mother, Dicksie Brown Cribb, was and is a vivacious Southern lady, who is much loved in the nation's musical circles for her unstinting work in support of classical musicians. Possessed of a fine singing voice and a flair for the dramatic, Dicksie Cribb had the lead in many amateur productions in Spartanburg. "I learned," says Ken Cribb, "how to speak in public from her."[13] He also learned the importance of a living faith from his parents, both prominent members of the Methodist Church.

When Ken was in the third grade, Dicksie Cribb took her young son to see Lawrence Olivier in *Richard III,* which made such a vivid impression that the boy carried a book of Shakespeare's plays to school every day for the next three years. "I carried that book," says Cribb, "until I could read and understand it."[14] The incident revealed the boy's precocious appreciation for great writing and his impressive perseverance. His entry into politics was occasioned by his reading—between the sixth and seventh grades—Allen Drury's best-selling Washington novel, *Advise and Consent,* a work with several "conservative lessons." His conversion to the Republican Party (the Cribbs had been loyal Democrats for generations) followed his watching on television the 1960 Republican GOP convention.

"I have been a Republican," Cribb explains, "ever since watching Walter Judd give the keynote address at that convention."[15] Political historians describe the Judd address—devoted almost exclusively to U.S. foreign policy—as part political speech, part history lesson, part sermon, part philosophical discourse, and all exhortation, intended to sway the millions of Americans watching the first gavel-to-gavel coverage of national conventions by the television networks. The *Omaha World-Herald* called the speech a "masterpiece" and "a beacon of truth in a dark and uncertain era."[16]

13. Author's interview with T. Kenneth Cribb, Jr., May 5, 2003.
14. Ibid.
15. Ibid.
16. *Omaha World-Herald,* July 27, 1960. Also see Lee Edwards, *Missionary for Freedom: The Life and Times of Walter Judd,* New York, 1990: 247-251.

Young Cribb went on to found the first chapter of Young Americans for Freedom in South Carolina—while in junior high school—and to devour every paperback distributed during the 1964 Goldwater presidential campaign, including the Arizona senator's *The Conscience of a Conservative.* But it was at Washington and Lee that Ken Cribb read the book that shaped "my political philosophy."[17] One of his very first extracurricular acts at the University was to join the Edmund Burke Society, a fortnightly dining club that discussed important books and was affiliated with ISI. Senior Jeffrey Gayner, the Society's president, was so impressed with the intellectual maturity of the always smiling freshman—who seemed to have a thousand tales about growing up in the South—that he arranged for ISI to give Cribb a copy of Russell Kirk's classic work on American conservatism—*The Conservative Mind.*

Like so many other young conservatives seeking confirmation of their beliefs, Cribb has never forgotten the epiphany of reading that extraordinary book. Until the advent of that landmark work in 1953, he now points out, there had been a disparate group of "nostalgic southerners," "Midwest isolationists" and "zealous anti-Communists" but no unifying theme among them. *The Conservative Mind* provided "an intellectual pedigree" for American conservatism going back to Edmund Burke and "made us all more reflective about the philosophical premises of our political opinions."[18]

As president of the Edmund Burke Society, Cribb brought such conservative luminaries as economist W. H. Hutt and author-lecturer Erik von Kuehnelt-Leddihn to W&L. He also traveled to the University of Virginia with a carload of friends to hear the venerable Ludwig von Mises lecture. Kuehnelt-Leddihn demonstrated his mastery of the riposte, Cribb remembers, when he was asked at his lecture about the "birth of democracy" during the French Revolution. Without hesitating, the Austrian-born scholar ("a liberal but a monarchist") responded: "There was no birth but an abortion in a forest of guillotines."[19]

17. Author's interview with T. Kenneth Cribb, Jr., May 5, 2003.
18. Ibid.
19. Ibid.

Graduating in 1970 with a degree in French literature, Ken Cribb worked for his father in Spartanburg for a year and a half until he heard from Richard Hines, a fellow W&L alumnus working at ISI, that there was a vacancy at the Institute. "ISI had been a considerable part of my life all through college," says Cribb. The possibility of joining the national organization seemed a logical move for the lively young conservative.[20] He traveled to Bryn Mawr and was interviewed by Vic Milione, who, along with John Lulves, was impressed by the young man's solid grounding in conservative principles and his considerable Southern charm. Schadler, then ISI national director, says that Cribb was obviously "a very bright guy and a quite capable organizer."[21] He was hired almost on the spot and immediately plunged into his duties as Eastern/Southern director. His first major event was a summer school with the Eliotish theme, "Up From the Wasteland," to which he invited Russell Kirk, who accepted, bringing ISI and the noted conservative author closer than they had been for several years.

Kirk was so pleased with the school, particularly the high quality of the students, that he and his wife Annette discussed with Schadler and Cribb, now national director, the possibility of ISI sponsoring a series of intellectual seminars at their Mecosta, Michigan, home, Piety Hill. By the spring of 1973, an understanding had been reached, and that Christmas the first ISI Piety Hill Seminar was held, featuring political philosopher Frederick Wilhelmsen. This tradition has continued for three decades, even following Russell Kirk's death in 1994. The Piety Hill seminars "were my babies," says Ken Cribb proudly, listing the main speakers during his time as Wilhelmsen, Thomas Molnar, Mel Bradford, and Malcolm Muggeridge. He particularly remembers the Christmas 1978 seminar when Kirk and Muggeridge sat side by side in front of the fireplace, talking and "looking into the future."[22]

An even more consequential event in Cribb's life was the summer of

20. Ibid.
21. Author's interview with Robert Schadler, February 27, 2003.
22. Author's interview with T. Kenneth Cribb, Jr., May 5, 2003.

1973 when he and Bob Schadler accompanied Russell and Annette Kirk
and their three daughters—Monica, Cecilia, and Felicia—on "a romp
through Scotland," featuring a sojourn in a haunted house, visits with the
Earl of Crawford and other members of the Scottish aristocracy, side trips
to St. Andrews University where Kirk had earned his doctorate and to
Abbotsford, the home of Sir Walter Scott, brisk forty-mile walks through
the Scottish countryside, and talks with Scottish intellectuals such as au-
thor-essayist-poet George Scott-Moncrieff, who treated his guests to a
carefully balanced diet of fried eggs and straight whiskey. Every day there
was "the constant discussion of books and ideas" with Kirk, "the father of
the modern conservative intellectual movement of America." It was "a
fabulous summer" which left an indelible mark on the mind and heart of
the twenty-five-year-old Southern conservative.

"As we walked the Scottish borders one day," recalls Cribb, "I asked
Dr. Kirk for a succinct definition of conservative doctrine. In correctly
refusing to give me one, he offered the insight that conservatism is a 'dis-
position of openness to reality'—that is to say, openness toward the world
as God has created it, rather than a blind allegiance to one of those hypo-
thetical worlds in whose name so many have been slaughtered."[23]

"Russell was a mentor to Ken," says Annette Kirk, introducing him
to the best in Scotland, which with its love of tradition and its respect for
the past was akin to the South. She remembers how the two of them
would mix serious talk with funny stories—"Ken was always so full of
life." Cribb got to know her husband, explains Annette, "in his two real
lairs—Scotland and Mecosta."[24]

Big-Tent Conservatism

Always the teacher, Vic Milione constantly sought to stretch the abilities
of Ken Cribb and the other members of the ISI staff with ever more
challenging tasks, like fund-raising. Before he visited a major donor, Wayne
Valis recalls that Milione would call him in and stress one thing: "Re-

23. Ibid.
24. Author's telephone interview with Annette Kirk, April 4, 2003.

member the mission—educating for liberty. If they start saying we should strive for 'relevance,' ignore them." At this point, Valis remembers, Milione would pause and say emphatically, "I hate relevance!"[25] Valis knows of at least one very large gift (from California conservative Patrick J. Frawley) that Milione rejected because it fell outside ISI's purview.

"Vic's vision," explains Robert Schadler, "was a broadly based intellectual conservatism. He was never comfortable with Frank Meyer's label of 'fusionism.' He preferred to talk about the different strains of Western civilization that were not given their due in the academy. His was a nondoctrinaire conservatism, a big-tent conservatism."[26] The tent was big enough, Schadler points out, to include arch-libertarian Ludwig von Mises and the anti-gnostic political scientist Eric Voegelin, Catholic philosopher Fritz Wilhelmsen, and prominent Protestant Howard Kershner, southern agrarian Robert Penn Warren and northern agrarian Russell Kirk. The ISI approach toward conservatism, fashioned by Milione, thus confirms George Nash's contention that the conservative intellectual movement since 1945 was anything but a monolith.

In the early 1970s, ISI shifted from a practice of campus clubs—which waxed and waned depending upon individual leadership—to one of campus representatives. And it expanded its list of publications. In 1970-71, George Carey of Georgetown University's Department of Government and James McClellan founded the respected academic journal, *The Political Science Reviewer,* with the support of William J. Baroody, president of the American Enterprise Institute. The two conservatives wanted to provide in-depth reviews of important works, past and present, that had either been "ignored or treated too summarily or unfairly" by mainstream journals.[27] AEI helped with library subscriptions and picked up the cost of printing and mailing, but offered no long-term guarantee. When Robert Schadler said that the Institute would like to be the *PSR's* principal sponsor, Carey immediately agreed, for reasons of financial stability and because

25. Author's interview with Wayne Valis, November 20, 2001.
26. Author's interview with Robert Schadler, September 6, 2001.
27. Mark Henrie to Lee Edwards, March 19, 2003.

ISI and the *Reviewer* were in fundamental philosophical agreement.

The first issue was "spectacular," recalls Schadler, and featured essays by, among others, Gerhart Niemeyer, Stanley Rothman, and Ellis Sandoz on Eric Voegelin.[28] Asked about the influence of the journal, its first and only editor, George Carey, responded that *The Political Science Reviewer* "occupies a unique place in the profession.... If someone is going to write about a leading thinker [like Voegelin] whose works we have reviewed, then that someone is going to have to check with us to see what we said."[29] *PSR* pays special attention to America's founding documents.

With George Carey's help, ISI organized panels at the annual conventions of the American Political Science Association, helping young faculty members of the conservative persuasion to enhance their reputation; it still does. "Why not do the same for other academic professions?" Schadler and others asked themselves. And so conservative historians such as George Nash, Forrest McDonald, Burt Folsom, and Leonard Liggio offered panels at the annual meeting of the American Historical Association. The Modern Language Association was judged too far gone, but ISI did talk to Michael Uhlmann, among others, about starting a Legal Forum for law students and young lawyers.

The idea of an organization of conservative lawyers and law students gestated for several years until 1981 when Steven G. Calabresi at Yale and Lee Liberman and David McIntosh at the University of Chicago founded the Federalist Society for Law and Public Policy. The three law students recruited Antonin Scalia, then a professor with a long-standing ISI association at the University of Chicago Law School, as an adviser. Within five years, the Federalist Society had seventy chapters at law schools throughout the nation, lawyers' divisions in Washington, D.C., New York, Los Angeles, and Chicago, and a membership of two thousand. As chief assistant to Edward Meese III in the White House and later as counselor to Attorney General Meese, Kenneth Cribb encouraged the development of the Federalist Society at every possible opportunity and used the group

---

28. Interview with Schadler, September 6, 2001.
29. Author's interview with George Carey, July 5, 2001.

as a wellspring of legal and judicial talent for the Reagan administration.

"Ken took enormous interest in the Federalist Society," says Calabresi, who worked under Cribb at the Department of Justice in the second Reagan administration and is now a professor at Northwestern University Law School. "He immediately saw it as a continuation of ISI," Calabresi recalls.[30] Among other things, Cribb persuaded General Meese as well as President Reagan to address Federalist Society events. "I remember," says Eugene Meyer, president of the Federalist Society, "that when we tried to get Reagan to speak to us in the fall of 1988, it was Ken who was instrumental in making it happen." As it happened, Reagan's appearance coincided with Ken Cribb's very last day at the White House, prompting the president to joke, "Liberals are breaking out the champagne all over town." Subsequently named counselor to the Federalist Society, Cribb has given "invaluable" advice to the society over the years in the areas of fund-raising and management. "One of Ken's favorite sayings," reveals Meyer, "is 'Disaggregate the problem.' That is, break it down, don't be overwhelmed by its size, look at A, then B, then C." He's a good manager, says Meyer admiringly, "because he doesn't get flustered but sets about solving the problem."[31]

In remarkably few years, wrote the liberal *New Republic,* the Federalist Society went from "a guerrilla force to a standing army." By the end of 2002, it had an annual budget of $3.2 million and nearly 30,000 members. At its annual meeting that year, twelve senior Justice Department officials, including Attorney General John Ashcroft and half of the ten top-ranking assistant attorneys general, gave speeches and attended seminars. Also in attendance were Supreme Court Justice Scalia, Whitewater prosecutor Kenneth W. Starr, former federal judge Robert Bork, Interior Secretary Gale A. Norton, and Energy Secretary Spencer Abraham.[32] "I'm

---

30. Author's interview with Steve Calabresi, April 26, 2003.

31. Ronald Reagan's quote taken from author's interview with T. Kenneth Cribb, Jr., May 5, 2003; Eugene Meyer's remarks taken from author's interview with Eugene Meyer, April 26, 2003.

32. Crocker Coulson, "Federalist Pipes," *The New Republic,* December 1, 1986: 23; Eric Lichtblau, "Conservative club comes out as a force in capital," *New York Times,* November 17, 2002.

pleased," says Ken Cribb modestly, "to have played a part in building an institution firmly committed to the Constitution of the Founders and especially to the principle of original intent."[33]

A Conservative Review

Since 1957, *Modern Age* had been "the principal quarterly of the intellectual right."[34] Founded by Russell Kirk, Henry Regnery, and David S. Collier, a political scientist from Northwestern University, the journal stated forthrightly in its first editorial that it intended to challenge the dominant "liberal temper," stimulate discussion of "the great moral and social questions of the hour," and search for means by which "the legacy of our civilization may be kept safe." For its first two decades, *Modern Age* was based in Chicago, close by its primary benefactor, Henry Regnery, but in editor George Panichas's words, the journal "transcended any regional identity or parochial affiliation." Its writers were primarily academics, but their contributions rejected narrow academic specializations. Above all, *Modern Age* was concerned with the crisis of modernity—"a crisis of disorder"—and looked for answers and guidance "in the light of eternal values and permanent truths."[35]

The first article in the first issue of *Modern Age* was "Life Without Prejudice" by ISI mentor Richard Weaver, who defended prejudice as a good and necessary thing, arguing that a "life without prejudice ... would soon reveal itself to be a life without principle."[36] Weaver provided a model of rhetoric and analysis which was met over the ensuing years by a long list of consequential conservatives (many of them ISI lecturers and/or contributors to ISI publications) who addressed fundamental questions such as the need to restore tradition to society (Stanley Parry), the West's proper response to communism (John Dos Passos), the development of a common conservative doctrine comprehending both the traditionalist and

33. Author's interview with T. Kenneth Cribb, Jr., May 5, 2003.
34. George Panichas, ed., *Modern Age: The First Twenty-Five Years, A Selection*, Indianapolis, 1988: xiii.
35. Ibid: xiv–xv.
36. Ibid: 16.

the libertarian (Frank Meyer), the inborn inequality of man (Ludwig von Mises), and the "uneasy" relationship between conservatives and libertarians (Robert Nisbet).

There was also an extended debate between Harry Jaffa and M. E. Bradford on—what else?—equality; a luminous paean to the Southern agrarians by Andrew Lytle, the lone survivor of the agrarian movement; an examination of the Supreme Court's "civil theology" by political scientist Francis Graham Wilson; and discussions of the place of Christianity in society by such diverse authors as John Courtney Murray, S.J., European economist Wilhelm Roepke, author-lecturer Erik von Kuehnelt-Leddhin, and sociologist Will Herberg. Vivid dissections of the countless crimes and victims of communism were made by William Henry Chamberlin, Gerhart Niemeyer, Thomas Molnar, and Russian historian David J. Dallin.

There were also discerning essays about the academy by Eric Voegelin ("The climate of our universities certainly is hostile to the Life of Reason ... but there are always young men with enough spiritual instinct to resist the efforts of 'educators' who pressure for 'adjustment'");[37] social philosopher Eliseo Vivas ("our urgent need is to slow up the wreckage that our revolutionary age is inflicting on our civilization and to salvage what is still serviceable where there is still time");[38]and author-poet-professor Marion Montgomery, who wrote of Alexander Solzhenitsyn's riveting commencement address at Harvard, "He is a prophet addressing the intelligentsia's responsibility" for the crisis in academe.[39]

And yet, for all its brilliant illumination of the immediate as well as the permanent things, *Modern Age* was by the mid-1970s in financial straits and imminent danger of closing down. It was John Lulves in particular, remembers Robert Schadler, who argued forcefully that ISI should assume the responsibility of publishing America's foremost conservative quarterly.[40] Vic Milione concurred as did trustee chairman Henry Regnery,

37. Ibid: 700, Eric Voegelin, "On Classical Studies."
38. Ibid: 706, Eliseo Vivas, "The Educated Man."
39. Ibid: 776, Marion Montgomery, "Solzhenitsyn at Harvard."
40. Author's interview with Robert Schadler, September 6, 2001.

although all understood the heavy financial obligations (the journal's annual production budget for a circulation of 6,500 was $57,000).

But once again ISI did what it thought it ought to do, trusting that, as in the past, funding would be found somewhere. And it was, in the person of Richard Larry, president of the Sarah Scaife Foundation, who strongly supported *Modern Age* becoming part of ISI. In fact, in conversations with editor David Collier, Larry laughingly described himself as the "midwife" of the merger, which took place officially in July 1976. The foundation executive believed the new partnership was mutually beneficial: it would "permanentize" *Modern Age* and deepen ISI's reputation as a key propagator of the ideas of liberty.[41] On the publication of a twenty-fifth anniversary anthology of *Modern Age*, editor George Panichas gratefully wrote, "Neither the quarterly journal nor this selection would now exist without the Institute's support."[42]

The issues from 1976-1983 were marked by a concentration on "conservative theory" at a time when the conservative movement was on the cusp of coming to political power in America. In effect, wrote a future editor, the kinds of questions being argued in *National Review* "at a journalistic level" were taken up at "a deeper intellectual and academic level" in *Modern Age*.[43] There were, for example, a long string of articles about the relationship between libertarians, traditionalists, and the then novel neoconservatives, by such authors as Robert Nisbet, Murray Rothbard, George Carey, Russell Kirk, and Paul Gottfried.

A signature theme of *Modern Age* was the protracted debate between Mel Bradford and Harry Jaffa over the American Founding, the role of equality, and the proper understanding of Abraham Lincoln. In a seminal essay published in late 1976, Bradford argued that "equality as a moral or political imperative, pursued as an end in itself—Equality with the capital 'E'—is the antonym of every legitimate conservative principle." The "we" in the Declaration's second sentence signifies the colonials "not as

41. David S. Collier to Henry Regnery, June 2, 1976, and June 18, 1976, Henry Regnery Papers, Hoover Archives, Stanford University, Stanford, California.
42. Panichas, *Modern Age: The First Twenty-Five Years:* xx.
43. Mark Henrie to Lee Edwards, March 19, 2003.

individuals but rather in their corporate capacity." Therefore, the following "all men" are "persons prudent together." "Nothing," he said, "is maintained concerning the abilities or situations of individual persons living within the abandoned context of the British Empire or the societies to be formed by its disruption." Bradford stated that, in his view, neither the Declaration of Independence nor the Revolution nor the Constitution was "very revolutionary at all."[44] To which, in *Modern Age* the following spring, Jaffa responded that "equality is a conservative principle because justice is conservative, and equality is the principle of justice." The Declaration of Independence, he said, was "a political act without parallel in the history of the world" because it says that "*all* men have a right to resist despotism, and because all Americans are men, all Americans have this right ... that is, the right *not* to be slaves, is possessed equally by every human being on the face of the earth." The rights of which the Declaration speaks, argued Jaffa, "are not civil or political rights [but] rights with which they had been 'endowed by their Creator.'"[45] The Bradford-Jaffa debate on the Founding is one of *Modern Age's* signal contributions to American intellectual history.

Regardless of the differing interpretations by Bradford and Jaffa and those who lined up on one side or another (Frank Meyer wrote that "the freedom of the individual person from government, not the equality of individual persons, is the central theme of our constitutional arrangements"), they were all united against the liberal interpretation that equality meant that "men should be *made* equal in a material way."[46]

Another of *Modern Age's* core themes was the role of Christianity in the thought of the Founders and the American regime. Russell Kirk, Gerhart Niemeyer, Ellis Sandoz, and George Carey all wrote extensively about how experience and faith propelled the founding. There was also frequent reflection about the lessons to be drawn from the works of Leo

44. M.E. Bradford, "The Heresy of Equality: Bradford Replies to Jaffa," *Modern Age,* XX, Winter 1976: 62-77.

45. Harry V. Jaffa, "Equality, Justice, and the American Revolution: In Reply to Bradford's 'The Heresy of Equality,'" *Modern Age,* XXI, Spring 1977: 114-126.

46. Nash, *Conservative Intellectual Movement in America Since 1945:* 236.

Strauss and Eric Voegelin, the two scholars credited by conservatives with the "recovery of political philosophy" in the twentieth century.[47] *Modern Age* was *the* place where the thought of these recondite professors was presented as the common intellectual property of all conservative intellectuals and not just their academic colleagues. John East (later U.S. senator from North Carolina), Harry Jaffa, Steven Maaranen, Dante Germino, and Paul Norton all authored articles about Strauss in the late 1970s and early 1980s. During the same period, Marion Montgomery, David Levy, and Gerhart Niemeyer explored Voegelin, with East and Jaffa demonstrating their philosophical versatility by joining in.

Throughout the intellectual *sturm und drang* of this period, *Modern Age* kept returning to a consideration of the history and development of conservative thought in America, with contributions such as "The Contemporary Conservative Intellectual Movement" by George H. Nash, "American Conservative Intellectuals, the 1930s, and the Crisis of Ideology" by Edward S. Shapiro, "American Conservatism and F. A. Hayek" by Philip Dyer, and "Kirk, Rossiter, Hartz, and the Conservative Tradition in America" by William C. Dennis.

The Gospel of Liberty

Even without *Modern Age*, the Institute spent almost $80,000 on publications in the budget year ending June 30, 1977, up from $31,000 in 1970. It also expended another $200,000 on the Weaver Fellowships, lectures and summer schools, book distribution, campus and alumni development. The total amount spent on program services was just over $339,000. Salaries, rent, office supplies, telephone, postage, and other support services were $235,000. Fund-raising expenses were a modest $39,567, about 6.5 percent of the total budget, a percentage few nonprofit organizations could match. ISI's total expenditures for 1976-1977 were $613,539—almost three times what they had been in 1966-1967. A 300 percent increase over a ten-year period is an impressive showing

47. Mark Henrie to Lee Edwards, March 19, 2003.

for any organization, let alone an educational institute like ISI. And yet again, there was a deficit of $62,602 as the Institute strove to respond to an ever-rising number of student requests for literature and other ISI services. ISI took out a loan from the Union National Bank (Charles Hoeflich's bank) and kept on spreading the gospel of liberty. But it also made some painful cuts, such as closing ISI's Midwestern office after seventeen years. The failure of a large donor in Indianapolis to renew previous support made it necessary, Vic Milione explained to Henry Salvatori. And the Institute decided to concentrate its speakers and seminars at "the more important schools" rather than using funds for programs "at what may fairly be termed minor schools."[48]

Accordingly, ISI sponsored a Dallas seminar on "Solzhenitsyn and the Human Spirit," featuring the eloquent British author Malcolm Muggeridge, and a heavily attended Dartmouth College symposium featuring Muggeridge and Russell Kirk, on "The True Crisis of Our Time"; it held a series of summer institutes on the "Role of Business in Society" for secondary school teachers ("I gained new enthusiasm for getting more economic content into the curriculum," one teacher commented)[49]; and it presented campus lectures by such prominent educators as Allan Bloom of the University of Toronto (over a decade away from publishing *The Closing of the American Mind*), Irving Kristol of New York University (not yet known as the founding father of neoconservatism), Southern agrarian M. E. Bradford of the University of Dallas, political philosopher Walter Berns (who would become a senior fellow at the American Enterprise Institute in the 1980s), Straussian Harvey Mansfield of Harvard University, and Eric Voegelin, who delivered well-attended lectures at Syracuse University on "The Truth of Reason" and "The Beginning and the Beyond."

In this same period, the Institute presented at the Claremont Colleges a prescient lecture by P. T. Bauer of the London School of Econom-

---

48. E. Victor Milione to Henry Salvatori, October 26, 1977, ISI Archives.
49. "ISI in Review," The Programs of the Intercollegiate Studies Institute During the 1976-77 Academic Year: 16, ISI Archives.

ics, entitled, "Aid to the Third World: Sacred Cow and Unlimited Commitment." Bauer was the first Western scholar of prominence to question the effectiveness of foreign aid, and although his analysis was rejected by Keynesian economists for years, he lived to see vindicated his argument that "the crucial elements for development are personal, social, and political attitudes, attributes and arrangements."[50]

Thirteen Weaver Fellowships, each providing a $2,000 cash stipend and payment of full tuition, were awarded for the 1977-1978 academic year; the winners included Thomas Silver of Claremont Graduate School, a future president of the Claremont Institute. In the same year, several ISI alumni achieved prominence in public affairs and the academy. Edwin J. Feulner, Jr., was named president of the Heritage Foundation; Angelo Codevilla joined the staff of the Senate Select Committee on Intelligence; Ronald Lehman became legislative assistant to Senator Dewey F. Bartlett of Oklahoma; and Robert Hessen, a research fellow at the Hoover Institution, convincingly rebutted John K. Galbraith about the role of corporations on "The Age of Uncertainty" television series. A reconstituted Alumni Committee, co-chaired by Representative Philip M. Crane and M. Stanton Evans, announced the following new members: Representative Jack Kemp, Republican of New York; Representative Robert E. Bauman, Republican of Maryland; R. Emmett Tyrrell, editor of *The American Spectator*; Michael Antonovich, Republican leader of the California Assembly; and Joseph Freeman, chairman of the Department of Philosophy at Brigham Young University.

One of the more eminent ISI alumni was Larry P. Arnn, a 1975-1976 Weaver Fellow at the Claremont Graduate School, who, while enrolled at the London School of Economics the following year, was appointed research assistant to Martin Gilbert, Winston Churchill's official biographer. Arnn was given access to all of Churchill's manuscripts, letters, and memoranda—a privilege previously and exclusively reserved for Gilbert. It was Churchill's grappling with "the problem of preserving lib-

---

50. Ashley Morrisette, "P. T. Bauer Presents Devastating Critique of 'Third World' Aid, *ISI Campus Report*, Vol. 8, No. 1, Fall, 1979: 1.

erty and decency in the age of totalitarianism," explained Arnn, that captured his attention. According to Arnn, Churchill believed that "no man may rule another except in the interest of both, and that the state exists to serve the individual, and not the individual the state." It was also Churchill, said Arnn, who declared that "while the vice of capitalism was the unequal distribution of its blessings, the virtue of socialism was the equal distribution of its misery."[51]

Arnn learned about the Weaver fellowship program from ISI's western director, Robert Reilly, whose office was located in the town of Claremont, a few minutes walk from the Claremont campus. "Bob Reilly attended many classes at Claremont," recalls Arnn, "and he scooped us all up in the summer to go to [ISI] seminars." The Weaver fellowship enabled Arnn to study modern philosophy with the "idiosyncratic and insightful" Harry Neumann and the American Revolution with Harry Jaffa. President of Hillsdale College since 2000—and before that president of the Claremont Institute—Larry Arnn says that ISI has been fortunate to have leaders like Vic Milione, "a gentleman scholar ... of serious and constant purpose," who inspires trust "in all that he does."[52] Bob Reilly's influence on Arnn and other students extended beyond the academic. "He would have little dances," Arnn recalls, "where he would try to teach us oafs how to waltz." He once coached a young woman graduate with a baton, "gently but with a German purpose." Robert Reilly is undoubtedly Irish, says Arnn, but "the waltz converts him to the *mitteleuropean.*"[53]

It was Reilly who persuaded Vic Milione in 1978 that ISI should underwrite Public Research Syndicated (PRS), a new press service for America's community newspapers. Conceived as an alternative voice to the intellectuals who incessantly criticized American principles and practices, PRS quickly expanded its service to 270 newspapers by the end of

51. "Larry Arnn Appointed Research Assistant to Official Churchill Biographer: Odyssey of a Weaver Fellow," Peter W. Schramm, *ISI Campus Report*, Vol. 6, No. 1, Winter 1977: 7.

52. Larry P. Arnn to Lee Edwards, August 24, 2001.

53. Ibid.

its first year. The service's first president was Thomas Silver, a Weaver Fellow; its first essay was "On Making Distinctions," by Bob Reilly, later reprinted in the *Wall Street Journal*.

"People who never read scholarly journals," reported the trade journal *Editor and Publisher*, "are informed on important issues by some of the best minds in the world."[54] PRS essays soon reached an estimated weekly audience of more than one million readers through some six hundred community and college newspapers in thirty-one states.

Within a year, PRS inaugurated a Publius Fellows program to instruct young scholars in the art of writing for "the public prints on matters of contemporary concern." ("Publius" was the *nom de plume* taken by James Madison, Alexander Hamilton, and John Jay as authors of *The Federalist Papers*.) In 1980, when Public Research Syndicated obtained tax-exempt status, PRS decided to end its formal affiliation with ISI and begin operating as an independent institution. But PRS president Tom Silver acknowledged that without ISI's early financial support, PRS would not have survived and then evolved into the Claremont Institute, one of the most important conservative think tanks in California and the country.[55]

An ISI report on the first ten years of the Richard M. Weaver Fellowship Awards Program, published in 1975, confirmed the increasing impact of the program on the intellectual and political life of America. Fellows included Annelise Anderson (Ph.D., Columbia University), today a senior research fellow at the Hoover Institution and co-editor of the best-selling *Reagan in His Own Hand*; William Barclay Allen (Ph.D., Claremont Graduate School), today professor of political science at Michigan State University; Robert Emmet Moffit (Ph.D., University of Arizona), now director of domestic policy studies at the Heritage Foundation; and Perry Michael Ratliff (M. A., Johns Hopkins University), who became a rear admiral and the director of naval intelligence before joining ISI in 2000

54. "P.R.S. Expands, Names Publius Fellows," *ISI Campus Report*, Vol. 8, No. 1, Fall, 1979: 3.
55. Thomas B. Silver, "P.R.S. Begins Operating as an Independent Corporation," *ISI Campus Report*, Spring 1980: 1.

as vice president for programs.

Mike Ratliff was a young conservative activist in the late 1960s at Towson State University when he read an ISI pamphlet, "Standardization Without Standards," by Russell Kirk, which inspired him to read Kirk's classic, *The Conservative Mind*. Ratliff realized there was something beyond "bumper sticker conservatism" and started an Edmund Burke Society at his school, along with another young conservative, Wesley MacDonald, a future professor of political philosophy at Elizabethtown College. Ratliff attended an ISI summer school at Grove City College, and heard one of the last public lectures by Ludwig Von Mises—an experience that stimulated his interest in economics. Encouraged by his professors and Vic Milione, whom he met at Grove City, Ratliff applied for and received a Weaver for one year's study at Johns Hopkins University which led to a year at the London School of Economics. "The Weaver was key," says Ratliff. "It opened doors and helped me" get a Fulbright and then a Woodrow Wilson scholarship. The Weaver Fellowship, he explains, was "not just a check in the mail. You felt there was someone [at ISI] interested in helping you to grow intellectually."[56]

A Profound Influence

Among the other Weavers in the first decade were Jeffrey D. Wallin (M.A., Claremont Graduate School), who later founded and is president of the American Academy for Liberal Education, which certifies colleges and universities; Roger G. Pilon (Ph.D., University of Chicago), now vice president for legal affairs at the Cato Institute; John C. Goodman (Ph.D., Columbia University), who started and is the president of the Dallas-based and nationally quoted National Center for Policy Analysis; William Kristol (Ph.D., Harvard University), who taught at Harvard University and Pennsylvania, and then served as chief of staff for Vice President Dan Quayle before becoming editor and publisher of the consequential Washington journal, *The Weekly Standard*. "I'm grateful to have been a Weaver Fellow," says Kristol, but "I owe much more to ISI than simply a year's

56. Author's interview with Michael Ratliff, February 27, 2001.

financial support, welcome though that was." ISI deserves praise, Kristol says, for "its hospitality to many different strands of conservative thought ... which makes it a particularly useful and admirable educational source."[57]

Judge Loren A. Smith (the chief justice of the Court of Federal Claims from 1985-2000) is not a Weaver Fellow but credits ISI, through its literature and summer schools, with exerting a "profound influence" on him as a college student and throughout his life. As a student at Northwestern University in the early 1960s, Smith organized the Young Conservative Club and arranged public lectures by Milton Friedman, Willmoore Kendall, and M. Stanton Evans. He read voraciously: "*The Conservative Mind* was the single most important book in my intellectual development—I read it line by line. ISI—and Vic Milione—helped me to understand that if you want a better world, you must act on your ideas."[58]

After graduating from law school, Smith worked briefly at a federal agency in Washington and then at the Nixon White House before becoming the general counsel for Ronald Reagan's unsuccessful 1976 effort to capture the Republican presidential nomination. In 1980, he again served as general counsel for Reagan's successful bid for the presidency and hired as his deputy Kenneth Cribb, just graduated from the University of Virginia Law School. The two conservatives had become good friends through ISI, and Smith knew he could rely on Cribb. "I was immediately attracted by [Ken's] lively spirit," says Smith of their first meeting. "Meeting him is the intellectual equivalent of popping a bottle of champagne." But there was also Cribb's deep interest in ideas—"we would sit and talk for hours."[59]

Through his years in the judiciary, Smith has taught law at several universities, including Georgetown and the Catholic University of America, and is active in the Federalist Society, which, with its many campus chapters, reminds him of his student days at Northwestern. "Like ISI," he says, "the Federalist Society is interested in the real truth, not popular slogans."[60]

57. William Kristol to Lee Edwards, June 3, 2002.
58. Author's interview with Loren A. Smith, April 1, 2002.
59. Ibid.
60. Ibid.

ISI alumni (spearheaded by Congressman Phil Crane of Illinois and chairman Stan Evans of the ACU Education and Research Institute) exhibited their ascendant political influence in January 1977 with an impressive Washington, D.C., conference featuring the first major address by Ronald Reagan after his 1976 presidential campaign. Following an afternoon seminar with Russell Kirk, Gerhart Niemeyer, and Arthur Shenfield on "Beyond Politics," which emphasized the importance of maintaining a free society's non-political institutions, Governor Reagan talked at an evening banquet about the essential interrelationship of politics and ideas. He said:

> The success of liberalism in the United States is due, in no small part, to the success of its adherents in the media and the universities in making liberalism attractive to young Americans and in serving as sources of ideas to liberal politicians. Conservatives in political life should make it a habit to keep in touch with, and hire as aides, conservative thinkers and academicians. We have great ideas. We have too often failed to put them into practice.[61]

The mass media, including the television networks and the *Washington Post*, gave full and respectful coverage to Reagan's remarks, and many of the five hundred people in attendance that evening helped the future president to put conservative ideas into practice during the 1980s. One of those listening intently was Kenneth Cribb, M.C. of the dinner. He would leave ISI as its national director that year to enter the University of Virginia Law School. "I had always intended to go to law school," says Cribb, and the accidental automobile death of a close friend made him realize it was "time to get on with my life and my plans." Those plans included public service, and he no sooner graduated three years later from Virginia, "where I was not shy about raising the conservative banner," than he became deputy counsel in Ronald Reagan's 1980 presidential campaign.[62]

61. "ISI in Review: The Programs of the Intercollegiate Studies Institute During the 1976-77 Academic Year": 41, ISI Archives.
62. Author's interview with T. Kenneth Cribb, Jr., May 5, 2003.

Conservatives' Progress

"It is the indelible word which celebrates the spirituality of man that ISI has propagated." The speaker was William F. Buckley Jr., the occasion an April 1978 banquet, again in Washington, D.C., marking ISI's twenty-fifth anniversary. Looking back at the consequences of a quarter-century of conservative thought, Buckley asserted that in economics, "conservatives have done the work." In political philosophy, "there has been a gradual apprehension of the rootlessness of liberalism." Overall, Buckley said, "conservatives have accumulated a concentrated patrimony of the permanent things such as no other twenty-five years have seen."[63]

Buckley recalled "the futility with which the Conservative Godfathers approached their task in the 1940s and 1950s." But Whittaker Chambers' pessimistic view that "progress isn't possible" no longer held true in the light of the achievements of ISI and conservatism in general since 1953. No celebration of ISI, added Buckley, would be possible without paying tribute to the leadership of Victor Milione, who despite his remarkable accomplishments as ISI's principal guide since its founding, "is possessed of humility of heart and has followed a singular policy of self-effacement."[64]

Earlier, Stan Evans had stated that while ISI was not the "only agent" in the movement of conservative ideas, "it has arguably been the central one." Russell Kirk, who spoke at more campuses from the mid-1950s through the mid-1970s than any other conservative, said simply, "I never cease to marvel at how much ISI accomplishes with a straitened budget. It has been more effective than all the radical student organizations put together."[65] And while the radical student organizations like SDS had long since faded into oblivion, ISI kept educating for liberty—still on a relatively modest flow of income, a flow that depended in large part on

63. "ISI Observes Its Twenty-fifth Anniversary," *ISI Campus Report*, Vol. 7, No. 1, Fall, 1978: 4.
64. Ibid.
65. "The ISI Story: Ideas Have Consequences," M. Stanton Evans, *ISI Campus Report*, Vol. 7, No. 1, Fall 1978: 5.

the special relationships that Vic Milione built with ISI donors such as Henry Salvatori.

Although he relied heavily upon the telephone, Vic Milione was also a brilliant letter writer who "poured himself" (in John Lulves' phrase) into his correspondence. Milione's letters to Salvatori were a remarkable dialogue between a master of political philosophy and a master of business whose curiosity about the ideas of Western civilization never seemed to be satisfied. In a May 1975 letter, for example, Milione offered reflections by William Penn on government ("as governments are made and moved by men, so by them they are ruined too. Therefore, governments depend upon men rather than men upon government") and by Tocqueville on rekindling an old faith ("patriotism which never abandons the human heart, may be directed and revived... [for] every fresh generation is a new people").[66]

Writing to Salvatori in March 1979, Milione quoted Leo Strauss, Richard Weaver, Harvard's Carl J. Friedrich, and T. S. Eliot on the need to read books like Simone Weil's *The Need for Roots*. Eliot described the Weil work as the kind of book "which ought to be studied by the young before their leisure has been lost and their capacity for thought destroyed in the life of the hustings and the legislative assembly." Responding to the California philanthropist's concern that ISI might be "overextending itself," Milione admitted that "ISI does operate close to the bone.... The fruits of its efforts are remote." But, Milione went on, there was a crucial need to combat "the pernicious influence of relativism" in the academy at many different levels and in many different ways, including publications like *The Intercollegiate Review* and *The Political Science Reviewer*, fellowships like the Weavers, and a more popular project like Public Research Syndicated, which greatly benefitted "the public understanding of the free society."[67]

Taking up a topic that the two men had often discussed—the role of religion in assuring a moral society—Milione wrote Salvatori that a belief

---

66. E. Victor Milione to Henry Salvatori, May 2, 1975, ISI Archives.
67. E. Victor Milione to Henry Salvatori, March 16, 1979, ISI Archives.

in God and in man as "a special creation endowed with reason and free will" was central to Western civilization. In contrast was Marx's interpretation—the Communist keystone—that "man is simply the product of ruthless and impersonal life forces." Therefore, any discussion of a core curriculum in higher education "must begin with the premise that theology is a source of valid cognition giving us a knowledge of one of the important aspects of reality."[68]

After referring to the ideas of a university expressed by John Henry Newman in the midnineteenth century and by Jacques Barzun in the midtwentieth century, Milione said that because "there is a wholeness to knowledge," we ought to be conveying to students "a comprehensive and overarching view" of life. Most of "modern education," wrote Milione, "is too fragmented and diffuse to serve this end."[69] After apologizing for the length of his letter—six single-spaced pages—Milione concluded: "You may well say, 'To hell with it, the issue is too involved.' You may, but I hope not and think not. You are one of the most thoughtful men I know and the only one to whom I would hazard sending such a letter."[70]

Milione had been sending such "hazardous" letters to Salvatori for years, and Salvatori had been carefully reading them for as long. In his response, the eighty-three-year-old Salvatori conceded that the issue of faith and society was indeed "involved" and that the "greatest problem" was how to present it to businessmen trustees who had "never contemplated these issues." He suggested that any reference to such a subject would have to be "formulated in a paragraph or two—otherwise their limited attention span would be surpassed." The aged philanthropist finished by expressing his deep gratitude to "Vic" for providing "much food for my thoughts."[71] Their personal meetings in New York, when the Californian came East on business, or in Los Angeles, when the Philadelphian visited trustees and supporters in the West, cemented an unusually intimate relationship that explains the generous support that Salvatori

68. E. Victor Milione to Henry Salvatori, November 10, 1983, ISI Archives.
69. Ibid.
70. Ibid.
71. Henry Salvatori to Victor Milione, December 8, 1983, ISI Archives.

and other entrepreneurs gave ISI year in and year out.

The Dark Seventies

The 1970s were a dark decade for America, disfigured by the tragedy of Kent State, the disgrace of Watergate and Richard Nixon's forced resignation, the ignominious withdrawal from South Vietnam, Communist advances in Central America, Africa, and Asia, the mounting disappointments of the Carter presidency that ended in rampant inflation, soaring interest rates, and unemployment, and the seizure of fifty-two Americans by the revolutionary Khomeini government of Iran. Modern liberalism reached its nadir as the policies of welfarism and détente multiplied severalfold America's problems at home and abroad.

Taking advantage of liberalism's free fall, the conservative movement constructed a powerful counterestablishment that by the end of the decade was poised to assume the reins of political power. It was able to do so because the philosophers (such as F. A. Hayek, Richard Weaver, and Russell Kirk) had laid the necessary intellectual foundation, the popularizers (such as Frank Chodorov, Bill Buckley, and John Chamberlain) had translated their ideas into a popular idiom, the philanthropists (such as Henry Salvatori, Richard Scaife, and Roger Milliken) had willingly financed the thinkers' books and the writers' journals, and the politicians (such as Barry Goldwater and Ronald Reagan) believed in the power of their ideas and were ready to implement them. ISI played a critical role in this act of creation. Although at Vic Milione's insistence, ISI was more *of* rather than *in* the conservative movement, it nevertheless served time and again as the connecting tissue between a philosopher like Kirk, a popularizer like Buckley, and a politician like Reagan—sometimes through a publication, sometimes through a public event.

Whatever the Left had accomplished in the world of politics and public policy, the Right now resolved to better. To counter the liberal Brookings Institution, conservatives created The Heritage Foundation. In response to the liberal National Committee for an Effective Congress, conservatives organized the Emergency Committee for a Free Congress.

Liberals had the Democratic Study Group in the U.S. House of Representatives and the Wednesday Club in the Senate, so conservatives started
the Republican Study Committee in the House and the Senate Steering
Committee in the Senate. The Conservative Caucus was launched to ri-
val the lobbying capabilities of the leftist Common Cause. The Moral
Majority was intended to answer the liberal pronouncements of the National Council of Churches. And the National Conservative Political Action Committee (NCPAC) and the Conservative Victory Fund would
counter the PACs of the Left such as COPE (the AFL-CIO's Committee
on Political Education). ISI was one of the first conservative organizations to learn from the Left—after all, the Institute was conceived as a
response to the Intercollegiate Socialist Society.

The 1970s also saw the conservative movement strengthened by the
addition of two quite different political groups. Led by fundraiser Richard Viguerie, political strategist Paul Weyrich, grassroots organizer Howard
Phillips, and communications impresario Tony Dolan, the New Right
was "a group of anti-establishment, middle-class political rebels more interested in issues like abortion, gun control, busing, ERA, quotas, bureaucracy, and the grassroots tax revolt than in capital gains taxation or
natural gas deregulation."[72] The New Right saw as its enemy the four
bigs of modern America: Big Government, Big Business, Big Labor, and
Big Media. Both Frank Chodorov and Richard Weaver would have sym-
pathized with many of their populist views.

At the same time, the anarchic events of the late 1960s and early
1970s jolted a small but potent group of old-style liberals and led them to
leave their Democratic moorings. The catalytic happenings included the
presidential nomination of ultraliberal George McGovern, the seeming
indifference of modern liberals to the fate of South Vietnam and other
countries threatened by communism, the refusal of too many Democrats
to criticize the United Nations for its anti-Israel and anti-American rhetoric

72. Kevin P. Phillips, "Notes on the New Right," *Baltimore News-American*, June 25,
1976; "The Growing Importance of the New Right," *New York Daily Press*, October 13,
1978.

and resolutions, and the revolution in sexual and social relations that produced the adversary culture. Equally shocking for these liberal intellectuals was the assault on the institution—the academy—that had contributed so much to their elevated position in American politics and society.

"Mugged by reality" (Irving Kristol's pungent phrase), the former liberals began calling themselves "neoconservatives" and launched an attack on the radicals as despoilers of the liberal tradition. Kristol called for a return to the "republican virtue" of the founding fathers and the idea of a good society. Like Russell Kirk, he endorsed the notion of a "moral and political order" and, borrowing from Adam Smith, conceded that the idea of a "hidden hand" has its uses in the marketplace.[73] The neoconservatives had a telling impact on conservatism and American politics because they were, as the political historian Theodore H. White put it, "action intellectuals" fully credentialed by the establishment.[74] They were directly connected (and at the highest levels) to America's leading universities, the mass media, national officeholders, union leaders, large foundations, and influential think tanks. They could carry the conservative message to places barred to most conservatives.

The New Right and neoconservatives were uneasy colleagues in the new coalition. The New Right was religious in objective, language, and membership, looking forward to the City of God; the neoconservatives were generally secular in outlook and rhetoric, focused on the City of Man. The New Right was skeptical of government; the neoconservatives argued for its usefulness. The New Right reveled in the mechanics of grassroots politics; the neoconservatives preferred the realm of public policy at the national level. But both hated communism and both scorned liberals, the New Right for what liberals had always been, the neoconservatives for what they had become. The political leader who brought these disparate groups together was Ronald Reagan, who understood that to be elected president, he needed the brainpower of the neoconservatives and the manpower of the New Right.

73. Nash, *The Conservative Intellectual Movement in America:* 314-315.
74. Theodore H. White, "The Action Intellectuals," *Life*, June 15, 1967: 35.

By 1980, then, twenty-seven years after the founding of the Intercollegiate Society of Individualists and the publication of Russell Kirk's *The Conservative Mind*, sixteen years after Barry Goldwater had been resoundingly defeated for the presidency, and only four years after Reagan had failed to capture the Republican presidential nomination, conservatives had forged an impressive political coalition committed to electing Ronald Reagan as president. Here was a vivid demonstration of the power of ideas. Reagan revealed his deep debt to the ideas of the conservative movement in late 1979 in the formal announcement of his candidacy, when he stated that America "hungers for a spiritual revival ... hungers to see government once again the protector of our liberties, not the distributor of gifts and privileges." A troubled nation, Reagan said, expects us "to uphold the principles of self-reliance, self-discipline, morality, and—above all—responsible liberty for every individual."[75]

The ISI Response

ISI responded to the resurgent conservatism by expanding its programs and publications in the late 1970s and declaring its intention to increase its budget from $600,000 to $1 million a year. National director Robert Reilly reported that according to an ISI survey, "Ten percent of all government, economics and philosophy professors in the country would like to receive *The Intercollegiate Review.*" That would require, Reilly estimated, more than doubling the *IR*'s circulation from its current 40,000 to about 100,000. The principal quarterly of the intellectual Right also benefitted from the rise of the political Right: the circulation of *Modern Age* rose from 8,000 to 10,000 by the spring of 1979, as a result of a subscription promotion funded by the Kemper Educational and Charitable Fund of Chicago. Publisher John Lulves properly described *Modern Age* as the only intellectual journal "concerned with furthering an understanding of the free society and conserving the values and institutions necessary to its continuance."[76] *Modern Age* maintained its high standard of editorial ex-

75. Lee Edwards, *Ronald Reagan: A Political Biography,* Houston, Texas, 1981: 190.
76. "ISI Begins Project to Increase Modern Age Readership," *ISI Campus Report,* Fall

cellence by naming George Panichas, a cultural critic and professor of English at the University of Maryland, as its literary editor, succeeding Joseph M. Lalley, who had served sixteen years as the journal's book editor.

A champion of such diverse authors as the Russian novelist Fyodor Dostoyevsky, the French mystic and martyr Simone Weil, and the British writer D. H. Lawrence, Panichas argued that even the best American writers had abandoned the examination of great moral issues and had concentrated instead on developing "journalistic habits of mind." In fact, in Panichas' opinion, "a spiritual bankruptcy" had overwhelmed America's literary life.[77] The search for a moral imperative would characterize Panichas's tenure as literary editor and then as editor of *Modern Age* when he assumed that position in 1984, upon the death of David Collier.

On the fellowships front, Robert Schadler, director of the Weavers program, said that ISI received as many as four hundred applications annually for Weaver Fellowships but because of financial constraints could award only ten. "At a minimum," said Schadler, "twenty Weaver Fellowships should be awarded annually" at a cost of about $100,000.[78] With Milione at the telephone and Reilly and others on the road, ISI increased expenditures on its programs and supporting services to $726,652 in 1979, but then slipped to $552,624 in 1980, as donors shifted their attention and their support to political action in a presidential election year.

An undaunted ISI kept on educating for liberty. In the summer of 1979, when funds were flowing rather freely, it held two summer schools and four "Role of Business in Society" (ROBIS) institutes in five different states. Often held in conjunction with the business school of a local university, the ROBIS institutes were aimed at secondary school teachers—attendance at each institute was limited to fifty teachers—and sought to further understanding of the critical contribution of economic institutions in a free society. Robert Finan, who taught at Pomona High School in Arvada, Colorado, said that for him the core idea of the ROBIS insti-

1979: 4.
77. Christopher Swan, "A 'dissident critic' on literary values today," *Christian Science Monitor,* December 5, 1985.
78. "ISI Charts Fund Raising Drive," *ISI Campus Report,* Fall 1978: 2.

tutes was that "business is to human societies what free will is to the individual."[79] By design, the ROBIS faculty included business leaders and economists such as Professor Andrzej Brzeski of the University of California at Davis.

The intellectual quality of the speakers at the summer schools and elsewhere continued to be high. Among those who spoke under ISI auspices in 1978 and 1979 were British journalist and television commentator Malcolm Muggeridge, who stated that man's responsibility in the face of civilization's decline is "to be true to the Lord. To remember our citizenship in the City of God"; Professor Harry Jaffa of Claremont Men's College, who described Shakespeare as the great teacher (through his plays) of Greek wisdom and Roman political experience; Austrian scholar and monarchist Erik von Kuehnelt-Leddhin, who argued that the Founding Fathers of the American Republic were too conscious of human weaknesses to place unlimited trust in "the people"; former Cambodian information minister Chhang Song, who decried Western indifference to the Communist genocide in Cambodia; and ISI Western director Peter Schramm, who wrote that today's student in contrast to his counterpart of the sixties "is able to study the past in order to conserve what is best and to fulfill his obligation to the unseen future."[80]

At the 1979 National Friends and Alumni Conference, held in Washington, D.C., speakers probed the most prevalent maladies of modern man. Professor Fritz Wilhelmsen of the University of Dallas described him as "disco man"—a hollow man "who drifts from bed to bed, from disco to disco, and in no sense has any commitment to anybody or anything." Disco Man, Wilhelmsen said, "is totally living publicly" and "has no inner life whatsoever." While Wilhelmsen presented Disco Man as the

79. Robert E. Finan, "An Eloquent Barrister and Some Hungry Professors," *ISI Campus Report*, Fall 1978: 6.

80. Harry Jaffa as quoted in "250 Attend Conference on 'Poetry and Politics in Shakespeare,'"; Erik von Kuehnelt-Leddhin as quoted in "Travels with a Gentleman," Chhang Song as quoted in "Former Cambodian Minister Decries Indifference to Communist Genocide," Peter Schramm as quoted in "Is Today's Student More Conservative," and Malcolm Muggeridge as quoted in "'Pilgrims in the Dark Wood' Is Theme of ISI Christmas Seminar," *ISI Campus Report*, Spring 1979: 4, 5, 6, 7.

perfect incarnation of the new man who believes in nothing, Thomas Molnar preferred to characterize him as "robot man." Robot Man, according to Molnar, "lives in a mechanized universe" and denies any spiritual dimension of life.[81]

Attendance at the Washington conference was good, helped by the fact that some two hundred ISI alumni were now working in the nation's capital—as aides on Capitol Hill, in think tanks and political organizations, and in journalism. Three alumni had successfully climbed the greasy pole of politics to become members of Congress—Republicans Phil Crane of Illinois and Jack Kemp of New York and Democrat Phil Gramm of Texas. ISI "graduates" could be found almost everywhere: Robert Turner in the office of moderate Republican Senator Robert Griffin of Michigan; John Carbaugh with the hard-right Republican Senator Jesse Helms of North Carolina; James Hinish on the staff of the Senate Republican Policy Committee; James Taylor with the National Right to Work Committee; Brian Benson, editor of Richard Viguerie's *Conservative Digest;* and Thomas Winter and Allan Ryskind as the principal editors of *Human Events.*[82]

ISI continued to concern itself with student publications, financially helping students at Hillsdale College in Michigan to launch, in 1979, *The Hillsdale Review.* Edited by Hillsdale senior Gregory Wolfe, the first issue presented previously unpublished essays by Gerhart Niemeyer and Southern agrarian Andrew Lytle and student essays and reviews on legal theory and literature. Wolfe noted that in the 1960s there existed student magazines such as *Analysis, The Harvard Conservative, Phalanx,* and *Politeia* (started by Angelo Codevilla while a Rutgers University undergraduate). "To my knowledge," Wolfe said, "there are no conservative student journals publishing at present—we want to fill that gap." *The Hillsdale Review,* the young editor explained, "is one way in which conservative students can learn from and stimulate each other. To me, that is what ISI is all about."[83]

81. Susan Marshner, "275 Attend Meeting on 'Modern Man's Twisted Image,'" *ISI Campus Report,* Fall 1979: 6.
82. Evans, "The ISI Story: Ideas Have Consequences": 5.
83. "ISI Students Publish Conservative Journal," *ISI Campus Report, Fall 1979:* 7.

The Pull of Politics

The Institute celebrated the November 1980 election of Ronald Reagan with a testimonial dinner for its unflagging president, Vic Milione. Robert Reilly, who organized the event, predicted an impressive turnout, and he was correct. Gathering in the Great Hall of the Folger Shakespeare Library on Capitol Hill, ISI alumni and friends, including Edwin J. Feulner, Jr., of The Heritage Foundation, Congressman Phil Gramm of Texas, and Dr. Russell Kirk, acknowledged the seminal influence of the Institute in their lives and the course of the nation. Angelo Codevilla, president of the ISI club at Rutgers University in the mid-1960s and now a top Senate staffer, remembers thinking that Reagan's election marked "the apotheosis of ISI when we discovered that a substantial percentage of the new president's transition team were ISI people." ISI, said Dr. Kirk, "is changing the face of the American commonwealth for the better through ideas." Feulner discussed the critical connection between intellectual developments on the campus and their manifestation years later in public policy.

T. Kenneth Cribb, Jr., assistant director of the Office of Cabinet Administration and future top aide to White House counselor Edwin Meese III, described Milione as "the personification of ISI," adding, "He insists that we take stock of the immutable and the eternal." Reilly, director of government information for Heritage, repeated what Milione had told him in their very first conversation: "Civilization is only ten years old." That is, Reilly remarked, "what we are involved in is an ongoing enterprise. We would be making a great error to think that this is a won battle."[84]

Milione modestly replied that the idea for ISI "was not mine but that of Frank Chodorov" and that it was predicated on the belief that education sets the tone of society. Many people, he noted, particularly in Washington, "like to think that politics leads the country, but it does not. The future is largely determined by the ideals and theories citizens acquire in

---

84. "ISI President Honored at Testimonial Dinner," *ISI Campus Report,* Spring 1981: 8; author's interview with Angelo Codevilla, May 16, 2003.

youth." That was why ISI worked "exclusively with students" and those who influenced them the most, their teachers. Milione stressed the role of principle in the American tradition. A devotion to principle, he said, "avoids the need for each generation to live by trial and error." It was this devotion to principle and to continuity, he concluded, that ISI would "continue to foster with each new generation of students."[85]

Those assembled rose and heartily applauded the man who was ISI— and then retired to the nearby bars for beer and brandy and cigars and the latest gossip about who would fill what office in the incoming Reagan administration.

85. Ibid.

CHAPTER VI

The Rising Right

The Institute's work with students is often perceived as long range with results that are remote.... Twenty-eight years of effort, however, is now producing significant results. The earlier generation of youth ... are in the forefront of leadership in every area of American life.

E. Victor Milione[1]

THE 1980 PRESIDENTIAL ELECTION RESULTS constituted not merely a rejection of President Carter's dismal domestic and foreign policy record but a mandate for President-elect Reagan to change the direction of American politics. Former Democratic presidential candidate George McGovern said that the voters had "abandoned American liberalism." The *Washington Post* titled its editorial on the Reagan victory "Tidal Wave."[2] Political historian Michael Barone wrote that the 1980 election showed that "most American voters wanted limits on the growth of government at home, a more assertive foreign policy abroad, and some greater honoring of traditional moral values in their basic institutions."[3]

1. E. Victor Milione, Introduction, "I Am Proud To Be an ISI Alumnus," published by the Intercollegiate Studies Institute, 1981: 1.
2. "Start of a New Era," *U.S. News & World Report*, November 17, 1980: 21-66.
3. Michael Barone, *Our Country: The Shaping of America From Roosevelt to Reagan*: 596.

To help in this formidable task, President Reagan could count on a broad-shouldered, assertive conservative movement that had come a long way since the founding of the miniscule Intercollegiate Society of Individualists nearly thirty years before. Reagan could look for programs and policies to think tanks like Heritage (headed by Weaver Fellow Ed Feulner), whose mammoth one-thousand-page *Mandate for Leadership* (co-edited by former ISI staffer Charles Heatherly) contained two thousand specific recommendations to move the federal government in a conservative direction. He could call on groups like the American Conservative Union (headed by ISI alumnus Representative Robert Bauman of Maryland) and the National Right to Work Committee (whose roster included one-time ISI regional director James Taylor) for political muscle. He could staff his White House with dedicated conservatives like Richard V. Allen, T. Kenneth Cribb, Jr. and Wayne Valis, and his administration with seasoned professionals like John F. Lehman, Jr. (secretary of the navy), Donald Devine (director, Office of Personnel Management), Paul Craig Roberts (assistant treasury secretary for economic policy), Charles Heatherly (special assistant of the secretary of education), Robert F. Turner (counsel for the President's Intelligence Oversight Board), William R. Robie (counsel to the associate attorney general for attorney personnel), and William Schneider, Jr. (associate director for National Security and International Affairs, Office of Management and Budget). Every one of them was an ISI alumnus. As Reagan himself would later note in an appreciative letter to ISI's president on the occasion of the Institute's fortieth anniversary, "By the time the Reagan Revolution marched into Washington, I had the troops I needed—thanks in no small measure to the work with American youth ISI had been doing since 1953."[4]

Vic Milione was proud of the Institute's manifold contributions to the Reagan administration, commenting in a 1981 brochure:

> The Institute's work with students is often perceived as long range with results that are remote. This was true in the early years of the ISI effort. Twenty-eight years of effort, however, is now producing signifi-

4. Ronald Reagan to T. Kenneth Cribb, January 30, 1993.

cant results. The earlier generation of youth with potential needed time to mature. They have matured, they are upwardly mobile, and they are in the forefront of leadership in every area of American life.[5]

At the same time, Milione could not forebear from pointing out—in a Heritage publication—that politics was only one of many aspects of American society, and not necessarily the most important. "The spiritual moorings of the country, the family, the ethical norms that create better character," he said, "all must be preserved. That's not going to be accomplished by government."[6] While Milione's admonition was justified—and it certainly reflected ISI's philosophy of addressing political, social, and cultural matters at their deepest level—it struck some conservatives, exuberant about the possibilities of a Reagan administration, as unduly cautionary. This was, they felt, a time to seize the day, not to worry about the coming of the night.

Milione's insistence on maintaining a certain amount of space between ISI and the rest of the conservative movement had kept the Institute separate from the philosophical wars between traditionalists and libertarians in the 1950s and the 1960s. Rather than taking sides, ISI had presented the views of prominent members of both strains of conservatism, from Ludwig von Mises and Milton Friedman to Richard Weaver and Russell Kirk. ISI's public stand of independence had made it difficult for liberal critics to link ISI with extremist groups, like the John Birch Society, as part of the "radical Right"—an early version of the Clintons' "vast right-wing conspiracy." But in the politics-driven 1980s, ISI's independent stance and its insistence on emphasizing education above all else hindered it from fully benefiting from the political ascendancy of the conservative movement.

ISI's non-political, even romantic character was reflected in an informal institution established early in the Reagan years by former ISI staffers working in the administration or on K Street or in Washington think

5. Vic Milione, Introduction, "I Am Proud To Be An ISI Alumnus": 1.
6. As quoted in "Training the Next Generation: Spotlight on E. Victor Milione," *The Heritage Foundation Newsletter*, Spring 1982: 10.

tanks. "The Committee to Save Western Civilization" was founded by ISIer Robert Reilly, together with Robert and Elaine Schadler. How did the committee intend to "save" civilization? To begin with, by organizing a white-tie Viennese Waltz Ball that signaled a renaissance of high culture and high spirits in the nation's capital after four years of Jimmy Carter's cardigan sweaters and hand-wringing malaise. And whereas Washington social events are usually exercises in networking, this civilizing event was held purely for its own enjoyment. The waltz ball has been held annually each February in the beautiful great hall of the Organization of American States ever since its successful debut in 1983.

No Longer Alone

Meanwhile, other and more aggressive organizations took full advantage of the Reagan years. Among them were two relatively new groups also committed to youth activities—Young America's Foundation, led by Ron Robinson, a former executive director of the activist Young Americans for Freedom, and the Leadership Institute, headed by New Right leader (and ISI alumnus) Morton Blackwell. Both began to compete with ISI on the campus—Young America's Foundation by sponsoring prominent conservative speakers such as William F. Buckley Jr. and Patrick J. Buchanan, the Leadership Institute by holding intense weekend seminars on how to organize a conservative campus club and a campus publication. Echoing language long used by ISI, Young America's Foundation declared that it "sought to build what amounts to an alternative academic establishment; an establishment that offers a full range of educational programs and services for American students."[7] The days when ISI was the only conservative organization on campus were over.

Accordingly, ISI's income increased only moderately in the early 1980s, reflecting the greater competition for donations, and perhaps some fatigue at the top, understandable after thirty years of knocking on the

7. Ron Robinson, "Building an Alternative Academic Establishment," introduction to the 1978-79 Report of Young America's Foundation, c. 1979, Private Papers of James Taylor.

doors of foundations and corporations. In 1980, the year in which Ronald Reagan was elected president, the Institute spent just under $690,000 and wound up with a disturbing deficit of $136,909. Over the next five years, the ISI budget fluctuated between a low of $778,876 in 1982 and a high of $922,543 in 1983. But it was unable to balance its budget, averaging an annual deficit between 1982 and 1985 of nearly $77,000, and it never topped $1 million, a long-time financial goal. In short, the conservative movement's moment of political triumph did not translate into significant institutional advancement for ISI.

Nevertheless, ISI not only maintained all of its current programs—without an endowment, cash reserve, or real estate—but added a few new ones, agreeing, for example, to help publish a new historical journal, *Continuity*, edited by Aileen Kraditor of Boston University and Paul Gottfried of Rockford College. The first issue, published in the fall of 1980, included articles by Alan J. Levine, "Some Revisionist Theses on the Cold War, 1943-1946"; by Lee Congdon, "Lukacs, Camus, and the Russian Terrorists"; by Louise L. Stevenson, "A Conservative Critique of Victorian Culture"; and by Paul Gottfried, "Hegel, Plato, and the Nature of Civic Religion." Co-editor Kraditor said she hoped that, like Lenin's early journal *Iskra, Continuity* would "spark" thought, organization, and influence. Consistent with its title, said Kraditor, the journal would explore through history "the continuity between the work of our philosophers and that of our policy-formulators."[8]

ISI held two summer schools and three "Role of Business in Society" institutes in 1981—in Boulder, Colorado; Claremont, California; Chattanooga, Tennessee; Stanford, California; and Rosemont, Pennsylvania. The two summer schools focused on national defense and U.S. foreign policy with Angelo Codevilla, arguing (at the former) for a laser weapon defense against Soviet ICBMs—two years before President Reagan announced his intention to research and develop a Strategic Defense Initiative (SDI). With remarkable foresight, Codevilla said that the impact of a

8. "First 'Continuity' Published," *ISI Campus Report,* Spring 1981: 4.

U.S. antimissile defense system would be "revolutionary," as indeed it was.[9] After the Cold War ended, former Soviet officials admitted that the American commitment to SDI convinced them they could not win an arms race and led them to negotiations and a peaceful end to nearly fifty years of U.S.-Soviet hostility. Beginning at 9 A.M. and officially ending at 9 P.M. (although informal libation-lubricated discussions continued until well after midnight), the five-man faculty at the other summer school examined "American Foreign Policy and the Problem of Will." Professor Harold W. Rood of Claremont College "stole the show," according to *Campus Report*, with his examples of the vulnerability of the American press to Soviet disinformation.[10]

Launched in 1973 in Oregon, ISI's "Role of Business in Society" program (ROBIS) had by 1981 reached 1,075 high school teachers through its summer programs. Using economists such as Robert Hessen, James Gwartney, William H. Peterson, and Walter Williams, ROBIS analyzed the nature and functions of the free market system, its relationship with a free society and "the key role of business" in the system. "Businessmen have come to look upon all intellectuals as enemies," said ISI Western director Peter Schramm, who coordinated the ROBIS programs in the West. But he reassured potential underwriters that ISI had enlisted a group of teachers, writers, and scholars capable of elucidating the principles of the free economy "in a way that appeals to both the moral imagination and the practical good sense of students and teachers alike."[11]

The evaluations of the attending high school teachers confirmed Schramm's statement: "One of the most beneficial learning opportunities that I have ever participated in"; "the Institute was superior to any similar workshop or method of instruction that I have experienced"; "I have never felt my mind was being stretched so much in a small period of time." In many instances ISI co-sponsored an institute with a local college or uni-

9. Christopher Harmon, "Expert Discusses Laser Weapons at Western Session," *ISI Campus Report*, Spring 1982: 6.

10. Ibid: Thomas F. Payne, "Fifty-five Students Attend Eastern Summer School."

11. "The Role of Business in Society," Summary Report and Fund Proposal 1980-81, edited by Peter W. Schramm, ISI Archives.

versity—for example, the University of Colorado at Boulder and the University of Tennessee in Chattanooga. Each five-day summer institute cost only $15,000, and attracted the support of what ISI called "far-sighted members of the business community."[12]

Two decades before presidential candidate George W. Bush campaigned as a "compassionate conservative," the Institute sponsored a National Friends and Alumni Conference on "The Humane Vision of Conservatism." Among the speakers who spanned the conservative spectrum were nuclear physicist Edward Teller; George Gilder, author of the best-selling *Wealth and Poverty*; neoconservative founder Irving Kristol; national security adviser Richard V. Allen; and Senator John East, Republican of North Carolina. At an evening banquet attended by more than three hundred people, Senator East said that the "great task of conservatism" is to "recover the idea of a moral and ethical base of society" and referred to Aleksandr Solzhenitsyn's belief that "a spiritual exhaustion" existed in the West. In his banquet remarks, Allen said that the Reagan administration's human rights policy was "linked with our survival as a free people." Allen pointedly confessed that the ISI literature he had read as a student at Notre Dame University along with the classes he took under longtime ISI lecturer Gerhart Niemeyer "changed my whole way of thinking."[13]

In pursuit of the truth, ISI co-sponsored with *Modern Age* a conference on "Conservatism and Libertarianism" that featured scholars such as Murray N. Rothbard, Stephen J. Tonsor, Dante Germino, and Gottfried Dietze. M. Stanton Evans (anticipating his seminal work of the 1990s, *The Theme Is Freedom*) argued that Western political values were a product of Western religion. Seeking common ground between conservatives and libertarians, Evans said that "our tradition is a tradition of freedom, and libertarian precepts are undergirded by the traditional values of our faith."[14] The Institute also presented a seminar on "Hearth and Home:

12. Ibid.

13. Gregory Wolfe, "Sen. East, Allen Address ISI Conference," *Conservative Digest*, June 1981.

14. Nancy Klinghoffer, "'Conservatism and Libertarianism' Debated at *Modern Age* Symposium," *ISI Campus Report*, Vol. 9, Nos. 1-2, Spring, 1981: 5.

The Family in American Life" at Russell Kirk's home in Mecosta, Michigan, during which Kirk argued that the current decline of the family could be traced to the decline of piety as well as "the material impoverishment of the family" from such devices as the inheritance tax.[15] Despite its nonpolitical stance, the Institute was mentioned more and more often in the mainstream media, struggling to understand the conservative emergence: *U.S. News & World Report* said that "ISI has become the right wing's major conduit to the nation's campuses," while a prominent Soviet journal attacked the organization as "a leading propaganda organ of American conservatism."[16]

In the spring of 1982, ISI reluctantly, and sadly, ended its summer school program after twenty-two years and some fifty schools on campuses, from New York City to Stanford, California. The decision did not affect the "Role of Business in Society" (ROBIS) summer conferences for high school teachers, generally underwritten by local business organizations. The reasons for shutting down the schools were programmatic and budgetary. A number of excellent summer programs were now available for students. Also, the college population had doubled, and doubled again: the primary need in the 1980s was to reach the ever-expanding student body. That was best accomplished, it was decided, through on-campus speakers and one-day or two-day seminars rather than weeklong schools. And while the summer schools had transformed the lives and careers of many of the over two thousand students who attended them, they were not cost-efficient. By using the summer school funds for lectures and other programs, Vic Milione explained, "we will be able to reach more students."[17] ISI alumni understood that the Institute had to be practical, and yet when they heard the news, more than one graduate's thoughts lingered on the intellectual excitement he had experienced at a summer school.

15. Donald J. Senese, "'Health and Home' Seminar Held at Home of Russell Kirk," *ISI Campus Report*, Vol. 9, Nos. 1-2, Spring, 1891, ISI Archives.

16. "The Conservative Network: How It Plans to Keep on Winning," *U.S. News & World Report*, July 20, 1981: 47; Yu Levchenko, "A 'Battle for the Minds' of the Younger Generation," *International Affairs*, May 1986: 122.

17. "ISI Ends Summer School Program," *ISI Campus Report*, Vol. 10, Nos. 1-2, Spring 1983: 1, 13.

Challenging Leviathan

ISI was required to change its methods of operating because the American campus had changed, and enormously, in the three decades since the founding of the Intercollegiate Society of Individualists. In 1950, the number of students in American colleges and universities was 1.863 million; the faculty numbered 246,722. The total income of American higher education was $2.375 billion, with $524 million coming from the federal government. According to the historian Christopher J. Lucas, the "typical" collegian in the late 1940s and early 1950s was male, white, and upper middle class. He was single, attended college full time, lived on campus, and "pursued a liberal-arts degree program bounded by extensive common course requirements."[18] He did not go on to an advanced degree but immediately went to work, usually in the private sector.

By the year 1985, the total enrollment of students in American higher education was 12.247 million, a sixfold increase since 1950. The faculty numbered 715,000, almost a threefold increase. College and university income was over $100 billion—almost fifty times what it had been three-and-a-half decades earlier. The federal government's share was $12.705 billion, a twentyfold rise. In 1985, the typical college student was likely to be female (over 55 percent), one in five was a member of a racial or ethnic minority, and an increasing percentage were in their midtwenties. Many students divided their time between working and attending college, were more apt to commute to campus rather than live in a dormitory or fraternity house, and took more than four years to finish their undergraduate degrees. And many of them were in no hurry to begin working: the nation's 2,000-plus colleges and universities were granting about a million bachelor's degrees, 300,000 master's degrees, and nearly 40,000 doctorates every year. Higher education was now big business, with the billion-dollar university a "commonplace."[19]

18. Christopher J. Lucas, *Crisis in the Academy: Rethinking Higher Education in America*, New York, 1996: 17-18.
19. Martin Anderson, *Imposters in the Temple: A Blueprint for Improving Higher Education in America*, Stanford, California, 1996: 28.

As the academy grew ever larger, educators like Linda Ray Pratt of
Nebraska insisted on asking fundamental questions: "Are we educating
good citizens, potential leaders, women and men with power over their
own faculties and mental resources to question and discern? Or are we
training a 'workforce?'"[20] A disturbing answer was provided by *A Nation
at Risk*, the 1983 report of the National Commission on Excellence in
Education, appointed by President Reagan. The report, wrote educators
John D. Pulliam and James J. Van Patten, had an effect "similar to that of
Sputnik in 1957."[21] Its blunt conclusion was that for all the billions of
dollars and the impressive infrastructure of administrators, teachers, and
buildings, an alarming number of young Americans could not read, write,
or do the most elementary sums.

On nineteen academic tests American students were never first or
second but often last when ranked with other industrial nations. About
13 percent of the nation's seventeen-year-olds and 40 percent of minority
youth were functionally illiterate. Some 23 million adults could not pass
simple reading or writing tests. SAT scores had declined steadily for sev-
enteen years. And the average achievement scores of college graduates
had fallen between 1975 and 1980. Public disquiet and demands for
reform of higher education were widespread and became even louder when
a 1985 National Assessment of Educational Progress (NAEP) examined
literacy levels among a large national sample of twenty-one to twenty-
five-year olds. The NAEP found that roughly half of the young adults
surveyed who had graduated from college with bachelor's degrees could
not perform such simple intellectual tasks as summarizing the content of
a newspaper article, calculating a 10 percent tip for lunch, and interpret-
ing a bus schedule.[22]

As ISI ended its third decade in 1983 (the year of the publication of
A Nation at Risk), it knew very well that, whatever conservatism's success
in the world of politics, liberalism still rode high in the saddle on the

20. Lucas, *Crisis in the Academy*: 146.
21. John D. Pulliam and James J. Van Patten, *History of Education in America*, 7th
ed. Upper Saddle, New Jersey, 1999: 243.
22. Lucas, *Crisis in the Academy*: 203.

campus and in the culture. The Institute had no choice but to increase its efforts to help the American college student obtain "that education necessary to good citizenship, the preservation of liberty, and the humane life."[23] And so it sought funding for conservative campus publications, pointing out to one potential donor that it was supporting *The Hillsdale Review,* the *Dawson Newsletter* (St. Louis University), *Above Ground* (Brandeis University), and hoped to assist a new student publication at the University of Dallas.[24] ISI moreover covered the bulk of the costs of two hundred lectures a year at colleges and universities, large and small— among them, Walter Berns on "Free Speech in a Democracy," Allan Bloom on "Quality and Equality," Russell Kirk on "T. S. Eliot," and Arthur Shenfield on "Capitalism and the Intellectuals."

Tacking ever to the right, *The Intercollegiate Review* published articles such as "The Urban Crisis Revisited" by Robert Nisbet, "The Hydra of Marxism," by Gerhart Niemeyer, "Robert Frost: The Individual and Society" by Peter J. Stanlis, "Islam on the Move" by Thomas Molnar, "The Social Role of Drama" by M. E. Bradford, and "Moral Rights and the Law" by Ernest van den Haag—and a book review by Representative Jack Kemp of New York. In 1987, the *IR* would mark the bicentennial of the United States Constitution with an impressive symposium featuring George W. Carey, Charles Kesler, William Campbell, Harvey C. Mansfield, Francis Canavan, and George Anastaplo. Through the *IR* reprint program, essays and book reviews were made available for classroom use— 250,000 reprints were ordered in the program's ten years of operation.

ISI also continued to distribute, at reduced cost, "mind-clearing classics" on the principles of freedom and the heritage of Western civilization, including *A Humane Economy* by Wilhelm Roepke; *Ancients and Moderns: Essays on the Tradition of Political Philosophy in Honor of Leo Strauss,* edited by Joseph Cropsey; *In Defense of Freedom* by Frank S. Meyer; and four essentials of the modern conservative canon—*The Road to Serf-*

23. Excerpted from the Minutes of the ISI Board of Trustees Meeting, May 15, 1981, Washington, D.C., ISI Archives.
24. E. Victor Milione to Richard M. Larry, August 9, 1982, ISI Archives.

dom by F. A. Hayek, *Ideas Have Consequences* by Richard M. Weaver, *Witness* by Whittaker Chambers, and *The Conservative Mind* by Russell Kirk.

In 1953, ISI's audience had been almost all undergraduates, but thirty years later, graduation and the accretion of teachers had expanded significantly two critical constituencies—faculty members and alumni. The Institute estimated that its faculty members constituted about one-fourth of the strongly conservative professors in America. ISI responded to their needs by providing publishing and lecturing opportunities and bringing speakers to their campuses. One of the main reasons why the Institute agreed to absorb *Modern Age* was to better serve its faculty members. ISI also took advantage of the critical mass of conservative academics in political science and history by helping to publish *The Political Science Reviewer* and, later, *Continuity,* establishing "self-supporting catalysts for change" in the two disciplines.[25]

Weaver Fellows continued to make their way up the academic ladder, acknowledging their debt to ISI all along the way. By the mid-1980s, they had published over one hundred books and several thousand essays and articles, placing the Western tradition at the center of their teaching. Among the many academics and their works were William B. Allen, associate professor of government, Harvey Mudd College (*Works of Fisher Ames*); Bruce Bartlett, deputy director, Joint Economic Committee of the U.S. Congress (*Reaganomics: Supply-Side Economics in Action*); Burton Folsom, assistant professor of history, Murray State University (*Urban Capitalists*); William Graebner, professor of history, State University of New York (*A History of Retirement: The Meaning and Function of an American Institution, 1885-1978*); Robert Hessen, senior research fellow, Hoover Institution (*Steel Titan: The Life of Charles M. Schwab*); Michael J. Malbin, resident fellow at the American Enterprise Institute (*Unelected Representatives: Congressional Staff and the Future of Representative Government*); David L. Schaefer, associate professor of political science, Holy Cross College (*Justice or Tyranny? A Critique of John Rawls' "A Theory of Justice"*;

25. Generic foundation proposal letter signed by E. Victor Milione, October 1982, ISI Archives.

and Jeffrey D. Wallin, associate professor of politics, University of Dallas (*Statesmanship and Rhetoric*).

The ISI Ethos

Swedish-born Claes G. Ryn first read *Modern Age* and *The Intercollegiate Review* as a twenty-year-old Gymnasium student in his native country and went on to write in 1968 the first book in the West on postwar American conservatism. He correctly predicted there would be "long-term electoral consequences" from "the intellectual ferment" of conservatism. In the spring of 1969, Ryn attended the national meeting of the Philadelphia Society in Chicago, meeting for the first time conservative scholars like Eric Voegelin, Eliseo Vivas, and Ernest van den Haag, about whom he had written. He enrolled as a graduate student at Louisiana State University and received a "most helpful" Weaver Fellowship in his last year there. Today a professor of politics at the Catholic University of America and chairman of the National Humanities Institute, Ryn continues to be impressed by what he and *Modern Age* editor George Panichas call "the ISI ethos." According to this ethos, politics and economics are secondary to moral and cultural issues, what Edmund Burke called "the decent drapery of life." Summing up the Institute's influence, Ryn reflects that it would be "hard to imagine what conservatism in America would be without ISI."[26]

ISI had sponsored its first alumni event—a public policy conference in Washington, D.C.—in 1973 and continued the tradition into the 1980s. The most significant change was that, in the past, most of the participants and guests had been professors and lawyers, but now they were drawn "from the upper reaches" of the Reagan administration. While such people could and did provide financial support to the Institute, the more critical fact, in Vic Milione's mind, was that their participation enabled ISI "to stitch together a national quilt of commercially and politically potent individuals" committed to the principles of liberty.[27] In rec-

26. Bracy Bersnak's interview with Claes G. Ryn, April 22, 2003.
27. Ibid.

ognition of the network's importance, Elaine Schadler was named alumni executive director.

At the same time, ISI continued to attract intelligent dedicated young people to Bryn Mawr to fill its various staff positions. In the late 1970s and early 1980s, for example, John Rao, George Forsyth, Donald E. Atkins, Jr., and Stephen M. Krason all served as Eastern director. Atkins was a 1972 graduate of Trinity College, where he majored in economics and political science; his interest in conservative thought started in junior high school. A mixer of the political and intellectual, Atkins was the founder and first chairman of the T. S. Eliot chapter of Young Americans for Freedom in Pennsylvania. During the same period, Peter Schramm was the ISI Western director, followed by Edward N. Peters. Another key staffer was Carol Russell, secretary and administrator of the Western office before becoming director of the Institute's lecture program. Married and with four children, Russell was a woman of many talents, including flying (she was a licensed pilot), sewing, and cooking—once, she invited thirty-four ISI students from Claremont and other nearby colleges to her home for Thanksgiving dinner.

As publications director, Gregory Wolfe edited *The Intercollegiate Review,* supervised the production of *Continuity* and *The Political Science Reviewer,* and administered the Richard M. Weaver Fellowship Awards program. A self-described "compulsive organizer," Wolfe also edited *The Hillsdale Review,* a conservative journal of cultural criticism, which he had founded as a student at Hillsdale College. Published in over a dozen journals, the young editor-writer talked about finding the time somehow to write a book on the fiction of Evelyn Waugh; in 1995, he would publish the biography of a somewhat different English man of letters, Malcolm Muggeridge.

In all these ways, wrote Vic Milione on the occasion of the Institute's thirtieth anniversary in 1983, ISI resisted the prevailing educational arguments that moral values were "arbitrary taboos," industry was nothing more than "institutionalized greed," and limited government was "an impediment to the immediate and ultimate solution" of the nation's problems. Board chairman Henry Regnery stated that ISI had never deviated from its purpose to help "guide and direct the future leadership of the country."[28]

Challenging the Academy

The 1980s were boom years for conservatives, as all the elements of a successful political movement came together—a time-tested philosophy, a national constituency, effective fund-raising, solid organization, media sophistication, and charismatic, principled leadership. At the center of the conservative movement was a remarkable political fusionist, President Ronald Reagan, who brought together dissatisfied Democrats and traditional Republicans, Irish Catholics and fundamentalist Protestants, anti-government Westerners and patriotic Southerners, free market libertarians and cultural conservatives. He did so by appealing, as he put it in his final Oval Office address, to their best hopes, not their worst fears. He did so by reiterating traditional American themes of duty, honor, and country. "In his evocation of our national memory and symbols of pride," said former education secretary William J. Bennett, "in his summoning us to our national purpose and to national greatness, he performed the crucial task of political leadership."[29]

But rapid growth, political success, and public acclaim breed rifts and divisions, and the conservative movement proved to be no exception as traditionalists and libertarians fiercely debated with neoconservatives and New Rightists about the present and the future intellectual direction of American conservatism. Stephen Tonsor of the University of Michigan, a conservative professor long associated with ISI, delivered a stinging rebuke of the neoconservatives at the April 1986 national meeting of the Philadelphia Society, saying:

> It has always struck me as odd, even perverse, that former Marxists have been permitted, yes invited, to play such a leading role in the Conservative movement of the twentieth century. It is splendid when

28. Messages from E. Victor Milione and Henry Regnery, Program of ISI's 30th anniversary dinner, Sept. 30, 1983, Washington, D.C.: 2,4.

29. William J. Bennett to the author, September 3, 1997.

the town whore gets religion and joins the church. Now and then she makes a good choir director, but when she begins to tell the minister what he ought to say in his Sunday sermons, matters have been carried too far.[30]

While traditionalists applauded loudly, neoconservatives protested just as loudly, unappeased by Tonsor's qualification that he and other traditionalists welcomed "the assistance of neoconservatives ... in the work of dismantling the failed political structures erected by modernity." The key word here was "political." The Michigan professor made it Kristol-clear that in his view the neoconservatives were cultural modernists despite their rejection of Marxism and some aspects of the modern welfare state. If neoconservatives wished conservatives to take their conservatism seriously, Tonsor wrote, "they must return to the religious roots, beliefs and values of our common heritage."[31]

So serious a subject required serious examination, and in the Spring 1986 issue of *The Intercollegiate Review,* editor Gregory Wolfe presented a symposium on "The State of Conservatism," featuring seven well-known conservative writers, all closely identified with ISI. In his introduction, Wolfe said the dangers that threatened the integrity of the conservative movement could be summarized in a single term: "politicization." He said that the contributors to the *IR* symposium largely agreed that at least four developments had contributed to "the current crisis of conservative identity and mission." First, the 1960s radicalization of the academy and the Democratic Party had forced a number of "liberal refugees" to cross political borders, with many of them becoming neoconservatives. The second factor, Wolfe wrote, was the rapid decay of America's social fabric over the last two decades which had spawned the populist, evangelical movement known as the New Right. Third, conservative successes in national politics had attracted "the inevitable groups of pragmatists and camp followers," motivated by self-interest rather than principle. And

30. Stephen J. Tonsor, "Why I Too Am Not a Neoconservative," *National Review,* June 20, 1986: 55.
    31. Ibid: 55-56.

finally, conservatives had acquiesced and even abetted the redefinition of "legitimate" conservatism by the liberal-dominated mass media. As a result, Wolfe concluded unequivocally, "the post-war conservative movement has been defined out of existence."[32] Wolfe made no claim that the symposium contributors largely agreed with this Spenglerian conclusion, and indeed several of them, including Russell Kirk and, surprisingly, paleoconservative Paul Gottfried, offered a measured degree of hope about the future of traditional conservatism.

Historian Clyde Wilson of the University of South Carolina agreed with Wolfe that what he called "intellectual conservatives" were in "a state of demoralization and discouragement" because they had been "crowded out" by ex-liberals and because of the "unraveling of the social fabric." But the task of the conservative intellectual, Wilson said, remained what it had always been, although it had acquired new urgency: "to keep alive the wisdom that we are heir to" and to hand it on. While not denying there had been a "fundamental change in the country's politics," a rather gloomy Gerhart Niemeyer wondered whether "in terms of ideas, there is such a thing as American conservatism."

Modern Age editor George Panichas wrote that in the last decade, "conservatism has experienced a spiritual decline even as it has made considerable political gains." No significant restoration of "an authentic conservatism," Panichas wrote, was possible without giving "first allegiance to spiritual principles of order—to the life of the spirit, as Eric Voegelin insists." George Carey offered three suggestions for conservatives: First, accept that even if the Soviet Union disappeared, "American conservatism would still be confronted with an internal liberalism which is eroding the foundations of the republic." Next, conservatives had to understand that "rolling back" the liberal excesses "can only come about by cultivating the popular roots of conservatism." And, anticipating the stunning success of Newt Gingrich's Contract with America in the 1994 elections, Carey argued that the future of conservatism rested with politicians

32. Gregory Wolfe, "The State of Conservatism: A Symposium," *The Intercollegiate Review*, Vol. 21 No. 3, Spring 1986: 3-4.

like Reagan who "can give expression of the discontents, identify their source, and thereby maintain and broaden the alliance."[33]

Opportunists and Statists

English professor and Philadelphia Society president M. E. Bradford (who had recently lost to William Bennett in a bid to head the National Endowment for the Humanities) variously described neoconservatives as "thieves," "interlopers," "opportunists," and "statists." The first priority of conservatives, he wrote, was to refuse to surrender "our hard-won identity to those who would use it as a cloak for policies contrary to what we intend." Bradford then turned to an issue of major concern to nearly all the symposium participants, the judiciary, saying that conservatives needed to encourage the administration "to concentrate its surviving reserves of conservatism on judicial appointments." Reiterating a favorite theme of Richard Weaver, Bradford said that conservatives had to correct a fundamental shortcoming, "our indifference to the art of rhetoric, our inability to deal with the ostensibly benevolent simplicities of the adversary, who hopes to win with language what he lost at the polls."[34]

Best known for his unrelenting criticism of neoconservatives, historian Paul Gottfried devoted almost equal time in his essay to dismissing the New Right, calling it "lowbrow," "naive," and "intellectually crude." Gottfried identified three common mistakes among interpreters of the American Right—confusing the visibility of both neoconservatives and New Rightists with "electoral clout"; treating neoconservatives as "genuine conservatives"; and "ignoring the continued vitality of the Old Right." Gottfried can be challenged on the first point—the New Right was directly responsible for the defeat of about a dozen liberal senators in the 1978 and 1980 elections (producing a Republican Senate in the first six years of the Reagan administration). Furthermore, liberal pollster Lou

33. Ibid: Clyde Wilson, "The Conservative Identity": 6, 8; Gerhart Niemeyer, "Is There a Conservative Mission?": 9; George Panichas, "Conservatism and the Life of the Spirit": 25; George Carey, "The Popular Roots of Conservatism": 12-14.

34. Ibid: M. E. Bradford, "On Being Conservative in a Post-Liberal Era": 15-18.

Harris credited the Moral Majority as a major factor in Ronald Reagan's presidential victory in 1980.

But Gottfried's point about the Old Right, or traditional conservatives, was on the mark. Members of the founding generation such as Kirk, Buckley, and Molnar were still busily writing and debating. The second generation including Stan Evans, George Nash, and George Panichas was "leaving its imprint on conservative thought." In the end, Gottfried predicted that the Old Right rather than the neoconservatives would have the greater impact, because it held to the concept of "a differentiated humanity," valued social diversity, and perceived the necessary relationship "between established custom and human nature." "The Old Right still lives," Gottfried said proudly, "reports on its demise have been greatly exaggerated."[35]

It remained for Russell Kirk, the man who had given the conservative movement its name, to offer a balanced assessment of American conservatism, conceding the remarkable political victories since 1953, but pointing out that "relatively few intellectual gains" had occurred. His major proof was that university and college staffs were "far more dominated by radicals" than they had been in the 1950s. "Ballot-box victories," Kirk wrote, can be quickly undone "if unsupported by the enduring art of persuasion." However, he was not alarmed by the various conservative factions because "enough common ground" could be cultivated to maintain unity on large questions. It was important, he said, ever the Burkean, that conservatives in politics "steer clear of the Scylla of abstraction and the Charybdis of opportunism." For all the factionalism within the conservative movement, Kirk insisted that "a conservative cast of character and of mind capable of sacrifice, thought, and sound sentiment" had survived.[36]

By reason of its timing, by the elevated tone of the essays, and by the participation of several of the most respected conservative intellectuals in America, the Spring 1986 issue of *The Intercollegiate Review* proved yet again how essential ISI was to the conservative movement. The move-

35. Ibid: Paul Gottfried, "A View of Contemporary Conservatism": 19-21.
36. Ibid: Russell Kirk, "Enlivening the Conservative Mind": 26-28.

ment that had begun in the 1950s had brought together disparate intellectual strands—anti-communists, libertarians, and traditionalists—but the thinkers of each strand had all understood that they faced a "total crisis" of civilization in the twentieth century. However, such cultural matters are often forgotten or left aside when the opportunity to exercise political power presents itself. If ISI had not published this symposium on the state of conservatism, no one else would have, and fundamental questions about the present and the future of conservatism would have gone unanswered, even unaddressed.

The Battle of Ideas

At about this time, ISI started on a road that would eventually lead to book publishing by establishing a relationship with the University Press of America to "co-publish" edited collections of selected conferences. Edited by George Carey of Georgetown University, the initial books were *Essays on Christianity and Political Philosophy*, which explored the relationship between Christian faith and the limitations it places on the role of the state, and *Freedom and Virtue: The Conservative/Libertarian Debate*, with new contributions on this perennial question by Walter Berns, Murray Rothbard, and Paul Kurtz.

All of this activity ISI undertook on an annual budget of about three-quarters of a million dollars and a full-time staff of ten, crowded into a small suite measuring just 2,145 square feet. The atmosphere was nearly Dickensian. "The entry door," Christopher Long remembers, "was metal, and the offices were piled high with decades of accumulated paper." Empty rectangles on the orange walls showed where artwork had once hung, and the smell of nicotine was everywhere.[37] And yet there were few complaints from the staff members who deferred the beautification of their surroundings in favor of educating as many students as they could about the value of liberty and the conditions of a good society.

They knew that ISI's contribution to what trustee Richard V. Allen called "the battle of ideas on the college campus" had been vital—and not

37. Christopher Long to Lee Edwards, September 5, 2002.

just on the campus.[38] Through the sponsorship of hundreds of lectures, seminars, and schools which had been attended by thousands of students, through the distribution of thousands of books, pamphlets, and journals which had been read by the tens of thousands, through the several hundred Weaver Fellows who had produced dozens of textbooks and thousands of scholarly articles on philosophy, economics, history, international relations, and nearly every other subject under the academic sun, ISI had helped conservatives transform themselves from a weak remnant into a powerful national movement.

In the 1950s and 1960s, wrote Allen in an ISI fund-raising letter, the conservative network was "small and fragmented, unfunded and described by liberals and leftists as the 'extreme right' and 'the radical right.'" In the mid-1980s, conservatives had "every reason to be optimistic." President Reagan headed a generally conservative administration that had restored the confidence of most Americans in the future, slowed the growth of government (and even reduced it in some areas), and declared that the United States was out to end the Cold War by winning it. Outside the administration, the conservative movement continued to grow in strength and stature. The Heritage Foundation had nearly doubled its annual income, and the Cato Institute had moved its national headquarters to Washington. New organizations like the Family Research Council and the Competitive Enterprise Institute had gained measurable influence. *National Review, Human Events*, and *The American Spectator* had reached new circulation highs. And the American Conservative Union attracted as many as 1,500 activists to its annual Conservative Political Action Conferences.

The rise of the Right was recognized by a leading organ of the Left— the *Washington Post*—which published "The Conservative Elite," a four-part series by investigative reporter Sidney Blumenthal, who later served as a key White House aide to President Bill Clinton. To movement conservatives, Blumenthal wrote, "the Reagan Revolution means more than the attempt to create an electoral realignment. Just as important to them

38. Richard V. Allen to R. J. Buckley, February 21, 1984, ISI Archives.

is the effort to give life to the conservative elite, the revolution's vanguard." The forging of a conservative policy-making elite that would run the government in Washington, he said, "could be this administration's lasting legacy in Washington." Featured in the September 1985 articles was T. Kenneth Cribb, then counselor to Attorney General Edwin Meese III, who commented, "This isn't merely a Republican regime but a conservative regime." And according to Blumenthal, the conservatives who carried the greatest weight were those who had affiliations with organizations like The Heritage Foundation and the "Intercollegiate Society of Individualists [sic]."[39]

But how long would the conservative ascendancy last? The answer, Dick Allen argued in his ISI fund-raising letter, lay in whether conservatives continued to generate "dynamic new ideas." And the generation of new ideas depended on what happened on the campus. "Political power comes and goes," Allen wrote, while "true values and worthy ideals never lose their strength."[40] For thirty years, he pointed out, ISI had provided a "unique and invaluable service," offering young men and women "the deeper philosophical foundation on which they could build their practical plans—the core values to help them organize their careers."[41] ISI believed with Russell Kirk that the future "will be decided in the minds of the rising generation—and within that generation by the minority who have the gift of reason."[42]

Embued with a reverence for the past and filled with a desire to shape the future, hundreds of ISI alumni had come to Washington, D.C. Navy Secretary John Lehman exaggerated, but not by much, when he said that "nearly every sensible young policymaker here in Washington has had some association with ISI."[43] They could be found in the White

39. Sidney Blumenthal, "Staying Power: Cadres for the Right Train for the Future," *Washington Post,* September 22, 1985.

40. Allen to Buckley, February 21, 1984.

41. Ibid.

42. E. Victor Milione, "A Message from the President," on the 30th anniversary of the Intercollegiate Studies Institute, Washington-Sheraton Hotel, September 30th-October 1st, 1983: 2. Henry Regnery, "The Purpose of ISI," Ibid: 4.

43. Ibid.

House and the Congress, in the executive branch, and in the private sector. In words that varied little, they echoed Heritage President Ed Feulner's statement that "were it not for the local ISI chapter during my undergraduate days, I would not have gained the philosophical underpinnings that are necessary for one to develop political knowledge and understanding."[44]

It seemed that everything was in place for ISI to take full advantage of the ascendancy of the Right—a seasoned principled leader in Vic Milione, a small but experienced staff led by John Lulves, a proven program centered on literature, lectures, and the Weaver Fellowships, a network of illustrious alumni willing to help open doors and wallets. ISI remained as it had been for more than thirty years—the only national conservative organization that directed *all* of its efforts to the college campus. "If the future is to develop within a society that is civilized, humane, and free," an ISI brochure declared, "it remains vital to continue 'to educate for liberty.'"[45]

And then one morning in February 1985, sixty-one-year-old Vic Milione was still at home when he began perspiring heavily and felt quite ill. Overriding Vic's objections, his wife Mali insisted that he go immediately to Bryn Mawr General Hospital. The requisite tests were followed by a swift decision to operate that resulted in a heart-bypass procedure. There were no serious complications from the surgery, but recovery required several months. It was not until the summer that Milione returned to work full-time in the office. His work schedule was much the same, and his mind could still wrap itself around the logic and rhetoric of Richard Weaver and Jacob Burckhardt. But there were new lines in his face and his carefully trimmed beard was noticeably more gray. Vic Milione's commitment to the cause of a free society and his beloved ISI was undiminished, but it was clear to all, including the man himself, that it was time to begin planning for the retirement of "Mr. ISI"—and for the se-

---

44. Edwin J. Feulner, as quoted in the brochure "Achievement Past & Present: ISI in the Fourth Decade," c. 1984, ISI Archives.
45. Ibid: 31.

lection of his successor. That person would have to be conservative, familiar with ISI and its programs, a good administrator, a proficient fundraiser, and someone who could take full advantage of the burgeoning conservative movement in leading the Intercollegiate Studies Institute in the post-Reagan years.

The new president would also be required to shape ISI's strategy of how to deal with the continuing deterioration of the American academy— whose critical condition was graphically described in the best-selling works of two of the Institute's popular lecturers.

CHAPTER VII

Change and Continuity

Politics is a surface phenomenon. Below the surface we have to renew
in each new generation the legacy of Western liberty.

T. Kenneth Cribb, Jr.

IN THE LATE 1980S AND EARLY 1990S, the works of two conservative
critics dominated the public debate about the decline of the American
university—*The Closing of the American Mind* by Allan Bloom, a distinguished University of Chicago classics professor, and *Illiberal Education*
by Dinesh D'Souza, a young scholar at the American Enterprise Institute
in Washington, D.C., whose biting antiestablishment rhetoric reminded
some observers of a young Bill Buckley. Both Bloom and D'Souza had
been frequent speakers at ISI events, Bloom since the 1960s when he
taught at the University of Toronto in Canada, D'Souza since the mid-
1980s and his graduation from Dartmouth where he edited the provocative *Dartmouth Review.*

The professoriate, Bloom claimed in *The Closing of the American
Mind*, had abandoned "liberal arts" (that is, classical liberal learning) and
adopted either the latest intellectual fads or retreated to their academic

specialties. Bloom held that a profound "crisis" confronted American higher education. His solution was simple—provide "a good program of liberal education" and feed "the student's love of truth and passion to live a good life."[1] *The Closing of the American Mind* rose to number one on the *New York Times* bestseller list and was described by one reviewer as possibly "the most important work of its kind by an American since World War II." Educational historian Christopher J. Lucas said that Bloom was extending an argument made earlier in the decade by E. D. Hirsch, Jr., a professor of English at the University of Virginia. Hirsch had charged that America was dangerously close to losing "its coherence as a culture" and that "we need to connect more of our students to our history, our culture, and those ideas which hold us together."[2] ISI, through its sponsorship of lectures and literature by Weaver, Kirk, and many others, had been making such connections since its founding.

Modern Age responded to *The Closing of the American Mind,* characteristically, by taking the long view. A symposium of twelve conservative intellectuals, while conceding the accuracy of much of Bloom's scathing criticism of the American academy, generally faulted his Great Books prescription as simplistic and lacking in appreciation for the function of the sacred in higher education. While Bloom gave a powerful account of the problem in American higher education, his solution fell short. As Stephen Tonsor put it, "Bloom is a man of the Enlightenment sentimentalized by Rousseau."[3] Peter Augustine Lawler observed that for Bloom, "the possibility of the truth of revelation is not a real one," although his teacher Leo Strauss had suggested that it might be "the secret to the reinvigoration of the West." Thomas Molnar, writing as usual from the perspective of European high culture, called Bloom's book a failure because it did not deal with the "trivialization of education at all levels." The American mind

---

1. Allan Bloom, *The Closing of the American Mind: How Higher Education Has Failed Democracy and Impoverished the Souls of Today's Students,* New York, 1987: 22, 345.

2. Lucas, *American Higher Education*: 295-296. Also see E. D. Hirsch, Jr., *Cultural Literacy: What Every American Needs to Know,* Boston, 1987.

3. Stephen J. Tonsor, "Uberstudiert in Chicago," *Modern Age,* Volume 32, Winter 1988: 58.

had not been "closed," insisted Molnar, because it had never been opened.

Marion Montgomery counseled conservatives to avoid euphoria about Bloom's book, despite its well-founded critique of the academy, as well as its dismissal, because Bloom was so clearly a creature of the Enlightenment. Better, Montgomery said, to realize that Bloom's view of the academy "is a very narrow one" and to seek "a larger wisdom about the nature of man in community." Tonsor concluded that Bloom's favorite, Plato, was an authoritarian with "no comprehension of sin, reconciliation, and salvation, and no realization of the humanity which is only possible when we share in God's divinity."[4] In his introduction to the symposium, publisher (and ISI chairman) Henry Regnery expressed doubt that *The Closing of the American Mind* would have any lasting effect on the academy, but noted that its extraordinary sales (half a million copies) was "a greater indictment of the American university than anything in the book itself."[5] While the media treated Bloom's argument as central to the conservative indictment of the academy, the *Modern Age* symposium demonstrated that even deeper reasons accounted for higher education's eclipse.

It was Dinesh D'Souza's *Illiberal Education*—and his vigorous promotion of the book on television and radio and in dozens of debates on college campuses—that brought to light the full impact of "political correctness" and helped make it a major academic and political issue. D'Souza reported that American universities had deliberately filled a "sizable portion of their freshman class[es]" with minority students with little regard for their qualifications; had diluted or displaced their core curricula to make room for new courses dealing with non-Western cultures, Afro-American Studies, and women's studies; and had set up and funded separate institutions of minority groups in the name of "pluralism" and "diversity." Quoting University of Wisconsin chancellor Donna Shalala (a future secretary of health and human services in the Clinton administration) D'Souza said the alarming result was a "basic transformation of

4. Ibid: Peter Augustine Lawler, "Bloom on Socrates and America": 29; Thomas Molnar, "Adding to Organized Misunderstanding": 37; Marion Montgomery, "Wanted: A Better Reason as Guide": 44; Tonsor: 59.
5. Ibid: Henry Regnery, "Foreword": 2.

American higher education."[6]

After studying conditions at the University of California at Berkeley, Stanford University, Howard University, the University of Michigan, Duke University, and Harvard University, D'Souza concluded that affirmative action had increased, not decreased, racial and gender tensions. Born in India and himself a person of color, D'Souza warned that if this "university model is replicated in society at large ... it will reproduce and magnify the lurid bigotry, intolerance, and balkanization of campus life in the broader culture."[7] As D'Souza knew full well—many of his campus talks were arranged by ISI—the Institute had been countering such a perverted university model for three decades.

The wide public attention accorded Bloom and D'Souza, notwithstanding, ISI knew that any meaningful reform of the academy would be exceedingly difficult. By the end of the twentieth century, American higher education had become a leviathan of 14.5 million students, nearly 4,000 four-year and two-year institutions, more than 900,000 faculty members and staff, and annual expenditures of over $175 billion. And yet for all these resources, the National Endowment for the Humanities revealed that one could graduate from 77 percent of the nation's colleges without studying a foreign language; from 45 percent of schools without completing a single course in American or English literature; from 41 percent without studying mathematics; and from 38 percent without having taken one history course.[8]

Against this creature of enormous size and power, ISI commanded in the spring of 1985 the following resources: a membership of 25,000, including an estimated ten thousand faculty members; four major publications—*The Intercollegiate Review*, edited by Gregory Wolfe, who also served as the Institute's publications director; the quarterly *Modern Age*, edited by the distinguished literary critic George Panichas; the annual *The Political Science Reviewer*, edited by George Carey; and the semi-

6. Dinesh D'Souza, *Illiberal Education: The Politics of Race and Sex on Campus*, New York, 1991: 2, 5, 8, 13.
7. Ibid: 230.
8. Lucas, *Crisis in the Academy*: 220.

annual *Continuity: A Journal of History*, edited by Paul Gottfried—and about two hundred campus lectures a year, coordinated by lecture program director Carol Russell.

Among the speakers were such leading conservatives as Russell Kirk discussing "The Roots of American Order"; Michael Novak on "The Spirit of Democratic Capitalism"; Harry Jaffa on "The Declaration and the Draft"; James Gwartney on "The Way the Market Works"; and Marion Montgomery on "Why Flannery O'Connor Stayed Home." Other ISI activities included one-day and two-day campus seminars, symposia, and conferences on topics ranging from "The Things of God and the Things of Ceasar," featuring a lecture by Claes Ryn, professor of politics at the Catholic University of America, to "American Conservatism: A Reliable Voice or an Uneasy Contradiction?" with presentations by Jeffrey Hart, Dartmouth College professor of English and senior editor of *National Review*, and former ISI national director Robert Reilly, now associate director of the White House Office of Public Liaison.

The Importance of Continuity

It was in this where-are-we-going atmosphere (and with ISI's thirty-fifth anniversary falling the following year) that ISI's board of trustees appointed in 1987 a six-member Evaluation Committee to undertake the most comprehensive examination of the Institute in its history. The committee members were Richard Allen, now president of an international consulting company; T. Kenneth Cribb, Jr., assistant to the president of the United States; Charles Hoeflich, ISI's long-time secretary-treasurer; Henry Regnery, chairman of the board of trustees; Wayne Valis, head of his own Washington lobbying firm; and Edwin J. Feulner, president of The Heritage Foundation and chairman of the evaluation committee. The committee met four times during the summer and early fall of 1987 and held a final telephone conference call in mid-September. Vic Milione was an ex officio member of the committee, while ISI executive vice president John Lulves also participated in every meeting.

As soon as the committee was formed, rumors began radiating inside and outside Bryn Mawr that plans were underway "to take over ISI," that "a coup was being attempted," and that "a purge was going to be exercised of the current staff of ISI." The activist youth group, Young Americans for Freedom, had become infamous in the conservative movement for its personality-driven purges, but ISI did not suffer any such ruinous process. Rather, the evaluation committee expressed its "continuing commitment" to a "freestanding ISI," independent of any other entity. The committee also endorsed "an intellectually serious ISI," "an enhanced program" for the organization, and "a stable process of succession" as Vic Milione made plans to step down as president in June 1988, after thirty-five years of service, and to formally retire in June 1989.[9]

In its introduction, the evaluation committee praised the Institute's present programs and activities but urged their expansion and endorsed a long-discussed need—a building for a national headquarters. The committee conceded that implementation of its recommendations "would require a substantial growth in annual revenue," but stated that such fund-raising was necessary "to assure the undergirding of ISI for the long term."[10] The committee members reiterated certain principles that had been "responsible in large part for [ISI's] success." First, the Institute respected "students *qua* students," never seeking to use them for political or "issue-of-the-moment" projects. ISI emphasized quality and substance, convinced that higher education "is a serious enterprise for the long run." The Institute added or subtracted programs "with great care," always respecting continuity, a fundamental conservative principle. And finally, ISI focused on the top students, believing that a culture is determined by "the intelligence and quality of those in leadership positions."[11]

ISI's monumental task, the evaluation committee stated, was no less than "the preservation of the Western heritage" in a society that maintained "only tenuous connections" to its patrimony. Fortunately, ISI's

9. "Report of the Evaluation Committee to the Board of Trustees of the Intercollegiate Studies Institute, Inc.," Edwin J. Feulner, Jr., chairman, October 1987: 2.
10. Ibid: 3-4.
11. Ibid: 5-6.

Top photo: Vic Milione presents an award to John Lehman on behalf of the ISI Alumni Association, 1982. Left: Friedrich Hayek chats with Gerhart Niemeyer later that evening. Right: Edwin Meese and William F. Buckley Jr. at ISI's 30th anniversary dinner. Previous page: Ronald Reagan gives the keynote address at a 1977 ISI alumni dinner. To Reagan's left: Ken Cribb, Vic Milione, and ISI trustees Cong. Phil Crane (R-Il.) and Henry Regnery.

Top photo: While a graduate student, Russell Hittinger (2nd from right) organizes an ISI lecture for Michael Novak (foreground) at St. Louis University, March 28, 1983. Below: Hittinger, who now teaches at the University of Tulsa, and Princeton University professor Robert George debate natural law at the 1991 ISI Western summer school. Long devoted to encouraging traditional scholarship, ISI embarks on a new book publishing effort in the mid-1990s that produces works by both Hittinger and George.

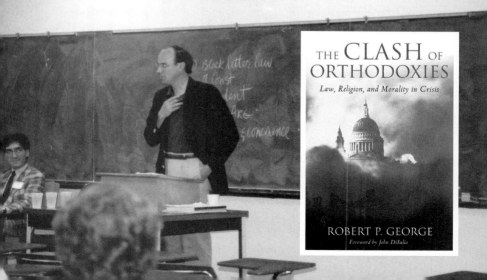

Counter clockwise: George Nash (l) speaks to a student after his lecture on "American Conservatism and the Reagan Revolution" at Yale University in 1988. Paul Gottfried an Aileen Kraditor become the first editors of ISI's journal of history, Continuity, *in 1980. Richard Pipes speaks at Yale in 1988. ISI alumnus and Reagan national security adviser Richard Allen (center) socializes with Vic Milione and J. William Middendorf. Gregory Wolfe (l) and Edward Teller at the 1977 ISI Western summer school. Milione with Supreme Court justice Antonin Scalia at an ISI-sponsored 1987 Villanova lecture.*

Counter clockwise: Weaver fellow Wilfred McClay (l) with Nicholas Capaldi (center) and Ellis Sandoz at the ISI National Leadership Conference in 1996. E. Christian Kopff and John Lukacs chat at the 1996 ISI summer school. Shelby Steele (r) speaks to students as part of ISI's prep school lecture program. ISI program staff circa 1997, from l to r: Paul Rhein, Bracy Bersnak, Gary Gregg, Jason Duke, Mark Henrie, and Michael Wallacavage. Vic Milione and Dinesh D'Souza at ISI's 40th anniversary gala.

Counter clockwise: ISI Books' founding publisher Jeffrey O. Nelson introduces the latest book catalogue at the 2002 Book Expo in New York City. Lady Thatcher with winners of the 1997 ISI Thatcher essay contest. Peter Augustine Lawler leads a seminar of ISI Honors Fellows. Ken Cribb (r) at ISI's 45th anniversary gala with keynote speaker Judge Robert Bork and former Delaware governor Pete Dupont. Whittaker Chambers biographer Sam Tanenhaus speaks at ISI's spring 2003 conference celebrating the 50th anniversary of Witness. Pat Gardner interviews Vice President Dan Quayle for CAMPUS magazine(1990).

Clockwise: 1993 Piety Hill seminar participants; Kirk home; 1999 Honors seminar, Kirk library; exterior of Kirk library; 1988 Piety Hill seminar lead by Dr. Kirk. Previous page, center photo: Richard M. DeVos, Louise Oliver, Ken Cribb, Helen DeVos, and F. M. Kirby dedicate ISI's new F. M. Kirby Campus in 1996. The Richard and Helen DeVos Freedom Center is located on the property.

Clockwise: 1998 Honors Fellows at Williamsburg listen to Tom West and Larry Arnn debate Barry Shain and Marshall DeRosa. Program VP Christopher Long (l) listens to long-time ISI treasurer Charles H. Hoeflich. 2002 ISI Honors Fellows at Oriel College, Oxford. Mel Bradford with students at the 1992 Southern Leadership Conference.

A flurry of activity at ISI's headquarters has accompanied the arrival of the new millennium with frequent lectures for West Point army cadets as well as for members of the public. Clockwise: James Kurth of Swathmore College; Rear Admiral Mike Ratliff (ret.) and ISI vice president of program speaks to cadets; Victor Davis Hanson, wearing an army cap presented to him as a gift, signs a book for a cadet; author Christina Hoff Sommers; political scientist Hadley Arkes; literary critic R. V. Young.

*ockwise: 2002 Collegiate Network
(CN) Foreign Correspondance Course
participants visit Radio Free Europe/
Radio Liberty headquarters in Prague.
Fred Barnes speaks to CN editors.
Prof. Alan Kors and CN students. CN
students visit a Prague television
studio. CN alumnus and* National
Review *national political reporter
John Miller with seminar participant
2000. Weekly Standard's Stephen
Hayes briefs CN editors. 1998 CN
editors' conference in New York City.*

INTERCOLLEGIATE SOCIETY OF IN

THE DEMOCRATIC PRINCIPLE
By CHARLES B. BROWNSON

FREEDOM,
TRADITION,
CONSERVATISM

FRANK S. MEYER

A
CONSERVATIVE
CASE
FOR
FREEDOM

M. STANTON EVANS

The ISI
Story as of
1961

CAMPU
AMERICA'S STUDENT NEWSPA

FOR
OUR
CHILDREN'S
CHILDREN
By
Frank Chodorov

Reprint from
HUMAN EVENTS, Inc.

Intercollegiate Society of Individualists, Inc.
For the Advancement of Conservative Thought on American College Campuses

ISI
Founded 1953

campus report
FEBRUARY 1962

The Individualist
Published by the Inter-Collegiate Society of Individualists

The National Student Associ
Does it Represent the American Studen

THE
ACADEM
REVIEW

THE ISI Leadership Conferences
d During First Semester

THE ISI GUIDE 2004

CHOOSING THE RIGHT COLLEGE
THE WHOLE TRUTH ABOUT AMERICA'S TOP SCHOOLS

MODERN AGE
A QUARTERLY REVIEW
Volume 26   SUMMER/FALL 1982   Number

SILVER JUBILEE ISSUE

"A GENERATION OF THE
INTELLECTUAL RIGHT"

RELATIVIS
AND
THE CRISI
OUR TIME

ISI CAMPUS REPORT

HE INTERCOLLEGIATE
REVIEW

NO. 1   JANUARY, 1965   SEVENTY-FIVE CENTS

"GROWTHMANSHIP": FACT AND FALLACY
Colin Clark

THE FALSEFACE OF SCIENCE
Albert H. Hobbs

THE DEPUTY: AN EXERCISE IN DRAMATIC IMPROPRIETY
Kenneth Paul Shorey

RENASCENT AMERICAN CONSERVATISM:
A CASE STUDY OF SCHIZOPHRENIA
Paul Cole Beach, Jr.

Malcolm Muggeridge Speaks on Solzhenitsyn
and Moral Crisis at ISI Seminars

WHAT IS CONSERVATISM?

A timely, important and
provocative examination of
American conservatism by
twelve leading conservative
thinkers and spokesmen
edited by FRANK S. MEYER

Contributors:
FRANK S. MEYER
RUSSELL KIRK
WILLMOORE KENDALL
WILHELM RÖPKE
F. A. HAYEK
M STANTON EVANS
STANLEY PARRY
STEPHEN J. TONSOR
GARRY WILLS
JOHN CHAMBERLAIN
STEFAN T. POSSONY
WILLIAM F. BUCKLEY JR.

UNDER 30

CAMPUS RE
Published by the Intercollegiate Society of Individ

Conservatism Examined at Pri

ISI BOOKS

A UNIVERSITY IN PRINT
FALL/WINTER 2003-2004

Everyday Graces
A Book of Good Manners

The American Way
and Community to the

ROCKFORD COLLEGE

SUMMER SCHOOLS

TO EDUCATE
ISI
FOR LIBERTY

the
Story in Brief

o-Week
o Be Co

e third consecutive y
which will cover all
before. ISI will offe
dwest, and the West.
nity lectureers for a
, William F. Buckle

THE
POLITICAL
REVIE

Vol. XX

program was "almost perfectly fashioned" to help accomplish the restoration of the American tradition of freedom and order in the institution that influenced every aspect of American society—higher education.[12]

The section on program goals and priorities stated that while "the decline of university learning" that characterized the 1960s had not abated, the campus situation in the 1980s was "quite different." On the negative side, the leftists who had entered academe during the Vietnam War were now in positions of power as full professors and even college presidents. "There ought to be no mistake," emphasized the program subcommittee, "about the determination of this opposition" to conservatism. The organized Left had in fact dedicated "money and cadre" to the development of selected campuses as staging areas for "left-wing agitation" on such contemporary issues as SDI, the Sandinistas and Nicaragua, and economic sanctions against South Africa. On the positive side was the "generation of young faculty members" in the 1980s who were conservative or open to conservatism. They constituted "a network" not found in the 1960s. And "the prominence of conservatism" in recent years—led by the political success of national leaders like Ronald Reagan and the intellectual success of academics like Nobel laureates F. A. Hayek and Milton Friedman—had finally made conservative thought "respectable."[13]

Specifically, the program subcommittee, headed by Ken Cribb, recommended that the Weaver Fellowship program, now twenty years old, be continued, and enlarged if possible; that *The Intercollegiate Review*, *Modern Age*, and *The Political Science Reviewer* be maintained, but close consideration be given to the discontinuance of *Continuity* and *The Hillsdale Review*. The subcommittee suggested that the network of campus representatives and faculty associates be expanded, the number of annual lectures be increased to over two hundred, the summer schools be restored, and the seminars, including the ISI Piety Hill Seminars at Russell Kirk's home in Mecosta, Michigan, be augmented. Acknowledging that books, reprints, bibliographies, and other printed materials were "at the

12. Ibid: 6.
13. Ibid: 8-9.

heart of the ISI enterprise," the Cribb subcommittee stressed that the publications program "should be enhanced." In particular, said the subcommittee, "ISI should make a strong effort to keep certain conservative classics available at all times."[14] In the years to come, particularly in its book publishing enterprise, the Institute would fulfill this directive, with honors.

The Cribb subcommittee also stated that recent financial constraints had "reduced ISI's core program," and that now was the time to reinvigorate the Institute by taking advantage of the "new situation" on campus and in conservatism. "ISI is positioned," the report said, "to be the premier conservative organization in the movement's most important long-term target beyond the Reagan Administration—the hearts and minds of the upcoming generation."[15] This was a telling description of ISI's place in the world of American conservatism. No longer would the Institute work primarily as an independent operator on the periphery of the conservative movement but henceforth as a prominent, integrated member of the movement.

The management subcommittee's contribution was brief and to the point: the board of trustees needed to be strengthened, a senior vice president responsible for fund raising ought to be hired, and "a serious effort" should be made to "buy a building to house the central office of ISI." The subcommittee, chaired by Henry Regnery, added that in order to preserve a measure of independence, the Institute "should not be located in Boston, New York City, or Washington, D.C." With regard to regional offices, ex officio member Milione argued that while the cost of reinstituting a Midwestern office could not be justified, the Western office in California should be continued.[16] The subcommittee agreed, unknowingly creating a controversial issue for ISI's next president.

The financial subcommittee, chaired by Dick Allen, said bluntly that the ISI staff (headed of course by Vic Milione) had not raised funds "as

14. Ibid: 12.
15. Ibid: 14.
16. Ibid: 15-16.

effectively as it should have." It then softened its criticism by saying that the board of trustees had not provided "the substantive support it should have" to the staff. In truth, ISI's 1987 budget of about $845,000 was the same in nominal dollars as it had been in the mid-1960s, meaning that "its purchasing power has been cut in half." The fact that many on-campus activities had been discontinued, that the Bryn Mawr office facilities were inadequate, and that publications were not regularly published, the subcommittee declared, "could be traced directly" to the inadequate fundraising efforts of "ISI management and the ISI Board of Trustees" in the 1980s.[17]

Expanding the Financial Pie

The solution, said the subcommittee briskly, was clear and mandatory— "an expanded fund-raising effort" that would require a senior vice president to manage the campaign, consultation with fund-raising experts, and "the close and continuing assistance of ISI trustees."[18] Everyone hoped that such "close" trustee assistance would include that of Ed Feulner, the most effective capital fund-raiser in the conservative movement. In order for ISI to achieve "penetration in depth" on the campus in the next decade, estimated the subcommittee, the Institute would have to spend $2 million annually, more than double its current budget. Exclusive of the funds needed to purchase a permanent ISI home, such a goal would necessitate $1.2 million in *new* revenue, to be acquired at the rate of $300,000 a year. The transition in ISI's leadership in the months ahead, concluded the finance subcommittee, would require close "continuity and cooperation among the staff and the Board."[19]

The presidential succession subcommittee, chaired by Ed Feulner with Cribb, Valis, and Regnery as members and Milione as an ex-officio member, considered several dozen candidates before winnowing the list down to twelve and then scheduling interviews with four people, all of

17. Ibid: 17.
18. Ibid: 18.
19. Ibid: 19.

whom had had a long association with the Institute. The final four were Charles Heatherly, Robert Schadler, John Lulves, and Robert Reilly. Ken Cribb was the first choice of several trustees and of Vic Milione as well, but Cribb declined because he had returned to the White House to help President Reagan set things right after the Iran-Contra crisis and had made a commitment to the president.[20] After being interviewed, John Lulves withdrew as a candidate because, as he put it, "In everyone's mind, including mine, I was the perfect number-two guy."[21] Reilly had reason to be optimistic about his chances, as both Milione and Feulner had telephoned him in Switzerland asking him "to put in my name as the new president of ISI."

First of all, the trustees wanted a chief executive who was familiar with and dedicated to ISI's mission. They also desired a good manager, an effective fund-raiser, a persuasive recruiter of ISI alumni and friends, and finally an articulate public spokesman who would promote "ISI's image, reputation and credibility as an organization vital to the preservation of our free society." It was natural that they looked inward, seeking a successor who understood the special educational role of the Institute in the conservative movement. After "considerable discussion" of the subcommittee's report, the evaluation committee unanimously recommended that Robert R. Reilly "be employed as ISI senior vice president and succeed E. Victor Milione as President of the Intercollegiate Studies Institute."[22]

At its October 1987 meeting, the full board of trustees approved the committee's recommendation (effective the following June), making Robert Reilly ISI's fourth president, following William F. Buckley Jr., Frank Chodorov, and Milione. The outgoing president described Bob Reilly as "one of the most talented individuals I have known during my many years with ISI. I am convinced that Bob will usher in a new era of growth and achievement as president."[23]

20. Author's interview with T. Kenneth Cribb, Jr., February 26, 2001.
21. Author's telephone interview with John Lulves, June 11, 2002.
22. Report of the Evaluation Committee: 21.
23. E. Victor Milione to John Howard, April 4, 1988, ISI Archives.

In Reilly, the board of trustees picked a 1968 graduate of Georgetown University who had served in the army for two years and then had been a professional actor in Baltimore and elsewhere on the East coast before deciding in 1973 that he wanted to work full-time in "the world of ideas." He first learned of ISI through his father, a friend of Henry Regnery who had given his son, as a Georgetown undergraduate, a subscription to *The Intercollegiate Review*. At Georgetown, Reilly met Bob Schadler, who invited him to an ISI summer school led by Will Herberg and Gerhart Niemeyer that "had a profound impact" on [me].[24]

Even more affecting was Bob Reilly's first meeting—in the summer of 1973—with Vic Milione at ISI headquarters. "I felt," recalls Reilly, "as though we had resumed a conversation we had been having all my life. There was an astonishing familiarity." What impressed the young conservative intellectual the most about Milione was his "profoundly religious" view of the world. "As much as Vic was for the freedom market," remembers Reilly, "he always saw its limits."[25] In the fall of 1973, Reilly became ISI's Western director in Claremont, California, where for the next four years he coordinated lectures, seminars, summer schools, and fund-raising, and acquired an M.A. in political philosophy at Claremont Graduate School. Through "The Role of Business in Society" schools, Reilly and his predecessor Charles Heatherly were able to "reeducate" dozens of secondary teachers in the West—including almost the entire roster of social studies high school teachers in Colorado. When Ken Cribb left ISI to go to law school, Milione asked Bob Reilly to take Cribb's place as national director in Bryn Mawr.

With Ronald Reagan's election as president in November 1980, Reilly moved to Washington, D.C., along with many other motivated conservatives, and for the next seven years he worked for the U.S. Information Agency, in the White House as a special assistant to the president for public liaison, and beginning in 1985, as senior advisor for public diplomacy at the U.S. Embassy in Bern, Switzerland. It was at the latter post—

24. Author's interview with Robert Reilly, August 30, 2001.
25. Ibid.

close to the increasing political tremors in Eastern and Central Europe reaching into the Soviet Union—that Bob Reilly's interest in international relations developed into something akin to a religious mission. He took to heart President Reagan's challenge to Soviet leader Gorbachev to tear down the Berlin Wall. And he became ISI president in the spring of 1988 when Reagan traveled to Moscow as "freedom's advocate" to speak to students at Moscow State University and one hundred dissident leaders at the U.S. Embassy.[26]

A New ISI

Reilly saw as his first task the revitalization of ISI ("it had atrophied seriously"), followed by the rebuilding of its stagnant finances. In fundraising, "the best thing I did," says Reilly, "was to 'steal' Spencer Masloff from Paul Weyrich and the Free Congress Foundation and make him the vice president overseeing development."[27] A graduate of American University, Herbert Spencer Masloff, Jr., worked at the National Foundation on Youth and Drugs as a program officer after college, and from there went to the Reagan-Bush Campaign in 1983 where he worked in fundraising and opposition research. After the 1984 election, Masloff joined the Free Congress Foundation as director of marketing and development. He was barely thirty at the time, but he had built an impressive track record at Free Congress—where he rose to vice president—when, in 1989, he moved his young family from Washington to take up the challenge of rebuilding ISI's financial base. Fifteen years later, Masloff remains ISI's highly valued and hard-driving vice president. His colleague John Lulves notes that "what is sometimes missed is that Spencer is a superb strategist, not only about raising donations, but also how to run a non-profit corporation and to develop projects." What is more, "he has a great, and often needed, sense of humor."[28]

The new CEO and the new chief fund-raiser worked hard to broaden

26. See Lou Cannon, *President Reagan: The Role of a Lifetime*, New York, 1991: 786.
27. Ibid.
28. Author's interview with John Lulves, August 25, 2003.

the donor base. In searching for new contributors—and shoring up old ones—Reilly went on the road and stayed there for much of the rest of the year. He discovered considerable interest in a national headquarters, and by late November, could report that he had raised $175,000 for the ISI "house," including $50,000 from the McKenna Foundation, $50,000 from William Regnery, $25,000 from Alex McKenna, and $25,000 from Charles Hoeflich.[29]

The new president was especially receptive to dramatic ideas that would raise ISI's visibility. Edward Lozansky, a one-time Russian dissident, approached Reilly about sponsoring a "freedom school" in Moscow in the summer of 1989. Reilly was captivated by the idea of presenting "the case for a free society in the heart of a totalitarian empire" at Moscow State University, the very school where in the spring of 1988, Reagan had delivered his nationally telecast speech about freedom to the Russian people.[30] In short order, Reilly and Lozansky lined up speakers such as neoconservatives Midge Decter and Norman Podhoretz, Republican Senator Philip Gramm of Texas, former ambassador Frank Shakespeare, and Father Stanley Jaki.

But from the beginning, several trustees were highly skeptical about the Moscow project, asking: Shouldn't ISI, in a time of organizational transition, tend to business at home? Will funding the Moscow conference mean less money for long-standing projects in the U.S.? Estimates of the conference's cost ranged widely from $50,000 to as high as $250,000.[31] Reilly responded that the program "would reap a publicity bonanza for ISI," and he reassured the trustees that he had obtained separate funding for the Moscow program.[32] His reassurances failed, however, when ISI found in the spring of 1989 that it had "a sizeable deficit," due to a sharply increased overhead—caused by higher salaries and travel expenses—the delay in the renewal of a key grant, and the partial loss of another grant. A preliminary estimate set the annual deficit at over

29. Robert R. Reilly to Mrs. Daniel Oliver, November 22, 1988, ISI Archives.
30. Robert R. Reilly to Edwin J. Feulner, April 5, 1989, ISI Archives.
31. See Robert F. Turner to T. Kenneth Cribb, Jr., March 30, 1989, ISI Archives.
32. Reilly to Feulner, April 5, 1989, ISI Archives.

$420,000, nearly one-half of the annual budget. (The actual deficit for 1988-1989 was $267,840.) Casting about for ways to economize, Reilly decided in early March to close the Institute's Western office in Claremont, California, saving an estimated $80,000 annually. But the action greatly upset trustee Harold Severance, who was not consulted although he was a California trustee and had long helped defray the expenses of the Western office.[33]

Seeking to mend fences, Reilly wrote Charles Hoeflich that the large ISI deficit had forced him to make the "painful" but "necessary" decision to shut the Western office which, however, he described as "a temporary measure." As soon as funds allowed, he said, "it is my intention ... to reopen an ISI Western office."[34] Earlier in the year, Reilly had also roiled the normally placid waters of ISI headquarters by clashing with Gregory Wolfe, the brilliant, strong-willed editor of *The Intercollegiate Review*, over the publication of an article by Clyde Wilson. Reilly vetoed its publication, and Wolfe abruptly resigned.

When Bob Reilly insisted on proceeding with plans for the controversial Moscow conference, Henry Regnery felt compelled as chairman of the board of trustees to telephone Reilly and follow up with an unusually blunt letter. At least four other trustees, Regnery wrote, were "strongly opposed" to the proposed Moscow meeting because "we don't have the money, it will divert us from the basic purpose of ISI, and it will require time and attention from you which could better be spent improving our finances." Conceding that cancellation would be "very disappointing" and even embarrassing to Reilly, Regnery said he could see "no alternative," given "the larger purposes of ISI and our present rather critical financial situation."[35]

But despite Regnery's pointed letter and communications from other trustees anxious about ISI's finances, Reilly refused to cancel the Moscow conference. "I intend," he informed Ed Feulner two days before the spring

33. Harold L. Severance to Robert Turner, March 13, 1989, ISI Archives.
34. Robert R. Reilly to Charles H. Hoeflich, March 30, 1989, ISI Archives.
35. Henry Regnery to Robert R. Reilly, March 28, 1989, ISI Archives.

board meeting, "to discuss all aspects of this situation with the board that elected me." After a full discussion, he added, "I will be glad to follow whatever course of action the board might direct."[36]

In fact, a majority of the board had already decided not only to cancel the Moscow meeting but to replace Robert Reilly as ISI president. The man whom many trustees had wanted in the first place—Kenneth Cribb—was now available with Ronald Reagan no longer in the White House. And Cribb had informed Vic Milione, Charles Hoeflich, and other trustees that he was willing, if asked, to assume the responsibility of heading the conservative movement's premier collegiate organization.[37]

An unusually large number of ISI trustees—twenty in all—personally attended the April 7, 1989, board meeting, held at the Union League in Philadelphia (there were also nine proxy votes, including that of chairman Henry Regnery, who could not attend for health reasons). Secretary-treasurer Charles Hoeflich presented a stark financial report that transfixed everyone. He revealed that ISI's liabilities totaled $597,000 (a sum equal to the Institute's entire annual budget just a few years earlier) and was only partially offset by $168,000 in special accounts. The "uncollateralized" liability of $429,000, said Hoeflich, had put the endowment fund "in jeopardy." Overall, summarized ISI's veteran secretary-treasurer, "the effect of the Institute's debt on fundraising is likely to be severe." It was critical, he concluded, to adopt a financial recovery plan.[38]

Robert Reilly responded by presenting the President's report, detailing his programmatic, personnel, and fundraising activities in the last ten months, and explaining that the deficit had risen to an historic high through an unexpected confluence of increased expenses and decreased income. He informed the board that as a result of his and Spencer Masloff's aggressive efforts, new sources of funding had been developed and the

36. Reilly to Feulner, April 5, 1989, ISI Archives.
37. See the letter of Henry Regnery to Charles H. Hoeflich, March 28, 1989, in which Regnery brings up, again, his wish to step down as chairman of the board of trustees. "I had thought that [my successor] was to be Ken Cribb, but if he is to succeed Bob Reilly ... we will need to think of someone else." ISI Archives.
38. Minutes of ISI Board Meeting of Trustees, April 7, 1989: 1-2. ISI Archives.

Institute's financial base had been expanded. He reiterated the "historic opportunity" the Moscow conference offered for ISI and the cause of freedom behind the Iron Curtain. Reilly was fervent and eloquent, but out of sync with the thinking of the majority of trustees who wanted no diversions from ISI's basic mission of educating for liberty in America. Following what the minutes termed a "wide-ranging discussion," Hoeflich offered the following resolution: "The President of ISI, Robert R. Reilly, for whom we all have affection, is invited to resign his position as President."[39]

The trustees decisively rejected a motion to table Hoeflich's no confidence resolution and then narrowly adopted it by a vote of 16 to 13. Reilly immediately resigned, as did trustees Faith Ryan Whittlesey and Alex Conroy, both strong Reilly supporters. Reconvening after lunch, the trustees, upon a motion made by Ed Feulner and seconded by Wayne Valis, elected T. Kenneth Cribb, Jr., as the fifth president of the Institute. Accepting the position, Cribb said it was his intention "to put ISI back on track and to secure the resources for it to prosper." ISI had to grow, he stated, in order "to address the increasingly perilous situation on campus."[40]

When they heard the news, some conservatives were surprised, aware of Ken Cribb's many options on leaving the Reagan administration. He could have become an influential Washington lobbyist, following the lead of fellow ISI alumnus Wayne Valis. He could have joined a prestigious New York or Washington law firm that would have paid him handsomely for his legal skills and his many contacts. Instead, after spending a few months as a senior fellow at The Heritage Foundation recharging his batteries, Ken Cribb became the president of ISI, believing in the power of the right ideas and committed to passing them on to what his mentor Russell Kirk called the rising generation. "What greater calling could there be," he asks, "than to educate young people in the idea of ordered liberty?"[41]

---

39. Ibid: 2.
40. Ibid: 3.
41. Author's interview with T. Kenneth Cribb, Jr., May 8, 2002.

The Reagan Connection

Forty-one-year-old T. Kenneth Cribb, Jr. brought to the ISI presidency a sharp intelligence, super-abundant energy, a quick wit that enlivened meetings, and eight years of top-level managerial experience in the Reagan administration. "Just thinking about Ken Cribb brings a smile to your face," says the Federalist Society's Eugene Meyer.[42] Cribb had been a deputy to Edwin Meese III when he was the counselor to the President and then was counselor to Meese when he was named attorney general. Cribb was at the very center of the Reagan administration because, as one observer commented, "Ed Meese was Ronald Reagan's right hand, and Ken Cribb was Ed Meese's right hand."[43] "Ken was in on everything I did," Meese says of his White House years from 1981-1985; "he was a confidant in the best sense of the word." During those years, Meese was with President Reagan every day, and in his absence Cribb "kept the office going." At Justice, Meese turned over much of the hiring to Cribb, who had, he says, "a very good sense about people." It was Cribb who brought "bright young lawyers" like David McIntosh and Steve Calabresi into the department. "I have not been surprised at all by his remarkable success at ISI," Meese says.[44]

"Ken Cribb and Brad Reynolds were the principal advisers on the selection of William Rehnquist [as Chief Justice] and Antonin Scalia to the Supreme Court," says Calabresi, who worked under Cribb for two years at the Department of Justice and later clerked for Justice Scalia. Cribb and Reynolds had recommended Scalia and Robert Bork as equally qualified for the Warren Burger seat, and the President had chosen Scalia on actuarial grounds, intending Bork for the next vacancy. Reagan also nominated a number of "staunch conservatives" to the lower courts, especially the U.S. Court of Appeals, including Chief Judge Douglas H. Ginsberg, David B. Sentelle, Laurence Hirsch Silberman, and Stephen F. Williams.[45] Again, it was Cribb and Reynolds who played key advisory

42. Author's interview with Eugene Meyer, April 26, 2003.
43. Author's interview with Steve Calabresi, April 26, 2003.
44. Author's interview with Edwin Meese III, April 8, 2003.
45. Author's interview with Steve Calabresi, April 26, 2003.

roles in their selection. "They advised Ed Meese, who advised President Reagan on judicial nominations." Echoing Ed Meese, Calabresi (now a professor at Northwestern Law School) says that Ken Cribb "is an extremely good judge of people. He understands the political maxim, 'Personnel are policy.' He saw how important it was to get movement conservatives into key positions."[46]

Indeed, in all he did, Cribb sought to advance the conservative cause, for as he told the *Washington Post* in a rare 1985 interview, "We're conservatives, not party people." And the man at the top was comfortable with that philosophical attitude. "It's unique," Cribb commented, "that you have a president who's a self-conscious conservative, approving of a body of thought and seeking policy that proceeds from that thought."[47]

In early 1987, as part of a White House reorganization following Chief of Staff Donald Regan's abrupt departure because of the Iran-Contra affair, Ken Cribb became (with new Chief of Staff Howard Baker's strong approval) assistant to the president for domestic affairs. Bill Buckley publicly (and correctly) predicted that the new White House assistant would serve Reagan "diligently, honorably, and ... inspiringly."[48] In welcoming Cribb back, President Reagan wrote to him, "You're no stranger to tough assignments, so I wasn't in the least surprised that you agreed to come back.... Your contributions to this Administration have been inestimable, and I know I'm going to owe you an even larger debt of gratitude before we're done."[49]

Cribb served as Reagan's top domestic adviser until the fall of 1988, paralleling Martin Anderson, who held the same post in the first two years. At a time when the president's approval ratings had sagged as a result of Iran-Contra and some Democratic partisans were even pushing impeachment, Cribb helped Baker and other Reagan advisers to get on with business and prepare the way for Ronald Reagan's concluding push to win the Cold War and consign communism to the dustbin of history.

46. Ibid.
47. Sidney Blumenthal, "Staying Power: Cadres for the Right Train for the Future," *Washington Post,* September 22, 1985.
48. William F. Buckley, Jr., "Baker's Mission," *National Review,* April 10, 1987: 61.
49. Letter of Ronald Reagan to T. Kenneth Cribb, Jr., June 29, 1987.

More Than An Adviser

Cribb was more than a key policy adviser to the president. He was also responsible for managing four White House units—the Office of Policy Development, the Office of Cabinet Affairs, the Office of Public Liaison, and the Office of Welfare Reform. When barely out of law school, the thirty-one-year-old Cribb had displayed impressive managerial skills as deputy chief counsel of the 1980 Reagan-Bush campaign and then supervisor of thirty of President-elect Reagan's transition teams. In all these circumstances, Cribb paid particular attention to promising young conservatives. "All these talented people who are in their mid-thirties now," Cribb said in the mid-1980s about the young conservatives serving in various posts in the administration, "will come back again in the future in more elevated positions."[50]

While observing the flow of decision-making from the White House, Cribb had concluded that "it was late in the game then for any consideration of ideas—the correlation of forces was already mostly decided." The experience led him to realize "how important is intellectual work on the minds of those between nineteen and twenty-five." He agreed to become ISI president, he later explained, because "politics is a surface phenomenon. Below the surface, we have to renew in each new generation the legacy of Western liberty."[51] Such an analysis reflected Cribb's experience as national director of ISI and his strong sense of the Institute's mission and its many possibilities in an era filled with challenge and change.

Eugene Meyer, the longtime director of the Federalist Society who has known and worked with Ken Cribb since the early 1980s, believes that Cribb "took on ISI" for several reasons. First was his deep loyalty to the organization—"he has been an ISIer since he was a freshman at W&L." He also understood, says Meyer, that "youth is all-important to building a movement, and he discovered in the Reagan administration how diffi-

50. Author's interview with T. Kenneth Cribb, Jr., May 8, 2002.
51. T. Kenneth Cribb, "The Reagan Legacy," Springfield, Virginia, 1992.

cult it is to find good young people." Finally there was a sense of "payback to Russell Kirk and others" who had taught him the first principles of conservatism—"he wanted to pass on what they had given him."[52]

Executive Vice President Phillip Truluck of The Heritage Foundation confirms Ken Cribb's life-long involvement with conservatism, pointing out, for example, that when Cribb was a Heritage intern in the summer of 1978, following his first year in law school, he worked closely with Heritage's Willa Johnson on the Resource Bank, a national network of conservative groups and individuals. The contacts that Cribb had made as ISI national director were "extremely useful" to Heritage in expanding the Resource Bank.[53] And when Cribb was in the White House, recalls Truluck, "you knew you had a friend. Ken was always working for the right ideas, even if he didn't always prevail. And his loyalty to Ronald Reagan was unwavering." Of his appointment as president of the Institute, Truluck says, "He was the right person at the right time. He had a great love for ISI. For him, it was like going home."[54]

That President Reagan was well aware of Ken Cribb's signal contributions to the conservative movement and his administration was demonstrated at Cribb's White House farewell on September 8, 1988. Three generations of Cribbs gathered in the Oval Office for a group photo with the president and then adjourned to the Roosevelt Room for a celebratory lunch. Standing next to his longtime aide, Reagan said (without relying on 4X6 note cards): "We're here to say goodbye to someone to whom we are deeply indebted, someone who has served nobly and above and beyond the call of duty—Ken Cribb. We know that where you're going you are going to continue to be of service to the public and to the things we believe in."[55]

In his brief but heartfelt response, Cribb summed up Reagan's uniqueness as a political leader: "What distinguishes the President," he said, "from the generality of humanity and from every other politician I know

---

52. Francis A. Clines, "Two Right Hands for the President," *New York Times,* December 9, 1983.

53. Author's interview with T. Kenneth Cribb, Jr., May 8, 2002.

54. Author's interview with Eugene Meyer, April 26, 2003.

55. Author's interview with Phillip Truluck, April 16, 2003.

is that he always asks first the question that other politicians never ask at all—'What is the proper role of government?'" His unequivocal answer to that essential question, Cribb said, "has led to less intrusiveness of government at home and that's brought with it prosperity," and "has led to strength abroad and that's brought with it peace."[56]

The departing presidential adviser noted that the debate about the government's proper role and its meaning for the future "is just starting," and he hoped to contribute to the debate "starting Monday." But, he emphasized, looking at Reagan, "the proudest thing in my life is the eight years I have been at your side." To which the president said simply, "We've been proud to have you."[57]

President Reagan summed up Cribb's achievements in a farewell letter:

Without your untiring efforts, loyalty, and professionalism, day in and day out, we could not have achieved as much as we did.

As Assistant to the President for Domestic Affairs, you have many accomplishments you can cite. One of the most important has been your contribution to changing the focus of the debate regarding the proper role of the judiciary in our constitutional system of government. In the area of crime, America's streets and homes are safer today than they were when we came into office. In the war on drugs, we're beginning to turn the tide. And we've managed to emphasize anew both the central importance of the family and the need to protect the unalienable right to life of the innocent unborn if we are to survive and prosper as a Nation.... As you move on to your new responsibilities, you'll be carrying on the fight for conservative principles.[58]

A New Chairman

The prospects for ISI growth turned brighter at the April 1989 board meeting when Ed Feulner, who had led The Heritage Foundation onto the top rung of Washington think tanks, was elected board of trustees chairman, following the reading of Henry Regnery's letter of resignation for reasons of health. Louise Oliver, at this, her first trustee meeting, was

56. Ibid.
57. Remarks by Ronald Reagan at the White House farewell to T. Kenneth Cribb, Jr., September 8, 1988.
58. Letter of Ronald Reagan to T. Kenneth Cribb, Jr., September 29, 1988.

elected vice chairman in recognition of her widespread connections and her contagious enthusiasm. The board took immediate steps to involve the trustees in fund-raising by setting up the first ever Finance Committee, with T. William Boxx of the McKenna Foundation as chairman. Anxious to prevent any enduring ill-feeling, the trustees expressed their gratitude to Robert Reilly "for his service to the Institute" and wished him success in the future. He was, beyond debate, an ISI "alum" of long and honorable standing.[59]

Upon adjournment, the board was confident it had made the right decision in selecting Ken Cribb as the Institute's new head, but no one denied that he faced a host of organizational and financial problems. The period following the stepping down of the founding generation is usually the most difficult and telling in the life of any institution. E. Victor Milione had been "Mr. ISI" for three-and-a-half decades. Could the Institute survive the retirement of a leader so closely identified with it and its mission? Was ISI a cult of personality or an institution of ideas?

There was also the broader philosophical question: What did ISI have to say to the post-Cold War generation? The Institute was a Cold War baby, born at a time when communism abroad and collectivism at home presented a clear and present danger to America and the West. For more than thirty years, the major threat to America and its liberties had been from without. Now even liberals like Arthur Schlesinger Jr. admitted that the greater threat came from within, in the undeniable fraying of American culture leading to a "disuniting of America."[60] But would ISI's prudential message of ordered liberty resonate with rootless students and professors in a post-Communist, post-modernist world, where, paradoxically, neo-Marxism was still taught on many campuses?

And what was ISI's true role in the American conservative movement? Ken Cribb was convinced that full integration of ISI into the movement would greatly enhance fund-raising and enable the Institute to of-

59. Author's interview with T. Kenneth Cribb, Jr., May 8, 2002.
60. See Arthur M. Schlesinger, Jr., *The Disuniting of America,* Knoxville, Tennessee, 1991.

fer a conservative educational alternative to thousands of additional students and professors. But the one-time White House adviser also saw an essential philosophical role for ISI within American conservatism. As the conservative movement became more politically powerful, there was the possibility, even the likelihood, that politics and public policy might crowd out principle. Means might be allowed, too often, to trump ends. It was the solemn duty of institutions like ISI to keep reminding conservatives, especially those laboring in Washington, of the permanent things.

CHAPTER VIII

The Best and the Brightest

ISI cannot stray, can't decompose; can only grow stronger, even as the government, under the shattering force of ISI's irradiations, grows weaker.

William F. Buckley Jr.[1]

ANY TALK ABOUT AN EXPANDED ROLE for ISI in the American academy or the conservative movement was no more than just that unless the Institute was able to break through the $1 million a year budget ceiling where it had been stymied for the past decade. Vic Milione had successfully sold ISI to far-sighted patriots like Henry Salvatori, Richard Scaife, and F. M. Kirby, who were already sympathetic to its mission, but Ken Cribb perceived that the ISI program required new packaging to attract new donors. As a former ISI student leader, national director, and long-time board member, observed a co-worker, Cribb was uniquely qualified to "transform the public image of ISI while maintaining intact its mission, programs, and proud history."[2] Only someone like ISI's new presi-

1. Remarks by William F. Buckley Jr. at ISI's 40th Anniversary Celebration, October 14, 1993, Washington, D.C., ISI Archives.
2. Christopher Long to Lee Edwards, September 17, 2002.

dent, with the wide contacts accumulated during eight years in the Reagan administration and the deep understanding of conservatism gained through an association with Russell Kirk and other giants of the movement, could have reshaped the organization without alienating its base.

Cribb and his colleagues resolved to renew ISI through a three-year "Campaign for Leadership," designed to expand the campus programs and double the annual budget. In remarkably short order, the Institute started a new national student newspaper, challenged political correctness and multiculturalism on such campuses as Stanford and Yale, committed itself to book publishing, and undertook a serious search for a building to house its national headquarters.

And it set about putting its finances in order. Within the first six months, accounts payable and loans payable were sharply reduced, so that the $150,000 cash flow shortfall for the period ending September 30 was cut by two-thirds. Substantial increases in contributions were obtained from the J. Howard Pew Freedom Trust, the Liberty Fund, the Phillip M. McKenna Foundation, and the Roe Foundation. Fund-raising ran $348,000 ahead of the previous year, thanks to the effective partnership of Ken Cribb and Spencer Masloff, and to "the largest single contribution" (excluding bequests) in ISI's history—a one-year grant of $150,000 from the Sarah Scaife Foundation. By October, ISI had raised half of its projected $1.36 million budget for the 1989-1990 fiscal year. Conceding that the budget was an "ambitious one" (it was the largest ever), Cribb said with justifiable satisfaction, "We are on target."[3]

Shortly thereafter, in his first published article as ISI president, Cribb analyzed the current state of the American academy and offered an "appropriate response" by the Institute and the conservative movement, deliberately linking the two. The long-standing problem of relativism "still stalked the corridors of the academy," Ken Cribb wrote in *The Intercollegiate Review.* He noted that Stanford University had decided to replace its

3. T. Kenneth Cribb, Jr. to Charles H. Hoeflich, May 18, 1989; T. William Boxx to Richard V. Allen, August 9, 1989; generic Cribb letter to trustees, October 7, 1989, ISI Archives.

required course on Western culture with a new course featuring "works by women and minorities and stressing non-Western accomplishments."[4] The Stanford shift symbolized relativism's unwavering opposition to "any notion of standards that proceed from a moral order and that form the basis of right conduct." Cribb described another phenomenon at work on the campus—the reappearance of "the Sixties-style hard Left radical, this time with the greying sideburns of the tenured professor." One of the more disturbing practices of this new/old hard Left was "its heavy-handed attempt to silence non-conforming opinion."[5]

Fortunately, Cribb said, there was a vehicle that could effectively respond to "the nihilism of the militant Left"—the American conservative movement, which had come into being "to strengthen the faltering institutions of the West against the hostile tides of the mid-twentieth century." For thirty years, the movement had concentrated on the winning of political battles culminating in the historic election of Ronald Reagan in 1980. Now, Cribb suggested, conservatives had to mount a "counteroffensive on that last leftist redoubt, the college campus."[6]

ISI's president outlined six factors enabling conservatism to contest the Left on its own turf, beginning with "a generation of young faculty members"—many of them nurtured by the ISI program—"who are conservative or open to conservatism." The political prominence of conservatism "has conferred a new respectability upon conservative thought within the academy." Liberalism had failed so miserably in the political realm that "the very word liberal has become an epithet." Students of every generation resist authority, and the authorities on many of today's campuses were the professors who struck only "politically correct" poses and the deans who "herd freshmen into required political indoctrination courses." A "conservative intellectual infrastructure" now existed, Cribb said, that was only a dream thirty years earlier. Finally, argued ISI's presi-

4. T. Kenneth Cribb, Jr., "Conservatism and the American Academy: Prospects for the 1990s," *The Intercollegiate Review,* Vol. 25 No. 2, Spring 1990: 24.

5. Ibid: 26.

6. Ibid: 29.

dent, there was the question of who had the superior ideas. The Left offered "turgid Marxist tracts," politically correct jargon, and false compassion that was only "thinly disguised lust for power in the people's name—but without the people's participation."[7]

In contrast, conservatives offered the inquiring student the rich and truly diverse traditions of the West. In *The Roots of American Order,* Cribb pointed out, Russell Kirk offered "a tale of five cities"—Jerusalem, with its prophets of monotheism and the Incarnation; Athens, the birthplace of democracy and philosophy; Rome and its republican fathers of the rule of law; London, the mother of parliaments; and Philadelphia, with its revolutionary idea that "good government could be preserved from the eventual corruption of power, by dividing power against itself." Cribb ended his analysis with a rhetorical flourish, offering to place the student "whose life of the mind is before him" on the shoulders of the giants of the West so that he "will see farther than any of us."[8]

The Cribb Way

The *IR* article set the tone of the Cribb administration, combining shrewd analysis and philosophical insight, concerned with the problems of the present but looking to the past to help solve them, and emphasizing that ISI was not only in but an integral part of the conservative movement.

Energized by its new leadership, ISI proceeded to provide its 33,000 members, including some ten thousand faculty, with a judicious mix of publications, lectures, seminars, and other programs. Two issues of *The Intercollegiate Review* and four issues of *Modern Age* were published in the 1989-1990 school year; 275,000 reprints of articles from the *Review* were distributed, most of them for classroom use by professors; 188 lectures on campus were sponsored, reaching an estimated audience of 20,000; some five hundred schools were served by campus representatives, faculty associates, and associated clubs; 140 college libraries participated in ISI's book program; and ten Weaver Fellowships were awarded. Two hundred stu-

7. Ibid: 29-30.
8. Ibid.

dent leaders received "advanced intellectual training" at small-group week-end seminars and summer schools. "Where many other groups merely spoon-feed their members the facts that support the campaign of the day," commented undergraduate Dennis Ebersole of Ohio State University, "ISI succeeds in educating its members for a lifetime of leadership."[9]

The fall 1990 issue of *The Intercollegiate Review* presented a special section on education with articles by Lynne V. Cheney, chairman of the National Endowment for the Humanities; Michael E. Allsopp and Michael W. Sundermeier, both professors at Creighton University; and John Silber, president of Boston University. Chairman Cheney suggested that the American academy could be "recovered" if, among other things, the study of history and literature were more encouraged and if the importance of the teaching mission was reaffirmed. Professors Allsop and Sundermeier argued that a return to John Henry Newman's idea of a university would help colleges become "centers of learning" again rather than places of "subjective and disconnected discussion of values, trends and issues." President Silber referred to "a new barbarism" that was "more difficult to iden-tify, easier to fall in with inadvertently," because Martin Heidegger and Paul De Man were far subtler and "more effective in undermining serious thought" than cruder sorts like Huey Long.[10]

ISI launched in the spring of 1991 one of its most ambitious publi-cations, *CAMPUS: America's Student Newspaper*, the only national news-paper written and edited entirely by college students. *CAMPUS* was the brainchild of Ken Cribb, who recognized the need to publicly challenge political correctness and multiculturalism and at the same time increase ISI membership and influence. The Institute had not published the *ISI Campus Report* from 1982 through 1989, for lack of money, and it needed to get back into the student publication field. In its maiden issue, co-

9. As quoted in letter of T. Kenneth Cribb, Jr. to Thomas M. Ferguson, December 14, 1993, ISI Archives.

10. Lynne V. Cheney, "The Recovery of the American Academy," Michael E. Allsopp and Michael W. Sundermeier, "Newman's Idea of a University," John Silber, "Free Speech and the Academy," *The Intercollegiate Review*, Vol. 26, No. 1, Fall 1990: 23-24, 30, 40.

edited by Stefan Norman of Vassar College and John-Peter Pham of the University of Chicago, *CAMPUS* examined the effectiveness of affirmative action, the treatment of Asian-Americans on campus, and how to find a Washington internship.

In an editorial titled, "Behind the Ivy Curtain," the editors criticized American colleges like Tufts and Vassar for adopting speech codes that violated academic freedom and the First Amendment while students in China and other totalitarian countries were "throwing themselves in front of tanks to promote liberty." Vassar's Jonathan D. Karl reported that according to a Gallup Poll, "twenty-three percent of college seniors" were unable to distinguish between Karl Marx and the U.S. Constitution. A ready corrective, said Karl, was a model core of courses suggested by *50 Hours: A Core Curriculum for College Students,* published by the National Endowment for the Humanities.[11]

With a circulation of 100,000 (the paper was mailed directly to ISI members and also distributed in bulk on hundreds of campuses), *CAMPUS* was "essential to the jump-starting of ISI" in the early 1990s, says Christopher Long, the newspaper's executive publisher, who had helped publish George Washington University's *Sentinel.*[12] Three Vassar students were especially helpful in launching *CAMPUS*: Marc Thiessen, later Senator Jesse Helms' press secretary on the Senate Foreign Relations Committee; Jonathan Karl, CNN's future White House correspondent; and Stefan Norman.

In every way possible, wrote Ken Cribb to a trustee, ISI was reaching out to educate the young men and women who would "constitute the mainstream leadership of American society in the next century."[13] No longer satisfied with preserving an intellectual remnant, as Frank Chodorov had proposed in his founding essay, ISI now sought to forge a counter-establishment within the realm of American higher education that was

---

11. "Behind the Ivy Curtain," Jonathan D. Karl, "Gallup Poll Finds College Students Culturally Illiterate," *Campus,* Volume 1 Number 1, Spring 1990: 9,3.
12. Christopher Long to Lee Edwards, September 27, 2002.
13. Ibid.

committed to the preservation of Western civilization. With John Lulves providing day-to-day financial and administrative oversight, and Spencer Masloff working miracles as ISI's chief fundraiser, Cribb increasingly utilized the talents of two young men, Christopher Long, who would become vice president for programs, and Jeffrey Nelson, who would serve as vice president for publications.

Long, who served brilliantly as ISI's national director in the first half of the 1990s, was a political activist at George Washington University and then George Mason University from 1984-1988 where he never saw ISI "on my radar screen." Weaver Fellow Christopher Manion—working on Capitol Hill for Senator Jesse Helms of North Carolina—was one of the first to mention ISI to Long at a "soiree" held in "The Right House," the name that Long and several other young conservatives gave to the Georgetown townhouse they shared. At an out-of-town event marking the anniversary of the Sharon Statement (the 1960 mission statement of Young Americans for Freedom), the young activist was taken aside by Ken Cribb, who attempted to recruit him to help "re-energize" ISI. Long declined, but Cribb kept in touch.

Shortly thereafter, Chris Long started working for The Heritage Foundation, directing its New Majority Project, and declared himself "very happy" to his bosses and his new bride Sheila.[14] "I can't imagine now," Long says, "how I convinced myself to give up a secure, prestigious post at the largest and most powerful think tank in the world to take up camp with a nearly bankrupt organization." Ken Cribb, he admits, was a "very compelling" salesman. Long still remembers his first impression of the Institute's Bryn Mawr headquarters—a "rabbit's warren of offices cluttered with decades of accumulated publications and paper." Ken Cribb had talked to the young conservative about the need to "jump-start" ISI. "One could argue," Long remarked years later, "that it would have been far easier to start from scratch."[15] But that was not the ISI way—patrimony, even if somewhat tattered and frayed at the edges, would be preserved.

14. Ibid.
15. Ibid.

"Chris Long was the catalyst of ISI's on-campus program growth in the early 1990s," observed Jeff Nelson. "Chris had energy, enthusiasm, and ambitious goals. He was committed to Ken Cribb's dream of rebuilding ISI into a one-stop resource for college students interested in the ideas of liberty, and he also shared Ken's tactical mind." Long and the rest of the young staff sought to repeat, Nelson said, "what a previous generation of ISI staff, students, and faculty accomplished in the 1960s: a counterrevolution on campus."[16]

For his part, Nelson had much in common with his hero and mentor, Russell Kirk: an affection for the school rooms and railroad tracks of Plymouth, Michigan (a Detroit suburb where both grew up), an abiding respect for the permanent things, and a love for his second daughter Cecilia, whom Nelson married in 1993. (Cecilia had her own ISI legacy that included a 1990 Weaver Fellowship to attend graduate school in St. Andrews University, Scotland.) Nelson attended the Jesuit-run University of Detroit and still remembers a class on "Marxism and Christianity" in which his priest-professor kept noting the similarities between the two "faiths" and Nelson kept bringing up the dissimilarities. One day the exasperated Jesuit remarked to the recalcitrant sophomore, "Please come see me in my office. I'm worried about your politics."

Two days later, Nelson was in the office of another professor, the economist Harry C. Veryser, Jr., a longtime ISI member. When Nelson informed Veryser, whose name he had seen in a Reagan-Bush political newsletter, that he wanted to start a conservative club at the University, the professor got up and closed his office door. "Will you be our faculty adviser?" Nelson asked. "Yes," replied Veryser, a layman, "but we need to agree on one thing—conservatism is about saving souls."[17] This, according to Nelson, was his "Damascus moment." Within a span of forty-eight hours he had encountered a priest troubled about his politics and an economist worried about his soul.

Veryser then introduced Nelson to the works of Thomas Aquinas,

16. Author's interview with Jeffrey O. Nelson, March 26, 2003.
17. Ibid.

G. K. Chesterton, John Henry Newman, F. A. Hayek, and Ludwig von Mises, and, personally, to Russell Kirk. Nelson attended ISI Piety Hill seminars as a Detroit student, learning from ISI stalwarts such as Peter Stanlis, Stephen Tonsor, Gerhart Niemeyer, and Claes Ryn and developing "my conservative consciousness." A pivotal opportunity came in the winter of 1986-1987, when Nelson was invited to become Kirk's research assistant and spent long hours in the working library of conservatism's first man of letters.

Nelson's interests were not, however, solely literary. In Michigan he ran key elements of statewide gubernatorial and U.S. senate races, serving on Michigan's Republican Central Committee under Spencer Abraham, and was elected a delegate to the 1988 Republican National Convention. And yet, Nelson recalled, the political life left him feeling incomplete. He knew from his reading and his ISI experiences that "ideas precede policy." And so he decided to go back to school, leaving a congressional campaign in North Carolina to attend Yale University and receive his Masters degree in religion. (He is currently in the final stages of his Ph.D. dissertation work at the University of Edinburgh, Scotland.)

After Yale, he taught economics at Walsh College in Michigan, and later that year became the Acton Institute's first academic director. It was during this period that he enjoyed another tour as a Kirk assistant in the summer of 1989, rooming with a future ISI editor, Christopher Briggs. His understanding of conservatism and Catholicism was also deepened in 1991 through a summer spent in Spain with ISI favorite and philosophy professor Frederick D. Wilhelmsen, and a year later a trip to Scotland with the Kirk clan. Traveling with Kirk and Wilhelmsen left an indelible mark upon Nelson. "These two legendary figures," Nelson recalls, "fired my imagination. They were realists *and* they were romantics. They were true individualists, liberty lovers, *and* champions of order. Neither had a positivist bone in their bodies." So when John Lulves invited Jeff Nelson in October of 1991 to become the Institute's director of publications, he readily accepted, thinking, however, it would be for only two years, and then he would return to Michigan and the world of politics. But Nelson soon discovered that ISI was the perfect place for him and action intellectuals like him—"a nexus of the intellectual and the political, where every day an employee has one foot in the world of business and affairs and another in the world of academe and ideas."[18]

Right from the start, Nelson did "an amazing job," says Chris Long, of enlivening ISI publications and getting *The Intercollegiate Review, Modern Age,* and *The Political Science Reviewer* back on a regular publication schedule, while his creation of the ISI Books imprint "brought an enormous amount of respect to the organization."[19] Nelson's appreciation for the uniqueness of ISI matured through the years. He came to understand how much the organization reflected the ideas and the imaginations of three "generous, warm, and wonderful men—Vic Milione, John Lulves, and Ken Cribb. They incarnate the spirit of ISI."[20]

The Best and Brightest

Without the several hundred faculty representatives already in place, ISI would not have been able to expand its campus programs as quickly as it did in the first years of the Cribb administration. And it was primarily John Lulves and James Gaston (then the Institute's Eastern director, now director of the humanities and Catholic culture program at Franciscan University of Steubenville) who through their personal relationships "kept the [faculty] involved even when there was little money for lectures and only sporadic publishing of the journals." Another key person in the transition was Hillsdale graduate Edward V. Giles, who almost single-handedly brought ISI into the technological world, setting up the servers, computers, and software that, for example, enabled *CAMPUS* and other journals to appear. Without Giles' assistance, Christopher Long says, "we would not have been able to track and service the thousands of new members and supporters that began to flood in."[21]

18. Ibid.
19. Christopher Long to Lee Edwards, September 17, 2002.
20. Author's interview with Jeffrey O. Nelson, March 26, 2003.
21. Long to Edwards, September 17, 2002.

Giles was a former assistant to Russell Kirk and a key member of the "Michigan diaspora" filling the ISI office at 14 S. Bryn Mawr Ave. Nelson remembers Giles' pivotal contribution: "Ed combined literary interest and sophistication with a childlike curiosity in and zeal for gadgets. Ken's coming to ISI corresponded directly with the information boom and the rise of networks, software, and desktop publishing. Ed brought the traditional ISI program into the new digital world, with sensitivity and skill because he appreciated both." Giles also served as managing editor of *Modern Age* and *The Intercollegiate Review.* "He was, like all of us at the time," Nelson recalled, "strong-willed and determined, but he kept it light. None of us will forget those years when Ed would stand near the door at the end of the day and salute each departing employee with an index finger pointed at them while saying wryly: 'Thanks for coming in today—you made all the difference.'"[22]

Other staffers of the period included membership director Ann (Douglas) Ritter (now re-united with her old ISI boss, Chris Long, at Foster Friess & Associates); lecture director Robert Erwin (now a marketing specialist at Unisys); Eastern director Stephen Krason (today director of the political science program at Franciscan University of Steubenville and founder of the Society of Catholic Social Scientists), conference director Mitch Muncy (now editor-in-chief of Spence Publishing), and conference director Stanley K. Ridgley, who would later become director of ISI's Collegiate Network.

ISI's renewed educational mission influenced rising young scholars like Bradley Birzer—now an associate professor of political history at Hillsdale College—who recalls that he was on a trans-Atlantic flight in December 1991 when he read the latest issue of *The Intercollegiate Review* that contained a symposium on cultural conservatism. "I'd never heard of or thought about cultural conservatism before," Birzer admits. "That issue [of IR] made me realize that markets were relatively unimportant if the citizenry lacked virtue."[23] John J. Miller (today *National Review's*

22. Author's interview with Jeffrey O. Nelson, March 26, 2003.
23. From Bradley Birzer's response to the author's ISI questionnaire, July 2001.

national political reporter) learned about ISI while writing for the conservative *Michigan Review* as a University of Michigan undergraduate. In the summer of 1990 he attended a seminar on Edmund Burke at Russell Kirk's home in Mecosta. "I met a legendary conservative mind," Miller remembers, "sat in his library, listened to his ghost stories, and went on a walk with him. I was already interested in [Russell Kirk] and his work, but that visit cemented an allegiance that I'm sure will be lifelong."[24]

In May 1990, one year after he assumed the presidency of ISI, Cribb proudly reported to Ralph W. Husted and other trustees that total revenues for 1989-1990 had reached $1.42 million, up from $932,855 the preceding year—the Institute had finally broken through the $1 million ceiling. Contributions were up 63 percent, "our best year ever."[25] The national headquarters fund increased by 64 percent to $243,000. The operating surplus for the year was $161,797, helping to reduce over half of the deficit from the previous year.

Enthusiastic approval of the new ISI administration came from one of the Institute's oldest supporters when Henry Salvatori pledged $1 million to endow the ISI Salvatori Center for American Founding Studies. In years when the endowment interest permits, a distinguished panel selectes the "person who has made the greatest contribution during the year in furtherance of American founding principles." The awardee receives a $25,000 prize and delivers the Salvatori Lecture at "a suitable banquet." The first honoree was Lynne Cheney, chairman of the National Endowment for the Humanities. The second honoree was Russell Kirk, followed in succeeding years by Supreme Court Associate Justice Antonin Scalia, historian Forrest McDonald, and author-jurist Robert Bork. In addition, two Salvatori Fellowships of $10,000 each are awarded to graduate students who intend to teach in the field of the American founding. The remainder of the annual income goes toward an enhanced version of the Salvatori Lecture series on campus. Borrowing from his former boss Ronald Reagan (who often remarked that it was "amazing"

24. From John J. Miller's response to the author's ISI questionnaire, July 20, 2001.
25. T. Kenneth Cribb, Jr. to Ralph W. Husted, May 3, 1990, ISI Archives.

how much you could accomplish if you didn't care who got the credit)
Cribb readily acknowledged that Vic Milione had been of "indispensable
help" in obtaining the Salvatori donation.[26]

Other timely support came from the John M. Olin Foundation, which
approved a $48,000 grant for a national lecture series on "the politicization
of the academy" by such scholars as Charles Sykes (author of *Profscam:
Professors and the Demise of Higher Education*); and from the Liberty Fund,
which provided $100,000 for a series of student colloquia and a full-time
conference director. Olin funding for ISI and other organizations, Cribb
said, helped create "a conservative intellectual infrastructure ... that was
but a dream in 1964."[27]

The Liberty Fund grant enabled the Institute to co-sponsor four small
group student colloquia each academic year, bringing together sixteen "of
our brightest undergraduates for three days of intensive discussion and
reflection" on the preservation of individual liberty and a free society.[28]
Faculty for the initial colloquia included James Gwartney, Charles Kesler,
and M. Stanton Evans. Among the colloquia themes were "The Moral
Basis of a Free Market," "Freedom and the Law," and "A Generation of the
Intellectual Right." In addition to the undergraduate colloquia, an annual
Liberty Fund colloquium for former Weaver Fellows was established; the
second Weaver meeting focused on the writings of Richard Weaver. According to coordinator Stan Ridgley, "participants have called the colloquia the most intellectually enriching experience of their college careers."[29]

From its earliest days, the Institute had wanted to educate young
men and women about basic American values and institutions even *before* they arrived on campus—particularly at the prep schools that produced so many of the nation's leaders—but it never had the funds. In his
two years with Americans for the Competitive Enterprise System, Vic

26. T. Kenneth Cribb, Jr. to Ralph W. Husted, July 6, 1990, ISI Archives.
27. "Funding the Right: Olin provides foundation for conservative infrastructure,"
Texas Observer, September 20, 1991: 8.
28. See Stanley K. Ridgley's report, "ISI Conference Program," to the ISI Board of
Trustees Meeting, March 5, 1993, ISI Archives.
29. Ibid.

Milione had often lectured at high schools in the Philadelphia area about the fundamentals of a free society and knew how receptive young minds could be to such ideas. Now in the early 1990s, through the generous support of the Allegheny Foundation, the Institute created the ISI Preparatory School Lecture Program, bringing speakers like Dinesh D'Souza, Russell Kirk, former navy secretary John Lehman, former education secretary William J. Bennett, English philosopher Roger Scruton, and Amherst professor Hadley Arkes to prep schools, big and small.

The articulate, quick-witted D'Souza received a standing ovation from one thousand students at Phillips Exeter Academy, where he dissected the many inconsistencies of multiculturalism. Administrators of the Desert Christian School were so impressed with Kirk's lecture on "The Roots of American Order" that they adopted the work as one of their textbooks. And John Lehman spoke with such eloquence at the Kent School about "The Role of Defense in a Free Society" that his lecture was extended one hour for student questions, and the headmaster later remarked that Lehman was "absolutely spectacular."[30] Former Weaver Fellow George Michos was an early director of the prep school effort. He organized yearly lecture series with titles as "Multiculturalism and American Society" that featured such speakers as *New Criterion* editor Hilton Kramer, philosophy professor Christina Hoff Sommers, and economist Walter Williams. From the program's inception, the Institute scheduled about fifty lectures each academic year, with an average lecture attendance of one hundred and eighty.

The Fourth Generation

Through all these programs (campus representatives and faculty associates, regional leadership conferences, student colloquia, prep school lectures, the Weaver Fellowships) ISI worked to identify and nurture a growing body of the students with an allegiance to the ideals of America and the West—"a fourth generation," in the words of Christopher Long, that would one day assume "positions of leadership in the conservative move-

30. As quoted in the program highlights of the ISI Preparatory School Lecture Program, Minutes of the ISI Board of Trustees meeting, October 14, 1993.

ment and the world of affairs."[31]

Increased income helped ISI to boost its membership in March 1991 to 36,031, the highest in the Institute's thirty-eight-year history. Part of the increase was caused by the negative reaction to "political correctness" on the campus (documented by Dinesh D'Souza and others) and part by the Persian Gulf War that produced "a wave of patriotism" that rolled "across the American campus." Christopher Long suggested that the 1990-1991 academic year "marked a watershed in the climate on the modern American university campus." As evidence he cited a call-in poll in the March 1991 issue of the liberal national collegiate newspaper, *U,* which reported that 71 percent of students did not support affirmative action. Long also noted that rather than opposing the Gulf War, as "liberal pundits" had predicted, many students hung American flags from the windows of their dormitories.[32]

The Institute's membership growth suggested that the goals set by the Campaign for Leadership—40,000 members by the end of 1991, 50,000 by the end of 1992—would be met. At the same time, ISI built up its network of student and faculty representatives to 1,770 on some one thousand campuses, up from six hundred campuses at the beginning of the campaign. To service the enlarged campus network, the Institute's field staff was expanded from two to seven full-time employees. John Lulves oversaw this staff growth, serving the Institute both as chief financial officer and as the day-to-day executive director. He was, as such, a model to the new generation of ISI employees. Jeff Nelson recalled how Lulves exhorted staff to maintain the high standards set by ISI's founders and encouraged them to cultivate "a bookish life," one that could provide the foundation for a reflective conservatism. "If Vic Milione and Ken Cribb are the two halves of the one ISI brain," says Jeff Nelson, "John Lulves is its generous heart."[33]

31. Christopher Long, "The Campaign for Leadership," Minutes of the ISI Board of Trustees Meeting, January 11, 1991.
32. "The Campaign for Leadership," Christopher Long, ISI Board of Trustees Meeting, June 7, 1991.
33. Author's interview with Jeffrey O. Nelson, March 26, 2003.

Encouraged by a first-time grant of $75,000 from the Grover Herman Foundation and increased grants from the Richard and Helen DeVos Foundation, the Allegheny Foundation and the Adolph Coors Foundation, ISI adopted a budget of $2.19 million for 1991-1992, including "a major circulation expansion" of *CAMPUS*. The Institute also launched a capital campaign to secure "a permanent ISI National Headquarters," with help from development consultant Robert Russell, who knew ISI well: he had been encouraged to start his own fund-raising business in 1976 by trustee Al Campbell and had been in steady contact with Vic Milione since the late 1970s.[34] "The Institute is on track," Ken Cribb reported to trustees, "to establish a vocal and visible presence at 1,100 schools," half of the 2,200 four-year colleges and universities in America.[35]

ISI's rapid ascent did not go unnoticed by the leaders of the conservative movement. "It was as though the preceding years had been a huge, wonderful but slow launch," commented William F. Buckley Jr. "Ken Cribb, with his vitality and his learned form of evangelism, sparked ISI into thinking of achievements which simply were not realized conceptually by us types or by Victor." "The kind of enthusiasm and optimism he gave to [ISI]," Buckley said, "was really Providential."[36]

Rise and Fall

In the political realm, things were not going as well for President Bush. Although the 1991 Persian Gulf War had ended in a spectacular victory—after only six weeks and at a cost of just 148 Americans killed in action—the public's attention had quickly turned inward. More rapidly than ever before in modern politics, a president seeking reelection went from overwhelming favorite to unpopular underdog. In less than eighteen months, Bush's approval plummeted nearly sixty points to the mid-thirties just before the national Republican convention in July 1992. The central reason was smoldering public dissatisfaction with a sinking

34. Author's interview with Robert Russell, April 8, 2001.
35. T. Kenneth Cribb, Jr. to Ralph W. Husted, March 1, 1991, ISI Archives.
36. Jeff Nelson interview with William F. Buckley Jr., July 7, 2003.

economy. Only 1 million new jobs were created during the first three-and-a-half years of the Bush presidency—the worst record of any administration since World War II. Unemployment hit 7.7 percent, the highest since the 1982-1983 recession. The president was also the victim of what has been called the Churchill syndrome, a term political scientists coined to describe the surprise defeat of British Prime Minister Winston Churchill in the 1945 elections after he had guided his country to victory over the Nazis. Like Churchill, Bush was being told by an unhappy electorate, "You're a wonderful global leader, but you don't seem to care about our problems here at home."

At the same time, political conservatives were still fuming over Bush's decision to increase taxes. A typical comment was that of analyst Charles Kolb, who wrote that the Bush administration had "agreed to raising taxes, renouncing Reaganomics, and acquiescing in major domestic spending increases, while simultaneously castigating GOP members of Congress who were willing to stand up for real spending cuts, economic growth and lower taxes!" A glum vice president Dan Quayle later conceded that Bush's broken promise about taxes "haunted" him for the rest of his presidency.[37]

Committed as ever to the long view, ISI decided that the time was right for an examination of conservatism's future. In a symposium entitled, "The Tasks Ahead: The Conservative Mission in the 21st Century," published in *The Intercollegiate Review,* nine recent Weaver Fellows unanimously stated that the West was "in steep [moral] decline" and might "yet fall." Yet, they added, recovery was possible if there were "an unflinching recognition of the plight of our culture."[38] Guest editor Gregory Wolfe noted that the young conservative scholars rejected the utopian notions of a New World Order or the "end of history" and preferred to underscore the "fragility of order, threatened as it was by moral relativism, an alienated radical intelligentsia, and pervasive materialism." The road to recovery they outlined, Wolfe said, was a renewal of what Richard

37. Dick Williams, *Newt! Leader of the Second American Revolution,* Marietta, Georgia, 1995: 126-127.
38. Gregory Wolfe, "Introduction to The Tasks Ahead: The Conservative Mission in the Twenty First Century," *The Intercollegiate Review,* Vol. 27 No. 1, Fall 1991: 3-4.

Weaver called the "metaphysical dream"—the "fundamental vision of order" inherited from America's Judeo-Christian tradition.[39]

Harvard doctoral candidate George Michos, echoing a remark by Frederick Wilhelmsen two generations earlier, wrote that, "the most important thing conservatives can contribute to society at present is their vision." If America is to have a healthy public philosophy, he said, "it must be predicated upon a realistic conception of man, ignoring neither his capacity for noble achievement nor his capacity for evil."[40] The collapse of communism, wrote the Claremont Institute's Steven Hayward, did not imply the prospect of a New World Order but more likely a return "to something like the *status quo ante* of the nineteenth century," when statecraft was based on balance of power considerations. Mark Henrie, studying for his Ph.D. in political theory at Harvard, posited that the "true vocation" of the conservative was not merely to preserve a "pre-modern past" but to serve as a pragmatic post-modernist. Conservatives, he said, "should be able to assert confidently that the road to the future runs through the past."[41]

"The conservative mission in the twenty-first century," wrote Gleaves Whitney, pursuing a doctorate in intellectual history at the University of Michigan, is to articulate "first principles" so that America's opinion makers will "retreat from the edge of the abyss to which they have been seduced." Conservatives have dangerously neglected the realms of art and culture, wrote symposium editor Gregory Wolfe, leaving them in the hands of liberals. Distressed by the "increasing politicization" of the conservative movement, Wolfe urged conservatives to tend "the roots of culture" lest they "wither and die from inattention." Accepting his own challenge, the young conservative declared his intention to start a new quarterly, *Image: A Journal of the Arts and Religion.*[42]

39. Ibid.
40. Ibid: George Michos, "'Up From Liberalism' Revisited": 9.
41. Ibid: Steven Hayward, "Conservatism in the Post-Modern Age": 14; Mark C. Henrie, "The Road to the Future": 17, 19.
42. Ibid: Gleaves Whitney, "Decadence and Its Critics": 23; Gregory Wolfe, "Beauty Will Save the World": 31.

Boston College doctoral candidate Kenneth Craycraft wrote that conservatism will only have a future if it affirms that "pluralism is not a blessing to be celebrated, but a problem to be overcome." Admitting that the moral "ruins" could be observed on all sides, Craycraft nevertheless pledged to teach "virtue, truth, beauty, goodness," if at a small "sectarian" college, hoping that such commitment would create witnesses to the truth. Daniel E. Ritchie, assistant professor of English at Bethel College, struck a more optimistic note, stating that because students "know" that ideological approaches to the humanities are wrong, they will respond to an alternative (conservative) structure where "they can encounter the living spirits of our tradition in all their severe virtue and hilarity."[43]

Addressing the constant American emphasis on self-interest and supply-and-demand, economist Ralph E. Ancil called for an economics that "reflects traditional values rather than the utilitarian and pragmatic orientation implicit in much of modern economic thought." It was the duty of conservatives like himself, stated Jonathan Mills, completing his doctorate in theology at Boston College, to challenge value-free legal theory and defend the tradition of "substantive law" which developed in the course of Western religious and political history.[44]

The essays by the nine young conservative scholars were striking in their intellectual force, measured realism, and common vision of an ordered liberty dependent upon faith as well as reason. They could have appeared nowhere else but in *The Intercollegiate Review,* attesting yet again to ISI's leading role in the conservative movement and the American academy.

Membership Record

In March 1992, ISI membership attained an all-time high of 47,375, impressive when compared with the Institute's level of 30,000 to 35,000 over the preceding decade. The ISI headquarters staff was confident that

43. Ibid: Kenneth R. Craycraft, "Virtue Among the Ruins?": 36-37; Daniel E. Ritchie, "If We Build It...":41.

44. Ibid: Ralph E. Ancil, "Prophets of Piety": 44; Jonathan Mills, "The Substance of Law": 47.

all of their ambitious goals for the school year (some trustees wondered whether they were too ambitious) would be met: 50,000 student and faculty members, 250 lectures, 20 conferences, 2,200 volunteer representatives at 1,100 campuses, and the printing of 500,000 copies of major publications. There was a purpose behind the numbers—to counter the imposition of a political ideology in the classroom that, Ken Cribb wrote to a potential donor, "was hostile to the values and institutions that have sustained and nourished civilization, freedom, and order in our great nation for more than 200 years."[45] The ideology in question was "political correctness."

In response, ISI started a three-year campaign that would have pleased founder Frank Chodorov—to marshal market forces in favor of reform at America's most politicized universities. "College alumni, trustees, and donors," Cribb pointed out, "can exercise real leverage through [their] funding decisions."[46] The first targeted school was Stanford, which under President Donald Kennedy had dumped much of Western civilization into the ash heap of academe. The new Stanford president, Gerhart Casper, had publicly expressed skepticism about his predecessor's PC policies, and ISI devoted an entire issue of *CAMPUS* to documenting the Kennedy follies, particularly a new sequence of required courses on "Cultures, Ideas and Values" (CIV), which offered not only Western perspectives but African, Japanese, Indian, and Middle Eastern ones. A philosophy teacher stated that the classics (Aristotle, Augustine, Shakespeare, etc.) were an "albatross" around the neck of the new generation of professors.[47] Some 20,000 copies of the ISI newspaper were mailed to alumni who had graduated from Stanford in the 1940s and 1950s and had given the largest annual gifts to the university. ISI believed that a large number did not know how much things had changed at their alma mater and would prefer that they had not. The Institute called the effort The Winds of Freedom Project.

45. T. Kenneth Cribb, Jr. to Dr. and Mrs. Charles Maxfield-Parrish, May 28, 1992, ISI Archives.
46. T. Kenneth Cribb, Jr. to Rich DeVos, October 5, 1992, ISI Archives.
47. "The Great Debate III," *Campus Report*, Stanford University, February 24, 1988: 13.

Another 12,000 copies of *CAMPUS* were distributed by ISI volunteers to "virtually every student, professor, and administrator on the Stanford campus." Each copy featured a letter from David Sacks, a Stanford junior and ISI's campus representative, who urged alumni "to support the repeal of politically correct policies." Also included was a response card that alumni could use to communicate directly with President Casper and "stay in touch with ISI."[48] More than five hundred aroused alumni did just that, including one who withheld a $250,000 grant and called for reform. Bolstered by such outside support, President Casper appointed conservative professor Condoleezza Rice as provost, denied tenure to a Maoist professor, and welcomed the resignation of Sharon Parker, the University's director of the Office of Multicultural Development. Casper also appointed a new committee to evaluate Stanford's PC curriculum.[49]

ISI also developed special editions of *CAMPUS* for Vassar College and Duke University. After receiving *CAMPUS,* several hundred Vassar alumnae wrote to the college's president, Frances Fergusson, urging a return to traditional education at their school. Fergusson quickly denied all charges of politicization and mismanagement in a letter to alumnae. ISI countered Fergusson's denials point by point in a mailing to nearly ten thousand Vassar alumnae and trustees, noting that the college had discontinued the sole remaining course devoted to the Western classics and quoting a recently retired senior professor of economics that "there has been no educational leadership on this campus for the past twelve years."[50] Several hundred miles to the South, more than five hundred Duke alumni sent postcards and letters calling for a return to balance and standards at their University. Professor Timothy Lomperis, initially denied tenure following a highly politicized review process, credited Duke's reversal of its decision to the response generated by a *CAMPUS* article.[51]

48. Ibid.
49. "Summary of Accomplishments and Goals," Intercollegiate Studies Institute, April 1994, ISI Archives.
50. As quoted in a letter to Vassar alumnae from Alex Steinberg, Vassar Class of '93 and senior editor, *CAMPUS,* July 19, 1993.
51. Report on *CAMPUS* Saturation Pilot Project, "The ISI Carrier: A Weekly Information Packet for ISI Employees," Number 7, July 29, 1993.

Just as *The Intercollegiate Review* afforded young scholars the opportunity to explore the permanent things in an academic setting, so *CAMPUS* allowed ISI members to apply their journalistic skills to the issues of the day. In 1991 and 1992, John Miller of the University of Michigan analyzed the wave of campus "speech codes" that limited student free speech, especially those students who dissented from "the left-wing academic line." Graduate student Gary Gregg of Miami University (who would later serve as ISI's national director and author of several books on the American Founding) challenged the study done by the Carnegie Foundation for the Advancement of Teaching for first criticizing the growing intolerance on the American campus and then proposing a series of reforms that would squelch debate, especially if it challenged the prevailing liberal, multiculturalist orthodoxy of a school.

Paul Scalia (son of Supreme Court justice Antonin Scalia and today a Catholic priest in the diocese of Arlington, Virginia) asked readers "How Catholic are America's Catholic Colleges?" and Alex Steinberg, a Vassar junior, showed how administrators and radical student groups prospered from the confiscation of student fees in a story called "Where Are Your Student Fees Going?" In a prescient introductory paragraph, Steinberg said: "One of the most serious battles that will be waged on college campuses over the coming years involves the use of student fees for the promotion of partisan political legislation."

In the spring of 1992, *CAMPUS* published a symposium of six outstanding students that moved from criticism to proposition. "Out of the Darkness" examined the present state of the academy from the aim of education to racial politics, college athletics, curricular reform, and university administration, offering prescriptions along the way. As editor John Lutz put it, "Only a concerted effort conducted on a dramatic scale will enable us to once again rejuvenate the moribund Western academy." *CAMPUS* also commissioned a series of articles on graduate programs, considering them by discipline—a foreshadowing of ISI's development as a guidance resource with the publication of its college guide and study guides to the major disciplines. Book and movie reviews, a popular P.C.

roundup called "Campus Wire," and interviews filled out the pages of *CAMPUS*. In one number, Duke sophomore Tony Mecia (today a staff writer for the *Charlotte Observer)* interviewed Hoover Institution scholar Thomas Sowell about the harmful effects of affirmative action. "'Diversity,' Sowell said, "is one of the great fraudulent words of our time."[52]

In the spring 1992 issue of *The Intercollegiate Review,* with Jeffrey Nelson as the new editor, author Robert Royal examined the savage attacks of the multiculturalists on Christopher Columbus during the quincentenary of his discovery of America. While a century ago Columbus was celebrated as "a modern man" liberating himself from Catholic Spain to "help create Protestant and democratic America," the same explorer and liberator was now presented as "the prototype of early white European capitalist oppression whose victims ... are a veritable multicultural litany."[53]

The same issue published original essays on Alexander Solzhenitsyn, Hilaire Belloc, C. S. Lewis, and Richard Weaver, and included new literary criticism on Faulkner's *Intruder in the Dust* by M. E. Bradford. "I recall the interest Dr. Bradford took in me as a new editor of an important conservative journal," Nelson noted. "We had frequent conversations about the role and duty of editor, especially one with the dual audience of professors and students such as the *IR* has. Among other things, he encouraged me to balance symposia with miscellany, and he underscored the need to frequently revisit seemingly settled questions because they are seldom so settled as supposed and because with every passing year the ISI college readership is changing."[54]

In the fall of 1992, Nelson commissioned his first *Intercollegiate Re-*

52. John Miller, "Radical Administrators Limit Student Free Speech," *CAMPUS,* Volume 2 Number 1, Fall 1990: 6; Gary Gregg, "Campus Community in Shambles, Says Report," Ibid: 3; Alex Steinberg, "Student Activity Fees Finance Fringe Agenda," *CAMPUS,* Volume 3 Number 2, Winter 1992: 2; "Out of the Darkness: Students Point Toward Campus Reform," *CAMPUS,* Volume 3 Number 3, Spring 1992: 3-7, 1; Tony Mecia, "Sowell Blasts Affirmative Action's Harmful Effects," *CAMPUS,* Volume 3 Number 1, Fall 1991: 6-7.

53. Robert Royal, "1492 and Multiculturalism," *The Intercollegiate Review,* Vol. 27, No. 2, Spring 1992: 3.

54. Author's interview with Jeffrey O. Nelson, March 26, 2003.

view symposium, "Technology and Ethics in a Brave New World Order." Former *IR* editor Gregory Wolfe, ethicist John Haas, biotechnology expert Andrew Kimbrell, and philosopher Frederick Wilhelmsen considered whether we were at a turning point in civilization, whether we have, "exchanged the old heaven of revelation for the new heaven of technology." The theme was vintage conservatism and vintage ISI. Ten years before it was fashionable, the *IR* warned that within a few short years, the modern project to reshape, even recreate, human nature through scientific technique would be upon us. As Kimbrell put it, "A technological revolution has begun. This revolution could affect each of us in the most intimate, yet permanent, fashion. It could indelibly change the destiny of mankind and other members of the biotech community…. [This] technology is not in any sense neutral…. The biotechnology revolution demonstrates that technologies can also have a metaphysical content…. The biotechnologists are attempting to recreate nature in the image of efficiency."

Wolfe worried that the advance of new computer and virtual reality technologies were not providing new levels of "participation" as much as they were "removing most of the challenges which imagination imposes on us." Wilhelmsen invoked Gabriel Marcel's belief that it is easy to take up a technology but very difficult to lay it down. He argued that "the West had all the philosophic principles needed to control the development of technology but ultimately surrendered to the internal dynamics of its own technics…. The ecological crisis confronting the planet today certainly will—indeed, is—calling back to public consciousness the primacy of man's good over the good and perfection of his artifacts."

In traditional ISI fashion, Wilhelmsen outlined for young and older readers alike the hierarchy which the good society depends on, one "built by sanity itself": "Religion ought to dominate Politics; Politics ought to dominate Economics; and Economics ought to dominate Science and Technology." However, "since early in the modern experience the hierarchy has been reversed. Science and Technology today dominate Economics; Economics dominates Politics; and Politics dominate Religion. It is to this inversion of the natural order that we owe our winter of discontent." Wilhelmsen did close on a note of hope: "We cannot undo the world of electronic wizardry surrounding us. We can, however, set up a few road-blocks from within the human spirit rendering it less difficult for these media to trick us."[55]

ISI was in the business of erecting such roadblocks and showing how an authentic education in liberty can strengthen the human spirit against all odds. A direct result of the special symposium was a feature story on the Christian Broadcasting Network (CBN) on the ethical dimension of technology.

In the same 1992 issue, the *IR* displayed the conservative "ecumenism" fostered by ISI in all its materials. After the technology section, essays by famed conservative adversaries M. E. Bradford and Harry V. Jaffa followed, the former on "How to Read the Declaration" and the later on "Inventing the Gettysburg Address." These were followed by an *In Memoriam* for classical liberal political economist F. A. Hayek by economist Harry Veryser. The issue was a typical cornucopia of conservative ideas—packed into a mere 64 pages of text.

Balancing the tension between order and liberty, between duties and rights, has been a hallmark of ISI publications. The spring 1992 *IR* presented Russell Kirk's address upon receiving the ISI Salvatori Prize for writings on the founding of the Republic, in which the master of letters praised George Mason for institutionalizing, through his work on the Virginia Declaration of Rights and the federal Bill of Rights, "America's civil liberties." Mason did so because he was displeased with "the degree of centralization settled upon near the Constitution's end." Kirk's topic was "The Marriage of Rights and Duties," and he found its personification in George Mason. "The gentleman who wrote most convincingly about Americans' rights," said Kirk, "was among the most zealous Americans in the performance of high duties." We ought, Kirk suggested, to emulate Mason as we worked "to set this country aright, in morals, in

55. *The Intercollegiate Review*, "Technology and Ethics in a Brave New World Order," Vol. 28 No 1, Fall 1992: 3, 11, 16, 17, 23, 24, 37, 38.

politics, in economic policy, in foreign policy, in education, at every level."
He offered a concluding exhortation from Orestes Brownson:

> Ask not what your age wants, but what it needs, not what it will re-
> ward, but what, without which, it cannot be saved; and that go and
> do; and find your reward in the consciousness of having done your
> duty, and above all in the reflection, that you have been accounted to
> suffer somewhat for mankind.[56]

Alarming Anarchism

In the summer of 1992, *Modern Age* marked its thirty-fifth anniversary,
prompting editor and distinguished moral critic George Panichas to note
"the alarming growth of moral anarchism in American life" that affected
"in the most damaging ways" every institution—economic, political, philosophical, educational, and religious. Although the world had much
changed since 1957, Panichas said, *Modern Age* in "very distinct ways"
continued to articulate the themes of Richard Weaver's "magisterial" *Ideas
Have Consequences* first published in 1948. "The decline of belief in standards and values," Weaver wrote, in a world "dominated by the gods of
mass and speed ... can lead only to the lowering of standards, the adul-
teration of quality, and, in general, to the loss of those things which are
essential to the life of civility and culture."[57]

One public servant who had not lowered his standards was Supreme
Court Justice Antonin Scalia, who "enthralled" a capacity audience at the
third annual Salvatori Lecture and Banquet in Los Angeles in January
1993. The attendees were also moved by a message from former President Reagan, who recalled that many ISI graduates had been "among the
real work horses of my two terms as president." Reagan counseled the
audience not to be "cast down" by the recent election in which Bill Clinton
had been elected president. Victory and defeat, he reminded them, were
"the natural rhythms of American public life." A more important and

56. Russell Kirk, "The Marriage of Rights and Duties," *The Intercollegiate Review*,
Vol. 27, No. 2, Spring 1992: 27-32.

57. As quoted in "Modern Age Thirty-Five Years Later: An Editorial Note," George
A. Panichas, *Modern Age*, Summer 1992: 4.

fundamental question was whether the people would remain committed "to the enduring principles that have made America strong and free." Reagan charged ISI to remain steadfast in its commitment to "instill in succeeding generations of young people an allegiance to the ideas that sustain American freedom."[58] Vic Milione had expected to attend and sit next to his old friend, Henry Salvatori, but a quintuple heart bypass operation just nine days before the dinner prevented him from doing so. However, reported Ed Feulner to the Los Angeles audience, Vic was recovering well and was "already on the telephone for longer, probably, than he should be."[59]

Milione had the satisfaction of knowing that his legacy remained firm in the minds of ISI's new leadership. In a 1991 *CAMPUS* article, Harvard graduate student and ISI Weaver Fellow George Michos echoed Milione's conviction that "One of the defining characteristics of a liberal education is that it doesn't cease the moment a student received a college diploma; rather it is pursued over the course of a lifetime." "Ideally," Michos observed, "we imagine, there would be a place we could visit to get together with young people of like mind to discuss the ideas of our favorite authors under more favorable circumstances" than the contemporary college or university offered.[60] Happily for Michos and countless other students, ISI had acted on the idea. For the Institute continued throughout this period to support a more intimate approach to learning, such as the Piety Hill Seminars held at the Mecosta, Michigan, ancestral home of Russell Kirk.

Students tired of the prevailing orthodoxies on campus found a liberating alternative in the wide-ranging seminar themes at Piety Hill, among them "The Achievement of Solzhenitsyn," "The Literature of Politics," "The Humane Economy," "Agrarianism and Southern Letters," "Our Conservative Constitution," and "Questions of Church and State in

58. Message of Ronald Reagan at the Third Annual Henry Salvatori Lecture, January 30, 1993, Beverly Hills, California, ISI Archives.

59. Remarks by Edwin J. Feulner, Salvatori Lecture Dinner.

60. George Michos, "Small Group Seminars offer Students Reprieve from Usual College Fare," *CAMPUS*, Volume 3 Number 1, Fall 1991: 10.

America." "To visit Piety Hill," Michos noted, "is to enter an enchanting world of old-fashioned hospitality." The format called for fifteen to twenty students—usually college seniors and graduate students—to spend an intense, television-less weekend with Kirk and one or two other guest lecturers, listening to formal presentations and participating in discussions that often lasted into the late evening—interrupted only by the ghost stories offered by Dr. Kirk amid flickering candlelight and the rustling of the trees against the windows. An especially eerie moment came when the conservative scholar commenced the game of Snapdragon (popular in England in the eighteenth century) by uttering other worldly sounds and plunging his hands into the blue flames of burning rum on a silver tray and gobbled down warm raisins without a wince; students and faculty then followed suit, hesitantly and then enthusiastically.

But it was the words of wisdom and not the fiery game of Snapdragon that attracted the students to Mecosta, as in June 1993, when Kirk, Russell Hittinger of the Catholic University of America, and Francis Canavan of Fordham University explored natural law. "The grand Natural Law tradition of Cicero and the Schoolmen," Kirk explained, "though battered by Hobbes and confused by Locke, re-emerges in all its strength in Burke's reply to the French revolutionaries; and through Burke, in large part, it nurtures today whatever is healthy in our civil social order."[61] The impact of these brief encounters was lasting. As Michos put it, "These are weekends in which fast friendships develop, of the sort that are maintained over the years."[62] And the benefits accrued not only to the young scholars who met there but to the academy and the conservative movement as well.

Meanwhile, in the here and now world, noted educator Jacques Barzun of Columbia University, Pulitzer Prize-winning author Edward O. Wilson of Harvard University, and a dozen other prominent scholars announced the formation of an accrediting association—the American

61. As quoted in a brochure, "The Natural Law," an ISI Piety Hill Seminar, June 11-13, 1993, ISI Archives.
62. George Michos, "Small Group Seminars," *CAMPUS*, Fall 1991: 10.

Academy for Liberal Education—to set academic standards for teaching liberal arts in the traditional way. "Our concern is with undergraduate education," explained Barzun, "because in the last decade it has been confused, misdirected or not directed at all."[63] The American Academy for Liberal Education (AALE), explained its president Jeffrey D. Wallin, would seek recognition from the government as a specialized accrediting agency for liberal arts colleges and for humanities programs within universities. It took a little while, but in 1995, AALE was officially recognized by the U.S. Department of Education. As AALE's impact on higher education continued to increase, ISI proudly noted that AALE President Jeff Wallin had been a 1969-1970 Weaver Fellow. Other ISI alumni were also making their mark in the academy: Weaver Fellow Paul Rahe's monumental work, *Republics Ancient and Modern: Classical Republicanism and the American Revolution,* was adopted by the mainstream History Book Club.

The Feulner Touch

In March 1993, Ed Feulner stepped down after four exceptional years as board of trustees chairman of the Intercollegiate Studies Institute, the only organization, he always stressed, other than The Heritage Foundation, for which he helped raise funds. During his tenure, ISI tripled its annual budget from less than $1 million to just over $3 million. It cancelled all debt and attained a healthy net worth of just under $1.6 million. The additional funds enabled the Institute to establish new highs in every programmatic category from membership to lectures to publications. "I believe," Cribb wrote to a trustee, "this record demonstrates that the donor community has come to see the importance and efficacy of ISI's work in bringing the best of the new generation to thoughtful conservatism."[64] The record was made possible in large part by Feulner, who assumed the chairmanship of ISI when there were doubts among some

63. "Traditionalist Scholars Plan To Rate Liberal Arts Colleges," Anthony DePalma, *New York Times,* March 3, 1993.

64. T. Kenneth Cribb, Jr. to Rich DeVos, May 19, 1993, ISI Archives.

trustees and donors whether the Institute would survive. The Feulner-Cribb partnership had quickly dispelled all uncertainty and ushered in the most successful years in ISI's history.

The Institute's new chairman was Louise Oliver, whom Cribb described as one of "the true powerhouses of the conservative movement." Richard Larry, president of the Sarah Scaife Foundation, succeeded Oliver as vice chairman, commenting as he did so, "There is no question that over the years ISI has been one of [the Scaife Foundation's] very best investments."[65] Oliver had long had a special interest in philanthropy and vigorously promoted ISI's Forum for University Stewardship wherever she could.

Writing in the magazine of the Philanthropy Roundtable, she urged alumni who were unhappy with the political correctness and multiculturalism trend at their alma mater to support reform efforts coordinated by ISI. "By giving to ISI rather than directly to the universities," Oliver wrote, alumni could underwrite projects denied funding by university administrations, including alternative newspapers and lectures by conservative speakers. The ISI chairman explained that the forum director worked with donors one-on-one, "placing concerned alumni in contact with one another, arranging meetings between alumni and trustees, and providing alumni with information and advice on how and where to direct funds to support traditional liberal arts education."[66] Mediating institutions such as ISI, Oliver concluded, "preserve donor intent" and enable donors to use their financial leverage "to reclaim the academy for the next generation."[67]

The Republican loss of the White House to Democrat William Jefferson Clinton in 1992 created a moment for conservative reflection and reassessment. ISI responded at the level of high theory, and in doing so anticipated some of the themes which would emerge nearly a decade later in George W. Bush's "compassionate conservatism." "What is, and

65. T. Kenneth Cribb, Jr. to Ralph W. Husted, March 16, 1993.
66. Louise V. Oliver, "Successfully Supporting Your Alma Mater: The ISI Approach," *Philanthropy,* Volume VII, Number 3, Summer 1993: 2-3.
67. Ibid.

should be the essence of conservatism in America?" asked Harvard graduate student and Weaver fellow Mark C. Henrie in the spring 1993 issue of *The Intercollegiate Review.* He proceeded to offer an authoritative answer, signaling the existence of a conservative intellect of impressive power. The central issue of modern political life, Henrie argued, "is *not* one of collectivism versus individualism or central planning versus the market." It is rather a cooperative venture between democracy and the market economy, founded on an "atomized individualism," that leads to "homogenization and therefore dehumanization." It is therefore the task of conservatism to resist this homogenization and preserve such things as "community, solidarity, and, indeed, even eccentricity."[68]

Conservatives, contended the future senior editor of *Modern Age,* must resist the view of "man-as-consumer," and oppose efficiency when it conflicts with "the human scale of life." They must restore to the states a "measure of their sovereignty" and encourage the freedom of association. Quoting Russell Kirk, Henrie wrote that conservatives must "recapture the rhetoric of diversity" and oppose the "narrowing uniformity, egalitarianism, and utilitarian aims" of the radicals. The young conservative scholar called for the creation and support of a variety of associations in the community and on the college campus (such as independent student newspapers) to resist homogenization.[69] Editor Richard H. Neuhaus of *First Things* called Henrie's article "bracing" for urging conservatives to be the "reforming party by accenting true diversity and pluralism in society."[70]

The future of conservatism in America was also the theme of the *IR's* next issue, graced by a new design. The issue contended forcefully that any future orientation of American conservatism must keep faith with the vision of the movement's founders. In a special section entitled "1953: The Year Liberals Began to Listen" editor Jeff Nelson attempted to em-

68. Mark C. Henrie, "Rethinking American Conservatism in the 1990s: The Struggle Against Homogenization," *The Intercollegiate Review,* Vol. 28, No. 2, Spring 1993: 12.
69. Ibid: 12-15.
70. Richard J. Neuhaus, "Subversive Conservatism," *First Things,* January 1994: 63-64.

phasize for a new generation "the importance of that much maligned decade of the 1950s—paying attention to the year 1953 as being central to the history of American conservatism (and consequently to the fabric of American economic, political, and cultural life)."[71] As Nelson pointed out, 1953 was notable not merely for Eisenhower's Presidential Inauguration, it also saw the publication of important books by Russell Kirk, Robert Nisbet, Leo Strauss, Richard Weaver, Daniel Boorstin, James Burnham, Garet Garrett, and Clinton Rossiter. And it was the year ISI was launched.

Contributor Richard Brookhiser pointed young conservatives to these primary sources, arguing that "what the founders can do is raise the awkward questions, show us what we missed the first time around."[72] One of those founders, Robert Nisbet, contributed a penetrating re-assessment of his classic 1953 work *The Quest for Community* in which he argued that "a conservative party (or other group) has a double task confronting it. The first is to work tirelessly toward the diminution of the centralized, omnicompetent, and unitary state with its ever-soaring debt and deficit. The second and equally important task is that of protecting, reinforcing, nurturing where necessary the varied groups and associations which form the true building blocks of the social order."[73]

Appropriately, Vic Milione penned an assessment of ISI four decades after its founding, contending in the pages of the journal he created that "ISI has played an important role, not simply in the development and influence of the conservative political movement, but more importantly on the students who have passed through its many programs.... Today, ISI is still actively promoting its original vision, still educating for liberty. My old friend Richard Weaver taught me that a liberal education was a prerequisite for living freely. Multiculturalism and political correctness are just the latest manifestations of an old impulse, an essentially centralizing or collectivizing impulse that many of us saw in the 1950s,

71. Jeffrey O. Nelson, "1953: The Year Liberals Began to Listen," *The Intercollegiate Review*, Volume 29 Number 1, Fall 1993: 28.
72. Ibid: Richard Brookhiser, "Back to the Scratch Pad": 40.
73. Ibid: Robert Nisbet, "Still Questing": 45.

and that Frank Chodorov, and others, had the vision and courage to strike out against."

Despite signs to the contrary, Milione did not agree that the future was all bleak. The rising generation, if properly educated in liberty, could reverse the tide and secure the foundations, and future, of the American republic. What such an effort needed, Milione argued, was "integrity, consistency, and perseverance," virtues he believed ISI had in abundance. If ISI's "past is prologue," concluded Milione, "I look forward to the next act."[74]

A Grand Celebration

The curtain was lifted on the next act in October 1993, when ISI marked its fortieth anniversary with a black-tie dinner at the upscale Willard Inter-Continental Hotel in Washington, D.C., featuring remarks by William F. Buckley Jr. and the Institute's Salvatori Distinguished Scholar, Dinesh D'Souza. Honor was also paid to ISI's "founding families," in particular the Campbell family of Indianapolis, without whose support, Ken Cribb said, "ISI could never have reached the millions of students and faculty it has served during the past 40 years." Richard Ware, now president emeritus of the Earhart Foundation and living in New Hampshire, sent his regrets along with the exhortation, "If the Republic and 'the vigorous virtues' are to remain strong and liberty is to prevail, ISI is an institutional necessity."[75]

The dinner attendees included leaders of nearly every prominent conservative organization in America, confirming Ken Cribb's success in making ISI a requisite member of the conservative movement. Among the groups represented and ISI's varying contributions to their activities were the Federalist Society (the Institute underwrote part of the society's 1990 national conference), Young America's Foundation (the Institute promoted the foundation's 1990 summer conference among its campus representatives), the National Association of Scholars (many NAS mem-

74. Ibid: E. Victor Milione, "Ideas in Action": 57.
75. Richard A. Ware to T. Kenneth Cribb, Jr., October 5, 1993, ISI Archives.

bers were ISI faculty associates—its executive director Bradford Wilson was a Weaver Fellow), and the exclusive Council for National Policy (CNP), whose members included many of the movement's most important spokesmen and donors (Chris Long organized a panel on "Retaking the American Academy" at the CNP's February 1990 meeting).

In his introduction of Bill Buckley, Cribb delivered a brief history lesson, pointing to three things in the early 1950s that had helped a disjointed American conservatism to "find its center of gravity"—the publication of Russell Kirk's *The Conservative Mind*, the founding of ISI, and the launching of *National Review*. While conceding that the magazine was justly celebrated for serving as "midwife" to a political movement, Cribb argued that even more important was the role of Buckley and *National Review* role in "crafting an intellectual consensus which accommodated the warring proponents of freedom on the one hand and those of moral order on the other." To put it another way, said Cribb, "Ronald Reagan's famed electoral coalition was made possible by an antecedent intellectual coalition forged by William F. Buckley Jr."[76]

Rarely at a loss for the plangent phrase, Buckley responded that great strides had been made "in Frank Chodorov's Fifty Year Plan to disassemble the planted axioms of socialism" and that the unremitting work of ISI was "greatly responsible for the progress made." "How very proud Frank Chodorov must be," he said, "of the organization he founded, which Victor Milione guided for so many years and now exudes strength under Kenneth Cribb."[77]

Looking to the future, and reflecting the "politics of prudence" long preached by Russell Kirk, Buckley said that "the job of the conservative" was to "distinguish between the normative and the doable." But not, he insisted, at the cost of our liberties. Orthodox libertarians were most useful in "reminding us of the perils of forgetting about the unnecessary inroads of the state." The conservative, Buckley said, should endorse the

---

76. Remarks by T. Kenneth Cribb, Jr., at ISI's 40th Anniversary Celebration, October 14, 1993, Washington, D.C., ISI Archives.
77. Ibid: Remarks by William F. Buckley Jr.

libertarian impulse to move as far as possible from government, but "restrain the libertarian this side of [the] civil disorder" that would ensue if government did not exercise "those functions Adam Smith acknowledged inhere in public order."[78] ISI's first president ended with a graceful tribute to Ken Cribb, Stan Evans, Ed Feulner, Charles Hoeflich, Richard Scaife, Richard Allen and Louise Oliver, commenting that with such leadership, ISI "cannot stray, can't decompose; can only grow stronger, even as the government, under the shattering force of ISI's irradiations, grows weaker."[79]

A Conservative Renaissance

Student dissatisfaction with the status quo on campus, reported national director Christopher Long to ISI trustees the following spring, was at a level "unparalleled since the 1960s." But now it was conservatives not radicals who sought alternatives to the two orthodoxies of the day—"dogmatic multiculturalism and welfare-state liberalism."[80] He pointed out that in January 1994, despite the worst ice storm in recent years, more than five hundred Yale students attended an ISI debate on "Reaganomics vs. Clintonomics," featuring Reagan adviser Arthur Laffer and Carter adviser William Nordhaus. Nearly four hundred ISI members and guests came to the Institute's Midwestern Leadership Conference in Indianapolis where they were treated to vigorous attacks on big government and multiculturalism by economist Walter Williams and muckraker Charles Sykes.

ISI's Lecture Director Robert Erwin reported the good news that the number of ISI educational events on campus would soar to 310—an all-time high. Erwin also highlighted a special ISI lecture series on the collapse of communism and the educational controversies associated with the rise of multiculturalism and speech codes.[81] "Erwin did a marvelous

78. Ibid.
79. Ibid.
80. Christopher G. Long, "To Educate for Liberty: An ISI Program Overview," ISI Board of Trustees Meeting, March 11, 1994.
81. Ibid: Robert Erwin, "Lecture Program Report."

job organizing, tracking, and providing resources for the hundreds of lectures he set up," noted Jeff Nelson. "His enthusiasm for the ISI mission was unsurpassed on staff. He had a deep understanding of the issues at hand and was able to match just the right lecturer with the requested or assigned topic."[82] Nearly 40,000 students attended the lectures Erwin planned, sowing conservative seeds in the fertile soil of the American campus.

The evidence that such seeds were taking root was beginning to emerge nearly everywhere. ISI's Winds of Freedom group at Stanford, according to Chris Long, was now setting the campus agenda and, in the words of the *Stanford Daily*, "may be the nation's largest group of conservative alumni and students." Apprehensive left-wing Stanford students launched not one but two groups to combat campus conservatives who they agreed had "too great an influence on campus politics."[83] Approximately 185 students and faculty from some fifty schools attended a Yale Leadership Conference, eliciting enthusiastic comments such as: "I liked it so much, I'd be willing to walk [to it] next time" (Colleen Hilliard, Kent State University); "The most informative and thought-provoking experience of my college career" (Mario R. Nacinovich, Manhattan College).[84] The small group colloquia co-sponsored with the Liberty Fund drew equally positive and sometimes surprising responses. Following a Boston colloquium on "Morality and the Free Market," led by professors William Campbell and Nicholas Capaldi, Jennie Shippen of the University of North Carolina remarked, "The colloquium gave me new respect for my father as a small business owner."[85]

Always seeking to improve public understanding of all that ISI was doing, Cribb introduced the ISI Program Ladder. The ladder was a major visual accomplishment, summarizing the Institute's many disparate projects on just one page. At the base of the ladder were the total pieces of litera-

82. Author's interview with Jeffrey O. Nelson, March 26, 2003.
83. Ibid.
84. Stanley K. Ridgley, "ISI Conference Program," ISI Board of Trustees Meeting, March 11, 1994.
85. Ibid.

ture distributed—about 867,000 in 1993-1994. At the next and slightly more narrow rung were the copies of ISI publications and books circulated—over 536,000. Next came publications readership (313,000), student and faculty members (55,000), attendees at 310 lectures (36,000), student and faculty volunteer representatives on 1,100 campuses (2,700), attendees at thirty-seven conferences (2,691), leadership conference participants (644), five small group seminars, two summer schools, thirteen Weaver and Kinsey Graduate Fellowships, and at the very top rung the ISI Salvatori Center for American Founding Studies. The complex and multifaceted ISI program could now be grasped at a glance by a busy businessman or a foundation executive.

Passing of the Guard

ISI's successes during this period were overcast by the death of several mentors—chief among them Russell Kirk, an irreplaceable friend and teacher to Ken Cribb and many other conservatives for four decades. "He erected guideposts for those who would follow," Cribb said at a May 1994 memorial service for Kirk in Washington, D.C., so "that we too could travel the path he had marked toward order in the soul and order in the commonwealth." Kirk taught as much by personal example as by the printed and spoken word. "He and Annette made their house a home," Cribb pointed out, "to the troubled, to the dispossessed, to great eccentrics seeking refuge from the commonplace world."[86]

The fall 1994 issue of *The Intercollegiate Review* was a fulsome tribute to Kirk—it was in fact the largest single issue in the *Review's* history. Editor and Kirk son-in-law Jeff Nelson organized a who's who of ISI scholars to reflect on the significance of Kirk's life and his multiple contributions to conservative thought and letters. George Panichas, Roger Scruton, Peter Stanlis, Gerhart Niemeyer, Frederick Wilhelmsen, Francis Canavan, George H. Nash, Bruce Frohnen, Clyde Wilson, Ian Boyd, Russell Hittinger, and William Campbell were some of the notable essay-

---

86. T. Kenneth Cribb, Jr., "Euology at the Memorial Service of Russell Kirk," St. Joseph's Catholic Church, Washington, D.C., May 27, 1994, ISI Archives.

ists. Ian Boyd stated that "the most obvious and important thing that must be said about Russell Kirk concerns the harmony that existed between his public and his private life. He was an integrated man who lived what he wrote." His domestic life at Piety Hill was an extension of his written work, "a lived parable which illuminated everything he wrote about the primacy of private life over public life, about the family as the essential human community, and about the basic loyalties to the villages, neighborhoods, and regions in which human beings were most likely to find fulfillment and a measure of happiness."[87] The truth of this observation was experienced by three generations of ISI students and staff who attended Piety Hill seminars. And this legacy lives on through ISI's commitment to supporting student seminars at the "home" of conservatism—Piety Hill.

Three other conservative giants passed away just prior to, or soon, after Kirk—publisher Henry Regnery, literary critic and historian M. E. Bradford, and political philosopher Gerhart Niemeyer. Each was a cardinal contributor to ISI's history—Regnery as a member and then chairman during almost thirty years on the ISI board of trustees, Bradford and Niemeyer as indefatigable ISI lecturers and penetrating contributors to ISI publications. The *New York Times* described Regnery as the one-time New Deal Democrat "who became the godfather of modern conservatism as the publisher of the movement's leading theorists after World War II," including William F. Buckley Jr. and Russell Kirk.[88] Jeff Nelson, in his *Intercollegiate Review* tribute, referred to Regnery as a "missionary of culture."[89] "Regnery was as much a dissident writer as publisher," wrote Nelson. "He wrote in determined opposition to 'this liberal age,' an epoch characterized by an inadequate conception of the nature of man, and a faulty system of values based on a naturalism...."[90]

87. Ian Boyd, CSB, "Russell Kirk: An Integrated Man," *The Intercollegiate Review*, Volume 30 Number 1, Fall 1994: 18.

88. Robert McG. Thomas, Jr., "Henry Regnery, Ground-Breaking Conservative Publisher, 84," *New York Times*, June 23, 1996.

89. Jeffrey O. Nelson, "Henry Regnery: Missionary of Culture," *The Intercollegiate Review*, Volume 32 Number 1, Fall 1996: 14-19.

90. Ibid., p. 18.

Regnery was the Institute's longest serving chairman and led the organization through early crises and lean times. His contributions were often anonymous, much like those of fellow trustee Charles Hoeflich. ISI mourned the passing of an original founder, but it has preserved Regnery's intellectual insights by publishing two volumes of his essays and has imitated his missionary spirit through ISI Books. The Goethe epigram in the first ISI collection of Henry Regnery's writings captures the philosophy of this ISI founder: "One ought, every day at least, to hear a little song, read a good poem, see a fine picture, and, if it were possible, to speak a few reasonable words."[91]

M. E. Bradford was a world-class Faulkner scholar, an intellectual historian of America's founding era, and a passionate defender of the best of the Southern tradition. In his eulogy, Ken Cribb stated that "Mel Bradford might be called the philosopher of memory. He counseled us to know ourselves, not through introspection, but through recollection.... Against the millenarian tides of this century, [he] taught us to live in piety toward the world as God created it." Longtime ISI faculty member James McClellan summarized Bradford's appeal when he observed that "in taking his stand, M. E. Bradford articulated and defended traditional values that are not uniquely 'Southern.' Limited constitutional government, local self-government, political and cultural diversity, protection of the rural environment and way of life, the encouragement of religion and promotion of family and community institutions: these are American values, values, to be sure, that are disappearing not just in the South, but in the United States at large."[92]

Famous for his eloquent and uncompromising anticommunism, Gerhart Niemeyer emphasized the connection between liberty and personal moral responsibility. A world without God, he insisted, was unnatural and would lead to a modern form of intellectual slavery of the

91. Henry Regnery, *A Few Reasonable Words* (Wilmington, Delaware, 1996).
92. T. Kenneth Cribb, Jr. "Remembering Mel Bradford," *The Intercollegiate Review*, Vol. 29 No. 2, Spring 1994: 36. James McClellan, "Defending the High Ground," *Ibid*: 47.

mind and heart. Tim Goeglein, who would later serve in George W. Bush's White House, wrote that Niemeyer was "one of the most important conservative political philosophers of the last half century."[93] What animated his conservatism? And what drew ISI and Niemeyer to each other for more than three decades? Michael Henry, in his *Intercollegiate Review* tribute, noted that "vigilance required Niemeyer to be a conservative, which he understood not as adherence to a dogma or even a specific set of principles, but simply as 'common sense.' Conservatives 'affirm life's reality rather than their own emotions. It follows that conservatism cannot be a doctrine. Conservatism cannot be defined because, in its essence, it is an attitude.'" Niemeyer, wrote Henry, was "among those rare individuals who, even in the midst of great disorders, radiate the profound love of truth which they nurture in the depths of their soul."[94] Appropriately, Richard V. Allen, his former student and national security advisor to President Ronald Reagan, presented ISI's lifetime achievement award to Niemeyer just before the legendary teacher's death.

Looking Forward

Kirk's passing, along with that of Regnery, Bradford, and Niemeyer, called for reflection. The first generation of conservative intellectuals was nearly gone, the second generation was graying. It was thus all the more necessary for ISI to identify and nurture the present and future intellectual leadership of the conservative movement. At the November 1994 ISI board meeting, Ed Feulner looked back over the Institute's last several years and then forward to where the Institute might be in 2000, the beginning of the twenty-first century. He pointed out that every one of the goals set in 1987 by the evaluation committee he headed had been exceeded. Promising that ISI's core mission "will not change," Feulner listed the objectives of the Institute's new Campaign for Integrity in Higher Education, including: (1) to increase ISI's membership by as much as 50

93. Tim Goeglein, "Another great thinker is gone," *Washington Times*, July 15, 1997.
94. Michael Henry, "The Heritage of Gerhart Niemeyer," *The Intercollegiate Review*, Volume 33 Number 1, Fall 1997: 8-9.

percent; (2) to "identify and nurture" annually one hundred "ISI Honors Fellows" at the undergraduate level through one-on-one faculty mentoring and other guidance; and (3) to expand the Institute's book publishing program to as many as twenty books a year.

Depending upon the funding obtained, he added, "it would not be a surprise" to see ISI conduct "independent research" on higher education issues, expand the network of alternative student newspapers, offer technical and other courses on the Internet, and create "a placement service" for young faculty members. With such a comprehensive program and operating out of its new national offices, Feulner stated confidently, ISI would be "a major force in academe" and "*the* primary source" for those in the academy interested in ordered liberty.[95] The force was already being felt, as attested by one school administrator who informed free market economist Walter Williams after his "electrifying" appearance: "I have *never* seen so much 'aftershock' from an assembly speaker. For the rest of the day, every corner of the building was occupied by students and faculty discussing and arguing your points."[96]

Political Aftershocks

At the same time, conservatives were coping with the nation's roller-coaster politics which included President George H. W. Bush's sky-high public approval ratings in 1990 followed by the humiliating defeat at the polls in 1992, a victim of an economic slump and the beguiling charm and keen political intelligence of New Democrat Bill Clinton. And conservatives were trying to cope with each other. No sooner had President Reagan left office in January 1989 and the Berlin Wall tumbled down than conservatives began building barriers between each other. Before long, there was open talk of a "conservative crackup."[97] Sharp disagreements erupted about trade, immigration, and the direction of U.S. foreign policy.

President David Jones of the Fund for American Studies and other

95. Edwin J. Feulner, remarks, ISI Board Meeting, November 22, 1994, ISI Archives.
96. T. Kenneth Cribb, Jr. to James H. Burnley IV, December 14, 1994, ISI Archives.
97. See R. Emmett Tyrrell, Jr., *The Conservative Crack-Up*, New York, 1992.

conservative leaders in Washington, D.C., began meeting in 1992 to discuss "the future of the conservative movement."[98] Jones, an educator and veteran political activist, pointed out that a successful political movement often attracted followers who did not have an adequate grounding in the history and central purpose of the movement. "Eventually," he said, "the movement loses a sense of mission. Inevitably confusion and chaos replace a cohesive movement." The answer, he said, lay in ISI, The Heritage Foundation, and similar organizations working together to revitalize "a common understanding of the basic principles of conservatism" among younger conservatives.[99]

Another veteran conservative argued that every political movement needed three kinds of people to be successful—"philosophers, popularizers and politicians." In the past, the conservative movement had thinkers like Russell Kirk, F. A. Hayek, and Richard Weaver; journalists like William F. Buckley Jr., James J. Kilpatrick, and John Chamberlain; politicians like Barry Goldwater and Ronald Reagan. "Who," he asked, "are our emerging philosophers, popularizers, politicians?"[100]

One telling outcome of these "renewing conservatism" meetings was a cadre-building task force chaired by ISI's Kenneth Cribb, who stated in the task force's April 1994 report that young people had to be given "a thorough reading program in the conservative classics, along with mentoring from conservative scholars." Specific task force recommendations included the distribution of classics such as *The Conservative Intellectual Movement in America: Since 1945* by George Nash, *A Humane Economy* by Wilhelm Roepke, *In Defense of Freedom* by Frank Meyer, and *The Federalist Papers* by Alexander Hamilton, James Madison, and John Jay; the publication of a "broad-based guidebook" to colleges and universities; bringing "the best and the brightest" college students together with faculty mentors; and helping to place young conservatives "in good teaching positions."[101] ISI happily, and dependably, implemented several of

98. David J. Jones to Kenneth Cribb, July 7, 1992, ISI Archives.
99. Ibid.
100. Memorandum of Lee Edwards to David Jones, June 23, 1992, ISI Archives.
101. "Renewing American Conservatism: Strategies to Develop Young Conservative

these recommendations in pursuit of its educational mission and as part of its expanded educational role in the conservative movement.

That role became all the more important in the wake of an extraordinary event in American politics. On November 8, 1994, Republicans gained fifty-two seats and assumed a majority in the House of Representatives for the first time since Dwight Eisenhower was president four decades earlier. The *New York Times* called the GOP victory "a political upheaval of historic proportions."[102] The political vehicle used by House Republicans was the Contract with America, conceived and co-authored by the historian turned politician, Newt Gingrich of Georgia. The contract proposed a balanced budget amendment, a presidential line-item veto, welfare reform, congressional term limits, a $500 tax credit for children, an enforceable death penalty, regulatory reform, litigation reform, and Social Security reform. The ISI connection was clear—several of the ideas had first been suggested by conservative academics such as Milton Friedman, a frequent ISI lecturer, and had been supported by conservative politicians such as Barry Goldwater and Ronald Reagan, longtime ISI favorites.

But the year 1995, which began with such shining promise, ended in dark disappointment. The Republican House's public approval sank from a high of 52 percent to the mid-20s following two shutdowns of the federal government. House Speaker Gingrich, the man of the hour in January, became the Grinch who stole Christmas in December. Only five of the twenty-one legislative priorities in the Contract with America were enacted by Congress because of President Clinton's skillful use of the veto, the Republicans' failure to respond adequately to the Democrats' well-financed propaganda offensive, and Gingrich's disregard for the politics of prudence. For Leonard Liggio, executive vice president of the Atlas Economic Research Foundation and an original ISI student member, Gingrich's most serious flaw was his inability to stay within any boundary of ideas. In fact, said Liggio, Gingrich had so many ideas that "he trip[ped] over them." In contrast, Ronald Reagan steadfastly relied on a few basic

Talent," T. Kenneth Cribb, chairman, April 1994, ISI Archives.
    102. "Dr. Fell's Election," *New York Times* editorial, November 10, 1994.

concepts for his policies and programs. Reagan was a great communicator, Liggio argued, because he believed in the great ideas of Western civilization and the American Founding—those which had guided ISI from the beginning and which the Institute continued to advance in all its programs.[103]

The Multi-Million Dollar Deception

ISI's programmatic commitment to the foundations of America and the West led to its central role in what came to be known as the "Bass Affair." In mid-1994, the Institute was approached by ISI member Pat Collins about underwriting a new conservative newspaper at Yale to be called *Light & Truth*. Inasmuch as the school already had two conservative publications—one served as the organ of the Tories, the other was published by the Conservative Party of Yale—and that Collins—a broad-shouldered water polo player from Southern California—had a scant background in journalism, ISI was, as Chris Long put it, "skeptical to say the least."[104] But Collins had something no other Yale undergraduate had—an explosive story involving a prominent alum's multi-million-dollar gift that had gone astray and an apparent cover-up by the administration.

The young muckraker wanted to expose through *Light & Truth* that the Yale administration had solicited and obtained $20 million from Fort Worth alumnus Lee M. Bass for a series of undergraduate classes about Western civilization but had then failed to follow through on the terms of the gift and had "covered up" their dereliction.[105] ISI agreed to fund Collins' student paper and the Bass exposé.

With considerable editorial help from ISI headquarters, *Light & Truth* published a carefully documented article entitled, "The $20 Million Deception." Cribb gave a pre-production exclusive to Robert Bartley, editor of the *Wall Street Journal*, who assigned the gifted and indefatigable Dorothy Rabinowitz to the story. On November 24, 1994, the first of five

103. Leonard Liggio to the author, July 29, 1997.
104. Christopher Long to Lee Edwards, September 17, 2002.
105. Ibid.

Wall Street Journal editorials on this fiasco appeared. It denounced Yale for giving in to "faculty ideologues" and accusing the University of "derailing the [Bass] initiative and, not incidentally, the intentions of the grant."[106] ISI blast-faxed press releases to hundreds of media outlets, and scores of news articles appeared all over the world. Even the *Washington Post* admitted that then-Provost Judith Rodin had been critical of taking the Bass grant from the very beginning.[107] ISI ensured that members of the Yale community were kept informed by distributing several thousand copies of the *Light & Truth* article on campus and mailing another 5,200 copies to the University's $1,000-plus donors. Unimpressed by intimidating overtures from Yale officials, ISI sponsored a January debate at Yale on "What Is the Proper Role of Western Civilization in American Higher Education?" An alarmed Yale administration countered with lame explanations and eleventh-hour attempts by Yale President Richard Levin and former Carter White House counsel Lloyd Cutler to convince Bass that the University was now prepared to carry out his wishes.

But when a skeptical Bass was refused reasonable guarantees that the original program would in fact be implemented, he demanded and received the return of his $20 million gift. The Bass family have been generous donors to ISI's initiatives in Western civilization ever since. Their contributions provide significant support for the ISI Honors Program and for lectures on America's most elite campuses. Each year, two or more graduate fellowships in Western civilization are awarded to doctoral candidates in the final stages of their dissertation work.

At about the same time, another Yale alumnus, Robert Eskridge of Coral Gables, Florida, announced that the $500,000 he had planned for Yale was going elsewhere. "Academic freedom" said Eskridge, "is being wiped out by a radical faculty who have an agenda of their own—of multiculturalism and activism."[108] Robert and Peggy Eskridge found in

106. "New Magazine, *WSJ*, Rekindle Western Civilization Blaze," *Yale Alumni Magazine*, February 1995.

107. David Karp, "A Whiter Shade of Yale?" *Washington Post*, June 4, 1995.

108. John Meroney, "Will Yale Alumni Close Wallets Over Western Civilization Flap?" *Human Events*, December 30, 1994.

ISI what was lacking at Yale: Chris Long sent them a copy of Russell Kirk's *The Roots of American Order* and they have been loyal supporters of the Institute ever since.

Long recalls fielding dozens of calls from the news media and from irate alumni and spending hours trying to coordinate the often helter-skelter activities of the Yale students. "It was draining," he admits, "running with a tiger like the Bass affair."[109] But it was a pivotal event in ISI's history, moving the Institute onto the front pages of major newspapers and attracting the attention of *Time, Newsweek,* and other magazines. It reflected Kenneth Cribb's successful strategy of developing an aggressive educational reform arm of the Institute without diluting or distorting its traditional mission. No longer content to engage in guerrilla tactics, ISI now launched an all-out frontal assault on the most vulnerable shibboleths of the American academy—political correctness and multiculturalism. And the Institute was soon to do so from an impressive new national headquarters in Wilmington, Delaware, providing further proof of its status as a major combatant in the nation's intellectual wars.

109. Long to Edwards, September 17, 2002.

CHAPTER IX

A Permanent Home

In the shrinking and increasingly troubled world of serious book publishing, ISI Books has been one of the most heartening success stories of the past decade.

Wilfred McClay[1]

SCARLET OAKS, A MAJESTIC STONE MANSION near Wilmington, Delaware, had overlooked a serene artificial lake and twenty-three acres of English country gardens and natural forest since the 1930s. But when the owners William A. and Jane Richards Worth died, the heirs of the steel company founder could not find the right buyer for the imposing property. Their hopes of selling the 9,000 square-foot house as a residence were not realized, and they did not want to sell to developers who would carve up the estate into predictable "faux chateaux." And then one day while Spencer Masloff and Christopher Long were travelling north from Washington to Bryn Mawr, they stopped to visit a realtor who mentioned this Delaware property that had been on the market for two years. "Once we set eyes on Scarlet Oaks," recalls Long, "we knew it was perfect."[2]

1. Wilfred McClay to Bracy Bersnak, May 29, 2003.
2. Christopher Long to Lee Edwards, September 17, 2002.

The Worth estate was located in the heart of Delaware's Chateau country and was the "perfect" location for ISI's national headquarters. "Scarlett Oaks" comprised a Colonial Revival stone mansion and twenty-three acres of country gardens and forest. Its conditional purchase was made possible through a supra-grant of $1.5 million from the F. M. Kirby Foundation, the largest single donation ever received by the Institute. ISI had long enjoyed Fred Kirby's bounty because of its conservative works and the close personal relationship between Vic Milione and Kirby, who like Henry Salvatori, appreciated Milione's insightful mind and direct manner of speaking. In December 1994, a somewhat giddy Cribb wrote, "This is truly a historic moment for our organization and for the overall movement to sustain ordered liberty in our great country."[3]

It took some creative zoning by the New Castle Country Council, allowing "significant" properties to be used as commercial space while retaining residential zoning; and additional energetic fund-raising for a $1.5 million renovation. But on May 31, 1996, President Kenneth Cribb, Board Chairman Louise Oliver, and principal benefactors Fred Kirby and Richard M. DeVos cut the ribbon for the F. M. Kirby Campus of the Intercollegiate Studies Institute. The Institute added to the occasion by awarding the 1996 Henry Salvatori Prize to master entrepreneur DeVos—who delivered the annual Salvatori lecture on the power of "compassionate capitalism"—and dedicating the Henry Regnery Library to its long-time chairman. For the first time in its forty-three-year history, ISI had a permanent home.[4] John Lulves explained to the *Times* that the house "manifested in a physical way what we believe in—the passing to each generation of our heritage."[5]

Ken Cribb elaborated on the "idea" of ISI a few months later at a staff orientation, sketching the "bleak" situation for conservative ideas that prevailed in the early 1950s when the Institute was founded and

3. T. Kenneth Cribb Jr. to Richard V. Allen, December 6, 1994, ISI Archives.
4. Maureen Milford, "Creative Zoning for Delaware's 'Chateau Country'", *New York Times*, March 26, 1995.
5. Ibid.

describing the three events pivotal to the development of American conservatism. They were the publication of Russell Kirk's masterful *The Conservative Mind;* the advent of ISI, which generated "a market for conservative scholarship" and a "direct link to its potential audience;" and the establishment of *National Review*—a journalistic and political act in one.[6]

Through the years, emphasized ISI's president, the Institute had worked with "any responsible element of the conservative coalition," enabling it to sponsor lectures "by thinkers as diverse as John Lukacs, Alan Kors, and Walter Williams." "There is no party line at ISI," Cribb elaborated, "and there never has been." He applauded "the shaping contribution" of Vic Milione, especially his insistence on "intellectual breadth and variety, so that any essential need of the rising young scholar could be met."

Unlike many organizations in the conservative movement, Cribb said, ISI "eschews the current battles in politics and public policy and instead focuses on securing the allegiance of the new generation to the values of America and the West." Such a mission, he admitted, was not "the task of a day," but the effort would "bear fruit for more than a day." And it would, he hoped, sustain a future generation "in the never-ending task of maintaining the foundations of our common life."[7]

A Monumental Presence

As it began its fifth decade, the Institute had become, in the words of a friendly publication, "a monumental conservative presence on the college campus." While continuing to publish intellectual journals like *The Intercollegiate Review* (which had celebrated its 30th anniversary in 1994), *Modern Age* (which would mark its 40th year in 1997), and *The Political Science Reviewer* (which observed its 25th anniversary in 1996), ISI now directly participated in campus battles about curriculum content, speech codes, sensitivity training, and other applications of political correctness.

6. T. Kenneth Cribb Jr., "The Idea of ISI," a luncheon address for an all-staff orientation, September 18, 1996, ISI Archives.
7. Ibid.

Major weapons included *CAMPUS* and targeted mailings to wealthy alumni. "We have made great strides in the past few years, no doubt," said twenty-eight-year-old Christopher Long, the vice president for ISI programs. But the campus Left, he warned, was shifting its tactics and "infusing their ideologies into the traditional curriculum." While not claiming that the majority of the faculty was composed of radicals, Long argued that at many schools, "the radicals are calling the shots."[8] In response, ISI defended a traditional curriculum based on the ideas and institutions of Athens, Rome, Jerusalem, London, and Philadelphia (to use Russell Kirk's formulation of the five great cities in *The Roots of American Order*).

"While radical intellectual trends have come and gone in higher education," said Ken Cribb, "what we have been espousing—ordered liberty— is permanent and something the bright, independent students continue to believe strongly in." Looking forward to the next fifty years, Cribb said that "for a society to stay free it needs to have certain values conveyed generation after generation." And ISI knew that those values came from the family, the church, and the school.[9] Addressing the ISI staff in September 1997, the ISI president said that the family teaches the mores "from which it is possible to achieve virtue." The church teaches truth "from which it is possible to achieve understanding." And the educators should teach knowledge "from which it is possible to achieve wisdom."[10]

But in the twentieth century, Cribb asserted, the university began to fail in its transmission of human memory from one generation to the next, and indeed, "actually became hostile" to what the historian Christopher Dawson called "enculturation" (a favorite theme of Vic Milione). ISI was founded, stated its president, to produce new generations of "enculturators," cognizant of Alexander Solzhenitsyn's remark that "a people which no longer remembers has lost its history and its soul."[11]

8. "Intercollegiate Studies Institute," *Human Events*, March 1995: 16; Ralph Vigoda, "Quiet Pa. institute stirs academic furor," *Philadelphia Inquirer*, January 9, 1995.
    9. Ibid.
    10. "The Idea of ISI," T. Kenneth Cribb, Jr., remarks to the ISI All-Staff Orientation, September 3, 1997, ISI Archives.
    11. Ibid.

Cribb was confident, as previous ISI presidents had been, that the brightest of the rising generation would welcome the Institute's programs because they offered a genuine alternative to the "politically correct jargon" and "turgid Marxist tracts" of the Left.[12]

For their part, the ISI trustees laid down in that same year of 1997 a framework for the Institute's operations for the rest of the 1990s and the early 2000s. They called it the Mendenhall Plan, after the Mendenhall Inn near the new ISI headquarters in Wilmington, Delaware, where ISI's senior staff had met to plan for the Institute's future. The plan had a lofty goal—to make ISI into "a one-stop resource" about the principles of freedom for "talented students" in American higher education. Three new undergraduate programs were launched: the ISI Honors Program, intended to identify and nurture the "rising generation of American leaders"—and help them follow in the footsteps of prominent ISI alumni such as Ed Feulner, William Kristol, Richard Allen, John Lehman, Paul Craig Roberts, and James Gwartney; the Collegiate Network, a group of independent student newspapers; and the ISI Internet Resource Center, which would use the latest technology to expand the Institute's outreach to students and faculty.[13]

Staffing the New Programs

Such ambitious program goals required a staff with exceptional skills and educational backgrounds. Eager, talented, and intellectually oriented young people had, of course, long been drawn to work at ISI. Typically just out of college, ISI staffers would dedicate a few energetic years to the Institute before going on to graduate or professional school. In the mid-1990s, however, the expanding ISI program began to attract more academically seasoned professionals. The new cadre were often themselves Ph.D.s or graduate students with advanced standing who had taught university students, sometimes for several years. Their presence on staff added to ISI's

12. Ibid.
13. Progress Report at Meeting of ISI Board of Trustees, Wilmington, Delaware, May 31, 1996:4-5, ISI Archives.

academic weight and greatly expanded the range of faculty actively involved with the Institute.

In 1994-1995, for example, Lenore Thomas, a Ph.D. candidate at Johns Hopkins and a Weaver Fellow, worked at the Institute. A former student of acclaimed historian Forrest McDonald, Thomas was instrumental in conceptualizing the ISI Honors Program, which provided intensive intellectual development and direct faculty mentoring for the most academically gifted undergraduates. In 1995, Thomas left ISI to marry Steven Ealy of the Liberty Fund—another Weaver Fellow—so that the task of implementing the first summer colloquium of the Honors Program fell to Amy Fahey, Thomas's successor.

Fahey was a doctoral candidate in English literature at Washington University in St. Louis and herself a Weaver Fellow. She was the wife of William Fahey, who also had been a Weaver Fellow while earning his Ph.D. at the Catholic University of America, and is now chairman of the classics department at Christendom College in Virginia. Amy Fahey, a Hillsdale alumna who had made frequent visits to the Kirk family in Mecosta, was well qualified to coordinate the week-long intellectual retreat. The students, many drawn from Ivy League and other top colleges, were treated to lectures by ISI faculty associates as well as seminars, one-on-one time with a faculty mentor, open discussions, and cultural events. The syllabus for the week included conservative classics by the likes of Richard M. Weaver and Russell Kirk and works of general culture such as Josef Pieper's *Leisure the Basis of Culture* and John Henry Newman's *Idea of a University*. The Honors Program provided top undergraduates with an introduction to the minds of the conservative movement and also demonstrated the movement's intimate connection with the main currents of Western civilization.

At the beginning of 1997, both Amy Fahey and Chris Long left ISI, Fahey to follow her husband into the academic world, Long to join Foster Friess & Associates, where he would oversee the philanthropic endeavors of one of the nation's premier evangelical Christian conservatives. Long's able successor was Dr. Gary Gregg, a young political scientist from Clarion University in Pennsylvania. Fahey was succeeded by Mark Henrie.

Gregg was a varsity baseball player at Davis & Elkins College in West Virginia with politically conservative leanings when one of his professors, ISI faculty associate Marshall DeRosa, gave him a copy of *The Conservative Mind*. It was a milestone in his life. Gregg went on to read many of Kirk's works as well as other classics of post-war conservative thought, and he devoured each issue of *The Intercollegiate Review*. Gregg resolved to attend graduate school at Miami University in Ohio, where with the help of both a Weaver and a Salvatori Fellowship, he completed a dissertation on the American presidency inspired by the work of Willmoore Kendall and James Burnham. As an ISI faculty associate at Clarion University, he had participated as a mentor in the first year of the Honors Program. Gregg was looking for a new challenge when he signed on as ISI's new academic director in 1997. But he got more than he bargained for when Cribb asked him to fill Chris Long's vacant position. He decided to seized the opportunity to lead the Institute's national program.

Mark Henrie had been active in ISI since 1987 when, as Dartmouth's valedictorian, he had published a chapter of his senior thesis in *Modern Age*. After receiving an M.Phil. at Cambridge in 1988 and entering graduate school at Harvard, he attended several ISI Piety Hill seminars at the home of Russell Kirk, with whom he kept up a cordial correspondence. As a doctoral candidate at Harvard in the early 1990s, Henrie published widely in such journals as *First Things*, *Crisis*, and *The University Bookman* as well as *Modern Age* and *The Intercollegiate Review*. An ISI Weaver Fellow and an award-winning teacher at Harvard, he also taught and lectured in Eastern Europe for the Jan Hus Foundation and in the annual summer program sponsored by Michael Novak, George Weigel, and Richard John Neuhaus.

A convert to Catholicism, Henrie resolved in 1995 to test a religious vocation with the Toronto Oratorians, but by the spring of 1997, he had come to the conclusion that he had no calling to the religious life. Perplexed about what to do next, he found in the mail one day an advertisement for a job opening at ISI which sounded very attractive——mentoring ISI students within the Honors Program and the larger Campus Leaders Program. Within a month of leaving the Toronto Oratory in 1997, he went to work at ISI, hoping he had found his true vocation. Six years later, Henrie acts as ISI's intellectual compass. While at the Institute, he found a different vocation: marriage to Claudia Pasquantonio, who had been Annette Kirk's, then Jeff Nelson's, personal assistant.

Together, Gary Gregg and Mark Henrie raised the bar for intellectual excellence in ISI programming. Two of the summer colloquia that Gregg organized—"America's Founding and the Western Tradition" and "George Washington: Patriot Sage"—were turned into scholarly volumes (*Vital Remnants* and *Patriot Sage*) that became critically acclaimed bestselling titles for ISI Books and main selections of the Conservative Book Club. The large number of faculty associates participating in the Honors conferences created the atmosphere of a socratic symposium, forging new bonds between faculty from disparate schools and disciplines, between faculty and a group of exceptional students, and between faculty and ISI. One senior faculty associate commented that the Honors colloquium at Williamsburg was "the most intellectually rewarding conference I have ever attended." Students too recognized they were experiencing something unusual.

For his part, Henrie offered the opening lecture of each summer colloquium, asking the question, "Why Go To College?" He then engaged the students in a probing dialogue that linked the problems facing young people today to first principles, a dialogue that he continued on an internet listserve throughout the academic year. Some students printed out the listserve postings after reading them to keep for permanent reference. For two generations, ISI had been organizing encounters between inquiring right-leaning students and conservative academics and intellectuals. Now ISI staff was being called upon to help cultivate the great debate about the role of liberal education as opposed to merely mediating it.

The Right Colleges

In the mid-1990s, three other new programs were aimed at the parents of students and the financial supporters of higher education: the Forum for University Stewardship, calculated to help alumni, donors, and trustees make financial choices that "foster traditional liberal arts standards of excellence;" the Templeton Honor Rolls for Education in a Free Society—underwritten by the prominent investment analyst Sir John Templeton—which honored selected colleges and universities, departments and programs, professors and textbooks; and the ISI guide to American colleges (*Choosing the Right College: The Whole Truth About America's Top 100 Schools*) which helped students and parents identify the schools that "offer a genuine university education."[14]

Given ISI's belief in the moral as well as the economic dimension of man, the Institute was a logical choice to administer the 1997-1998 Templeton Honor Rolls. "The scholarship recognized in these Honor Rolls seeks not to tear down or 'debunk' our nation's founding principles, but to inculcate in young people a sense of the profound moral and political wisdom of those principles," William E. Simon, chairman of the twenty-seven-member executive committee that made the selections, said.[15] Simon, president of the John M. Olin Foundation, also served as a trustee for the John Templeton Foundation. Legendary financier Sir John Templeton had asked Simon to head a search for an appropriate institution to administer his "honor rolls" program.

Simon tendered ISI the high compliment of selecting the Institute to administer Sir John's important program. Bill Simon and his close associate, James Piereson of the John M. Olin Foundation, worked effectively with Ken Cribb and his staff to assemble and direct the notables who composed the Honor Rolls' executive committee. In addition to the insti-

---

14. Ibid: 5-6.
15. William E. Simon, "Foreword," *The Templeton Honor Rolls for Education in a Free Society 1997-1998,"* John Templeton Foundation/The Intercollegiate Studies Institute, 1997: viii.

tutions, scholars, and books the program honored, two special awards were given—a Lifetime Achievement Award to Nobel laureate Milton Friedman, "who has done more to communicate clearly and persuasively the virtues of a free economy than almost any other scholar over the course of the last half century;" and an Outstanding Contemporary Book Award to scholar Gertrude Himmelfarb for her "seminal work," *The De-Moralization of Society*.[16]

Some eight hundred nominees were narrowed down to one hundred eighty finalists and then to the final honorees—thirteen colleges and universities (from Boston University to Washington and Lee University), twenty-eight departments and programs (from the Honors College at Adelphi College to the program of directed studies at Yale University), twenty-four scholarly books and textbooks (from Allen Bloom's *The Closing of the American Mind* to James Q. Wilson's *American Government*), forty-seven professors (from Henry J. Abraham of the department of government and foreign affairs at the University of Virginia to Catherine Zuckert of the political science department at Carleton College).

The awards were presented at a star-studded luncheon in the U.S. Senate's Russell Caucus Room. Milton Friedman addressed the honorees live via satellite television, and William Bennett observed that the Templeton/ISI honorees could themselves form a world-class university. Gregory Wolfe returned to ISI to administer the many details of the Templeton awards, assisted by Micki Gorman and directed by Jeff Nelson. The John M. Olin Foundation also provided staff assistance for the initiative derived from the belief that "true liberty is derived not from the state, but from the individual's adherence to God-given moral laws."[17]

Even more ambitious than the Templeton Honor Rolls, the ISI college guide is the consummate example of a work that could only have been produced by ISI. It drew from both the Institute's four decades of experience in the vineyard of higher education and from its on-the-ground membership and alumni to provide fresh analysis and context. It was a

16. Ibid.
17. Ibid.

Herculean undertaking for the relatively small ISI staff. Ken Cribb was
the primary force behind the idea, authorizing Chris Long to acquire the
rights to the Madison Center's *Commonsense Guide to American Colleges*.
Cribb and Long initially thought that ISI could simply update the content of that early conservative college guide and publish it under the
Institute's imprint. However, when Long and ISI editor Jeff Nelson examined the text carefully, they realized much more work was needed if it
were to be a true ISI college guide.

It so happened that Gregory Wolfe was ending his tenure as director of
the Templeton Honor Rolls and was looking for a new challenge. Long and
Nelson considered several possible editors for a revised and renamed ISI
guide, but agreed that they could do no better than the immensely talented
Wolfe, who had a long ISI pedigree. Nelson assumed the position of project
director and with Wolfe began to construct a new outline for what was to
be the ISI guide, together with a comprehensive editorial, writing, and publishing plan. Wolfe tapped promising writer Jeremy Nafzinger to oversee
the drafting stage of the guide, while Nelson assembled a team of research-
ers composed of former ISI members and staff to conduct the kind of on-
campus interviews that would give the guide an "insider's" feel.

The guide was to be comprehensive and candid about institutions
from Amherst to Yale, disclosing, as William Bennett observed in his
introduction, "the good, the bad, and the ugly in American higher education." Although *Choosing the Right College* did not make the *New York
Times'* best-seller list when it appeared in 1998, it rose to number 34 on
Amazon.com, the largest online bookstore, and was in the top 30 on
barnesandnoble.com's list of education bestsellers. It was reviewed or featured in thirty-five major newspapers and magazines and dozens of smaller
newspapers and journals and mentioned on several national TV and radio programs, including ABC News, the Fox News Channel, and CBS
News. Readers liked its straightforward assessment of each school's history, academic life, political atmosphere, and student life. "This is an
outstanding resource for prospective students," commented a Minneapolis buyer, "and for parents of prospective students that want honest infor-

mation and direct analysis, NOT marketing pabulum from college admissions and P.R. departments."[18]

The guide attracted widespread and largely enthusiastic attention in both the conservative and mainstream media. "A godsend for anyone who wants to know how to beat the academic establishment and actually get an education," wrote the *National Catholic Register*. "This guide is a must for parents who care more about their kids' integrity than about their credentials," enthused radio talk show host Dr. Laura Schlessinger. "This book," wrote columnist and author Thomas Sowell, "presents a rounded picture—warts and all—of the pluses and minuses of 100 colleges, rather than trying to reduce everything to some numerical ranking.... *Choosing the Right College* is by far the best college guide in America." Popular syndicated columnist Cal Thomas observed that "American parents (and students) have long needed a reliable 'review' of our nation's universities so that they can be sure they will not be supporting the systematic destruction of the values, faith, and worldview they have spent so many years building up. *Choosing the Right College* is the right book for them." Author and philosophy professor Christina Hoff Sommers called the ISI guide "definitive and indispensable."

Although the *New York Times* termed the ISI guide "frankly conservative," it was impressed enough to devote fifteen paragraphs to the Institute's criticism (Harvard "now marches in lock step with the dominant trends of the intellectual world") and praise (the University of Dallas is "one of the few genuinely counter-cultural universities in the nation"). Until now, commented the highly regarded *Library Journal,* "no single publication has attempted to analyze and evaluate universities, academic programs, and professors on the basis of principled instruction and intellectual rigor."[19]

18. As quoted in "Making an Impact," August 1999 report about *Choosing the Right College,* ISI Archives.

19. Thomas Sowell, "Detailed guide to colleges sets higher standard," *Atlanta Journal,* September 25, 1998; William H. Honan, "A Right-Wing Slant on Choosing the Right College," *New York Times,* September 6, 1998; Samuel T. Huang, "Choosing the Right College: The Whole Truth About America's Top 100 Schools," *Library Journal,* November 1, 1998.

The ISI guide became required reading for parents, and not just con-servative parents, seeking the right school for their high school graduate children. The work confirmed what the National Association of Scholars and other groups had reported—that less than a quarter of the nation's universities had a "core curriculum." But it was still possible, the ISI book stated, to obtain a good liberal arts education even at PC colleges by taking courses offered by departments that were less politicized and taught by more traditional but still respected professors. *Choosing the Right College*, wrote graduate student David J. Bobb of Boston College, was a valu-able resource in the battle "to restore the liberal arts to their proper place" on the American campus.[20]

In many ways the guide amounted to a comprehensive survey of the state of higher education. Alumni sent copies of the guide to the trustees of their schools asking that it be used as a guideline for reviewing under-graduate instruction at their alma mater. Several schools that received favorable reviews forwarded copies to prospective students. The new presi-dent of the Catholic University of America even quoted the guide in his inaugural address. The ISI college guide sold an impressive 50,000 copies in its first two editions—a third edition is scheduled for the 2003-2004 academic year, and annually thereafter, in response to the pleas of many readers for a regular and wider survey.

Operation Self Reliance

ISI has stressed the virtue of self-reliance from its earliest days. The Institute's goal, founder Frank Chodorov pointed out, was not "to *make* individualists but to ... help them *find* themselves."[21] It was fitting, there-fore, that ISI students convinced a skeptical faculty at a 1997 summer honors conference that on today's progressive campuses, undergraduates seeking a true liberal education needed a bibliography of "must-read" books. The result was the Student Self-Reliance Project and the instantly

20. David J. Bobb, "The Good, the Bad, and the Politically Correct," *CAMPUS*, Fall 1998: 21-22.
21. See William F. Buckley Jr., "Death of a Teacher," eulogy delivered on Frank Chodorov's funeral, December 31, 1966.

popular series of student guides to history, philosophy, English, and other major disciplines.

Organized with a special grant from the William H. Donner Foundation, the title of the 1997 honors conference was "The Western Civilization Summit," and it attracted a record number of faculty to Snoqualamie, Washington. At one of the most heavily attended sessions, Gary Gregg presented a bibliography of essential reading in the arts and sciences that ISI had published years before and invited faculty comments. To Gregg's mounting disappointment, professor after professor criticized the bibliography, some even ridiculing the idea itself. Undergraduate Bracy Bersnak of Miami University, sitting in the audience, was aghast that "so many professors were oblivious to what seemed to me the dire need for such a resource." He raised his hand and informed the faculty that before encountering ISI, "[I] had searched in vain for a list of books that would give me a deeper appreciation of conservatism and the principles undergirding the U.S. Constitution and Western civilization."[22]

It would be "immensely useful," Bersnak said, to have a list of recommended literature because so much of what students were assigned in their coursework "was tainted by progressivist ideologies." How, he asked, would an undergraduate brought up in the post-Cold War world appreciate "the horrors of communism" if he had been taught that it was "a noble failure" and had no recourse to the works of, say, Robert Conquest and Martin Malia, who had exposed Communist myths? The right bibliography, Bersnak emphasized, "would be invaluable to undergraduates intellectually adrift in colleges corrupted by leftist ideology."[23] According to Gary Gregg, "the tide of the discussion immediately turned around," and the faculty, previously dismissive, began talking seriously about the possible contents of a bibliography. Upon returning to Wilmington, Gregg and Mark Henrie expanded the bibliographic idea into a series of student guides and asked Jeffrey Nelson to have his publications team design the series, and work out the details of discipline topics, authorship, organiza-

22. Bracy Bersnak memo to the author, April 1, 2003.
23. Ibid.

tion, production, and marketing.[24]

By 2001, the Self Reliance Project had produced a "first series" of guides—basic introductions to the most important fields of knowledge in the liberal arts by some of the nation's leading scholars—beginning with James V. Schall's *A Student's Guide to Liberal Learning* and concluding with Harvey C. Mansfield's *A Student's Guide to Political Philosophy.* The other titles were *A Student's Guide to the Core Curriculum* by Mark C. Henrie, *A Student's Guide to U.S. History* by Wilfred M. McClay, *A Student's Guide to Philosophy* by Ralph M. McInerny, *A Student's Guide to the Study of History* by John Lukacs, *A Student's Guide to Literature* by R. V. Young, and *A Student's Guide to Economics* by Paul Heyne. A second series was launched in 2002 with Daniel N. Robinson's *A Student's Guide to Psychology* followed in 2003 by Gerard V. Bradley's *A Student's Guide to the Study of Law* and Bruce Thornton's *A Student's Guide to Classics.*

Nothing like the student guides—clearly written, quietly erudite, attractively printed—had ever been seen by most students or professors, and they were enormously popular: 200,000 copies were sold, distributed, or downloaded from ISI's web page in the first three years. *The Chronicle of Higher Education,* the organ of the education establishment, respectfully noted their appearance, calling them "pocket mentors." The review in the conservative *Weekly Standard* was titled, "Guiding the Perplexed: What a liberal arts education ought to be."[25] "These slim volumes," the *Wall Street Journal* wrote, "come close to constituting mini-great books in themselves."[26]

Another key element of the Self-Reliance Project was the creation of the ISI Library of Modern Thinkers. Jeff Nelson had wanted to establish an ISI alternative to university press fare such as the Oxford Past Masters series, and proposed that as an element of the Self-Reliance Project, ISI

24. Ibid; Jeffrey O. Nelson memorandum to the author, January 20, 2003.

25. "Hot Type: Pocket Mentors," *The Chronicle of Higher Education,* October 11, 2002: A19; Diana Schaub, "Guiding the Perplexed: What a liberal education ought to be," *The Weekly Standard,* September 17, 2001: 38.

26. "ISI Guides Help Students Help Themselves," *The Canon: Reports from the Battlefield of Ideas,* Spring 2001: 1, an ISI publication.

commit itself to publishing a series of short, critical intellectual biographies of twentieth-century thinkers often neglected by the mainstream academy. Ken Cribb shared Nelson's sentiments and enlisted the support of former ISI vice chairman Richard Larry to help make the project financially viable. Cribb and Larry understood that university courses on twentieth century intellectual currents often dwelt on the minute disagreements of a coterie of Communist party intellectuals or championed the work of progressive social scientists whose intellectual contributions were usually more fantasy than fact. ISI sought to produce a resource that might bring to the academy much needed balance.

The ISI Library of Modern Thinkers was designed for classroom adoption, or at least to be easily accessible to students. The biographies were intended to begin the hard work of filling in the gaps of the academic mind—to say nothing of classroom reading lists. The first volumes in the Library, on Robert Nisbet, Eric Voegelin, Ludwig von Mises, and Wilhelm Roepke, met with immediate critical acclaim in journals such as *National Review*, *Booklist*, *Choice*, *First Things*, *The American Enterprise*, and the *Washington Times*. Series editor Nelson has arranged a heavyweight list of modern thinkers to be featured in forthcoming titles, including Will Herberg, Michael Oakeshott, Andrew Lytle, John Courtney Murray, Richard Weaver, Wilmoore Kendall, Francis Graham Wilson, John Lukacs, and Christopher Lasch.

All these programmatic successes facilitated fund-raising. ISI spent over $4 million in 1996 and 1997, and almost $4.5 million in 1998 on new and old programs that reached 51,500 student and faculty members on one thousand campuses. Over half a million copies of ISI publications and books were circulated; a grand total of 846,100 pieces of literature were distributed. The Honors Program provided forty undergraduates in 1997 with individual faculty mentoring, the Institute serving as "a matchmaker between the student and the professor," while twelve Weaver and Salvatori Fellowships were awarded to graduate students.[27] The Institute

27. Author's interview with Gregory Wolfe, October 27, 2002.

estimated that the number of books and articles produced by ISI graduate fellows was now in the thousands.

The Collegiate Network

For decades, ISI had offered its encouragement and resources to assist conservative student activists to publish their views on local college campuses. Already in the 1960s, ISI had been involved with *The New Individualist Review* at the University of Chicago, *Analysis* at Penn, *Phalanx* in Southern California, and many other student journals and newspapers. In the Reagan 1980s, a new generation of students launching papers across the country—starting with *Counterpoint* at the University of Chicago and *The Dartmouth Review*—gravitated to the well-financed Institute for Educational Affairs (IEA), under the direction of Irving Kristol, William Simon, and Michael Joyce of the Bradley Foundation.

But by 1995, the IEA had dissolved, and the Collegiate Network of independent student newspapers was being administered by the Madison Center in Washington, D.C. Taking advantage of ISI's expanding resources and administrative expertise, the CN was brought that year under ISI management. Once again, ISI was at the center of college conservative journalism. For the remainder of the 1990s and into the first years of the new century, the CN was supervised by executive director Stanley K. Ridgley. With a background in U.S. Army intelligence and a working knowledge of Russian, Ridgley had been active as a graduate student at Duke with the CN paper there—the *Duke Review*. He was mainly responsible for enlarging the network from thirty-five papers in 1995 to eighty papers today. He cultivated student talent with commitment and a sense of humor, while attracting the involvement of leading conservative journalists with his consistent professionalism. Under his sure hand, the Collegiate Network expanded to a total annual distribution of about 2.4 million.

In the second half of the 1990s, the CN annually sponsored two "Start the Presses" conferences for its student editors which included issue briefings, roundtables on practical questions in student publishing, and one-on-one writing sessions with leading journalists. Both summer-long and year-long internships were made available for the most promis-ing student journalists—including a position as an intern on the editorial pages of *USA Today*, and opportunities at *The Weekly Standard, U.S. News & World Report,* the *Detroit News,* the *Washington Times,* the *Wall Street Journal, National Review,* and *Voice of America*. By the turn of the new century, the CN was even able to offer a "foreign correspondent course" in Prague.

With Jeff Nelson's assistance, Ridgley did yeoman's work directing the editorial side of *CAMPUS* magazine for nearly a decade. He was an effective spokesman for the integrity of the written word, speaking fre-quently on good writing habits and skills, arranging intensive writing workshops for young college editors, and contracting with *Writer's Digest* editor William Brohaugh to republish with ISI Books his instructive *Write Tight,* to which Ridgley contributed a foreword. "Ridgley was an im-mensely talented editor and manager," noted longtime colleague Jeff Nelson. "The unprecedented growth of the Collegiate Network is due in large part to his commitment to excellence in collegiate journalism and his dogged pursuit of ideological balance on campus."[28] Ridgley today serves as president of the Russian-American Institute.

Continuing an ISI tradition, several Collegiate Network alumni en-tered the field of journalism, among them, David Masteo at *USA Today*; Lila Arzua at the *Miami Herald* and *Washington Post*; John Miller and Sarah Maserati at *National Review*; Matt Rees, Lee Bockhorn, Steve Hayes, Pia Zadora, Beth Henary, and Kathrine Mangu-Ward at *The Weekly Stan-dard*; acclaimed authors Wendy Shalit and Michael Fumento; Jonathan Karl at the *New York Post* and then CNN; and Matt Robinson at *Investor's Business Daily*. In the political field, attorney Marc Wheat became coun-sel for the House Commerce Committee, Marc Thiessen became a speech writer for Donald Rumsfeld, Bruce Frohnen assumed similar duties for Spencer Abraham, while Alex Steinberg took up speech writing for Mayor Rudy Guiliani of New York City.

28. Author's interview with Jeffrey O. Nelson, August 18, 2003.

Making a Literary Difference

The first book that ISI published on its own (in 1993) had been Russell Kirk's *The Politics of Prudence*, a collection of the conservative historian's speeches at The Heritage Foundation. Its success (by the fourth edition, it had sold more than 15,000 copies) encouraged Jeffrey Nelson to press for the formation of an ISI imprint. In a May 1995 memorandum to John Lulves, Nelson outlined how the Institute could publish as many as twenty-four books a year.[29] The Institute had been "inwardly directed," Nelson said, focusing on the editing, production, and marketing of in-house publications. To become a serious book publisher required ISI to be "outwardly directed," concerned with acquisitions, contacting authors, arranging for exhibits at conventions and conferences. The biggest challenge, stated Nelson, would be to come up with "new and exciting manuscripts."

The young editor and aspiring publisher envisioned six categories of books: reprints of classic conservative texts; introductions to the leading conservative thinkers of the twentieth century; reprints of books in the ISI Canon of Western Civilization; translations of principally European scholars whose books were not available to an American audience; original manuscripts relevant to "ISI's core mission;" and more scholarly books that would contribute to a particular academic field.[30] Both Ken Cribb and John Lulves were supportive of Nelson. "One of Ken's strengths is his willingness to listen to his staff, help develop what he deems are good ideas, and then leave his program directors to work out the details," Nelson said. "Such a style encourages creativity and it is great for staff morale. It is also based on a very conservative insight that one cannot control the direction and flow of information bureaucratically." ISI Books, commented Nelson, "bears the mark of Ken's intellect and, I hope, will be a lasting monument to his presidency."[31]

Nelson also credits John Lulves for being a principal force behind the

29. Jeffrey O. Nelson to John F. Lulves, May 11, 1995, ISI Archives.
30. Ibid.
31. Author's interview with Jeffrey O. Nelson, March 26, 2003.

creation of the press. "John Lulves," noted Nelson, "is the godfather of ISI Books." Lulves, a longtime owner with his wife, Carolanne, of a local used bookstore, especially guided Nelson on the financial aspects of the book program.[32] Nelson's vision, with Cribb's encouragement and Lulves's mentoring, was an audacious undertaking for a comparatively small organization that had co-published only a handful of books in its forty-year history.

And yet, in less than a decade, *National Review* literary editor Michael Potemra would say admiringly, "ISI Books publishes more books worth reading than any other publisher."[33] Some of these early titles included both original works and new editions such as George H. Nash's *The Conservative Intellectual Movement in America: Since 1945*, Willmoore Kendall's Oxford letters, Gerhart Niemeyer's *Within and Above Ourselves,* Richard Weaver's *Visions of Order,* and *A Few Reasonable Words* by Henry Regnery. The program's success was due to Nelson's editorial acumen and that of the editors he hired, former Weaver Fellows Christopher Briggs and Jeremy Beer, as well as certain long-term trends in New York and academic publishing. In a 1998 memo to Ken Cribb, Nelson argued that changes in the book business—including financial pressures stemming from huge cash advances to celebrities for books that did not return the investment and intellectual bias—had impeded conservative gains within the publishing industry. This was especially true for conservative authors of more serious books.

As a result, Nelson argued, "what the book industry calls a 'mid-list' book—a work printed in limited quantity and expected to bring in only modest profits—is becoming an endangered species." Largely political, mid-list books make a serious contribution to public knowledge and often help professors obtain tenure. "Such books," Nelson explained, "give conservative thinkers direct access to the public, allowing them in many cases to speak to people across the political and philosophical spectrum."[34]

32. Ibid.
33. Author's interview with Michael Potemra, May 19, 2003.
34. Jeff Nelson memo to Ken Cribb, June 1998, ISI Archives.

The young editor's insights were borne out by future events.

Grudgingly receptive to popular conservative authors like William F. Buckley Jr. and Rush Limbaugh, most major New York houses in 1995 expressed little interest in books that challenged left-wing orthodoxies. Penguin Putnam and the Crown Publishing Group finally launched small conservative imprints in the spring of 2003—years after ISI detected the trends and established ISI Books. University presses for their part happily pandered to politically correct trends and their advocates. Without embarrassment, prestigious academic publishers like Oxford, Johns Hopkins, and Duke offered such trendy works as *The Body in Late-Capitalist USA, Our Vampires, Ourselves*, and *Drag: A History of Female Impersonators*.[35]

While conservative philanthropy had directed a lot of resources to combating multiculturalism and political correctness, and the corresponding denigration of Western and American civilization, ISI hoped to convince far-sighted philanthropists that resources were also needed to provide fresh alternatives to academic and mid-list trade publishing—so often the source for the ideas that animated radical movements. However, Lulves and Nelson believed that, regardless of outside support, ISI Books could cover a substantial amount of its costs through aggressive and creative marketing—which for the most part it has been able to do through impressive year-to-year revenue growth.

ISI Books' remarkable track record is a testament to the soundness of their analysis. With the help of the widely respected University of Chicago Press, which, through the efforts of Brooke Daley Haas, assumed both the distribution and trade sales of ISI Books in 2000, the Institute published fourteen books in 2002 and will publish an estimated twenty books in 2003. The announcement by the mammoth Book-of-the-Month Club in May 2003 that it was forming a new club devoted to works with a conservative point of view was sobering news for the Conservative Book Club—which has long enjoyed a monopoly among conservative readers—but good news for ISI Books, which will now have two book clubs

35. "ISI Books: Countering the Academic Left with Conservative Principles," circa 2001, ISI Files.

as potential distributors of its books.

The consistently high quality of ISI Books has helped secure its reputation, a fact reflected in such recent works as *The Clash of Orthodoxies: Law, Religion, and Morality in Crisis* by Robert P. George, described by one reviewer "as one of the most important books of the last decade in the area of moral theory;" it sold an impressive 7,000 copies in its first year;[36] *The First Grace: Recovering the Natural Law in a Post Christian World* by Russell Hittinger; *Bonfire of the Humanities: Rescuing the Classics in an Impoverished Age* by Victor Davis Hanson, John Heath, and Bruce S. Thornton; and *Patriot Sage: George Washington and the American Political Tradition*, edited by Gary L. Gregg II and Matthew Spalding.

Classic reprints have included *A Humane Economy* by Wilhelm Roepke, Christopher Dawson's *Dynamics of World History*, Russell Kirk's *Edmund Burke: A Genius Reconsidered* and *The American Cause*, Orestes Brownson's *The American Republic*, Ellis Sandoz's *Political Apocalypse*, and *The End of the Modern World* by Romano Guardini. ISI has also produced biographies of important modern conservative figures such as James Burnham, Frank Meyer, Ludwig von Mises, Robert Nisbet, and Eric Voegelin as well as studies of J. R. R. Tolkien, Malcolm Muggeridge, and George Orwell.

One ISI book, Trace Lee Simmons' *Climbing Parnassus: A New Apologia for Greek and Latin,* was selected by the library journal *Choice* as an outstanding academic title for 2002. The award solidified "Tracy's position as a national standard-bearer for classical humanism," Nelson commented. The same could be said for ISI and ISI Books. *Aliens in America: The Strange Truth About Our Souls* by Peter Augustine Lawler was favorably reviewed, among other places, in *Booklist, First Things,* and the *Philadelphia Inquirer.*[37]

36. Jack Wade Nowlin, "Reason's Culture, Life's Defense," *Touchstone,* November 2002: 45.

37. For Jeffrey Nelson quotation, see Hillsdale College news release, "Book by Hillsdale College Journalism Professor Selected as Top Academic Title," January 13, 2003; Patrick J. Deneen, "Examining ourselves, our nation, our souls," *Philadelphia Inquirer,* October 24, 2002.

As a contribution to the ongoing discussion about terrorism, ISI Books commissioned a short but powerful book by the eminent conservative British philosopher Roger Scruton—*The West and the Rest: Globalization and the Terrorist Threat.* The central difference between the West and Islam, Scruton says, can be traced to "the contest between the religious and the political forms of social order." In the West, the contest has been resolved through the "separation of religious and secular authority." In the Islamic world, he says, it has not yet been resolved. A principal concern of this work, "is to understand the kinds of order and disorder" that have emerged in the West as result of its having "left behind its religious belief and its sacred text."[38] Rather than suggesting how to fight terrorism, said one review, Scruton urges the West to examine its present positions about multiculturalism, free trade, and secular law. *The West and the Rest,* commented the *Philadelphia Inquirer,* "is a marvel of clarity and concision."[39]

Of course, this kind of productivity cannot occur without consistent financial support. Nelson credits farsighted philanthropists such as David Kennedy of the Earhart Foundation and Gary Ricks at the Wilbur Foundation (Santa Clara, California) for supporting ISI Books and journals "year in and year out."

As the 1990s drew to a close, ISI Books received a boost with the arrival of a new senior editor, later appointed by Nelson as editor-in-chief: Jeremy Beer. An Indiana native, Beer earned a Ph.D. in psychology at the University of Texas, where he was actively involved with a conservative newspaper, and he did further graduate work in the liberal arts at the University of Dallas. He also spent several months as a research fellow at the Russell Kirk Center for Cultural Renewal in Mecosta, absorbing the classic works of the conservative tradition as well as the writings of the agrarian critic Wendell Berry.

38. Roger Scruton, *The West and the Rest: Globalization and the Terrorist Threat,* Wilmington, Delaware, 2002: x-xi.
39. Frank Wilson, "A philosopher compares the Western and Islamic worlds," *Philadelphia Inquirer,* September 8, 2002.

A highly efficient and energetic professional, Beer commissioned manuscripts about biotechnology and cloning which he believes will be major concerns in the future. Beer is also looking for authors who can deal with globalization and theology, capitalism and the family, and the new urbanism. "It is important to ISI Books' mission," he says, "that we only respond to important, enduring issues because we are engaged in the struggle with modernity for the long haul."[40] Assisting Beer are Alexandra (Xandy) Gilman, managing editor and first full-time editor of the ISI college guide; and Nancy Halsey, books production manager and a former *Washington Times* editor.

Both Beer and Nelson credit Brooke Daley (now Haas) with a significant role in ISI Books' success. As the first full-time book employee in 1997, Daley produced the first catalogue and persuaded the University of Chicago Press to distribute the Institute's books. "She was a master," says Beer, "of oft-unappreciated detail work."[41] "We quite simply would not be where we are today as a press were it not for Brooke's creativity, drive, and intelligence," added Jeff Nelson.[42] Daley was succeeded by Douglas Schneider, who has proven to be a dependable manager of the complex business of book sales and distribution. Schneider, a graduate of Messiah College, has a "deeply conservative sensibility," observed Nelson. "He is building the sales, marketing, and publicity arms of the press, taking us to new heights in all of these areas."[43]

Typical of the favorable reviews that ISI Books routinely received was the *Wall Street Journal's* August 2003 comment about *The Literary Book of Economics*, edited by Michael Watts. From the Rabelais story about charging for smoke produced by a roasting goose to the egg-pricing scheme in *Catch-22*, said the *Journal*, "the *Literary Book of Economics* illustrates theories and delights readers." *Boston Globe* columnist Jeff Jacoby wrote that Watts' "wonderfully rich and vivid survey of the economic realm"

40. Bracy Bersnak's interview with Jeremy Beer, April 11, 2003.
41. Ibid.
42. Author's interview with Jeffrey O. Nelson, March 26, 2003.
43. Ibid.

was "far more likely to kindle an interest in economics than [Allan] Greenspan's jargon-filled sludge."[44]

By mid-2003, the ISI list comprised more than seventy-five titles, justifying the comment of historian Wilfred McClay that "in the shrinking and increasingly troubled world of serious book publishing, ISI Books has been one of the most heartening success stories of the past decade."[45] But it was William F. Buckley Jr., acknowledged master of the written word and author of more than forty books, who paid ISI's publishing arm the ultimate compliment: "ISI Books is one of the blessings of this century," he said, for its "beautiful production" of works that are "rather studiously neglected by contemporary publishing" because of "their long-term moral, intellectual and strategic appeal." If ISI were to die tomorrow, Buckley said, "it has, in my judgment, brought out books which would preserve its memory for a century."[46]

Presidents and Pollys

When Arthur Schlesinger Jr. and the usual collection of liberal academics released a presidential poll in the winter of 1996, ranking Ronald Reagan as a "low average" president and John F. Kennedy and Lyndon B. Johnson as "high average" presidents, ISI decided that the best response was its own presidential survey. Enlisting Forrest McDonald, Donald Kagan, Martin Anderson, Harvey Mansfield, George Carey, Walter A. McDougall of the University of Pennsylvania, Herman Belz of the University of Maryland, and twenty-five other historians, political scientists, and economists, ISI reported that its group ranked Reagan as "near great"—along with Jefferson, Theodore Roosevelt, Franklin D. Roosevelt, and Dwight Eisenhower. Bill Clinton was judged a "failure," as were Johnson and Jimmy Carter. In the judgment of the ISI historians, wrote the Olin Foundation's James Piereson in *The Weekly Standard*, Ronald Reagan was "the only genu-

44. William McGurn, "Illuminating Looks at the Dismal Science," *Wall Street Journal*, August 13, 2003; Jeff Jacoby, "The unbearable dullness of economic writing," *Boston Globe*, August 21, 2003.

45. Wilfred McClay to Bracy Bersnak, May 29, 2003.

46. Interview with William F. Buckley Jr. for ISI's video history, July 7, 2003.

inely successful president" in the period between 1960 and 2000.[47]

Seeking to hoist the radicals with their own petard, ISI initiated the annual Campus Outrage Awards (or "Pollys") to expose the politically correct excesses of students, faculty, and administrators. The most egregious outrage in 1997-98 was judged to be Arizona State University's denial of tenure to drama professor Jared Sakren, a graduate of Juilliard and a former Yale professor. Sakren's unforgiveable offense: teaching Shakespeare, Aeschylus, and other classic playwrights whom his colleagues characterized as "sexist" and "offensive to feminists." Instead, the department required the inclusion of a play titled "Betty the Yeti: An Eco-Fable," in which, among other grotesqueries, a logger has sexual intercourse with a yeti (a kind of abominable snowwoman) and is transformed into an environmentalist. Rachel Alexander of the University of Arizona law school received a prize of $1,000 for documenting Sakren's story.[48]

U.S. News & World Report columnist John Leo praised ISI for highlighting what "the American campus does better than any other institution: screw up its people with soul-crunching correctness." "Academic freedom in America," wrote syndicated columnist Suzanne Fields, "has had tough times before, but today's ideological assault is bizarre, indeed." One feminist philosopher, Fields noted, has argued that holding a "seminar" is sexist, and suggested replacing the term with "ovular." Film star Annette Bening, a one-time student of Jared Sakren, declared in an interview with *CAMPUS* that discouraging the teaching and performing of Shakespeare "is like taking a painting or art student and saying, 'Don't study Rembrandt because he lived in a patriarchal society.'... It's absurd." The "ultimate losers" from such stifling political correctness, Bening said, are the students.[49]

47. James Piereson, "Historians and the Reagan Legacy," *The Weekly Standard*, September 29, 1997: 22.

48. Eric S. Cohen, "Professor Fired for Teaching Shakespeare! Announcing the 1998 Campus Outrage Awards," *Campus*, Spring 1998: 10.

49. John Leo, "Ready for Betty the Yeti?", *U.S. News & World Report, March 30, 1998;* Suzanne Fields, "Theater of the Absurd," *Insight,* December 7, 1998: 48; For Annette Bening quotes, see Julie Cart, "Professor's Suit Says Using Bard Got Him Fired," *Los Angeles Times,* January 19, 1999.

Amid the daily crises, the Institute took time in November 1998 to award its Henry Salvatori Prize to Robert H. Bork, the noted author and jurist and John M. Olin Scholar in Legal Studies at the American Enterprise Institute. It was presented during the Institute's 45th anniversary celebration held in its Wilmington headquarters. Judge Bork responded with a keen analysis of American culture in which he asserted that "we are now two cultural nations"—one that embodied the anarchic counterculture of the 1960s and was dominant, the other that reflected a traditional culture and was required to be dissident. Although not someone who had been religious for most of his life, Judge Bork argued that a reversal of the present moral crisis, with its "culture of death," depended upon "a revival of biblical religion."[50]

Taking back the culture, he admitted, would not be easy, but "religion rejects despair." The four cardinal Christian virtues of prudence, justice, fortitude, and temperance, he said, are enough to do the job, led by the virtue of fortitude—"the courage to take stands that are not immediately popular, the courage to ignore the opinion polls." That is what "true conservatism means," he said, "or it means nothing."[51] Judge Bork later acknowledged the Institute's pivotal role in defining true conservatism when he said, "By fighting for the soul of the university, ISI is performing a very valuable function to America as a whole."[52]

Covering the Campus

CAMPUS was taking note of PC follies in other areas of campus life as well. In a 1996 issue, Cornell junior Kenneth Lee exposed the hypocrisy of many schools in their call for more "diversity." While faculty and administrators routinely call for "diversity," their commitment to this goal fell short when applied to faculty hiring. *CAMPUS* substantiated how Cornell and other schools have systematically discriminated against Republicans.

North Carolina journalism graduate student Tony Mecia reported

50. Robert H. Bork, "Conservatism and the Culture," *The Intercollegiate Review,* Vol. 34, No. 2, Spring 1999: 3-7.
51. Ibid: 7.
52. Christine O'Donnell interview with Robert H. Bork, July 14, 2003.

in a 1997 *CAMPUS* about a growing discrimination problem at American law schools. Many schools, he found, discriminated against military recruiters for the JAG corps (Judge Advocate General), not allowing them onto campus because of the military's policy dealing with homosexuals in the ranks. Mecia pointed out that such schools "greedily accept defense department handouts while barring military recruiters from their campuses." This hypocrisy was and is widespread. As a direct result of the *CAMPUS* investigation, North Carolina legislators introduced a bill to bar state funds from any college or university that discriminates against military recruiters. UNC grudgingly reversed its policy within six months of the appearance of the *CAMPUS* exposé, and the Law School dean responsible for the policy was eventually ousted from the school. Legislators in other states, such as Alabama, began acting against schools found to be discriminatory, opening up the recruitment process and increasing employment options for all students.

In the same year, a *CAMPUS* article on campus crime revealed that, among other things, the University of Pennsylvania's accounting practices denied the horrendous crime problem at that school. The exposé by University of Pennsylvania sophomore David Kalstein helped spotlight a problem that was finally addressed by the Higher Education Act of 1998, which included provisions about the accounting of crime and security statistics.

In 1998, *CAMPUS* chronicled an imaginative tactic against the illogic of affirmative action. Students at the University of Texas developed and produced a "pledge" for proponents of affirmative action to sign. Since the victims of affirmative action—the qualified students rejected because of their race—are never seen on campus, the UT students publicized the real costs of racial discrimination by asking white affirmative action supporters to give up their slots at UT *now* to make room for qualified and government-approved minorities. The tactic was copied by many conservative student publications and used effectively across the nation.

In the winter of 1999, *CAMPUS* celebrated "Ten Years of Impact."

The anniversary issue was filled with accolades from conservative leaders in journalism and the media. "*CAMPUS* has proved an invaluable and indispensable resource in the war to maintain Western values and educational freedom," said syndicated columnist Robert Novak. *National Review* editor Richard Lowry, a former editor of a conservative student paper, commented that "for 10 years, *CAMPUS* has been there—a lively, fearless guardian of freedom. It's indispensable." Professor Alan Charles Kors at the University of Pennsylvania summed up *CAMPUS*'s contribution: "*CAMPUS* almost single-handedly has maintained a national, undergraduate voice against the campus orthodoxies and injustices that threaten the essential values of individual rights and responsibilities, critical mind, due process, and the sanctity of private conscience."[53]

Scholarship and Opinion

Throughout the second half of the 1990s, *The Intercollegiate Review* published a series of provocative and timely articles, reinforcing its place as one of the Institute's most valued programs. The spring 1997 issue, for example, featured a symposium on communitarianism, then a popular subject among academic political theorists seeking solutions to the arid abstractions of modern liberal theory. While generally sympathetic with the moral aspirations of this new "third way," the contributors—Brad Lowell Stone, Bruce Frohnen, Wilfred McClay, and Peter Augustine Lawler—pointed out that much of the new communitarian thought amounted to nothing but warmed over socialism, and that whatever was healthy in this academic movement had already been better understood and articulated by conservatives many years before. The symposium was something of a turning point, for thereafter conservative interest in communitarianism—which had been significant—declined, and the purported "third way" has become a special interest of the Left.

Reflecting the fact that the *IR*'s most devoted readers were often faculty, the spring 1999 issue featured a special section on "The Professor as

---

53. "Ten Years of Impact," *CAMPUS*, Volume 10 Number 2, Fall 1999: 4-8.

Company Man." Bruce S. Thornton, Peter Augustine Lawler, and Hugh
Mercer Curtler took stock of the current malaise of university faculty, but
also offered practical advice for the remoralization of the profession. Introducing an international dimension to the discussion, the issue also
contained a translation of "The Professor," by Alvaro d'Ors, one of Spain's
leading conservative thinkers.

The *IR* also took the occasion of George W. Bush's election in 2000
to examine "The Foundations of Compassionate Conservatism." While
most journalistic commentators considered this phrase a mere campaign
slogan designed to appeal to suburban "soccer moms," contributors to a
special section—Kenneth L. Grasso, Bruce Frohnen, and Allan Carlson—
discerned a deeper intellectual current that drew on traditional conservative insights. The symposium attracted the attention of the *Chronicle of
Higher Education*, the White House Office of Public Liaison, and *U.S.
News & World Report* columnist John Leo.

Beyond the theme issues, the *IR* editors have carefully maintained
ISI's eclectic intellectual tradition. Thus, readers in the late 1990s were
treated to such diverse articles as Robert R. Reilly discussing "The Music
of the Spheres, or The Metaphysics of Music," Louise Cowan arguing for
"The Necessity of the Classics," Steven J. Schloeder addressing "A Return
to Humane Architecture," Catherine Brown Tkacz examining feminist
appropriations of the Biblical story of Susanna—and even a symposium
on the comic films of Whit Stillman.

Relying upon a group of exceptional academics and a sly wit, *The
Intercollegiate Review* marked the turn of the century by publishing its list
of the fifty worst (and best) non-fiction books of the twentieth century.
The "worst" list, noted the editors, revealed a "remarkable number of
volumes of sham social science of every kind" and "a persistent attraction
to a dehumanizing statist administration of society." The "best" persuaded
the editors that "fine writing and clear-mindedness are perennially possible."[54] The "very worst" books were Margaret Mead's *Coming of Age in*

54. "The Fifth Worst (and Best) Books of the Century," *The Intercollegiate Review*,
Vol. 35 No. 1, Fall 1999: 3.

Somoa ("so amusing did the natives find the white woman's prurient questions that they told her the wildest tales—and she believed them!"); Beatrice and Sidney Webb's *Soviet Communism;* Alfred Kinsey's *Sexual Behavior in the Human Male* ("a pervert's attempt to demonstrate that perversion is 'statistically' normal"); Herbert Marcuse's *One-Dimensional Man*; and John Dewey's *Democracy and Education.*

The "very best" books of the twentieth century were Henry Adams' *The Education of Henry Adams,* C. S. Lewis's *The Abolition of Man,* Whittaker Chambers' *Witness,* T.S. Eliot's *Selected Essays, 1917-1932,* and Arnold Toynbee's *A Study of History.*[55] While intentionally humorous, the ISI "50-50" list, as it came to be called, had a serious purpose: to come to a preliminary judgment about the intellectual enthusiasms of the twentieth century and to help students to discriminate between the nourishing wheat and the worthless chaff. The list was the subject of much national and international coverage—the Associated Press and *Time* discussed it, as did several European and Australian publications. After the Modern Library's much-anticipated list of the best books of the century, ISI's was the most frequently cited such list—proving that in the world of ideas, ISI could more than hold its own.

British scholar Roger Scruton concurred, praising the Institute's books and journals as being "of the highest intellectual quality" and helping to ensure that "the conservative voice" is heard from generation to generation. While not optimistic that conservatism had a future among the educated elite in his own country, Scruton said, "I think it still does here, thanks largely to institutions like [ISI]."[56]

Continuing Growth

In 1999, ISI's operating budget almost reached $5 million for the first time in its history—excluding the $3.5 million received in contributions and outstanding pledges of $300,000 for the headquarters building. Accordingly, the Institute ratcheted up its activities. Remarked author/lec-

55. Ibid: 4-13.
56. Interview for ISI's video history, May 4, 2003.

turer Robert Royal, "The way ISI ... is going, a man could get a decent education reading you alone."[57]

The number of students seeking out ISI's resources and guidance continued to grow. In the 1998-1999 academic year, ISI held two summer schools, nine small-group seminars, and thirty-nine conferences; sponsored 292 lectures drawing 40,575 attendees; circulated 576,000 copies of major publications and books; and distributed almost 850,000 total pieces of literature. The Collegiate Network of student newspapers increased to seventy publications with a total annual circulation of 2.9 million. Through its Honors Program, thirty-nine ISI Fellows received faculty mentoring, counseling, and guidance in career placement.

The 1998-99 Honors Fellows were an exceptional group, including Tom Brown of Harvard, who won a Marshall Scholarship to study medieval literature at Oxford University; William Norris of Princeton, who won a Luce Fellowship for study and work in Asia; and Lynsey Morris of Berry College, who won the Carl Albert Fellowship to study political science at the University of Oklahoma. Other Fellows included Eric Cohen (Williams), later named managing editor of the prestigious journal, *The Public Interest,* and who went on to become a fellow at the Ethics and Public Policy Center and the founding editor of *The New Atlantis*; Hunter Campaigne (Notre Dame), who joined the Heritage Foundation as coordinator for civil society projects and is now with William Bennett's K-12 program; and Ilya Shapiro (Princeton), who entered the London School of Economics to study international relations.

"I know," said a Honors Fellow at Stanford, that "the program will be of lasting value to me throughout the rest of my education and as I head into professional life."[58] 1999-2000 Honors Fellow Austin Bramwell (Yale University), a recent Harvard Law School graduate now working on Wall Street, summarized the impact of the ISI Honors Program on him: "Before being an Honors Fellow, despite having three years of college, I was living amongst the shadows and waiting to receive the light,

57. Report of the Meeting of the ISI Board of Trustees, May 7, 1999: 3, 25.
58. "Preparing the Next Generation of American Leaders," *The Canon,* Spring 2001: 5.

intellectually speaking. I don't really feel I had ever learned anything terribly important before I had done the Honors Program."[59] For Sarah Maserati, another Yale student and now an editor at *National Review*, ISI acted "in loco universitatis," bringing conservative speakers to the campus that the university did not, giving "us the books that we didn't read in our classes." Of all organizations, said Maserati, ISI showed the conservative student that "you have an advocate, there are people behind you—a veritable army marching behind you—that you are not alone."[60]

And understanding full well that today's graduate student is tomorrow's professor, ISI expanded its fellowship programs. In 2002-2003, eight Weaver Fellowships, each providing a grant of $5,000 plus tuition, were awarded to those young scholars who appreciated there can be no free society without a genuinely liberal education. Two Salvatori Fellowships, worth $10,000 each, were given to graduate students doing work in a field related to the American Founding. Two graduate students studying the institutions, values and history of the West received a Western Civilization Fellowship in the amount of $20,000.

Two new fellowship programs were established: the Bache Renshaw Fellowship, providing full tuition and a living stipend of $12,000 for a student intending to pursue doctoral work at the University of Virginia's Curry School of Education; and the Richard and Karna Bodman Scholars in Science, who attended a weeklong, expenses-paid summer retreat at Oriel College, Oxford. The Bodman Scholars were science majors who explored the major themes of Western civilization with an ISI Mentor, a professor who has volunteered to make himself available for intellectual and career guidance. "My favorite part," commented a Bodman mentor at North Carolina State University, "was simply interacting with the other faculty and the students."[61]

59. Interview for ISI historic video with Austin Bramwell, July 7, 2003.
60. Interview for ISI historic video with Sarah Maserati, July 7, 2003.
61. As quoted in "Bodman Scholars in Science," ISI brochure, ISI Files.

The ISI Family

All these programs did not just happen: they were coordinated by a team of efficient, dedicated young staffers—almost every one in his or her twenties and thirties. In the second half of the 1990s, they included Kara Björklund Beer, former managing editor of *Modern Age* and assistant in the development office and later chief-of-staff to Jeffrey Nelson; Chris Briggs, formerly senior editor of ISI Books and today executive director of Aid to the Church in Russia; Brian Brown, one-time ISI director of campus leadership and now executive director of the Family Institute of Connecticut; Jason Duke, former director of the Prep School and Lecture Program and later director of Academic Projects for the Institute from 1996; chief financial officer Lori Halpern, who departed to pursue an M.B.A.; John M. Vella, managing editor of *Modern Age* and maestro of ISI's layout and graphics work from 1995; Chad Kifer, director of campus leadership since June 1999; Paul G. Rhein, conference director and later director of internet education from 1997; Jeffrey Cain, a former Marine and a former ISI Honors Fellow and Weaver Fellow, (with a Ph.D. in literature at Washington State) who had run a small think tank before coming to ISI to work first in program and then in development; and Michael Wallacavage, ISI's lecture director for almost a decade and now program officer for the International Institute for Culture in Philadelphia.

For many students and faculty in the 1990s, Michael Wallacavage was the always-overworked but irrepressibly cheerful face and voice of ISI, as he made thousands of telephone calls to touch base with student groups and logged as many air miles accompanying speakers to campuses across the country. Before beginning work at ISI in 1994, Wallacavage had earned a master's degree at the International Academy of Philosophy in Liechtenstein after doing his undergraduate work at Villanova University and Christendom College. "When Michael left ISI," says Mark Henrie, "it really took two people to replace him. In fact, his inspiring optimism is irreplaceable."[62]

62. Author's interview with Mark Henrie, August 21, 2003.

As the Institute's lecture director, Wallacavage got to know such intellectual giants as the eminent historian John Lukacs and the polymath Erik von Kuehnelt-Leddihn, who toured American campuses under ISI auspices until he was almost ninety. "I do not mind to be 'overworked,'" Kuehhelt-Leddihn once wrote Wallacavage at age eighty-eight, "but not more than three lectures a day."[63] Among Wallacavage's most popular speakers were Dinesh D'Souza, touring on behalf of *Illiberal Education,* and Christina Hoff Sommers when she was promoting her controversial book, *Who Stole Feminism?* Despite the constant pressure and invariable crises, Wallacavage loved his work—"ISI is what a university is supposed to be."[64]

Among those responsible for the high quality of ISI publications are designers Glenn K. Peirce and Sam Torode. But the single most important staffer in this area has been John Vella, a graduate of Louisiana State University where he published a student journal entitled *Faith & Culture.* Several of conservatism's leading thinkers—including Marion Montgomery, Gerhart Niemeyer, and Russell Kirk—contributed to the LSU journal. After a short stint at the Acton Institute, Vella has been a steady hand for ISI publications for nearly a decade, managing all aspects of production and design. "John has a deep commitment to the ideas that animate ISI," explained Jeff Nelson. "He understands the central importance of conservative publications to advancing those ideas."[65]

The Oxford Connection

There are several reasons why the Institute now has far more applicants than it can accept into its Honors Program, suggests academic projects director Jason Duke, including better public relations. But the most important development, undoubtedly, was to move the program to Oxford University, regarded by most American undergraduates as "the most prestigious university on earth." Duke, who suggested the move, notes that in

63. Michael Wallacavage to Bracy Bersnak, May 15, 2003.
64. Bracy Bersnak interview with Michael Wallacavage, April 25, 2003.
65. Author's interview with Jeffrey O. Nelson, March 26, 2003.

though only fifty were accepted into the program. Receiving a BA from the University of Seattle in 1996, Duke had his first ISI encounter at a Liberty Fund colloquium that included as faculty George Carey and M. Stanton Evans. Christopher Long was so impressed by a subsequent talk that Duke gave on the history of opera that he offered the recent college graduate an ISI job—director of the Prep School Lecture Program. "I did not envision staying long at ISI," recalls Duke. But over the next seven years, he built up the prep school lecture program to as many as eighty talks a year, organized Liberty Fund colloquia on Richard Wagner and William Shakespeare, ran the Weaver Essay contest, wrote for the College Guide, and instituted the move of the Honors Program to Oxford.[66]

Just past thirty, Kara Björklund Beer has seen many changes in her years with the Institute, having first worked in the cluttered but cozy confines of the Bryn Mawr office. Staffers often did the *New York Times* crossword puzzle together, she remembers, "and you could walk anywhere to shop or go to lunch." After thirty years in one place, people were a little set in their ways. She notes that when Spencer Masloff wanted to paint the office to make it more presentable to visiting donors, John Lulves "wouldn't move his things, so they painted around him." The staff was smaller then—one-third the size of today's staff—which encouraged camaraderie. David Burns, now Fr. Basil Burns, OSB, trying to encourage ISI employees to recruit new members, placed a box for names and addresses in the common room and pasted footprints on the floor leading to the box. Beer is grateful to ISI for helping her to learn so much about editing and publishing—and for meeting her husband, Jeremy Beer, now editor-in-chief of ISI Books. The Institute, she says, "has been an immense good in my life."[67]

As the 1990s came to a close, ISI had built up an impressive staff of professionals although there were the inevitable departures of good people. At the end of 1999, Gary Gregg left his position as director of ISI's national program to pursue a once-in-a-lifetime opportunity—an endowed

66. Bracy Bersnak's telephone interview with Jason Duke, May 19, 2003.
67. Bracy Bersnak's telephone interview with Kara Björkland Beer, April 11, 2003.

tional program to pursue a once-in-a-lifetime opportunity—an endowed chair and directorship of the McConnell Center for Political Leadership at the University of Louisville. When he came to ISI in 1997, Gregg had feared that after taking a job with "the vast right-wing conspiracy," he "would never be able to get a job in academia again." But Gregg's experience at ISI enabled him "to pole vault ahead" of far better known scholars to be appointed—at age thirty-two—to lead a major new educational program at a Louisville. "ISI made me," Gregg says, attesting to the Institute's beneficial reputation, at least in some regions of the country.[68]

Gregg's successor, and immediately named vice president of the Institute, was Rear Admiral P. Michael Ratliff, who had just retired from a naval career that culminated in the post of Director of Naval Intelligence. A 1969-1970 Weaver Fellow at the London School of Economics, Ratliff had another tie to the ISI family: he had met his wife Gracia in Mecosta, where she had been for many years the babysitter for the Kirk family, as well as friend and confidante to Annette Kirk. Ratliff brought to ISI's program side a strong commitment to his country and its young people, along with the skills of a seasoned manager. Throughout the Cold War, ISI had sought to defend the West intellectually; Ratliff played a more direct role, keeping track on the movements of Soviet submarines through the long twilight conflict. Of his new colleagues, he said that they compared "favorably with the best with whom I served in the Navy-Marine team over the past thirty years."[69]

As the Institute rapidly expanded under Ken Cribb's leadership—growing, for example, from $960,000 to an estimated $11 million in revenue in 2003-2004, from eleven to forty-three employees, and multiplying its programs—there was a crucial need to build an appropriate support system. The expansion of the accounting system was undertaken by Lori Halpern, a literature student who began at ISI as a receptionist and had achieved the position of chief financial officer when she left in 1999. Halpern, largely self-taught in the subject, kept ISI's accounting

68. Bracy Bersnak's interview with Gary L. Gregg II, April 26, 2003.
69. Spencer Bjorklund, "From the Pentagon to ISI," *Campus*, Fall/Winter 2000: 22.

systems in accord with the continuing expansion. Her successor, Elaine Pinder, had a degree in the field and wide experience from a variety of accounting positions. Pinder's mandate as manager of accounting was to establish systems that would serve the Institute through 2010. By 2003, in a world of complex and expensive systems software and in an era that requires extensive budgeting and unimpeachable accounting, Pinder had put ISI ahead of the curve.

Under the direction of Mary Ehart and her successor, Christine Singles, the pioneering work of Ed Giles in setting up ISI's internal network and external web sites was expanded and developed as required by ISI's increased campus activity. In 2002, the ISI DataCenter was established by Benjamin Schools, with a broad directive to utilize the huge amount of information accumulated by the Institute's publications, program, and development departments.

Spencer Masloff had long shouldered the burdens of fundraising almost alone, excepting Ken Cribb. Given the behind-the-scenes nature of much of his work, Masloff's efforts could be overlooked, but that, according to John Lulves, would be a grave mistake: "Spencer's work is central to producing all of the books, journals, lectures, fellowships, and all the other parts of ISI's widespread activities. His vast knowledge and long experience in development are apparent in the steady upward march of the Institute's revenue."[70] Understanding that "program drives fundraising," Masloff stood by as program staff grew while his staff remained essentially static. It was an understandable policy, but for the Institute's sake it had to change.[71]

And so in the mid-1990s, Masloff could look for help to Justin Haas, a Temple University graduate and workhorse development program officer (now leading the development efforts of the Philadelphia-based International Institute for Culture) and gifted writer Kevin McNamara (currently at Drexel University). More recently, Masloff has benefited from the addition of the unflappable Jennifer Connolly, who assists him in

70. John Lulves to author, July 2003.
71. Author's interview with Jeffrey O. Nelson, March 26, 2003.

directing ISI's development efforts. Connolly is a Mount St. Mary's College graduate recently awarded a Master's degree in literature from West Chester University. Her even temperament is especially welcome in the high-pressure environment that is endemic to institutional fundraising. Connolly is complemented by grant-writer Scott Rubush, a University of North Carolina graduate, former Collegiate Network editor, and ISI Honors Program alumni. Rubush's writing skills in particular have been a boon to ISI's development. The erudite and personable Jeffrey Cain accepted a career challenge to move from directing the ISI academic program to overseeing ISI's individual donor relations and taking on a new planned giving effort. Cain's success is crucial, the Institute's top management agrees, to current and future growth.

With Kenneth Cribb as president and CEO, John Lulves as executive vice president and COO, Spencer Masloff as vice president, Michael Ratliff as vice president for programs, and Jeffrey Nelson as vice president for publications, ISI had a seasoned, resourceful management team prepared, with the guidance of the board of trustees, to lead the Institute into the twenty-first century.

A Constant Mission

The trustees held a strategic planning session in May 2000 at which they concluded that, first, ISI's mission "must remain constant." The mission could and should be clarified, defined and "refreshed" for each new generation, but its substance "ought never to be changed." Second, ISI must develop even more of a national presence so that it could become "*the* national resource for those interested in traditional liberal arts education." Third, ISI's primary focus was college students and teachers. Fourth, in recognition of the communications revolution occurring in the nation and the world, ISI must utilize the Internet "to the fullest." Fifth, ISI must "push conservative ideas" into the intellectual mainstream of the campus—"the Institute's publishing program is central to accomplishing" this objective. Sixth, ISI should develop a national survey program to determine "the concerns, needs, and motivation points of students, teachers, and donors." No conservative educational organization had ever before attempted so ambitious an analysis of American higher education. Seventh, ISI must use its fiftieth anniversary in 2003 to significantly raise the level of its finances and the impact of its programs.[72]

The board of trustees took time out from its strategizing in August 2000 to travel to Souderton, Pennsylvania, to present its Lifetime Achievement Award to trustee Charles H. Hoeflich. Hoeflich, who turned the Union National Bank of Souderton into Univest Corporation, one of the most successful financial institutions in Pennsylvania, is a charter ISI trustee and served as secretary-treasurer for over forty years. The board subsequently and unanimously renamed the award the "Charles Hoeflich Award for Lifetime Achievement." "Naturally," Hoeflich later wrote his fellow trustees, "one cannot feel worthy of such recognition but please be assured this one is so completely grateful the euphoria has continued unabated."[73] The board also welcomed as a member Alfred S. Regnery, president of Regnery Publishing (now publisher of *The American Spectator*) and the son of the late Henry Regnery, who gave so generously to ISI and the conservative movement throughout his life.

The Closest Election

A presidential election is normally a referendum on continuity or change, but in the fall of 2000, Americans seemed to vote for continuity *and* change. The public's desire for change frustrated the Democratic candidate, Vice President Al Gore, who should have been able to win the presidency by promising to continue the peace and prosperity of the Clinton-Gore years. But Clinton was so personally unwelcome in the living rooms of most Americans that Gore distanced himself from Clinton throughout the campaign, insisting, "I am my own man." The desire for continuity hampered the Republican candidate, Texas Governor George W. Bush, who had to be careful not to be overly critical of the generally popular record of the Clinton-Gore administration. He instead promised to solve the

72. Summary of ISI Trustees' Strategic Planning Session, May 12, 2000, ISI Archives.

73. "Hoeflich Receives Lifetime Achievement Award," *The Canon*, Spring 2001: 2.

major problems—too high tax rates, a weakened military, ineffective education—that had not been sufficiently addressed by Clinton and Gore. Bush also sought to reassure the electorate that he was not an uncaring, unfeeling Gingrich conservative but a "compassionate conservative."

The ambivalent mood of the electorate produced the closest presidential election since 1960 when John Kennedy defeated Richard Nixon by only two-tenths of 1 percent of the popular vote—about the same margin by which Gore topped Bush. But Bush won the electoral vote and the presidency by accruing 271 electoral votes (one more than needed) to Gore's 267—or did he? Bush was preparing to announce the first members of his cabinet—beginning with Colin Powell as secretary of state—when Florida with its twenty-five electoral votes suddenly became too close to call. The nation was plunged into a political and legal battle that did not end until a month later when Bush—following a crucial ruling by the U.S. Supreme Court—secured Florida after a series of recounts and was officially declared the winner.[74]

For the next ten months, America was divided. Etched in most Americans' mind was a twin-hued map—the "blue" Gore nation of the secular, elitist East and West coasts and the "red" Bush nation of the observant, populist heartland. Politics became increasingly rancorous and partisan, fueled by politicians who could not let go of the last election or stop plotting for the next. The economy, after eighteen years of unprecedented prosperity, teetered on the edge of recession, and picking whom to blame for the economic stall became the favorite game of the mass media. Americans seemed obsessed with the absurd (lottery payoffs) and the trivial—such as whether President Bush was spending too much time on his Texas ranch.

By the fall of 2001, the nation was mired in an unhappy, unsettled mood, seemingly unable to get on with life, questioning the meaning of liberty, finding scant satisfaction in the pursuit of happiness, and casting about for a *raison d'etre* in the post-Cold War world. What could unite a divided nation and give its people a sense of purpose for the new millennium?

74. For a full discussion of *Bush v. Gore,* see *The Vote: Bush, Gore and the Supreme Court,* eds. Cass R. Sunstein and Richard Allen Epstein, Chicago, 2001.

ISI decided to contribute to the debate through a special edition of *CAMPUS*. In the late summer of 2001, *CAMPUS* devoted almost an entire issue to the decline of academic standards, tracing it in large measure to the failure of universities "to teach their students to distinguish truth from falsehood with rigorous rational analysis and research." Spectacle and drama, wrote editor-in-chief Katherine Mangu-Ward (a Yale senior and now a reporter at *The Weekly Standard*), have replaced rhetoric and logic as "the dominant mode of communication."[75] Caught up in the idea of the world as a spectacle, university administrators and professors rewarded students for "embracing showmanship and emotion" over "respect for facts" and "principled responses to important questions."[76]

In "Mickey Mouse History," Sean Salai of Wabash College described the revised, oversimplified history presented at amusement parks, national monuments, historical battle sites, and even in upper level history texts. It was not surprising, therefore, that a Roper survey of America's elite colleges and universities revealed that only 34 percent of the students surveyed could identify George Washington as the American general at the battle of Yorktown while just 23 percent knew that James Madison was the "Father of the Constitution."[77]

Spotlighted in *CAMPUS* were the 2001 Polly Awards—the top five politically correct outrages on the American campus. Among them was the abject reversal of UC-Berkeley's student paper, the *Daily Californian*, which printed ex-radical David Horowitz's advertisement, "Ten Reasons Why Reparations for Slavery Is a Bad Idea—and Racist Too," and then apologized for running the ad *after* student radicals stole all the papers they could find and stormed the *Californian's* offices, demanding a public apology for the offending message. Topping the Polly list was Dr. Peter Singer of Princeton, DeCamp Professor of Bioethics at the University Center for Human Values [sic], who wrote a favorable review for nerve.com of Midas Dekker's *Dearest Pet: On Bestiality*. Singer's enthusiastic endorse-

75. Katherine Mangu-Ward, "The Decline of Standards," *CAMPUS*, Fall 2001: 3.
76. Ibid.
77. Sean Salai, "Hollywood History Lessons: Who's Imitating Whom?" *CAMPUS*, Fall 2001: 21.

ment of human-animal sex followed his earlier advocacy of euthanasia for the handicapped of every age. "Killing a disabled infant," he wrote, "is not morally equivalent to killing a person. Very often it is not wrong at all."[78]

ISI's measured response to this psychotic amorality was to hold fall conferences on "The Roots of American Order: Markets, Morality, and Civil Society," featuring Dinesh D'Souza and Burt Folsom (a former Weaver Fellow), and "Winston Churchill: A Leadership Model for the 21st Century," with Sir Martin Gilbert, Churchill's official biographer. It also presented lectures by Richard Brookhiser on George Washington, Robert George on academics and ethics, E. Christian Kopff on America's classical tradition, Christina Hoff Sommers on contemporary culture's war against boys, and Victor Davis Hanson and Bruce Thornton on the "bonfire" of the humanities. Asked by a *CAMPUS* interviewer what advice he had for conservative students in a liberal land at the dawn of a new century, William F. Buckley Jr., ISI's first president, responded: "Read widely.... It is very, very important in my experience for conservative centers and students to do their homework, to give as much time to reading as to protesting."[79]

78. Nick Felten, "'Pollys' Spotlight PC Excess," *CAMPUS*, Fall 2001: 17-18; Peter Singer, "Taking Life: Humans," excerpted from *Practical Ethics*, 2nd edition, Cambridge, 1993: 8.

79. Paul Glader, "Novelist, TV Personality, Intellectual: William F. Buckley, the Quintessential Conservative," *CAMPUS*, Fall 2001: 26.

CHAPTER X

The Rising Generation

We are the institution of first resort on the philosophical side of conservatism.

T. Kenneth Cribb, Jr.[1]

I N ITS FIRST FORTY-EIGHT YEARS, ISI had survived the Cold War and the
Great Society, SDS and the JBS, affirmative action and
multiculturalism, declining SATs and accelerating PC, closed minds and
illiberal educators, the deaths of founder Frank Chodorov and mentors
Richard Weaver and Russell Kirk, Jimmy Carter's malaise and Bill Clinton's
charisma, but nothing had prepared the Institute for the unprecedented
terrorist attacks of September 11, 2001.

By coincidence, the entire ISI staff was to meet that morning for the
annual preview of the Institute's programs in the coming academic year.
Ken Cribb was expected to give his usual "state of ISI" talk, but immediately cancelled the meeting as the horrific pictures from New York City
and Washington, D.C., filled the TV screen. The next day, the Institute's
senior management gathered to discuss how the organization's mission

1. Author's interview with T. Kenneth Cribb, Jr., May 8, 2002.

might have to be modulated in response to the changed political land-
scape. But the new reality turned out to be a very old one—how to balance liberty and order in an insecure world. ISI sponsored a series of
campus lectures by prominent conservatives under the theme, "The Roots
of American Order." The Collegiate Network hosted a flag-waving Rally
for America on the steps of the Texas Capitol Building in Austin. And the
cover of the Spring 2002 *CAMPUS* was dominated by a stern-visaged
Uncle Sam asking, "Where Do YOU Stand?" "People of all faiths and
ethnic origins," remarked ISI vice president Mike Ratliff, "have come
together in a way not seen in generations."[2]

The Islamic extremists who smashed hijacked airplanes into the silver towers of the World Trade Center in New York City, the side of the
mammoth Pentagon in Washington, D.C., and the Pennsylvania countryside killed three thousand innocent people, and in the aftershock swept
away the political and social detritus of the previous ten months. The
signs of a new America surfaced everywhere: the overnight surge in military enlistments; the thousands lining up to give blood; the tens of millions of dollars in donations pouring into the Red Cross, the Salvation
Army, and other charitable organizations for the victims and their families; the doubled and tripled attendance at churches, synagogues, and
mosques; the runaway sale of American flags—one Chicago store sold
more flags in one day than it had in all of the past year.

The campus mood was especially revealing. A memorial service for
the terrorist victims at the University of California at Berkeley (birthplace
of the student demonstrations of the 1960s) drew an impressive 12,000
students, over a third of the student population. A rally against military
retaliation attracted 2,500, but was followed the next day by an almost
equally large "Rally for America." "This is 2001, not 1968," said student
Randy Barnes, the chief organizer of the pro-America rally. "This is not
Vietnam, but an act of aggression upon us as a nation."[3]

2. Email memorandum from Mike Ratliff to ISI Alumni, September 26, 2001.
3. Thomas D. Elias, "Berkeley breaks from anti-war past," *Washington Times*,
October 1, 2001.

A poll by Harvard's Institute of Politics found that 75 percent of college students trusted the military to "do the right thing" all or most of the time, while 92 percent considered themselves patriotic. "We're so used to thinking in terms of the 60s generation," remarked Shelby Steele, a fellow at the Hoover Institution at Stanford University, that "it's just stunning to see college students who like their country."[4] Surveys showed that on campuses across the country, support for President Bush and the war against terrorism was as high as 85 percent. At a patriotic rally at the University of Texas in Austin—the most liberal school in the state—senior and active ISI member Marc Levin described September 11 as "a wake-up call" for many of his generation who once cared more about music than mujahideen. "Now," he said, "so many more students are focused on politics and the world around them."[5]

While there were antiwar demonstrations and teach-ins on approximately one hundred campuses, at which speakers fulminated against American "imperialism" and "racism," the crowds usually numbered in the hundreds, not the thousands as in the 1960s. There were several reasons for this. To begin with, there was no draft and no immediate prospect that students would be fighting an entrenched Taliban in the snowy mountains of Afghanistan. Second, this was not a debate about U.S. involvement in a "civil" war halfway around the world, but the appropriate response to a direct and unprovoked terrorist attack on America and Americans. Third, the anti-war demonstrations of 2001 did not have the organization, commitment, and finances of the anti-war movement of the 1960s. Finally, 1960s students—and their leftist professors—had romanticized the outposts of communism like North Vietnam, viewing them as utopian alternatives to Western capitalism and colonialism. But few students, aside from those on the extreme Left, could justify or identify with Islamic terrorists like Osama Bin Laden.

But beyond this, some conservatives perceived systemic change in

4. Liz Marlantes, "After 9/11, the body politic tilts to conservatism," *Christian Science Monitor*, January 16, 2002.

5. Kris Axtman, "College campuses are a hotbed of ... pro-war fervor?" *Christian Science Monitor*, November 27, 2001.

America. Thanks to Osama bin Laden, wrote Dartmouth professor Jeffrey Hart, a veteran ISI lecturer, "the cultural wars of the '60s are over." In plotting the murder of thousands of innocents, bin Laden had destroyed "anti-Americanism, even among liberals." Unlike the 1960s, said Hart, there were no 2001 counterculturalists wearing bin Laden T-shirts or displaying his poster on dormitory walls. The veteran professor even sensed "a return of civility and good manners on the college campus."[6]

In the weeks following September 11, conservative cultural critic Terry Teachout could find statements by only two liberal celebrities—the artistic director of Harvard's American Repertory Theatre and singer-songwriter James Taylor—criticizing the United States or speaking out in opposition to a military reprisal. Instead, wrote Teachout, there was "an outpouring of support" for the families of the victims of the attacks. Actors and musicians across the country donated their services to benefit performances, among them a gala by the Metropolitan Opera at which $2.5 million was raised in a single evening. More than thirty television networks and channels simultaneously aired *America: A Tribute to Heroes*, an all-star, fund-raising telethon featuring such politically liberal celebrities as Tom Hanks, Julia Roberts, Paul Simon, and Bruce Springsteen. In a cover story of the trendy *Entertainment Weekly*, Jeff Gordinier argued that far-reaching cultural shifts were in the making:

> If America is a nation held spell-bound by fantasy, if we've spent a lot of the past 25 years getting our kicks from catty irony and glib sadism and empty fizz, it took only an instant of excruciating reality to render our old appetites moot, piddling, even nauseating.[7]

While applauding the efforts of pop-culture stars to help the families of the September 11 victims, Teachout cautioned that a "much tougher challenge" awaited them—"a deep reconsideration of some of the fundamental tenets of the adversary culture from which so many American artists have sprung and by which they take their bearings."[8]

6. Jeffrey Hart, "The day the 1960s died," *Washington Times*, November 5, 2001.
7. Jeff Gordinier, "How We Saw It," *Entertainment Weekly*, September 28, 2001: 12.
8. Terry Teachout, "Prime-Time Patriotism," *Commentary*, November 2001: 52-54.

"Umpteen" professors and college administrators, according to columnist John Leo, were flunking the challenge. The American Association of University Professors pompously promised to "continue to fight violence with renewed dedication to the exercise of freedom of thought and the expression of that freedom in our teaching." Leo wondered whether that meant, for example, that the professors of 1941 should have responded to Pearl Harbor "by giving longer lectures." Brad Wilson of the National Association of Scholars termed the AAUP statement "fatuous nonsense."[9] At Yale, six hand-wringing professors focused on the underlying causes of the September 11 attack and America's many faults, including its "offensive cultural messages." Yale professor Donald Kagan responded that the panelists seemed intent on "blaming the victim" and asked why the University couldn't find one panelist who would discuss the enemy and "how to stamp out such evil."[10]

The Right Response

Because ISI members had done their homework and knew who they were and what America was, they were able to respond correctly to the horrific events of September 11, 2001—burning candles and not flags, placing the blame on the terrorists and not on U.S. foreign policy, distinguishing between government censorship of anti-Americanism, which is illegal, and public censure, which "is healthy."[11] At Amherst, one hundred students gathered at a pro-American rally hosted by the Amherst Assembly of Patriotism. The rally was interrupted by a handful of students from nearby Hampshire College who burned a large American flag—patriotic students countered by singing "God Bless America." At Princeton, Lynne Cheney urged students to recognize the difference between the Vietnam War and the present war against terrorism. "This is not a war in which we get to choose whether or not to fight," said Cheney—"thousands of

9. John Leo, "Learning to love terrorists," *Newsweek*, October 8, 2001: 48.
10. Ibid.
11. Katherin Mangu-Ward, "September 11 Offers Opportunity for Reflection," *CAMPUS*, Spring 2002: 3.

Americans were killed on the very first day of conflict here at home."[12]

With the airplane missiles, wrote editor Jeff Nelson in *The Intercollegiate Review,* "an era came to an end—a decade of feeling-your-pain, actions without consequences, and anti-culture multiculturalism." Freedom, Nelson said, "was again recognized for the complex and delicate achievement that it is."[13] ISI's leading journal offered essays on such important questions as: Why is our civilization worth the fight? Why has the reaction of the intellectual class been so mixed, and often hostile, to American actions and interests? What constitutes a legitimate, reflective, and honorable patriotism? Forty copies of the special *IR* issue were requested by the White House for internal use.

While the attacks on America produced a wave of vilification from some intellectuals in America and abroad, Professor Donald Kagan of Yale, writing in the *IR,* quoted an Englishman with a quite different view:

> Let us ponder exactly what the Americans did in that most awful of all centuries, the twentieth. They saved Europe from barbarism in two world wars. After the Second World War they rebuilt the continent from the ashes. They confronted and peacefully defeated Soviet communism, the most murderous system ever devised by man.... America, primarily, ejected Iraq from Kuwait and stopped the slaughter in the Balkans while the Europeans dithered...."[14]

Kagan argued in the *IR* that patriotism is essential to democracy because, of all political systems, democracy "depends on the participation of its citizens in their own government" and "their own free will to risk their lives in its defense." And the civic sense that America needs, he said, can come "only from a common educational effort." Predicting "a long and deadly war that will inflict much loss and pain," Kagan stated that Americans "must be powerfully armed, morally as well as materially, if we are to do what must be done."[15]

12. Ibid.
13. Jeffrey O. Nelson, "In This Issue," *The Intercollegiate Review,* Spring 2002: 2.
14. Donald Kagan, "Terrorism and the Intellectuals," *The Intercollegiate Review,* Spring 2002: 5.
15. Ibid: 8.

We are also defending, wrote Professor Bruce Frohnen of the Ave Maria School of Law in the *IR*, the "civilization stretching back thousands of years, which shapes our culture, giving it meaning and permanence." That civilization had its basis in our religious and philosophical outlook—in what Matthew Arnold characterized as "the creative tension" between Jerusalem and Athens and what Russell Kirk termed "the roots of American order."[16]

For the pacifists and moral relativists who rejected any notion of an American military response against terrorists and their sponsors in Afghanistan and elsewhere, Keith Pavlischek of the Center for Public Justice provided an essay on "just and unjust war in the terrorist age." He concluded that "just war thinking begins with the belief that in a fallen world, the use of coercion and force, including the use of lethal force by legitimate public authority, is not only permitted but also morally required under certain circumstances." "For governments *not* to use lethal violence to protect the innocent," Pavlischek said bluntly, "is unjust and dishonorable."[17] His article on just war doctrine was adopted for classroom use at the Air Force Academy.

But in responding to the crisis, ISI eschewed the merely political. In the words of one trustee, the Institute would not serve as a "cheerleader" for the Bush administration and its policies. Rather, ISI would make its contribution, as it always had, by teaching the "values, principles and ideas of Western civilization" through its publications and programs.[18] In the spring of 2002, for example, 125 students and professors representing seventy-five schools participated in ISI's spring regional conference on "Building Communities of Character: Prospects for the Future." After

16. Bruce Frohnen, "What We Are Fighting For," *The Intercollegiate Review*, Spring 2002: 10.

17. Keith Pavlischek, "Just and Unjust War in the Terrorist Age," *The Intercollegiate Review*, Spring 2002: 32.

18. At the October 26, 2001, board of trustees meeting, Wayne Valis responded to trustee Tom Pauken's comment that ISI must remain "non-political" by saying that ISI was "no cheerleader for the [Bush] administration and its policies." Board chairman Louise Oliver emphasized that ISI could help most by teaching "the values, principles, and ideas of Western civilization." Author's notes.

listening to Professor Bradley Birzer of Hillsdale College expound on the theme that "good education, like a good society, must be built on faith and morality," one student remarked that the weekend "opened my eyes to the moral battle our country faces now and in the future."[19]

Dozens of campus lectures were presented under the theme, "The Roots of American Order." A typical response was that of philosophy professor Phil Goggins at Seattle Pacific University, who said of Professor Alan Kors' talk at the University of Washington: "I'm still floating.... We had 300 people.... Alan Kors was interrupted by applause several times and received a standing ovation at the end."[20]

Utilizing the Internet

ISI's Internet Education Project, directed by Paul G. Rhein, took a big leap forward, making available transcripts from selected lectures by Robert Royal and Peter Lawler, among others, as well as audio versions of speeches by Alan Kors, Richard Brookhiser, and George Nash. The Institute also began the formidable process of placing all thirty-five years of *The Intercollegiate Review* on the Internet. On-line chat and message boards for ISI alumni were also initiated in the early summer of 2002. That fall, the Institute "rolled out" the ISI Online Community that allows ISI members to talk with old friends, network for jobs, debate ideas, and receive the latest information about ISI activities.

At the same time, ISI members could still pick up and read, and thousands did, two of the Institute's oldest and most intellectually cogent publications. The summer 2002 issue of *Modern Age* was a strong one, featuring a major article by A. Owen Aldridge on John Adams, a sensitive remembrance of the poet and longtime *Modern Age* associate editor Robert Drake, and a timely reconsideration of the work of Paul Hollander, author of the seminal work, *Political Pilgrims*. Literary critic R. V. Young returned to the journal with a trenchant examination of the new *Norton*

---

19. "Character is as Relevant as Ever:" ISI's Spring Regional Conference Brings Students to Their Feet," ISI email newsletter, May 9, 2002.

20. Jeffrey Cain, "ISI Lecture Program," Minutes of Meeting of ISI Board of Trustees, May 9, 2002: 33.

Anthology of Theory and Criticism. Young agreed to write a series of essays on major contemporary critics, beginning with the post-modernist guru, Stanley Fish.[21]

The 2002 volume of *The Political Science Reviewer* presented a symposium on the work of the late Gerhart Niemeyer, who had made a lasting intellectual impression on many ISI members, including Richard V. Allen, Wayne Valis, and Tim Goeglein. Niemeyer symposium contributors included Weaver Fellow Bruce Fingerhut of St. Augustine Press and Gregory Wolfe of *Image*. Other *PSR* articles included Paul Seaton's insightful analysis of Vaclav Havel's *Summer Meditations* and Kenneth Whitehead's comprehensive critique of ten recent books about the relationship between the Catholic Church, Pope Pius XII, and the Holocaust.

At their May 2002 board meeting, trustees received a highly encouraging report about the financial and programmatic expansion of ISI. Despite the drop in the stock market following the terrorist attacks of September 11, the 2002 budget was $6.1 million. The estimated budget for 2003-the Institute's fiftieth year—was $7.6 million. Thanks to careful management, programming consumed 82 percent of expenditures, administration 7.2 percent, and development (i.e., fund-raising) a modest 10.8 percent. ISI membership was 53,000, including some 20,000 faculty members. The Institute had grown at the rate of over one thousand new members a month during the past academic year—the fastest growth in ISI history. As a result, the Institute had one thousand student representatives, 1,200 faculty associates, and seventy student groups on one thousand campuses.

Because of ISI's unremitting efforts, along with the founding of such groups as the Historical Society and the Association of Literary Scholars and Critics (ALSC), and the continuing impact of the National Association of Scholars, erosion of political correctness on campus could clearly be detected. The leftist orthodoxies still dominated the universities, com-

21. Mark C. Henrie and John M. Vella, "ISI Journals," prepared for the November 2002 board meeting of ISI: 37-38.

mented one ISI faculty associate, "but there is increasing room for students and faculty to dissent."[22]

Several ISI professors, however, disagreed with even this guardedly optimistic assessment. "There's no hope for America's 'great universities,'" said John Agresto, former president of St. John's College, Santa Fe. "They've destroyed the humanities, destroyed literature, and they wonder why students gravitate to the practical and the monetary." He conceded, however, that there was still hope "for small, independent, especially church-related colleges." Philosophy professor Peter A. Redpath of St. John's University in New York was equally pessimistic about the future of the university: "It no longer has the critical mass of people on the faculty and administration who understand the nature of the liberal arts and how they relate to higher education." Paul Rahe, professor of American history at the University of Tulsa, agreed, remarking, "I am extremely pessimistic about American academe. The new Stalinists are in control and their agenda is very ugly indeed."[23]

But other professors, like Noel B. Reynolds, associate academic vice president at Brigham Young University, argued that the climate of the campus had definitely improved since the 1960s. "Who would have believed in 1968," he asked, "that the American academy would be *more* conservative in 2001; that neo-classical economics would have triumphed over Marxists and socialists, and permeated most social science disciplines at the theoretical level?" Robert C. Rice, chairman of the department of English at Christendom College concurred, saying, "When I compare the condition of academe in 2001 with its condition 25 or 30 years ago, I find some reasons for cheerfulness to break in"—including the rise of independent orthodox Catholic liberal arts colleges like Christendom and Thomas Aquinas College. "The public response to the September 11 attacks," reported political science professor and ISI Salvatori Fellow Howard L. Lubert at James Madison University, "across the nation and

22. "ISI Faculty: Teaching, Researching, and Enriching America's Campuses," *CAMPUS*, Spring 2002:4-5.
23. Excerpted from responses of John Agresto, Peter A. Redpath, and Paul Rahe to the author's ISI questionnaire, July 2002.

on our campuses has been encouraging. I'm witnessing serious debate about serious issues, with a sensitivity to the need to balance liberty with order."[24]

Then, too, according to a May 2003 cover article in the *New York Times Magazine,* "student conservatism is increasing in many areas." The *Times* based its assertion on the latest poll of the UCLA Higher Education Research Institute, which has been tracking college freshman attitudes since 1966. Asked their opinion about casual sex, 51 percent of freshmen were for it in 1987; now 42 percent are. In 1989, 66 percent of freshmen believed abortion should be legal; today, only 54 percent do. In 1995, 66 percent of young people agreed that wealthy people should pay a larger share of taxes; the number is now 50 percent.[25]

Contributing to the spreading debate was the Collegiate Network, which today compromises 80 student newspapers with about 800 student editors and writers and a combined annual distribution of approximately three million copies. (Edwin Feulner still marvels at Ken Cribb's "masterful integration" of the campus newspapers into the mission of ISI.)[26] Seeking to expand its postgraduate impact, CN expanded its internship program, sponsoring yearlong internships at leading news media, continuing a ISI tradition that began in the mid-1950s.

Preparing New Generations

In November 2002, ISI formally adopted "Educating for Liberty ... In Each New Generation," a strategic plan for 2003-2007, calculated to "renew the American tradition of teaching each new generation of college students the principles that sustain a free and humane society." The selection of the title was deliberate—it was the phrase that inspired the young Vic Milione many years ago in Philadelphia and has served ever since as ISI's motto. The 2003-2007 plan, building on the Feulner Plan of 1987

24. Responses of Noel B. Reynolds, Robert C. Rice, and Howard L. Lubert to the author's ISI questionnaire, June 2002.

25. John Colapinto, "The Young Hipublicans," *New York Times Magazine,* May 25, 2003: 33.

26. Author's interview with Edwin J. Feulner, August 22, 2001.

and the Mendenhall Plan of 1994, had five "landmark objectives": (1) to provide students and teachers the necessary resources to understand basic economic thinking, the moral and political tradition of the West, and the U.S. constitutional system; (2) to employ the latest technology, particularly the Internet, to communicate the case for the free society to the greatest possible number of students, teachers, and parents; (3) to develop an institutional communications and marketing effort; (4) to launch a Center for the Study of American Civic Literacy; and (5) to endow critical elements of ISI's educational program through a $54 million multi-year fund-raising campaign.[27]

The boldest objective was the Center for the Study of American Civic Literacy, which will measure higher education's success in transmitting core civic principles to America's students. The Center will go inside leading colleges and universities to obtain concrete evidence of what students are learning, and not learning, about America's history and its free institutions. Colleges will be ranked objectively as to their ability to transmit the "wisdom of the ages" in fields such as history, political philosophy, economics, and international relations. The findings will be widely publicized to "encourage" universities to improve their transmittal of core knowledge of the American heritage. Such a comprehensive and recurring measurement of the effectiveness of a college education has never before been attempted.

"The failure of American colleges to do their job," says Ken Cribb, "is ultimately the trustees' failure. It should not be the responsibility of a third party [like ISI] to correct the situation but rather that of the schools themselves, led by the trustees. The Center for the Study of American Civic Literacy will give the trustees and other members of the academic community the tools with which they can do this job."[28] Among the tools will be an annual report to the nation on higher education and frequent white papers on civic literacy in the academy.

The initiative received a significant boost when retired Lt. General

27. Minutes of November 1, 2002, Board of Trustees meeting, ISI Archives.
28. Ibid; author's interview with T. Kenneth Cribb, Jr., May 5, 2003.

Josiah Bunting III, superintendent emeritus of Virginia Military Institute, agreed to serve as chairman of the National Civic Literacy Board which will help to guide and oversee the new Center. "If the rising generation and its successors are not educated to their responsibilities as citizens," said Bunting, "the world's greatest continuing experiment in human liberty will fail."[29] Bunting has been joined on the board by such prominent educators and intellectuals as Victor Davis Hanson, visiting professor of history at the U.S. Naval Academy; James Daughrill, president emeritus, Rhodes College; James Hester, president, H. Frank Guggenheim Foundation; Roger Kimball, managing editor, *The New Criterion*; John Marsh, former secretary of the army; Ross McKenzie, editorial page editor, *Richmond Times-Dispartch;* Carlos Mosley, chairman emeritus, New York Philharmonic; Robert P. George, professor and Madison Center director, Princeton University; retired Vice Admiral John Ryan, president, SUNY Maritime College. Professor Gary Scott left a tenured professorship at St. Mary's University in Texas to become the Center's first research fellow in civic literacy. Mike Ratliff will serve as director of the Center, which will be housed in an office facility on ISI's Kirby Campus, reflecting the Institute's long-range commitment to the project.

Just as widespread public dissatisfaction has produced significant reform in K-12, including such measures as educational vouchers and charter schools, says Ken Cribb, so reform of higher education can be effected by proving to the public—"with hard evidence"—that the American university is failing to transmit the "core knowledge necessary for citizenship."[30]

ISI also expanded its traditional programs. Under program director Chad Kifer (Honors Fellow, 1996-1997), 190 lectures on college and prep school campuses were presented in the 2002-2003 academic year. Including online as well as media programs, more than 360 educational

---

29. Statement of Purpose, Center for the Study of American Civic Literacy, ISI Archives.
30. Author's interview with T. Kenneth Cribb, Jr., May 5, 2003.

events were offered, among them lectures by Alan Kors of the University of Pennsylvania, student conferences led by academics Peter Lawler and Daniel J. Mahoney, internet appearances by Hillsdale College's Brad Birzer, and C-SPAN coverage of talks by rising scholars Matthew Spalding and Mark Henrie. At the end of the year, ISI campus membership exceeded 50,000, a new record.

At the Institute's annual Indianapolis conference in the spring of 2003, students and faculty representing more than fifteen states and fifty colleges and universities convened to discuss Whittaker Chambers' magisterial autobiography, *Witness*. In cooperation with the Liberty Fund, undergraduate and faculty colloquia were held in California, Rhode Island, Virginia, and Georgia. ISI celebrated the fiftieth anniversary of the publication of Russell Kirk's masterwork, *The Conservative Mind*, with a reception for alumni and friends at the annual Conservative Political Action Conference in Washington, D.C., the annual fellowship retreat at Piety Hill, Kirk's ancestral home, and two conferences at Oriel College, Oxford.

Sixty thousand copies of a new ISI brochure for college-bound students and their parents, entitled *Asking the Right Questions in Choosing a College*, were sent in the 2002-2003 school year to targeted high schools. Twelve thousand copies of *A Student's Guide to U.S. History* by Wilfred M. McClay were specially prepared and provided to participants in the American Legion Boys and Girls State program. Mike Ratliff, the vice president for programs, stated that the growing range of resources available through "ISI Interactive" and the Online Community "are bringing the Institute closer to being able to offer an online university education in liberty."[31] Conference coordinator Julia Austin (Honors Fellow, 2001-2002) said that a series of colloquia on such topics as "Liberty and Liberal Education" and Tocqueville's *Democracy in America* had brought over one hundred students and faculty associates together, inspiring one Bowdoin College undergraduate to enthuse, "Tocqueville became more clear for

31. Mike Ratliff, "The Student Self-Reliance Project," May 8, 2003 meeting of the ISI Board of Trustees: 30.

me and more applicable to today's America through these seminar-style classes."[32]

ISI's web sites recorded 454,000 user sessions in 2002 and will easily exceed that number in 2003. Launched in the fall of 2002, the Online Community has already become, according to Paul Rhein, director of educational outreach, "a dynamic platform" for a wide variety of programming. In December 2002, for example, ISI provided context for extended online discussions of J. R. R. Tolkien, a major national topic because of the release of the second installment of *The Lord of the Rings* movie trilogy. Tolkien scholars Joseph Pearce and Brad Birzer were featured in chat sessions. The ISI lecture library offered more than one hundred video, audio, or text files completely accessible online.

In early 2003, ISI formed a public relations committee which promptly decided that the Institute's websites should be "the chief tactic" in a marketing strategy to achieve the objectives of the fiftieth anniversary and to "highlight the Institute's role as a thought leader in higher education." Jeff Nelson was given oversight responsibility for the new institutional marketing/publicity effort in addition to his other duties. A key message of the anniversary celebration, Nelson explained, would be: "ISI is the conservator of the American tradition of ordered liberty among the rising generation."[33]

As part of the reorganization, Nelson tapped Christine O'Donnell, a graduate of Farleigh Dickinson University and currently studying constitutional government at Princeton, to be named director of communications and public affairs and the Institute's spokesperson. With over 300 appearances on various television programs and articles in the *Washington Post* and other leading publications, O'Donnell made an immediate impact, increasing mentions of the Institute in the news media. At the same time, Paul Rhein was named manager and editor of ISI's Internet resources, including www.isi.org, www.isibooks.org, www.collegeguide.org,

32. Julia Austin, "Conferences," May 2003 board meeting: 33.
33. "A Plan for Improving the Identity of the Institute," Jeff Nelson, January 13, 2003, ISI Archives.

and www.collegiatenetwork.org, and was charged to help make the ISI web into a more comprehensive "mini-university" site. "There is a pool of talented faculty," points out Ken Cribb, "that can be featured and from which we can present essays and articles that are updated regularly."

Under new executive director Brian Auchterlonie, a 2001 graduate of Kenyon College, where he edited the *Kenyon Review*, a CN paper, the Collegiate Network reached in 2003 a new high of eighty member newspapers. The CN also supervised the sixth annual Campus Outrage Awards—the 2003 Pollys. Tied for first place were Duke University, which offered a lecture by Laura Whitehorn—who served fourteen years in a federal prison for bombing the U.S. Capitol in 1983 and advised her student audience, "It's easy to do a bombing"—and Columbia University, whose professor Gayatri Spivak offered the following rationalization about suicide bombings: "Suicidal resistance is a message inscribed on the body when no other means will get through. It is both execution and mourning, for self and other."[34] For some academic institutions, it was as though September 11, 2001, had never occurred.

Among the forthcoming offerings of ISI Books, the most anticipated was perhaps the "revised, expanded and enhanced" edition of *Choosing the Right College.* With Jeremy Beer as editor-in-chief and Alexandra Gilman as senior editor, the 2004 College Guide will examine 125 schools, fifteen more than the last edition. It will also advise students at schools that have no genuine core curriculum (over 90 percent of the schools surveyed) what eight courses they should take as substitutes. This "build-your-own curriculum" was supervised by Mark Henrie and is based on his *Student's Guide to the Core Curriculum.*

Other forthcoming ISI books included a revisionist history of the American family by sociologist Allan Carlson; Peter Stanlis's study of Robert Frost, a widely anticipated book by a personal friend of the celebrated poet that will be the apex of a lifetime of scholarly reflection; a monumental reference work, *American Conservatism: An Encyclopedia,*

34. Bryan Auchterlonie, "Sixth Annual Campus Outrage Awards," May 2003 board meeting: 54.

edited by Bruce Frohnen, Jeffrey Nelson, and Jeremy Beer; *The Conservative Mind* Today, an in-depth examination of Russell Kirk's magnum opus with particular reference to the guidance it provides for current and near-future conservatism; and *Russia in Collapse* by Alexander Solzhenitsyn, the first English translation (by Olga Cooke of Texas A & M University) of the work and the first book the Russian Nobel laureate has published in America since 1995.

The conservatism encyclopedia, a decade in the making, contains more than 630 entries totaling almost half a million words and including essays on such varied topics as Protestant evangelism, the Cold War, Austrian economics, and states' rights. Contributors include Russell Kirk, Gerhart Niemyer, Forrest McDonald, George Panichas, George Weigel, George Carey, M. E. Bradford, and dozens more. Only ISI, says Jeff Nelson, with its national network of academics and other resources could have produced what will be "the definite reference work of conservatism."

Publication of *The National Review Treasury of Classic Children's Literature,* selected by William F. Buckley Jr., marked the 2003 debut of ISI Books' "Foundations" series, the Institute's entry into the world of children's literature. The second Foundations volume was *Everyday Graces: A Child's Book of Good Manners,* a literary anthology edited by Karen Santorum, wife of U.S. Senator Rick Santorum of Pennsylvania. The anthology, explains Santorum, the mother of six children, "grew out of the frustration of not being able to find a book on manners that instructs through stories rather than by rules of dos and don'ts."[35]

Summing up the Institute's accomplishments in the last decade-and-a-half, Ken Cribb stated that "our single greatest accomplishment has been to put ISI on a permanent footing. It is here for all time, with a financial base, an intellectual base, a physical base. Now the right ideas have a permanent home."[36]

---

35. Memorandum of Jeffrey Nelson to the author, August 10, 2003.
36. Author's interview with T. Kenneth Cribb, Jr., May 5, 2003.

A Monumental Challenge

"Educating For Liberty ... In Each New Generation" is the most ambitious campaign in ISI's fifty-year history. Is the Institute up to it? Does it have the necessary people with the necessary skills, commitment, and vision? Can the Institute raise more money than it has ever before dreamed of—six times its current annual budget? Is ISI taking the next logical step in its decades-long commitment to educate for liberty, or is it, like its quixotic founder, tilting against the $230 billion windmill known as American higher education?

Success or failure depends, in part, on ISI's performance in four areas—mission, management, members, and money. History is replete with idea-oriented organizations that have diverged from their original mission, foundered, and failed. "There has been zero mission creep in ISI," insists Ken Cribb, "because of Vic Milione, whose genius was his single-minded determination to educate for liberty." Cribb is similarly focused. "We want to grow and retool our tactics where necessary," he says, but at the same time "stay true to the mission." And that mission, Cribb explains, is to develop a comprehensive program "to meet the intellectual needs of every student and scholar in the study of liberty."[37]

Since 1989, when Ken Cribb became president and Ed Feulner chairman of the board of trustees, ISI has developed and refined a management style that reflects their Washington, D.C., background—but with one essential exception: they are careful about spending other people's money. ISI managers are philosophically sound and when necessary politically savvy. They are conscious of ISI's role as an anchor of the conservative movement. "We are," says Cribb, "the institution of first resort on the philosophical side of conservatism."[38] ISI managers are mature but still youthful. They are committed to educating this and future generations about liberty and restoring the ideals of Western civilization to an honored place in American higher education.

37. Author's interview with T. Kenneth Cribb, Jr., May 8, 2002.
38. Ibid.

During his eight years as a top adviser at the White House and the Justice Department, Ken Cribb learned the importance of numbers—in preparing a budget (just how much would a proposed program cost?), crafting a campaign (you go where the most votes are), setting public policy priorities (health care reform affects everyone). As ISI president, Cribb has stressed the relevance of membership size as a means of determining whether the Institute is expanding or contracting. He is not interested in preserving a remnant but reaching out to the majority.

And in the last fourteen years, ISI membership on campus has increased almost one hundred percent from 32,616 to over 63,000, the number of campus representatives from 715 to more than 1,000, and faculty associates from 899 to approximately 1,200. The number of faculty on American colleges and universities who read ISI publications and participate in its programs has also nearly doubled to some 20,000 (about five times the membership of the influential National Association of Scholars). The faculty growth, said one professor, suggests "that a number of academics are not only fed up with the excesses of race, class, and gender, but are willing to do something about it."[39] Frank Chodorov was "a voice in the wilderness," says ISI trustee Alfred Regnery, "today there is a large chorus of conservative voices everywhere."[40]

As encouraging as the growth of the Institute is, it must be balanced against the overall size of the American academy with its 15 million students (undergraduates number 12.5 million) and nearly one million faculty (of whom 60 percent are full-time). "The conservative task," wrote ISI's Mark Henrie in a seminal article for *The Intercollegiate Review*, "is to work toward developing smaller bodies on campus to resist [liberal] homogenization." Such associations include fraternities, dining clubs, literary societies, interest-oriented group houses, religious houses, and independent "think-tanks."[41]

---

39. Ibid: 5.
40. Author's interview with Alfred Regnery, July 16, 2001.
41. Mark C. Henrie, "Rethinking American Conservatism in the 1990s: The Struggle Against Homogenization," *The Intercollegiate Review*, Spring 1993: 16.

ISI's financial growth has been striking, increasing sixfold from just over $1 million in 1989 to an estimated $7.6 million for the fiscal year ending March 2003. The projected revenue for 2003-2004 is $11.3 million—including early gifts from the Fiftieth Anniversary Campaign—although expenditures for the year have been set at $8.1 million. All ISI revenues from 1989-1993, according to Robert Russell, fund-raising consultant to the Institute, went up an amazing 556 percent. ISI donors, stated Russell, comprise the "most impressive list in the country" among conservative organizations. They give generously, he said, because they believe that ISI "can make a difference in higher education."[42] They are confident, in the words of foundation executive Richard Larry, that "ISI knows its mission and will not change."[43]

At the same time, ISI has adjusted impressively to changing circumstances in higher education and the conservative movement. Publications like the "splendid" Student Guides, says Michael Joyce, the longtime head of the Lynde and Harry Bradley Foundation, were inconceivable in the 1960s because conservatives "did not have the necessary resources." What ISI did do in those years was nevertheless crucial—"it held together the traditional and libertarian strains" of conservatism, preserving the intellectual foundation for today's political successes. ISI and *National Review*, says Joyce, instructed the faithful like the "catechumens of the early Christian era."[44] "Throughout its fifty years," says James Burnley, who served as chairman of the board of trustees for most of 2002, "ISI has nurtured the conservative movement." But for the presence of the Institute, Burnley believes, "the voice of conservatism would have been almost obliterated on most campuses."[45]

ISI acknowledged the consequential contributions of the "greatest generation" to American conservatism by naming Preston A. (Dick) Wells as its new chairman and J. Bayard Boyle, Jr., as its new vice chairman at

---

42. Robert Russell, remarks at ISI board of trustees meeting, May 9, 2002, author's notes.
43. Author's interview with Spencer Masloff, May 11, 2001.
44. Author's interview with Michael Joyce, September 17, 2001.
45. Author's interview with James Burnley, July 17, 2001.

the October 2002 board of trustees meeting. Former Marine Dick Wells fought on Iwo Jima during World War II before returning home and starting what has become one of Ft. Lauderdale's most successful land development/real estate companies. "Ever since I served our country in the South Pacific as a young man," said Wells, "I have concerned myself with the defense of American liberty, both abroad and at home." Wells saw the chairmanship of ISI as the culmination of his lifelong effort because "ISI's work lays a firm foundation on behalf of liberty in America and ultimately the Western world." The American way of life, he stated, will not be secure "without a sound culture shaped by a sound education for ordered liberty."[46] Head of a family-owned real estate development company whose roots date back to the founding of Memphis in the early 1800s, vice chairman Bayard Boyle values especially the role of education in building a better and freer society. He is a trustee of Rhodes College, listed among the Institute's one hundred best colleges.

Unfortunately, Dick Wells was obliged to resign for health reasons as chairman and trustee in the summer of 2003, and then died in September, depriving the Institute of his quiet, principled guidance. The sense of loss over Wells' unexpected passing was succeeded by a sense of relief when his successor was announced—Edwin J. Feulner, ISI member and chapter organizer at the London School of Economics, Weaver Fellow, trustee, and board chairman from 1989 to 1993. Who better to help Ken Cribb and the rest of the ISI management team in the celebration of the Institute's fiftieth year than the person who played so critical a part in its history? "I am deeply honored," Feulner said, "to serve again as chairman of an extraordinary organization whose salutary influence on young minds is crucial to the future of the conservative movement and America."[47]

Asked to explain ISI's remarkable growth during the 1990s and into the 2000s, Feulner replied that the first reason was "the deconstruction and rot of the popular culture, as shown in the conduct of President Clinton, requiring students to look for alternatives." The second was that

46. Preston Wells to the author, May 21, 2003.
47. Edwin J. Feulner to the author, August 10, 2003.

ISI benefitted from what Feulner called the three "I's"—institution, ideas, and individuals. "ISI now has a permanent presence in a beautiful campus in Delaware. It has the right ideas, the permanent things that Dr. Kirk wrote about so eloquently. And it has a great individual heading it. That Ken Cribb was willing to give up a career as a very successful lawyer and devote his life to sharing the vision of a free and humane society with college students all over the country, Feulner said, "is the magic component that has made ISI into the force it is on its fiftieth anniversary."[48]

As it prepares for the next fifty years, then, ISI finds itself, by reason of its clear mission, competent management, expanding membership, and strong financial resources, among the handful of institutions that may be called indispensable to the conservative movement.

The Academic Archipelago

And what of the Leviathan that ISI confronts—the American academy? Higher education is one of the largest industries in the country—Americans spend over $230 billion annually on their colleges and universities, about twenty times what they spend on Hollywood movies. Over 60 percent of that amount comes from tuition fees and other school income, 12 percent from the federal government, 23 percent from the states, and 3 percent from local government. The academy has come to regard the 38 percent government subsidy as an entitlement. Of the 12.5 million undergraduate students in the year 2003, 56 percent are women and 66 percent are full-time. Most of the part-time students hold jobs and attend classes at night. They seek their education in a vast, diverse academic archipelago that is the envy of the rest of the world—in 2000 there were nearly 4,000 public and private colleges and universities in America. The fastest growing segment is what used to be called the community college: since 1960, enrollment at public two-year colleges has increased from less than 500,000 to nearly 6 million in some 1,800 schools.

But the total number of students in higher education has leveled off

48. Interview for ISI historic video with Edwin J. Feulner, July, 14, 2003.

in the last decade at about 15 million, meaning, among other things, that schools are facing a painful choice: either reduce expenses or raise the cost of matriculation. Almost all have chosen to increase tuition and other fees at a rate several times faster than that of inflation. Academic demographers have estimated that over the next decade, the total college population will increase to only 17.5 million.[49] Such limited growth provides scant comfort to school financial officers seeking revenue wherever they can.

College education in America is not cheap. In 2000, according to the U.S. Census Bureau, the average annual cost of tuition, fees, room and board at all *public* institutions—four-year and two-year—was just over $7,000. The average annual charges at all *private* institutions—four-year and two-year—were almost three times that, $19,410. The total annual expenses at a private four-year college in 2001-2002, the *Chronicle of Higher Education* estimated, was $26,093. An Ivy League university like Harvard or Stanford charged almost $40,000 each year—the equivalent of the average American's annual income. In 2002, according to a survey by *Insight* magazine, a top-ranked private college like Hillsdale cost $21,386, St. John's College in Annapolis (well known for its Great Books curriculum), $34,380. Grove City College, ranked in the top one hundred private schools by most college guides, was a bargain at $14,302.[50] As a result, parents and/or their children are required to mortgage a good part of their homes or their future for a BA or BS.

And so, given the ever rising costs, a level student population, the often fierce public debates about the curriculum, the increasingly arcane scholarship and intellectual isolation of many professors, the uneasiness and even unhappiness of many alumni about their alma mater, how does the education establishment see the future of higher education in America? When asked this question by the author, four prominent educators, including the president of the American Council on Education, were opti-

---

49. "Projections of College Enrollment, Degrees Conferred, and High-School Graduates, 2002 to 2012, *Chronicle of Higher Education*, August 30, 2002: 24.

50. Stephen Goode, "2002's Best Colleges," *Insight*, September 9, 2002: 10-14.

mistic, seeing enormous potential in the new technology and encouraged by what one called the spread of "humanistic values" in American society.[51] All shared the conviction that government should play the same major funding role in the first half of the twenty-first century it did in the last half of the twentieth century. None mentioned curriculum content or multiculturalism as issues of concern. Typical of such insular thinking is Donald N. Michael's influential work, *The Unprepared Society*, in which the author asserts that although the people are not ready for the future, "utopia" is possible through careful planning by the establishment.[52]

Liberal educators' preoccupation with process, reflecting the still dominant influence of John Dewey's progressivism, opens the academic door wide for ISI, with its commitment to John Henry Newman's idea of a university—a place where "Why?" is the most important question of all. What the distinguished educational historian Diane Ravitch has said about secondary education applies with equal force to higher education in America. Throughout the twentieth century, Ravitch wrote, progressives claimed that "the schools had the power and responsibility to reconstruct society," and attempted to impose "their social, religious, cultural, and political agendas on the schools."[53] But their century-long effort diminished and in some cases eliminated the intellectual purpose of schools. Progressives, Ravitch said, urged the schools to "de-emphasize" reading, writing, history, mathematics, and science; to drop foreign languages; to replace history with that pedagogical grab-bag, "social studies"; to "eliminate high-quality literature and substitute for it uninspired scraps from textbooks"; and to teach only what was "useful" and "immediately functional."[54]

The progressive prescription has been a disaster leading, in the words of President Reagan's 1983 Commission on Excellence in Education, to

51. Author's interview with Malcolm G. Scully, editor at large, *The Chronicle of Higher Education*, December 7, 1998.

52. John D. Pulliam and James J. Van Patten, *History of Higher Education in America*, seventh edition, Upper Saddle River, New Jersey, 1999: 289.

53. Diane Ravitch, *Left Back: A Century of Failed School Reforms*, New York, 2000: 459.

54. Ibid.

"a nation at risk." "The educational foundations of our society," the commission warned, "are presently being eroded by a rising tide of mediocrity that threatens our very future as a Nation and a people."[55] And the foundations will not be restored by the magic of some new technology but by schools concentrating on their historic mission to teach the fundamentals, such as science and mathematics, U.S. history and Western civilization, the principles of self-government, the glories of great literature and art and music. "A society that tolerates anti-intellectualism in its schools," wrote Ravitch, "can expect to have a dumbed-down culture that honors celebrity and sensation rather than knowledge and wisdom."[56] ISI, through its journals, student guides, books, lectures, and seminars, offers a rigorous intellectual alternative to the dumbing down of the curriculum. With its campus representatives, faculty associates, associated clubs, honors fellows and mentors, the Institute provides a verdant oasis for independent-minded students unwilling to accept the forced homogenization that prevails at many schools.

The essential role of ISI—and the timeliness of the Center for the Study of American Civic Literacy—was proven in a national poll of public opinion of higher education conducted in February-March 2003 by *The Chronicle of Higher Education,* the weekly newspaper of the American academy. Although the poll discovered strong general support for colleges, it also found that Americans disliked many things that colleges love and questioned the priorities of college administrations. According to the *Chronicle,* the respondents were "highly skeptical" about affirmative action and tenure. They urged universities to "focus less" on economic-development and research missions and more "on the basics" such as general education, leadership, and responsibility.[57]

Whither Conservatism?

And what of the conservative movement with which ISI is so closely con-

55. Ibid: 412.
56. Ibid: 466.
57. Jeffrey Selingo, "What Americans Think About Higher Education," *The Chronicle of Higher Education,* May 2, 2003: A10.

nected? Historian George Nash has written that by the end of President Reagan's second term in the late 1980s, the American Right encompassed "five distinct impulses"—traditionalism, libertarianism, anti-communism, neoconservatism, and the Religious Right. As the movement reached maturity, said Nash, many conservatives shifted from "a search for self-definition and philosophic coherence" (characteristic of the 1950s and 1960s) to an absorption with the programmatic.[58] The theoretical essay was supplanted by the policy paper. The focus on the here and now was accelerated by the emergence of supply-side economics and its successful application by the Reagan administration in the 1980s and by the triumph of the 1994 election manifesto—the Contract with America.

It was a time of contradictions. The world, Nash wrote, was a far less lonely place for conservatives than in 1953 when a young Michigan professor named Russell Kirk published a book he originally titled *The Conservatives' Rout*. By 1996, conservatism had built "an elaborate infrastructure that was nonexistent a generation earlier."[59] And yet, editor-publisher William Kristol of the conservative *Weekly Standard* could write in the spring of 2000 that the conservative movement "which accomplished great things over the past quarter-century is finished."[60] Kristol's obituary—written before the startling November 2000 elections and the galvanizing events of September 11, 2001—echoed the earlier gloomy conclusions of conservative editor R. Emmett Tyrrell, political analyst David Frum, and conservative strategist Paul Weyrich. Are these eminent authorities correct? Is American conservatism headed for the ash heap of history or primed to remain a major political and intellectual influence in America for the foreseeable future?

In the spring of 2003, Frum declared war on the so-called paleoconservatives calling them "unpatriotic" conservatives who should be read out of the movement for "turning their backs on their country"

58. George Nash, *The Conservative Intellectual Movement in America Since 1945:* 332, 335.

59. Ibid: 340.

60. William Kristol, "The New Hampshire Upheaval," *Washington Post*, February 2, 2000.

and failing to support the U.S.-led war against Saddam Hussein. Among the many letters responding to Frum's *National Review* cover article was one by David Keene, chairman of the American Conservative Union, who charged that the author had painted "with far too broad a brush." Disputing that Robert Novak and Llewellyn H. Rockwell were soul brothers, Keene said that while he supported the war in Iraq he didn't like "nation-building." "Frum seems to see himself as the conscience of a new conservatism," wrote Keene, but unlike Frank Meyer and other founders of the modern conservative movement, "he seeks a far more exclusive club." Another reaction to the "split on the right" came from Donald Devine, a former high-ranking official of the Reagan administration and veteran conservative, who called for a policy of inclusivity rather than exclusivity—a return to Meyer's "fusionist conservatism"—as well as a return to the "limited-government position represented by *National Review* in the 1960s."[61]

A persuasive variation of the fusionist theme was offered by senior fellow John Fonte of the Hudson Institute, who suggested that along with the traditional pillars of economic conservatism and social conservatism, a third pillar had reemerged since September 11, 2001—patriotic conservatism. In the 2002 elections, Fonte wrote, as in the days of Nixon's "silent majority" and the Reagan years, "it was an emphasis on the nation, national security, and patriotism (rather than on the market or morality) that proved crucial to conservatism's success."[62] Fonte argued that patriotic conservatism, like anticommunism in the days of the Cold War, could be the cement that strengthened the other pillars, unified the conservative movement, and served as the key to electoral victory.

Such spirited debate is not a sign of distress but a sign of vitality. Sharp differences and sharper rhetoric have characterized the conservative movement since its first stirrings in the late 1940s and early 1950s. Those who say that the conservative movement is badly split or burned

61. David Frum, "Unpatriotic Conservatives: A War Against America," *National Review*, April 7, 2003: 40; David Keene, "Frum Forum," *National Review*, May 19, 2003: 17; Donald Devine, "Revitalizing Conservatism," May 13, 2003, ACU Email.
62. John Fonte, "Homeland Politics," *National Review*, June 2, 2003: 27.

out should consider the elements of political success.

First, a political movement must have a clearly defined, consistent philosophy relevant to the problems of today. And whatever their differences, conservatives of all dispositions honor the Constitution and its carefully constructed system of checks and balances. They favor a government that is limited and a people who are free to make their own decisions. They understand there can be no lasting liberty without virtue, public and private, and that peace is most surely guaranteed through military strength.

Second, a political movement must have a national constituency with members able and willing to work together. Although conservatives are often individualistic to a fault, they have come together under the right political leadership—under Robert A. Taft in the 1950s, Barry Goldwater in the 1960s, Ronald Reagan in the 1980s, Newt Gingrich in the 1990s, and, somewhat conditionally, under George W. Bush in the 2000s. Moreover, conservatives proved their national importance in Reagan's presidential victory in 1980, the capture of the Congress in 1994, and the Bush-led victories of 2000 and 2002.

Third, a movement must have a sound financial base. Thanks to technical proficiency—particularly in the use of direct mail, and, increasingly, the Internet—and political success, the number of conservative donors has grown from a few thousand in the 1950s to an estimated 5 million in the 2000s.

Fourth, a political movement must be media savvy, and although conservatives are understandably wary of the media, today prominent conservatives are to be found in every part of the news media. The number one columnist in America (measured by the number of newspapers that carry his column) is conservative Cal Thomas, followed closely by George Will. The number one radio talk show host for years has been the redoubtable Rush Limbaugh. The opinion journal with the largest circulation (at 150,000) is *National Review,* followed by the lively *Human Events* and the reconstituted *American Spectator,* whose prospects for a comeback under editor-in-chief Bob Tyrrell were improved considerably when Alfred Regnery became its publisher. The fastest growing cable news network is the right-of-center Fox News—led by anchors Tony Snow and Brit Hume, and popular hosts Sean Hannity and Bill O'Reilly—which continues to widen its lead in ratings over second-place CNN. In contrast, the broadcast networks' share of the viewing audience has dropped dramatically, from close to 90 percent thirty years ago to barely 40 percent today.

The final element of a successful political movement is charismatic, principled leadership. Over the past fifty years, conservatism has been blessed with a remarkable quartet of political leaders, the like of which have not been seen perhaps since the Founding of the Republic. I refer to "Mr. Republican," Robert A. Taft; "Mr. Conservative," Barry Goldwater; "Mr. President," Ronald Reagan; and "Mr. Speaker," Newt Gingrich. Whether George W. Bush will join their eminent ranks is yet to be determined, although his leadership to date has been strongly endorsed by the American people with approval ratings as high as any modern president has ever received.

Far from being finished or fading away, then, the conservative movement appears to be poised for new political victories in Congress, the courts, and the states, sustained today as it has been for the past fifty years by a remarkable group of philosophers, popularizers, politicians, and philanthropists. Today, young scholars build on the ideas of Hayek, Kirk, Strauss, and Voegelin, emerging journalists emulate the rhetoric of Buckley, Will, Limbaugh, and Snow, elected officials imitate the principled politics of Reagan and Bush, new entrepreneurs take the long view of Pew, Coors, Noble, Scaife, Earhart, Olin, and Bradley.

But it is the duty of ISI to remind conservatives that in politics there are no permanent victories or defeats, only permanent things like wisdom, courage, prudence, and justice. The Institute must continue to serve, in George Nash's words, as an institution of reinforcement and recruitment—to sustain "the morale and intellectual foundations" of conservative students and to recruit the best of them "for intellectual leadership after graduation."[63] Such a rising generation will lift all hearts.

63. George H. Nash to Lee Edwards, October 17, 2001.

Fifty years ago, the editor and teacher Frank Chodorov had an incandescent idea about the need to educate his children and all the children of America about the free market and individual freedom. His idea became the charter of the Intercollegiate Society of Individualists. ISI metamorphosized under the leadership of Victor Milione and then Kenneth Cribb, who both recognized the spiritual as well as the material side of man, into the 50,000-member, $8 million-a-year Intercollegiate Studies Institute, which today promotes in a hundred different ways on a thousand different campuses its unwavering belief in ordered liberty and a humane economy. Today, ISI is not only the educational pillar of the conservative movement—one of the Indispensables—but the leading source of information about a free society for the tens of thousands of American students and teachers who reject the post-modernist zeitgeist. Today, as it has for the past fifty years and as it looks ahead to the next fifty years, ISI continues the work of not only preserving but of extending liberty, knowing that such work is never finished because the road to liberty is never ending.

Appendix

Board of Trustees 1953-2003

†Deceased.
*The original name of ISI, from 1953 to 1966, was the Intercollegiate Society of Individualists. The name was changed to the Intercollegiate Studies Institute in 1966. (See Chapter 3 for details.)

Dr. William H. Peterson (1957-1960, 1968-1988)
U.S. Steel Corporation
Senior Economic Advisor, U.S. Department of Commerce, Social and Economic Statistics Administration
Director, Center for Economic Education, University of Tennessee

Dr. Anthony T. Bouscaren (1960-1980)
Professor of Political Science, LeMoyne College

†Albert M. Campbell, Esq. (1960-1988)
Vice Chairman, Intercollegiate Studies Institute, 1976-1988
Attorney

†Louis H.T. Dehmlow (1960-1962)
President, Great Lakes Terminal and Transport Corporation

M. Stanton Evans (1960-present)
Chairman, Education and Research Center

Peter O'Donnell, Jr. (1960-1966)
Trustee, University of the South
Trustee, American Enterprise Institute
Chairman, Texas Republican Party

James A McConnell (1960-1964)
Director, Corn Products Company

Dr. Hans F. Sennholz (1960-1968)
Professor of Economics, Grove City College

†Dr. Richard F. Staar (1960-1964)
Fleet Admiral Chester W. Nimitz Chair of Social and Political Philosophy, Naval War College

†Dr. Richard M. Weaver (1960-1963)
Professor of English, University of Chicago

†Charles Dana Bennett (1962-1987)
Consultant, Foundation of American Agriculture

†Lemuel R. Boulware (1962-1975)
Vice President, General Electric

†Brigadier General Bonner F. Fellers (1962-1965)
Vice Chairman and Recording Secretary, Americans for Constitutional Action

Dr. Thomas Molnar (1963-1981)
Professor of French and World Literature, Brooklyn College

†Dr. William S. Stokes (1963-1966)
Senior Professor of Comparative Political Institutions, Claremont Men's College

†Dr. James W. Wiggins (1963-1976)
Professor of Sociology, Emory University

†William T. Brady (1964-1966)
Former President and Chairman, Advisory Committee of the Board of Directors of Corn Products Company
Chairman, National Association of Manufacturers

R. H. Borchers (1965)
Executive Vice President and Director, Armour & Company

Dr. John H. Davis (1965-1975)
Chairman and Chief Executive Officer, American Near East Refugee Aid, Inc.

J. Jerome Thompson (1965-1966)
Group Vice President and Director, Charles Pfizer & Company
Board of Directors, American Farm Foundation

†Harold L. Severance (1965-1991)
Secretary, Executive Committee,
Standard Oil Company of
California

†Henry Regnery (1966-1995)
Chairman, the Intercollegiate
Studies Institute 1971-1990
Chairman, Regnery Publishing

Richard C. Holmquist (1966-1987)
President, Diversified Industries
Group, Lone Star Industries

Richard V. Allen (1968-present)
Senior Fellow, The Hoover
Institution
Former National Security Advisor

William P. Bogie (1968-1971)
American Bankers' Association

Dr. Philip M. Crane (1968-present)
U.S. Representative from Illinois

Mrs. John Loor Locke (1968-1970)

Dr. H. E. Michl (1968-1980)
H. Rodney Sharp Professor of
Economics and Business,
University of Delaware

†Hon. George H. Murphy (1968-1975)
U.S. Senator from California
G.M. Washington Consultants,
Inc.

†Henry Salvatori (1968-1988)
Founder and President, Western
Geophysical Company

Dr. Richard J. Whalen (1968-1969)
Center for Strategic Studies,
Georgetown University

Robert H. Miller (1970-present)
President, Leading Edge Technologies

Chris F. Moersch, Jr. (1971-1976)
President, Vulcan Mold and Iron
Company

†James V. Smith (1971-1972)
Administrator, Farmers Home
Administration, U.S. Department
of Agriculture

†Ralph W. Husted (1973-1995)
President, Indianapolis Power and
Light Company
Trustee, Liberty Fund

†Kersey Kinsey (1973-1979)
President, Kersey Kinsey Company

†Russell Kirk (1973-1994)
Writer and lecturer

†Edward A. Prentice (1975-1987)
President, E. V. Prentice Company

†John L. Ryan (1975-1995)
Business Consultant

Hon. Jack F. Kemp (1977-1988)
U.S. Representative from New York

Dr. George W. Carey (1977-present)
Professor of Government,
Georgetown University
Editor, *The Political Science Reviewer*

†Dr. David S. Collier (1977-1980)
Editor, *Modern Age*

Hon. W. Philip Gramm (1978-1989)
U.S. Senator from Texas

Alexius Conroy (1979-1989)
President, Cadillac Fairview
Shopping Center, Limited

William H. Regnery (1979-present)
Former President, The Joanna
Western Mills Company
Former President, Caroline House
Consultant

Richard F. Baum (1980-1987)
Writer

Dr. Edwin J. Feulner (1980-present)
Chairman, the Intercollegiate
Studies Institute, 1989-1993,
2003-present
President, The Heritage Foundation

Edward Littlejohn (1980-1983)
Vice President, Public Affairs,
Pfizer, Inc.
University of California–Los
Angeles Graduate School of
Management

Mary Ann Blatch (1982-1987)
Vice President, Consumer Affairs,
Reader's Digest Association

†Dr. John P. East (1982-1986)
U.S. Senator from North Carolina

James R. Evans (1984-2000)
President, L.G.E., Limited

†Thomas A. Roe (1984-1999)
Chairman, Builder Marts of
America

Beverly V. Thompson (1984-1987)
President, Texas Educational
Association

Hon. Wayne Valis (1984-present)
President, Valis Associates

T. William Boxx (1988-present)
Chairman, Philip M. McKenna
Foundation

Dr. William F. Campbell (1988-present)
Professor Emeritus of Economics,
Louisiana State University

Hon. T. Kenneth Cribb, Jr., Esq. (1988-present)
President, the Intercollegiate
Studies Institute, 1989-present

E. Victor Milione (1988-present)
President, the Intercollegiate
Studies Institute, 1963-1988*
President Emeritus, 1988-present

Louise Oliver (1988-present)
Chairman, the Intercollegiate
Studies Institute, 1993-2001
Trustee, George E. Coleman, Jr.
Foundation

Hon. Thomas W. Pauken, Esq. (1988-present)
Chairman, Tutogen Medical, Inc.

Hon. James H. Burnley IV, Esq. (1989-present)
Chairman, the Intercollegiate
Studies Institute, 2001-2002
Attorney, Partner, Venable, LLP
Former U.S Secretary of Transportation

Robert R. Reilly (1988-1989)
President, the Intercollegiate
Studies Institute, 1988-1989
Chairman, The Committee for
Western Civilization

Robert F. Turner, Esq. (1989-1990)
Associate Director, Center for
National Security Law, University
of Virginia School of Law

Hon. Faith Ryan Whittlesey (1988-1989)
Former U.S. Ambassador to
Switzerland
Chief Executive Officer, American
Swiss Foundation

Hon. Richard M. DeVos (1990-2000)
President, Amway Corporation

†Dr. Robert H. Krieble (1990-1997)
Former Chairman, Loctite
Corporation

Index

All photos appearing on the dustjacket of **Educating for Liberty** were taken at ISI-sponsored events.

Richard M. Weaver

Eric Voegelin

Will Herberg

Forrest McDonald

Ludwig von Mis

Stephen Tonsor

Antonin Scalia

Thomas Molnar

Jeane J. Kirkpatrick

Walter E. Williams

Russell Kirk

Robert Nisbet

Frank S. Meyer

Erik von Kuehnelt-Leddihn

M. E. Bradford

William F. Buckley Jr.

Henry Regnery

Robert P. George

Israel Kirzner

Ernest van den Haag